6/30/97

For Reference

Not to be taken from this room

Biography Today

Profiles of People of Interest to Young Readers

1995
Annual
Cumulation

Laurie Lanzen Harris
Executive Editor

Cherie D. Abbey
Associate Editor

Omnigraphics, Inc.

Penobscot Building
Detroit, Michigan 48226

Laurie Lanzen Harris, *Executive Editor*
Cherie D. Abbey, *Associate Editor*
Helene Henderson, Kevin Hillstrom, Laurie Hillstrom, Margaret W. Young,
Sketch Writers
Barry Puckett, *Research Associate*

Omnigraphics, Inc.

* * *

Matt Barbour, *Production Manager*
Laurie Lanzen Harris, *Vice President & Editorial Director*
Peter E. Ruffner, *Vice President, Administration*
James A. Sellgren, *Vice President, Operations and Finance*
Jane Steele, *Vice President, Research*

* * *

Frederick G. Ruffner, Jr., *Publisher*

Copyright © 1996 Omnigraphics, Inc.

ISBN 0-7808-0063-X

Printed in the United States

Contents

3

Preface

Biography Today is a publication designed and written for the young reader—aged 9 and above—and covers individuals that librarians and teachers tell us that young people want to know about most: entertainers, athletes, writers, illustrators, cartoonists, and political leaders.

Biography Today is available as a magazine and as a hardbound annual. In its first year (Volume 1, 1992) *Biography Today* was published four times. Beginning with Volume 2, 1993, *Biography Today* will be published three times a year, in January, April, and September. We have made this change to adapt our publishing schedule more closely to the school year. Despite this change in frequency, the total number of pages will not change. We had initially planned to produce four issues of approximately 100 pages each; now we plan three issues of approximately 150 pages each, with a hardbound cumulation of approximately 400 pages.

The Plan of the Work

The publication was especially created to appeal to young readers in a format they can enjoy reading and readily understand. Each issue contains approximately 15 sketches arranged alphabetically; this annual cumulation contains entries on 46 individuals. Each entry provides at least one picture of the individual profiled, and bold-faced rubrics lead the reader to information on birth, youth, early memories, education, first jobs, marriage and family, career highlights, memorable experiences, hobbies, and honors and awards. Each of the entries ends with a list of easily accessible sources designed to lead the student to further reading on the individual and a current address. Obituary entries are also included, written to provide a perspective on the individual's entire career. Obituaries are clearly marked in both the table of contents and at the beginning of the entry.

New Feature—Brief Entries

Beginning with Volume 3, *Biography Today* will include Brief Entries of approximately two pages each. These entries cover people who may not have had as much extensive media coverage as the subjects of our other profiles. Examples of people profiled in Brief Entries in Volume 4 include Vicki Van Meter, who became the youngest person to pilot a plane across the U.S. and to Europe. All brief entries are clearly marked in the table of contents and at the beginning of the entry.

Biographies are prepared by Omni editors after extensive research, utilizing the most current materials available. Those sources that are generally available to students appear in the list of further reading at the end of the sketch.

Indexes

To provide easy access to entries, each issue of *Biography Today* contains a Name Index, a General Index covering occupations, organizations, and ethnic and minority origins, a Places of Birth Index, and a Birthday Index. These indexes cumulate with each succeeding issue. The three yearly issues are cumulated annually in the hardbound volume, with cumulative indexes.

Our Advisors

Biography Today is reviewed regularly by an Advisory Board comprised of librarians, children's literature specialists, and reading instructors so that we can make sure that the concept of this publication—to provide a readable and accessible biographical magazine for young readers—stays on target. They have evaluated the title as it developed, and their suggestions have proved invaluable. Any errors, however, are ours alone. We'd like to list the Advisory Board members, and to thank them for their efforts.

Sandra Arden	Assistant Director, Retired Troy Public Library Troy, MI
Gail Beaver	Ann Arbor Huron High School Library and the University of Michigan School of Information and Library Studies Ann Arbor, MI
Marilyn Bethel	Pompano Beach Branch Library Pompano Beach, FL
Eileen Butterfield	Waterford Public Library Waterford, CT
Linda Carpino	Detroit Public Library Detroit, MI
Helen Gregory	Grosse Pointe Public Library Grosse Pointe, MI
Jane Klasing	School Board of Broward County, Retired Fort Lauderdale, FL
Marlene Lee	Broward County Public Library System Fort Lauderdale, FL
Judy Liskov	Waterford Public Library Waterford, CT
Sylvia Mavrogenes	Miami-Dade Public Library System Miami, FL

Carole J. McCollough	Wayne State University School of Library Science Detroit, MI
Deborah Rutter	Russell Library Middletown, CT
Barbara Sawyer	Groton Public Library and Information Center Groton, CT
Renee Schwartz	School Board of Broward County Fort Lauderdale, FL
Lee Sprince	Broward West Regional Library Fort Lauderdale, FL
Susan Stewart	Birney Middle School Reading Laboratory Southfield, MI
Ethel Stoloff	Librarian, Birney Middle School, Retired Southfield, MI

Our Advisory Board stressed to us that we should not shy away from controversial or unconventional people in our profiles, and we have tried to follow their advice. The Advisory Board also mentioned that the sketches might be useful in reluctant reader and adult literacy programs, and we would value any comments librarians and teachers might have about the suitability of our magazine for those purposes.

New Series

In response to the growing number of suggestions from our readers, we have decided to expand the *Biography Today* family of publications. Five new series—*Biography Today Author Series, Scientists and Inventors Series, Artists Series, Sports Series,* and *Leaders of the World Series*—will be published in 1995 and 1996. Each of the special subject volumes will be 200-pages and will cover 20 individuals of interest to the reader aged 9 and above. The length and format of the entries will be like those found in the regular issues of *Biography Today,* but there will be *no* duplication among the series.

Your Comments Are Welcome

Our goal is to be accurate and up-to-date, to give young readers information they can learn from and enjoy. Now we want to know what you think. Take a look at this issue of *Biography Today,* on approval. Write or call me with your comments. We want to provide an excellent source of biographical information for young people. Let us know how you think we're doing.

And here's a special incentive: review our list of people to appear in up-coming issues. Use the bind-in card to list other people you want to see in *Biography Today*. If we include someone you suggest, your library wins a free issue, with our thanks. Please see the bind-in card for details.

And take a look at the next page, where we've listed those libraries and individuals that received a free issue of *Biography Today* in 1995 for their suggestions.

Laurie Harris
Editor, *Biography Today*

CONGRATULATIONS!

Congratulations to the following individuals and libraries, who received a free issue of *Biography Today,* in 1995 for suggesting people who appear in Volume 4:

Tiffini-Jenelle Bates
Machesney Park, IL

Bettendorf Public Library
Bettendorf, IA

Birmingham Public Library
Birmingham, AL
Patricia Kyser

Bixby Spartan Media Center
Bixby, OK

Bluffton Elementary School Library
Bluffton, OH
Marcia Thomas

Jennifer Bonelli
Elmhurst, NY

Brownsburg Public Library
Brownsburg, IN
Nancy Gwin

Laura Caggiano
Ft. Wayne, IN

Central Elementary School
Clear Lake, IA

Central Middle School Library
Dover, DE

Charlene Chan
Scarsdale, NY

Cimarron Middle School
Edmond, OK

City of Inglewood Public Library
Inglewood, CA
Katy Ikuta

Joann and Ruth Collier
San Jose, CA

Crawford Middle School Library
Lexington, KY
Robin Fannin

Rachel Cunningham
Auburn, IN

Stephanie Davis
Toledo, OH

Dike Elementary
Dike, IA

East Detroit High School Library
East Pointe, MI
Susan Kott

Linda Eveleth
Valencia, CA

Fauquier County Public Library
Warrenton, VA
Sharon Hanlon

Emma R. Fernandez
Victora, TX

Flat Shoals Library
Decatur, GA
Gina Jenkins

Franko School Library
Mt. Vernon, NY

Tyler Gates
Hutchinson, KS

Elizabeth Gist
Indianapolis, IN

Henry Inman Branch Library
Colonia, NJ
Marsha Quackenbush

Hialeah Middle Community School
Hialeah, FL

Highland Park Public School I.M.C.
Highland Park, MI
Sheila Jones

Angelica Maria Jimenez
Queens, NY

Alana Geneel Johnson
Machesney Park, IL

Andrea Kaufmann
Milwaukee, WI

Keigwin School
Middletown, CT

Yelena Kleblanskaya
Queens, NY

Cassandra Laurent
Miami, FL

Lake Dolloff Elementary
Auburn, WA
Melissa Zastrow

Lindbergh Elementary
Dearborn, MI
Barbara J. Moore

Livonia Civic Center Library
Livonia, MI
Barbara Lewis, Kimberly Koscielniak

Augusta R. Malvagno
Ridgewood, NY

Kerry McKiwstry
Canton, OH

Miami-Dade Community College
Miami, FL

Missouri School for the Blind
St. Louis, MO
Mary Dingus

Monrovia Public Library
Monrovia, CA
Melinda Steep

Jibril Muhammad
Jersey City, NJ

Erin Murphy
Sterling Hts., MI

Linda Nicholes
Caldwell, ID

Noth Pocono S.D.
Moscow, PA
Marianne Cummings

Northside School
Newnan, GA
Laura Glise

Matt Phelphs
Niskayuna, NY

Carly Plonka
Torrance, CA

Dana Reinoos
Milwaukee, WI

St. Benedict Joseph Labre
School Library
Queens, NY
Patricia Singh

St. Clair Shores Public Library
St. Clair Shores, MI
Rosemary Orlando

Frances Shih
Woodhaven, NY

Sharda Singh
South Ozone Park, NY

Maggie Solis
Brandon, FL

Springfield Greene County
Main Public Library
Springfield, OH
Lynn Ann Robinson

Stacie Stults
Wyoming, MI

Tinker Elementary Media Center
TAFB, OK
Sandra Austin

Sacheen A. Torres
Pico Rivera, CA

Jacinda Treadway
San Jose, CA

Katherine West
Mt. Laurel, NJ

Wisconsin Rapids Public Schools,
Wisonsin Rapids, WI

Dorothy Wolff
Valley Forge, PA

Wyndcroft School
Pottstown, PA
Jeanne M. Havrilla

Ybor City Public Library
Tampa, FL,
Marc Rod

Troy Aikman   1966-
American Professional Football Player with
the Dallas Cowboys
1993 MVP of the Super Bowl

BIRTH

Troy Kenneth Aikman was born November 21, 1966, in West
Covina, California, east of Los Angeles. The only son of Charlyn
and Ken Aikman, he has two older sisters, Tammy and Terri.
While Troy was growing up his father, Ken, welded pipe in the
oil fields of California and Oklahoma. Troy was born with a birth
defect that caused his feet to grow crooked. He wore casts on both
feet until he began to walk, then heavy orthopedic shoes 24 hours
a day. By the age of three he was able to walk and run around
like other children.

EARLY MEMORIES

When Troy turned nine, he was already five-foot-seven inches tall and weighed 110 pounds, the right size to play some serious football. He tried out for a local football team and in no time mastered running, throwing, and ball-handling, the skills of a quarterback. He began to dream of being a professional football player. "I used to practice my signature, working on the way I wanted to sign my autograph," Troy remembers, "I'd say to myself, 'One day I'll be somebody.'"

While Troy dreamed and soaked up the sun in southern California, his father hoped, too, to return to his roots in Oklahoma. In 1978 when Troy was 12, Ken piled the family in his pickup and moved them to a 175-acre farm outside the small town of Henryetta, Oklahoma. Troy missed his friends and the big city. He didn't even have neighbors. But before long the simple pleasures of getting to know people, going fishing, and listening to country music stole his heart. Even today that has not changed.

TOOLS FOR SUCCESS

Troy's father taught him that "a man doesn't whimper, cry, or complain. He gives an honest day's work for a day's pay. Friends, family, and church come first." He learned a quiet kind of confidence, rising to his parents' expectations of completing his homework and helping with the chores. Later, in the leadership role of quarterback, he guided his teammates by example rather than words. Seeing how hard his dad worked made him take more knocks than usual on the football field. These attributes have helped shape him into the success he is today, not only as a great quarterback, but also as a person.

EDUCATION

At Henryetta High School, Troy Aikman played three major sports, quarterbacking in football, centering for basketball, and playing pitcher and shortstop on the baseball team. Despite Aikman's proficiency in football, the Henryetta Fighting Hens rarely won a game until his junior year when the Hens made it to the first game in the state playoffs. Senior year the team finished with the respectable record of 6-4. During high school, Aikman passed for 3,208 yards and 30 touchdowns and rushed for 1,568 yards and 15 touchdowns. He earned All-Conference and All-State honors, and honorable mention on the *USA Today* All-American high school team. The combination of good grades and football talents, especially his strong throwing arm, did not go unnoticed by college football coaches. Offers poured in from Missouri, Tennessee, and from a coach who had been interested in him since his sophomore year, Jimmy Johnson from Oklahoma State University. But the most powerful draw came from Coach Barry Switzer from the University of Oklahoma in Norman, one of the best college teams in the country. Switzer offered a scholarship and a promise that the team would switch from a running offense, or wishbone, to drop-back passes better suited to his passing ability. Aikman succumbed, explaining, "In the state of Oklahoma, OU football is everything. Everybody wants to go to OU."

In 1984, Troy Aikman graduated from high school with his class of 100, and in the fall, as biographer Carl R. Green put it, "packed his blue jeans and cowboy boots and left for Norman."

CAREER HIGHLIGHTS

UNIVERSITY OF OKLAHOMA SOONERS: 1984-1986

Early on, Aikman discovered how quickly plans can change when he realized that his ambition of going to medical school was not going to mix with playing football in college. He changed his major to sociology. On the football field, Coach Switzer changed, too, beefing up the wishbone offense with a few more pass plays rather than dropping it as he said he would. Not a quitter, Aikman took Switzer's decision in stride.

Typical for first year "rookies," Aikman sat out the first six games, then unexpectedly started against Kansas. He completed only two passes and threw three inteceptions. The Sooners lost 28-11. "Our whole team laid down that day and didn't give Troy any help," Switzer said in the young quarterback's defense. The 1985 season seemed more promising, as Aikman returned as a starter and led the Sooners to three victories, completing 21 of 40 passes for 317 yards. The streak ended during the fourth game against Miami of Florida, when Aikman broke his leg. He watched from the sidelines as a new quarterback, Jamelle Holieway, led the team to eight final wins and the national championship.

A team can have only one starting quarterback, and Holieway fit the job. Aikman decided to transfer. Switzer called coaches at Stanford University, Arizona State, and the University of California at Los Angeles (UCLA). Coach Jimmy Johnson tried again, this time from the University of Miami, but UCLA was the clear choice. Looking back Aikman said, "I couldn't have hoped for any better. It was a big decision to leave Oklahoma and start over. You never know if things will work out."

UNIVERSITY OF CALIFORNIA AT LOS ANGELES BRUINS: 1986-1988

Before Troy Aikman could prove himself at UCLA he had to "redshirt," or sit out the first year to fulfill the National Collegiate Athletic Association (NCAA) requirement for college transfers. Aikman spent the time familiarizing himself with the UCLA playbook, working out with weights, and practicing. In 1987, Coach Terry Donahue gave him the starting position. Off to a slow start in the first few games, Troy improved over the next seven games, completing 69 percent of his passes for 1,663 yards, 15 touchdowns, and three interceptions. A stunning loss of 17-13 against the Bruins' arch-rival, the Trojans from the University of Southern California, booted the Bruins out of the Rose Bowl. Devastated, Aikman said, "I didn't sleep for two weeks after that." UCLA finished by playing the University of Florida in the Aloha Bowl, placing ninth in the national rankings. Aikman achieved second place nationally in passing efficiency and was honored as a second-team All-American and runner-up for the Davey O'Brien National Quarterback Award.

A more confident Troy Aikman emerged in his senior year. According to Rich Neuheisel, a former Bruins quarterback who practiced with Aikman, "Physically there wasn't much to improve on." But Aikman had learned the offense and what was expected of him. He led the Bruins to a 9-2 finish. Though the Bruins lost their game to USC, and their chance to go to the Rose Bowl, the team received an invitation to play in the Cotton Bowl. Aikman played the best game of his college career. The landslide victory of 17-3 over the Arkansas Razorbacks boosted the Bruins to a No. 6 national ranking. At UCLA Aikman completed 64.8 percent passes for 5,298 yards and 41 touchdowns, ranking third best passer in college history. And that year he won the Davey O'Brien Award. Viewed by scouts as one of the best quarterbacks in the college draft, he was snapped up as the Dallas Cowboys' No. 1 pick.

DALLAS COWBOYS: 1989—

At the start of Troy Aikman's pro career, the Cowboys were undergoing a reorganization. A new owner, Jerry Jones, bought the franchise for a reported $140 million, fired the legendary Coach Tom Landry, and hired the coach from the University of Miami, Jimmy Johnson. "The Cowboys have lost some of their luster," said Gil Brandt, the Cowboys' director of player personnel, "but hopefully Troy Aikman can restore some of that." Aikman was offered the largest rookie contract in NFL history, $11.2 million for an unusually long period of six years. The contract took only two weeks to negotiate. "It's pretty much a dream come true. It's beyond words. I wanted this so badly," Aikman said. In Dallas, Texas, he would be close to home, family, and friends. He would feel comfortable there.

Aikman's moment of glory was short-lived. Within two short months Steve Walsh, a talented quarterback who won 23 of 24 games and a division title for Jimmy Johnson at the University of Miami, joined the team. the quarterbacks shared playing time during practice and competed for the starting position in the fall. Johnson chose Aikman to start, but kept Walsh in the wings. It was unnerving for Aikman. He started in 11 games, but

Dallas lost every one. Then he broke the index finger on his left hand and watched Steve Walsh lead six games, including the only win of the season. Aikman had passed for 1,749 yards and threw nine touchdown passes, but he also threw 18 interceptions. The team finished with a dismal record of 1-15. That kind of beginning could short-circuit a career, and at times Aikman wanted to quit. In the long run he admitted that he had grown stronger, saying "I grew up a lot that year." Johnson relieved the pressure by trading Walsh to the New Orleans Saints and promised that help would be on the way.

The 1990 season opened to an improving team with Aikman in charge. The Cowboys won seven games, six featuring come-from-behind finishes led by Aikman. They finished 7-9, just missing the playoffs. A shoulder injury on December 23, 1990, ended Aikman's season and required surgery before he could return. Help came in 1991 with Emmitt Smith—"the superweapon of the Dallas running attack"—and a new offensive coordinator, Norv Turner. Turner's system favored short passes that enhanced Aikman's throwing capabilities. In the system's first year, Aikman had the most passing yards and highest completion rate, 65.3 percent, in the National Football Conference (NFC) and in Cowboys' history. The playoffs became a reality for the first time in six years after Dallas closed the season at 11-5. A sprained knee in late November cut his

season short, but Aikman was able to play in the playoffs and his first Pro Bowl. Critics called the successful season a fluke. They did not expect a turnaround this fast.

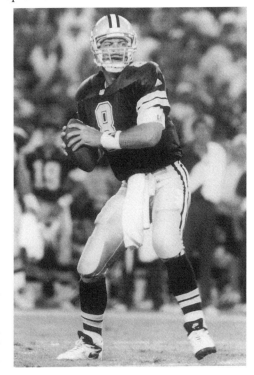

The critics were wrong. "America's Team" bounced back in 1992, beating the defending Super Bowl champions, the Washington Redskins, 23-10 in the season's first game. Three losses and 13 wins bought the division title and a ticket to the playoffs. In a playoff game on January 10, 1993, the Philadelphia Eagles met Dallas on its own turf at Texas Stadium. The Cowboys won it, 34-10, in what Aikman called "the biggest win I ever experienced." Next was the formidable task of winning the playoff game against Steve Young and the San Francisco 49ers, who had ruled the league during the 1980s and won the Super Bowl four times. Fans wondered how far the Cowboys had really come. Aikman led the Cowboys to a 78-yard score, and *Sports Illustrated* said the next 79-yard drive, ending with a scoring pass to Emmitt Smith, "was possibly Aikman's finest as a pro." With a final score of 30-20, the Cowboys were on their way to the Super Bowl!

Super Bowl Day, January 31, 1993, was Troy Aikman Day in Henryetta, Oklahoma, as the Cowboys prepared to play the Buffalo Bills. The sheer emotional impact of being in the Super Bowl made Aikman feel like passing out. When his head cleared he took control, helping his team to a 52-17 victory. Aikman completed 22 of 30 passes for 273 yards and four touchdowns. His playoff performance was the best in NFL history. And his stats earned him the game's Most Valuable Play (MVP) award. He was on top, his dream come true. "No matter what happens in my career from here on out," Aikman told *Newsday,* "at least I can say that I took a team to the Super Bowl and we were able to win it." The Super Bowl MVP award propels a player to stardom, and Aikman quickly learned that being famous was not going to be easy. Big companies competed for his endorsements, and he walked around bleary-eyed for days from so many interviews after the game.

Aikman took the Cowboys to a second Super Bowl in 1994, after posting one of the finest seasons for an NFL quarterback. He started all 16 season games and finished second in the NFL in passing. Completing 63 percent of his passes for 3,445 yards, Aikman had the best touchdowns-to-interceptions ratio of his career—23 to 14. In the playoffs, the Green Bay Packers and San Francisco 49ers were no match, and Dallas beat the Bills again in the Super Bowl, 30-13. "It's the greatest feeling in the world," he told the *Philadelphia Daily News.* "The second time feels better than the first. And I can't wait for the third time." In January 1994 Aikman signed a $50 million, eight-year contract that would finish out his career with the Cowboys and make him the highest paid player in football history.

The 1994 season brought changes as Aikman adjusted to a new coach, Barry Switzer, and a new offensive coordinator, Ernie Zampese. Injuries sidelined teammates Emmitt Smith and Michael Irvin and interrupted Aikman's season with three split chins, a concussion, knee sprain, and sprained thumb. Hopes to be the first team in NFL history to tie together three straight Super Bowl wins were dashed when the Cowboys lost to San Francisco, 38-28, in the NFC title game. In that game, Aikman completed 30 of 53 passes for 380 yards and three touchdowns. He admitted that the 1994 season had been "less fun" than the previous two. After all, he places a premium on winning football games, as he recently told a reporter from the Los Angeles *Daily News.* "That's how ultimately we're all judged."

FUTURE PLANS

Troy Aikman has talked about an early retirement. He has had numerous injuries, including a shoulder separation, six concussions, and a herniated disk from weight lifting. "The last couple of years have taken a toll," he said. "It's been a long grind." He once told an interviewer, "When I'm done playing I envision getting a ranch somewhere and no one may hear from me again."

MARRIAGE AND FAMILY

Troy Aikman lives in a western-style house in Dallas. He is single. His idea of a good time is to have barbecues with family and friends. The people Aikman feels most comfortable with are his teammates or old friends from college. "It takes a while for someone to gain my trust," he said. "Loyalty and trust are important to me." Because he dresses in jeans and boots and drives a pickup truck he looks like a cowboy, but he does not know how to ride a hourse. The image changes in his elegant white BMW. His six-foot, 230-pound physique, blond hair, and blue eyes merited a vote as one of *People* magazine's 50 Most Beautiful People in 1993, but his head never swelled. Instead he said, "Well, they don't know that many people."

HOBBIES AND OTHER INTERESTS

Outside of football, Aikman has many interests. He loves working on his computer and listening to music, especially country and western. He helped form a country and western band called the Super Boys with tight end Jay Novacek, special teams coach Joe Avezzano, and former Cowboys Walt Garrison and Randy White. The band recorded an album titled *Everybody Wants to Be a Cowboy*, with Aikman signing a ballad called "Oklahoma Nights." He is also involved in numerous charities. For young people he helped fund the Troy Aikman Athletic Complex, scholarships at Henryetta High School and UCLA, and the Troy Aikman Foundation to support childrens' charities.

HONORS AND AWARDS

All-Conference and All-State: 1984
All-American College Team: 1988
Davey O'Brien National Quarterback Award: 1988
College Quarterback of the Year: 1988
NFL Offensive Player of the Week: 1991
Pro Bowl: 1991, 1992, 1993
Super Bowl MVP: 1993
All Pro Honors (*Sports Illustrated* and *Sporting News*): 1993
All-NFC (*Football News*): 1993
Dallas All Sports Association Pro Athlete of the Year: 1993
Super Bowl Championship Team: 1993, 1994

FURTHER READING

BOOKS

Brady Games Staff. *Troy Aikman NFL Football Official Playbook*, 1994
Dippold, Joel. *Troy Aikman, Quick-Draw Quarterback*, 1994
Green, Carl R. *Troy Aikman*, 1994
Lincoln Library of Sports Champions, Vol. 1
Who's Who in America, 1995

PERIODICALS

Boston Globe, Dec. 28, 1988, p.25
Boy's Life, Oct. 1993, p.8
Daily News of Los Angeles, Apr. 20, 1989, p.S10; Apr. 21, 1989, p.S1; June 4, 1989, p.SB1; Jan. 15, 1995, p.SB4
GQ, Sep. 1993, p.268
Houston Post, Jan. 10, 1993, p.B15; Feb. 2, 1993, p.B1
Los Angeles Times, Nov. 19, 1987, p.1; Jan. 31, 1993, p.C1
New York Times, Nov. 7, 1994, p.C3
People, May 3, 1993, p.73
San Francisco Chronicle, Sep. 9, 1991, p.B3; June 23, 1993, p.E3; Dec. 24, 1993, p.G1
San Francisco Examiner, Jan. 15, 1993, p.E1
Seattle Post-Intelligencer, July 21, 1991, p.72; Feb. 2, 1993, p.D1; Nov. 26, 1994, p.C8
Sport, July, 1993, p.38
Sporting News, Jan. 10, 1994, p.13
Sports Illustrated, Aug. 21, 1989, p.30; Feb. 15, 1993, p.24
TV Guide, July 2, 1994, p.25
Washington Post, May 7, 1989, p.C1

ADDRESS

Dallas Cowboys
Cowboys Center
1 Cowboys Parkway
Irving, TX 75063-4727

Jean-Bertrand Aristide   1953-
Haitian President and Former Catholic Priest
Recently Returned from Exile and Reinstated
as President by the U.S. Invasion

BIRTH

Jean-Bertrand Aristide was born on July 15, 1953, in Port-Salut,
a small fishing village on the southwestern coast of Haiti. His
father, Joseph Aristide, a farmer, died when he was just three
months old. His mother, whose name has not been released to
the press, soon decided to move the family—herself, Jean-
Bertrand, and his two-year-old sister Anne Marie—to the capital
city, Port-au-Prince, to make sure that her children could get a
good education.

YOUTH

In Port-au-Prince, Aristide's mother set herself up as a merchant. She would buy produce or crafts from area peasants to resell in the city. They were certainly never wealthy, but they weren't desperately poor, either, and they always had enough—enough room in their home, enough dinner in the pot—to take in a few strays. His mother ran a lively household, as Aristide recalls in his memoir, *Aristide: An Autobiography*: "We never lived alone, just we three, a mother and two children. We were never less than ten people under one roof: family members, cousins (sometimes quite distantly related), but for the most part friends, peasants from the hill country in search of a roof for the night, a month, or even longer. The house was always full. It was there that I found the sense of, or rather the taste for, community. I feel even today that that brotherhood and sisterhood are something authentically biblical. When Jesus defined his sisters and brothers not as those who came from the womb of his mother, but as his companions, I felt myself molded by those words, immersed in their practice. They were all my brothers and sisters, just as my companions in struggle would later be, both the young intellectuals and the starving people from the slums."

The family often returned to Port-Salut to stay with Aristide's maternal grandfather. He owned a small plot of land, which he shared with those who didn't own land. Together they would work the hilly, barren soil to provide enough food for the entire community. For Aristide, the time spent in Port-Salut made a deep impression on him: "That village of scattered huts, so much like all the others, was my point of reference. There are my roots."

EARLY INFLUENCES

His greatest influence while growing up, Aristide has said, was his grandfather. A respected man in his community, he played the role of justice of the peace. "He was not invested with financial or political power, but he had power because of the confidence people had in him. I remember how, on many occasions, I saw peasants bring a petty thief to see my grandfather. He would pretend to be severe, as if he were going to punish, and would retain the thief. Then in the night, he would give him something to eat and send him away. Because, he would say, 'When you are hungry, [everyone's] food belongs to you.'

"It is a gesture that inhabits my memory. Why? Because it is the expression of a critical consciousness at a high level. It guided me throughout my life, this sensitivity toward the victims, the weak ones." As Aristide explains in his memoir, "He knew that the real thieves were not the ones who were brought before him. This humanist was revolted by injustice, whether of birth or of life. I did not have to look far for the sources of my inspiration, the feeling of revolt that began to move me when my conscience was stirred during my adolescence."

EDUCATION

Aristide's mother was a deeply religious woman, and she raised her son in the Catholic faith. When it came time for him to attend school, it was natural that he would attend a Catholic school. She sent Aristide to a school run by the Society of St. Francis de Sales, or the Salesians, a group known for serving the poor. Aristide describes a tough regime there. He grew up speaking Creole, the language used by over 90% of the population of Haiti. At school, though, Creole was forbidden, and the children had to speak French, the language of the elite. Any child who forgot was beaten and humiliated in front of the other students. Aristide was a good student who excelled in his studies. His teachers, the Fathers, were very demanding of him. They expected him to be first in the class—and if he wasn't, they beat him for that as well. But they also encouraged him.

By the time he finished primary school, Aristide had decided to become a priest, wanting to emulate the examples of service that he saw around him. "I saw my aunts organizing religious celebrations; I admired my grandfather for living and defending human rights every day, and my mother providing by her self-sacrifice for the needs of the household. I myself had also cultivated a taste for service, for saying to others: 'I am here for you.' My vocation became more and more clear."

Aristide entered the Salesian seminar at Cap Haitien in 1966. In addition to regular high school classes, there were conferences, daily talks, and evening mass, as well as soccer, Scouts, and music lessons. Aristide also began studying languages, learning Latin, Greek, English, Spanish, and Italian. In 1974 he completed his studies and started his novitiate in the Dominican Republic. For Catholics, the novitiate is a year during which the novice takes his or her first vows.

ADVANCED STUDIES

After a year in the Dominican Republic, Aristide returned to Port-au-Prince and entered the state university, the Universite d'Etat d'Haiti. There he studied philosophy and psychology. He earned his B.A. in psychology in 1979. He went on to advanced studies in Biblical theology in Israel, taking intensive courses in Hebrew and Arabic, and also studied in Egypt, Italy, and Great Britain.

ORDINATION

Returning to Haiti in 1982, Aristide was ordained to the priesthood on July 3, 1982. He was assigned to the parish of St. Joseph in Port-au-

Prince and started to speak out against injustice. "I had been away for some time," he has said about his reaction to returning to Haiti, "and so my eyes were reopened to the squalor and misery." He quickly became known for his fiery sermons criticizing the regime of Jean-Claude Duvalier and challenging his parishioners to stand up and protest against the government.

HAITIAN HISTORY

The Haitian people have had good reason to protest throughout much of their history. Their island (Hispaniola, which contains the countries of Haiti and the Dominican Republic) is believed to be the site of the first landing of Christopher Columbus on his voyage to the New World. After the arrival of Columbus and subsequent European explorers, the Native American Indian population was virtually wiped out—by disease, by warfare, or by being worked to death in the foreigners' gold mines and plantations. Both the Spaniards, who originally controlled the island, and the French, who later took it over, kidnapped Africans and forced them to work as slaves on the thriving sugar, cotton, coffee, and cocoa plantations.

In 1804, Haiti declared its independence, becoming the first independent nation in the West Indies. Throughout its history since then, Haiti has seen many different forms of leadership, all with certain similarities: there has been an elitist power structure, with just a few people ruling the country and reaping its financial rewards while most Haitians lived in poverty and desperation; the military and the Catholic Church have been prominent players in the country's political life; there has been widespread unrest and chronic political instability, including coups and assassinations; and, with a few notable exceptions, there has been a rapid succession of political leaders, with each government lasting just a short while. One exception was the occupation by the U.S. Marines, from 1915 to 1934. President Woodrow Wilson sent the Marines to Haiti out of fear that its unstable political situation would allow another country to take over and develop a stronghold close to U.S. shores. The U.S. occupation lasted for almost twenty years, and many Haitians came to resent it bitterly.

But by far, the most important government in recent Haitian history was that of François Duvalier (Papa Doc) and later his son, Jean-Claude Duvalier (Baby Doc). President of Haiti from his election in 1957 until his death in 1971, François Duvalier ruled as a complete and total dictator. He decimated the armed forces and created the feared and hated "Tontons Macoutes" (the Haitian Creole term for bogeymen), a secret police force that terrorized and killed anyone who criticized Duvalier. He silenced all avenues for dissent, including newspapers, radio, and television. He even manipulated the hierarchy of the Catholic Church, exiling or killing those who criticized him until the only Catholics left were either under his control or afraid to speak out.

Some people profited from the Duvalier regime. The light-skinned elite, a group of old Haitian families plus a few newcomers, makes up just 1% of the country's population but holds the vast majority of the country's wealth. This group continued to send their children to American Ivy-League schools, to wear designer clothes, to drive Mercedes and BMWs, and to eat in fancy French restaurants. But most Haitians suffered miserably under Duvalier. The peasants lived in unspeakable poverty in slums in the cities or tried to eke out a living from barren land in the countryside. Average income for the peasants was on the order of $120 per year. Unemployment was high. Malnutrition and hunger were widespread. Running water and indoor plumbing were rare. Infant mortality was high, and average life expectancies were low: Haitians died, on average, by the age of 50. There were few schools and few clinics, and typhoid and tuberculosis were epidemic. When François Duvalier died in 1971, his son ascended to the Presidency. Under Jean-Claude Duvalier, political corruption, repression, economic collapse, desperation, despair, and hopelessness continued unabated.

THE PRIESTHOOD

These were the conditions in which Aristide began his work as a priest. Certainly he had been aware of this political reality for years, but it was not until he began preaching in Port-au-Prince in 1982 that he began to challenge it publicly. He lasted three months in the St. Joseph parish before the church hierarchy sent him to Montreal, Canada, in what many have derided as an exile arranged by the Haitian military. He was transferred to what he calls "a pastoral institute that specialized in theological reprogramming." He spent almost three years there pursuing graduate studies at the University of Montreal. He completed his master's degree in biblical theology as well as the course work for his doctorate in psychology before returning to Haiti in January 1985.

There, he was assigned to the parish of St. Jean Bosco, in the slums of Port-au-Prince. He soon became one of the most vocal and prominent of the progressive priests in "Ti Legliz," Creole for "Little Church." Ti Legliz is part of the liberation theology movement, which has developed throughout Latin America. Its adherents believe that social and political freedom are essential to spiritual fulfillment; that the Church should be involved in the struggle for justice; and that the clergy are morally obligated to work on issues like poverty and racism. With such beliefs, Aristide, like the other priests of Ti Legliz, often found himself at odds with the hierarchy of the Catholic Church in Haiti.

At St. Jean Bosco, Aristide continued giving fiery speeches that incited his parishioners and organized a youth group to encourage more youth participation in the church. In the fall of 1985, discontent with Baby Doc Duvalier escalated after pro-government forces killed three students. Preaching fearlessly against the hated Tontons Macoutes, Aristide was instrumental in organizing the people to rise up against Duvalier. On February 7, 1986, the tyrant Jean-Claude Duvalier was driven into exile in France.

LIFE IN HAITI AFTER DUVALIER

What followed, for almost five years, was ongoing chaos: economic stagnation, repression, terror, and political turmoil. There were five different governmental regimes during that time, all unelected, unpopular, and imposed by the military. At first, many Haitians hoped that Duvalier's departure meant that they had won their freedom. But after a brief period of celebration, violence exploded throughout the country as the people began to demand the overthrow of the latest military regime. "Dechoukaj," a Creole word that means "to uproot," became the people's cry as they exacted vengeance on anyone associated with Duvalier.

From the beginning, Aristide argued that the new military government was simply "Duvalierism without Duvalier." There would be no true freedom, he maintained, until the Tontons Macoutes were disarmed and brought to justice. Unfortunately, he was soon proved correct, as the next few years brought more terrorism. The summer of 1987 saw widespread

protests and violence, including the massacre of over 200 peasants in just one incident. Aristide's scathing criticism of this and other events prompted the Salesians in August 1987 to try to transfer him out of the city, to a parish that was home to many Tontons Macoutes. Several members of Aristide's parish youth group staged a hunger strike in the city cathedral, forcing the order to cancel the transfer. Shortly afterward, he was the victim of two unsuccessful assassination attempts. In one, a gunman shot at him while he was preaching. In the other, he and several other priests traveling in a convoy of cars were pulled over by a gang, believed to be Tontons Macoutes, who said they were looking for Aristide. Several of the priests were beaten, but they managed to get away.

An even more hideous assassination attempt occurred the following year. On September 11, 1988, Aristide was beginning morning mass at St. Jean Bosco when a gang of about 100 armed Tontons Macoutes burst into the church and began firing on the approximately 800 parishioners. For several hours, the gang beat the churchgoers and eventually burned down the church, while members of the army and the police looked on without intervening. Aristide escaped, but 13 people were killed and at least 70 were injured. The appalling attack shocked and outraged Haitians at all levels of society. In October 1988, the Salesians again attempted to transfer Aristide, ordering him to leave Haiti. In response, thousands of protesters filled the streets of Port-au-Prince and blocked all routes to the airport. Again the Salesians backed down, but in December 1988 they expelled him from the order. That was a very difficult time for Aristide; he had considered the Salesians his family since childhood. Although he continued to minister to youth groups and set up a shelter for homeless boys, he was, for a time, withdrawn from the political world.

ELECTION TO THE PRESIDENCY

In 1990, presidential elections were scheduled for December. Recent history gave the Haitians no reason to hope that a fair election would take place. But their hopes rose when Aristide declared his candidacy for the presidency. He called his movement "lavalas," meaning a flood or avalanche that would wash away the former regimes' corruption and tyranny. His mother, then living in Miami, Florida, objected to his campaign out of fear for his life. "It is terrible," Aristide confided, "that in order to help the people, you have to hurt your mother." The elections were monitored by United Nations observers, and on December 16, 1990, Aristide won with almost 70% of the vote, becoming the first democratically elected president in the nation's history. Haitians took to the streets, elated. An attempt to take over the government was made before Aristide even took office, but thousands of Haitians again filled the streets and paralyzed the capital, and the army stepped in to foil the coup attempt.

Aristide took office on February 7, 1991. Despite widespread elation, there were some who opposed him during both the campaign and his administration. They challenged his qualifications to be president, saying that he knew little about economics, foreign relations, and the workings of government. They doubted his ability to work effectively with business leaders, whom he had often criticized. They also questioned his ability to control the army. But most importantly, they abhorred his failure to denounce mob violence. In several speeches, Aristide had seemed to condone street justice, including the hideous "Pere Lebrun," the flaming necklace, in which a tire soaked with gasoline is placed around someone's neck and set on fire. His detractors' concerns became moot just seven months into his term. On September 30, 1991, Aristide was ousted when a military faction overthrew his government. Protected by the U.S. Ambassador, Aristide and several associates were flown to Venezuela and then to Washington, D.C.

EXILE

Aristide spent the next three years in exile in Washington, D.C. There were ongoing attempts in the international community to negotiate with the military rulers in Haiti and to return Aristide to power. An economic blockade and trade ban were enforced against Haiti, making it impossible for the country to buy and sell goods. As a result, the economy ground to a halt, making the already impoverished people even more desperate. Many attempted to leave on small boats and sail to the United States, creating a refugee crisis in the U.S. when President Bill Clinton ordered U.S. ships to pick up the boat people and return them to Haiti. According to a report by the monitoring group Americas Watch, over 14,000 Haitians have applied for asylum in the United States since 1992, when President Clinton took office; only 307 have been allowed to immigrate to the U.S., causing charges of racism against the immigration policy on Haiti.

RETURN TO POWER

When diplomatic negotiations and economic sanctions failed to return Aristide to power, President Clinton declared that he was ready to use force to oust the military leaders and return Aristide to the post to which he was legally elected. Clinton ordered the Haitian military leaders to leave and warned them that U.S. forces would invade if they did not. In September 1994, warships began bringing thousands of U.S. soldiers to the area, preparing for an invasion. At the last minute, a team of U.S. negotiators—former President Jimmy Carter, former Chairman of the Joint Chiefs of Staff General Colin Powell, and Senator Sam Nunn—arrived in Port-au-Prince. On September 18, 1994, they convinced the junta—led by Lt. Gen. Raoul Cedras, the de facto military leader; Brig. Gen. Philippe Biamby, the army chief of staff; and Michel François, the chief of police in Port-au-Prince—to step down. The timing was so tight that 61 American planes were already in the air ready to launch the invasion when the agreement was reached. The following day, 3,000 U.S. troops landed and began policing Haiti, disarming the junta's army. One month later, Cedras and the others resigned and left the country.

The country erupted in joyous celebration. Aristide returned triumphantly to Haiti on October 15, 1994, three years after he was driven into exile. People thronged the area around the National Palace, waiting to hear him speak. His message was clear. After starting with the words "Honor, Respect," a greeting used in Haiti's rural villages, Aristide spoke the same words over and over, in Creole, French, English, and Spanish: "No to violence, no to vengeance, yes to reconciliation." Then he continued. "This is a day of national reconciliation, a day for the eyes of justice to open and never close again. Never, never, never again will blood be shed in this country."

Aristide had voiced that sentiment in an interview just before his return, reflecting on Haiti's future. He emphasized the importance of remembrance, not vengeance: "When I was in Israel, I had a chance to visit a museum that commemorates the Holocaust. The point it makes is 'Never again.' Never again seems to me to be the most important lesson Haitian children can learn. We must transcend the past without drowning ourselves in forgetfulness or vengeance or impunity."

Aristide has given other indications of his future plans. He plans to decentralize the government; to cut the army to about 1,500 people; to remove those loyal to the former junta from the police force and create a professional force controlled by civilians, not the military; to reduce the civil service; to create retraining programs for those who lose their jobs; to lower tariffs and increase imports of food and other supplies; to build up the private sector; and to seek out foreign investment to fund this ambitious economic reconstruction plan.

Observers also point out that Aristide will have to rebuild the justice system, which was decimated under the military regimes; to make peace with business leaders and work together to get the nation's economy going again; and, perhaps most importantly, to reconcile with the army, to make good on his promise to end the bloodshed. Reconciliation, reconstruction, and justice—these are the building blocks Aristide will use to try to create a just, democratic society in Haiti.

WRITINGS

In the Parish of the Poor: Writings from Haiti, 1990
Aristide: An Autobiography, 1993 (with Christophe Wargny; originally published in French in 1992)

FURTHER READING

BOOKS

Aristide, Jean-Bertrand, with Christophe Wargny. *Aristide: An Autobiography,* 1993 (originally published in French in 1992)
Wilentz, Amy. *The Rainy Season: Haiti since Duvalier,* 1989

PERIODICALS

America, Mar. 9, 1991, p.260
American Spectator, July 1994, p.32
Current Biography Yearbook 1991
Current History, Feb. 1992, p.65
Interview, Oct. 1991, p.88
Miami Herald, Nov. 26, 1990, p.A1
National Catholic Reporter, Feb. 21, 1992, p.9
The New Leader, Jan. 14, 1991, p.9
Newsweek, Sep. 26, 1994, pp.20, 26, 33, 35; Oct. 3, 1994, pp.22, 28, 34; Oct. 24, 1994, pp.22, 30
New York Times, Sep. 19, 1994, pp.A1, A8, A9; Sep. 20, 1994, pp.A1, A10, A11, A13, A14; Sep. 21, 1994, p.A1; Sep. 22, 1994, p.A1; Oct. 15, 1994, pp.A1, A4; Oct. 16, 1994, pp.A1, A4, A5, A6
New York Times Magazine, May 1, 1994, p.38; Nov. 6, 1994, p.52
Time, Oct. 14, 1991, p.36; Sep. 26, 1994, pp.20, 28, 31; Oct. 17, 1994, p.32; Oct. 24, 1994, pp.28, 33
Vanity Fair, Feb. 1994, p.74

ADDRESS

Haitian Embassy
2311 Massachusetts Avenue NW
Washington, DC 20008

Oksana Baiul   1977-
Ukrainian Figure Skater
Gold Medalist at the 1994 Winter Olympics

BIRTH

Oksana Baiul (Bye-OOL), the teenager from Ukraine who captivated the world at Norway's 1994 Winter Olympics, was born
November 16, 1977, in Dnepropetrovsk, Ukraine, then part of the
Soviet Union. Her parents, Sergei and Marina Baiul, separated
when she was only eight months old and divorced when she was
two. Sergei then disappeared from her life. Oksana's grandparents
died in the late 1980s, and her mother died of cancer in 1991 when
Oksana was 13. The young skater eventually was taken in by
renowned coach Galina Zmievskaya (Smy-ef-SKY-a), who has
become both her trainer and her surrogate mother.

EARLY LIFE

Few details are known about the earliest years of Baiul's childhood, and her tragic losses have made her reluctant to talk about those days at all. She longed to be a ballerina. At three, though, she was too young for ballet training, so she was steered in another direction. Oksana's grandfather bought her a pair of skates, and the ice rink became first her playground, and then her stage. By the time she turned seven and would have been eligible to switch to ballet, she had already won her first skating competition. Her course was charted.

Marina, Oksana's mother, was a French teacher in the large, industrial city of Dnepropetrovsk. The little girl was cared for during the day by her grandmother. Although there has been no mention of her education, it is certain that she went to school, at least until she was 15.

Baiul's world began to unravel when her grandparents died in the late 1980s. Even greater tragedy came in 1991 when her mother died of cancer, almost without warning. "At 13," reports Jere Longman of the *Vancouver Sun*, "she was without any family. And soon Baiul would be even without a coach." Her trainer, Stanislav Koritek, had taken care of her after her mother's death. But he could no longer make a living wage in the newly independent Ukraine's declining economy, so he accepted an offer from a skating club in Canada. Once again, Baiul was without home or family, and it was left to Koritek's father, a vice president of the Ukrainian skating federation, to find help for the orphaned girl. The person he turned to was the highly acclaimed Galina Zmievskaya, who had coached Olympic skater Viktor Petrenko to a gold medal in 1992.

YOUTH

Petrenko would soon be instrumental in helping Baiul. He himself was almost part of coach Zmievskaya's family; he was soon to marry her eldest daughter, Nina. Petrenko was so moved by Baiul's story that he befriended her and convinced Zmievskaya to give her a home and to be her coach. As Zmievskaya later said, "Oksana had nobody. I felt chills when I heard [her] story."

Baiul moved into their three-room flat in Odessa. There she lived with her new adopted family: her surrogate parents, Galina, her coach, and her husband Nicolai, president of a shipping and construction company, and their younger daughter, Galya, with whom Oksana happily shared a room crammed with stuffed animals and decorated with needlework and posters. Galina's mother lived there, too, plus the family dog and a cockatoo. No one complained about the daily confusion—except the family on the floor below, who had to put up with noise from the girl's stereo and the sounds of their active horseplay.

CAREER HIGHLIGHTS

Baiul soon began to practice at the ice rink in Odessa, with Zmievskaya as her coach. Skating conditions there were awful. For years, under the Communist system, the Soviet Union had run an elaborate government-supported system to train athletes. Their athletes were among the world's best. In recent years, since the break-up of the Soviet Union, the state-supported athletic system has also broken down. There is little money to pay most athlete's training expenses, or even to maintain the facilities that they need. One example of this disrepair is the ice rink in Odessa. The ice was often half melted, there was algae growing around the edges, and the two giant Zambonis (ice-smoothing machines) rarely worked. The rink was so run down that skaters often had to pitch in and smooth the ice before they could start their routines.

Despite these conditions, Baiul showed unmistakable promise. Her training was intense, but her love of skating was so great that she cooperated with a cheerfulness and focus that surprised even her demanding coach. Off the rink, her form was perfected by Nina Stoyan, the prima ballerina of the famous Odessa Academy theater.

Baiul was already a seasoned performer when Galina took over her training. She had been competing in regional contests for several years, and had skated to twelfth place in the Soviet nationals in 1991. But, in January 1993, after less than a year under Galina's wing, Baiul burst into the spotlight by placing second in the European championships at Helsinki, Finland. Two months later, she claimed the coveted world title in Prague. At 15, she became the youngest skater to win first place since 1927, when Norway's legendary Sonia Henie skated her way into the record books at the age of 14. It was Baiul's first try for a world championship, and she had never even competed in the world juniors. Her win surprised even Petrenko, her biggest booster, who was quoted by *People* magazine afterward: "I was shocked when she got second at the Europeans. It was unbelievable when she won the worlds."

Baiul went on the 1993 Tour of World Champions, performing in Europe and North America with 35 other skaters, and savoring every exciting new experience on and off the ice. At the end of the tour, she flew back to Ukraine to prepare for the 1994 Winter Olympics. Baiul's surprise first place at the World Championships the previous spring made her a serious challenger, and she was also under tremendous pressure to prove that her win had not been a fluke. She and Galina settled down to purposeful training, concentrating on the jumps that had been giving her trouble all season. She was beaten by France's Surya Bonaly in the European Championships a month before the Olympics were to open in Lillehammer, Norway, so her training sessions became even more focused.

1994 OLYMPICS

American skater Nancy Kerrigan was in top form and expected to win the gold medal. She had just recovered from being clubbed on the knee during the U.S. championships in Detroit, Michigan, in a brutal attempt to keep her out of Olympic contention. The media attention surrounding the crime, and Kerrigan's determination to put the trauma behind her, made her a fairy-tale favorite with the crowd. Baiul, however, was also ready for the challenge.

Figure skating titles are determined by the combination of marks a skater receives on the short, or technical program, and the long program. Oksana, costumed as the Black Swan and skating to music from *Swan Lake*, placed second to Kerrigan in the technical program. Then a frightening collision with Germany's Tanja Szewczenko during a practice session threatened to dash Baiul's chances of skating at all in the all-important long program. Her back was badly bruised, and several stitches were needed to close a gash on her right leg. Her final practice on the big day was dismal, and she left the ice in tears.

The final night of competition arrived. Nancy Kerrigan, skating next to last, performed an elegant, nearly flawless, program to the thunderous applause of the audience and high marks of approval from the judges.

Then Oksana took the ice. Because of her injury the day before, she had been given a legal pain-killer that was approved by the Olympic officials. She put the incident behind her and did her best. She skated magically that night, making her astonishing jumps look effortless, except for one flaw when she two-footed a landing on a triple flip. She performed with precision and perfect phrasing, and in the final moment before her performance ended, she slipped in an unplanned triple-toe-loop.

In the words of *Sports Illustrated*'s E.M. Swift, Baiul "beguiled both judges and crowd with that magic that cannot be taught." In a stunning and controversial upset, Baiul's marks gave her the gold medal by the narrowest margin in Olympic history. Five out of nine judges had voted for Baiul, those from China, the Czech Republic, Poland, Germany, and her native Ukraine. The decision stunned many in the crowd, including Kerrigan's supporters, some of whom accused the judges of bias. But as James Deacon in *Maclean's* wrote, "No one told Baiul that history was supposed to write a different ending—one scripted in Hollywood and featuring a gold medal around Kerrigan's neck."

THE PROFESSIONAL CIRCUIT

Baiul is now in the U.S. as one of the featured attractions at the new International Skating Center of Connecticut in Simsbury, near Hartford. ISCC will be her home base, at least for the immediate future. Since her victory at Lillehammer, she has been on a hectic schedule, skating in the Tour of World and Olympic Champions and headlining on the "Nutcracker on Ice" circuit. She has appeared in a variety of other professional events as well, with time out only for athroscopic knee surgery last September and a short period of rehabilitation. Baiul is reaping the rewards of her new-found celebrity with millions of dollars in earnings from pro competition, a TV movie about her life that aired on CBS in 1994, and a book deal now in discussion.

The 1996 Winter Olympics will draw her back into amateur competition, though. She intends to apply for reinstatement in 1995, and to defend her title.

MAJOR INFLUENCES

Rudolph Nureyev, the late, great Russian ballet dancer, was a source of inspiration for Baiul. Jill Trenary, whose skating she calls "an example of grace and femininity," is her model. And Viktor Petrenko is her friend and mentor. But it is Galina Zmievskaya who has been most influential in bringing Baiul to stardom. Galina has guided her young protégé with a mixture of discipline and motherly affection, and it is under this noted coach's tutelage that Oksana has been transformed from an eager, talented athlete into a skater of extraordinary artistry.

FAMILY LIFE

Baiul lives with her coach and adopted family in a townhouse in Simsbury, luxury quarters compared to the crowded apartment in Odessa that became Baiul's home soon after her mother died. Yet a more somber part of the household scene was depicted by *Life* last year in a feature story about the young woman who has become Ukraine's national heroine: "Snapshots of Oksana at the Olympics, Oksana at the World Championships, Oksana and Viktor in costume decorate a bookcase [in her room], but here in Oksana's private world there are no pictures of her parents and grandparents, no mementos of her early life. It's as if all those years had vanished or been shut away somewhere in a locked drawer."

Baiul's lifestyle is different now that she has turned pro and made her years of hard work and competition pay off financially. But she has not forsaken her homeland, and says she will never give up Ukrainian citizenship. Her emotions are close to the surface when she talks about the life she has so recently left behind her and the friends she rarely has time to visit.

The closeness between Baiul and her surrogate family is heartwarming to observe. Oksana looks to Petrenko and his ballerina wife, Nina, as her big brother and sister. She and Galya (whose real name is Galina, like her mother's) are best friends as well as foster siblings. There is true affection in the household, where Oksana is called "Mouyla," an endearing term that seems to have no direct English translation. Her representative, Michael Carlisle, told a *Boston Globe* interviewer last autumn that "to the untrained ear of a North American, [the nickname] sounds like moo-lah. A recent visitor to the Zmievskaya-Baiul home here," he added, "brought down the house when telling them that moo-lah in America is slang for money." A good name, they agreed laughingly.

HOBBIES AND OTHER INTERESTS

Perfecting her English, studying for her U.S. driver's license, and shopping at malls have been Baiul's main interests in her first year of residence in the United States. She has all the enthusiasms of a normal teenager, and she indulges in them with obvious glee. Her coach once told a *Sports Illustrated* feature writer that Oksana acts like "a young goat" (he realized then that he finally appreciated the derivation of the word "kid").

Baiul likes to watch horror movies on television, and she admits that chocolate and pizza are her favorite treats. Now that she is thousands of miles away from her homeland, she is nostalgic about Russian music and plays it frequently on her stereo. When she lived in Odessa, she could hardly get her fill of American music.

HONORS AND AWARDS

European Championships: 1993, second place
World Championships: 1993, first place
Olympic Figure Skating: 1994, gold medal

FURTHER READING

PERIODICALS

Boston Globe, Nov. 9, 1994, Sports section, p.75

Chicago Tribune, Feb. 27, 1994, Sports section, p.1; Feb. 9, 1995, Sports section, p.10
Life, June 1994, p.72
Maclean's, Mar. 7, 1994, p.72
Newsday, Nov. 9, 1994, p.B4
New York Times, Feb. 26, 1994, p.A1; Feb. 27, 1994, Section 8, p.1; Apr. 7, 1994, p.B1
People, Dec. 6, 1993, p.93; Nov. 7, 1994, p.53
Sporting News, Feb. 14, 1994, p.S5
Sports Illustrated, Mar. 22, 1993, p.22; Feb. 7, 1994, p.79; Mar. 7, 1994, p.20
Time, Jan. 24, 1994, p.55; Mar. 7, 1994, p.62

ADDRESS

Michael Carlisle
William Morris Agency
1325 Avenue of the Americas
New York, NY 10019

Halle Berry 1967?-
American Film and Television Actress
Played Title Role in TV Miniseries
"Queen"

BIRTH

Halle Berry was born in Cleveland, Ohio, on August 14, either
1967 or 1968. Inconsistencies have been noted in the published
dates for Halle's birth, but the year 1967 seems to be accurate. The
second child of Jerome and Judith Berry, Halle (pronounced HAL-
lee) was given her unconventional given name by her English-
born mother. Judith Berry took it from the shopping-bag logo of
a Cleveland department store, Halle Brothers, because she thought
it went well with the name of her elder daughter, Heidi.

YOUTH

Berry, the product of an interracial marriage, was reared in a single-parent home after her father left the family when Halle was only four. Her mother, a registered nurse at a Veterans Administration hospital, struggled to provide a stable life for her children. "When my father left, she had two little black kids and she was a white woman," says Berry. "I remember it not being easy for her . . . but we were everything to her. So she sacrificed, and she worked hard, and she made it through." It gives the actress great pleasure now to be able to "turn it around" and do nice things for her mother.

For the most part, the Berry sisters remember a happy childhood, despite the cruel taunts of other children about their mixed racial heritage. Being called "zebra" by schoolmates was an especially hurtful slur. At one time, someone started leaving Oreo cookies in their mailbox, and Judith Berry had to explain the significance to her perplexed young daughters. Counseling helped to sort out the confusion about racial identity, as did the compassion of a mother who had been disowned by her own family when she married a black man. Halle eventually chose to regard herself as African-American, not biracial, and took pride in that choice.

EDUCATION

Accepted in mostly white Bedford High School (suburban Cleveland), where it was "in" to be a good student, Berry nevertheless had problems in those years. "It was okay for Halle to be vice-president, editor of the school paper, and head cheerleader," the actress remembers. "Then I was voted prom queen," she adds with lingering bitterness, "and they accused me of stuffing the ballot box, although there was no proof. So I had to be co-queen with the runner-up, a blue-eyed blond." Even more devastating for Berry was the lack of support from so-called friends who backed the decision of the school administration. After her graduation from high school, Berry studied broadcast journalism for two semesters at Cuyahoga Community College.

FIRST JOBS

By then, Berry had already started her modeling career. In 1985, when she was 17, a boyfriend entered her in the Miss Teen Ohio competition, which she won. She went on to compete in several other pageants. In 1986, she was first runner-up for the title of Miss USA. "I spent a lot of time with a crown on my head," she now says. Her success in beauty pageants opened the door to modeling, so after leaving Cuyahoga Community College she moved to Chicago to begin a modeling career.

Modeling jobs and acting lessons in Chicago led to a an audition for a television pilot and a screen test, although the TV show never aired.

Undeterred in her quest to become an actress, Berry signed with an agent and moved to New York City, where she was cast as a brainy model on the short-lived television show, "Living Dolls." Guest spots followed on other programs until a steady role came along on "Knots Landing."

CAREER HIGHLIGHTS

Berry's first real break, though, came when director Spike Lee chose her to play Sam Jackson's crackhead girlfriend in his 1991 feature film, *Jungle Fever*. "Up until that film," Berry reveals, "I was fighting with the image of beauty-queen-turned actress. I would walk into auditions and people would read my résumé and say, 'Oh, Miss USA.' For *Jungle Fever*, I shed the makeup and gave a real performance for the first time."

Other roles followed in quick succession. She played a sexy nightclub owner in the low-budget comedy *Strictly Business*, an exotic dancer in *The Last Boy Scout*, and had a feature role as Eddie Murphy's love interest in *Boomerang*. During the filming of these movies, Berry kept her recurring role on "Knots Landing" and began to write a script of her own, which she has titled "Inside Out," but which she has not yet found time to develop.

A PLUM ROLE IN A MAJOR MINISERIES

In 1993, Halle Berry was cast in the lead for "Queen," a television miniseries based on a book by the late Alex Haley about his paternal grandmother. Portraying the daughter of a black slave and her white master was a role made to order for the young actress, who drew on her own feelings as a child of mixed racial parentage. "Queen could have been me if I had been alive then. . . . I got so caught up in the moment. I just felt so over-come with emotion," she revealed afterward. There was more turmoil for Berry than just the anxiety of doing justice to a part for which she had passionately campaigned: added pressure came from having top billing in an imposing cast of actors—Danny Glover, Paul Winfield, and Ossie Davis among them. Also, during the filming of a riding sequence, Berry fell from her horse and bruised her tailbone, stirring up even more stress with actual physical pain, and shutting down production for several days. The $16 million miniseries, however, was wrapped up close to schedule, with Berry turning in a strong performance.

After "Queen" came roles in *The Program*, *Father Hood*, and *The Flintstones*. In the latter, a film adaptation of television's hit cartoon series of the 1960s that became one of the biggest movies of 1994, Berry plays a seductive, conniving secretary. With her acting career firmly established, the beauty queen turned model turned actress continues to work at a dizzying pace. She currently is appearing with Jessica Lange in *Losing Isaiah*, a movie that addresses the controversial issue of black children reared by white adoptive or foster parents. Berry's latest role is in *Solomon and Sheba*, a made-for-TV movie filmed in Morocco. She was especially motivated to take the part, even against the advice of show business insiders who warned her that she should stay away from television if she intends to make it in the movies. Her clipped response was, "Listen, the same rules that apply to Julia Roberts don't apply to me. Black actresses don't have the same choices as white actresses. The Queen of Sheba was Ethiopian, yet this is the first time a person of color has ever played the lead in a major biblical production." Berry sees her acceptance of roles like this more as an obligation to her black heritage than as an opportunity for her own career.

MAJOR INFLUENCES

Halle Berry speaks of a number of role models in her life—a fifth-grade teacher who introduced her to black history, activist Angela Davis, the actress Cicely Tyson and, above all, her mother. "The great thing about my mother," says Berry, is that even though she is white, she was really concerned about what would happen to me as I grew up as a black woman in this country." Judith Berry inspired her daughter to have the best revenge, "to succeed," says Halle, "where maybe people don't want to see us as a race succeed."

MARRIAGE AND FAMILY

In the past, relationships with men were difficult for Berry, a fact that she attributes to growing up without a male figure in the household and to witnessing her father's violence against her mother. Until recently, Berry was involved in a string of relationships with abusive men. "Practically every relationship was either mentally abusive, physically abusive, or violent," she confides. "I got hit so hard by one of my boyfriends he broke the eardrum in my left ear. I have no hearing there." Recently, Halle has spoken candidly about her past in interviews with the press. "Once I broke the cycle in my own life," she explains, "I felt obligated to share my experiences with others. And It's been work it. I can't tell you how many letters I've received since the *Ebony* article [in April 1993]—I mean, really heartfelt letters from women who say, 'You've changed my life.' To feel that I'm helping someone has given me the greatest satisfaction when it comes down to it. That feels better than any movie role."

Berry broke that abusive pattern when she met David Justice, star outfielder for the Atlanta Braves baseball team. They married in the early hours of New Year's Day, 1993, after a storybook meeting and a nine-month, mostly long-distance, romance. Berry first spotted Justice on an MTV celebrity "Rock and Jock" show, and was taken with his looks and demeanor. Within weeks, a newspaper interviewer and old friend of the ballplayer engineered an introduction. At the time of the couple's first meeting, Justice was in a slump and suffering from a bad attitude problem, but marriage has been a major element in turning his life around. "Berry," says *Sports Illustrated*, "who's at home in the spotlight, has helped Justice get used to life in the public eye too."

They have no children, but two toy Maltese dogs make up the rest of the couple's household. Bumper and Petey go everywhere with the actress, around town and around the world. As for Berry's domesticity, she readily admits that she's not a standout in the kitchen, but her husband says that he's willing to learn and to become the family cook.

Berry and Justice divide their time between two homes—their first, a six-bedroom house in Atlanta, and now another place in Los Angeles.

HOBBIES AND OTHER INTERESTS

When Berry is in Atlanta, she faithfully works out four times weekly in the state-of-the-art gym she and Justice have built in their home; she hires a personal trainer whenever she is away on a movie or TV shoot. "I have diabetes," she explains, "so for me the exercise is a vital part of feeling good and staying healthy." Berry's diabetic condition was discovered several years ago after she passed out on the set of "Living Dolls," her first television job. Now learning to live with an illness for which no cure has been found, she has become a frequent spokesperson for the Juvenile Diabetes Foundation.

CREDITS

TELEVISION

"Living Dolls," 1989
"Knots Landing," 1991-92
Queen, 1993
Solomon and Sheba, 1995

FILMS

Jungle Fever, 1991
Strictly Business, 1991
The Last Boy Scout, 1991
Boomerang, 1992
The Program, 1993
Father Hood, 1993
The Flintstones, 1994
Losing Isaiah, 1995

HONORS AND AWARDS

Miss Teen Ohio: 1985
First Runner-Up, Miss USA: 1986
One of "Fifty Most Beautiful People in the World" (*People* magazine): 1992, 1993
Image Award (NAACP): 1994, for Best Actress in a television movie or mini-series, for *Queen*

FURTHER READING

BOOKS

Who's Who Among Black Americans, 1994-95

PERIODICALS

Cosmopolitan, Sep. 1993, p.186
Ebony, Feb. 1992, p.37; Apr. 1993, p.118; July 1993, p.68; Dec. 1994, p.114
Essence, June 1994, p.60
Jet, June 6, 1994, p.60
People, Mar. 2, 1993, p.35; May 9, 1993, p.90
Philadelphia Inquirer, Feb. 14, 1993, p.4
Redbook, July 1994, p.46
Sports Illustrated, June 6, 1994, p.66
TV Guide, Feb. 13, 1993, p.12

ADDRESS

Jonas Public Relations
417 South Beverly Drive
Suite 211
Beverly Hills, CA 90212

Benazir Bhutto 1953-
Pakistani Political Leader
Prime Minister of Pakistan

BIRTH

Benazir Bhutto was born on June 21, 1953, in Karachi, Pakistan. The name "Benazir" means "without comparison" in Urdu, the official language of Pakistan. She was the first child of Zulfikar Ali and Nusrat Bhutto. Her father, Zulfikar, was prime minister of Pakistan from 1971-77. She has a sister, Sanam, and two brothers, Shah Nawaz (deceased) and Mir Murtaza.

THE FORMATION OF PAKISTAN

Benazir Bhutto's family history is intimately tied to the history of her nation. The land now known as Pakistan used to be part of northwestern India. For centuries, India has been home to both Hindus and Muslims (followers of the Islamic faith), as well as smaller groups from other religions. Although Hindus formed a clear majority in India as a whole, the region now known as Pakistan has been home to Islamic people since the eighth century. Beginning in the sixteenthth and seventeenth centuries, European invaders were active on the Indian subcontinent; by the eighteenth century, India was part of the British Empire, with Britain holding effective economic and political control through their colonial government.

By the early twentieth century, two different independence movements were taking place simultaneously in this region: India was seeking independence from Britain, and the Muslims were seeking independence from India. Because of longstanding conflicts between Muslims and Hindus, Muslim leader Muhammad Ali Jinnah led a movement during the 1940s to establish a separate Islamic state. One of the early supporters of a Muslim nation was Benazir Bhutto's grandfather, Sir Shah Nawaz, who held several prominent positions in the British colonial government in India. Due to popular Muslim support, the Islamic Republic of Pakistan was created after India achieved independence from England in 1947. The new republic actually consisted of two territories located 1,000 miles apart on either side of the Indian subcontinent—West Pakistan and East Pakistan. Later, civil war followed when East Pakistan declared its independence. It became an autonomous country, Bangladesh, in 1971.

Since independence, Pakistan has struggled to achieve democracy. The country has been fraught with inconsistencies in its government (military dictatorships as well as democratically elected assemblies and prime ministers), civil war between the east and west portions of the country (until 1971), wars with India, violence between various ethnic groups, illiteracy, high birth rates, and poverty.

EARLY YEARS

Benazir Bhutto comes from a wealthy family that has owned land in Larkana in the province of Sindh for 350 years. At the beginning of her father's career, before he became prime minister of Pakistan, Zulfikar had a law practice in Karachi, located on the shores of the Arabian Sea and now Pakistan's leading city of commerce. Benazir's mother, the former Nusrat Ispahani, was born into a liberal Iranian family, that was prominent in the business world, they educated their daughters and allowed them to serve in the women's National Guard.

Nusrat is Zulfikar's second wife. The Bhuttos belong to the Islamic faith, which allows a man to take up to four wives. His first marriage, to a cousin, took place when he was twelve and she was eight years old. Each then returned home to live with their families, and they never lived together

45

as husband and wife. Arranged marriages are not unusual among land-owning families in Pakistan and are often performed to guarantee the family's continued hold on its land. When Zulfikar was 23 years old and home on vacation from Oxford University in England, he met and fell in love with Nusrat. His family, given to breaking tradition, gave him permission to marry her.

When Benazir was born, her father, Zulfikar, was completing his studies at Oxford University and didn't see his daughter until she was three months old. As a baby, her skin was of such an unusually rosy complexion that her family immediately began calling her "Pinkie," a nickname friends and relatives used through her college years.

YOUTH

Benazir entered Lady Jenning's Nursery School in Karachi when she was three years old. At five, her parents enrolled her in the Convent of Jesus and Mary School, a prestigious Catholic school. At home, tutors instructed her and her brothers and sister in secular subjects, the Islamic faith, and the Arabic language (because it is the language of the Holy Koran, the sacred book of Islam).

As Zulfikar embarked on the political career that would have so much impact on young Benazir, he and Nusrat traveled often, so they retained an English nanny to care for Benazir and her siblings. Benazir's parents expected her to take a role in looking after the other children because she was the oldest.

Her father doted on Benazir and began priming her at an early age in the intricacies of the political world. When she was as young as six years old, Zulfikar read to her from books about the great French military and political leader Napoleon Bonaparte, whom he greatly admired. He would tell all the children stories about the family's history and the history of the region from which they came. When U.S. President John F. Kennedy was shot by an assassin in 1963, Zulfikar woke ten-year-old Benazir up in the middle of the night to sit by his side while he read bulletins on the medical condition of the American president he personally knew and respected. While she and her younger sister, Sanam, attended primary school out of town, Zulfikar would "continue our political education by mail," Bhutto writes in her memoir, *Daughter of Destiny.* "Shortly after he returned from the Summit of Non-Aligned Countries in Jakarta [the capital city of Indonesia], he wrote us a long letter elaborating on the self-interest of the superpowers in the United Nations and the resulting neglect of third world countries. One of the nuns sat Sanam and me down on a bench in the school garden and read the letter to us in its entirety, though we understood little of its content."

At 14, she was a dues-paying member of the Pakistan People's Party (PPP), founded by her father in 1967. But, Benazir recalls, "When I was a child, there were many attempts on my father's life. Politics *scared* me. I remember the hushed voices when we would tiptoe into the drawing room, where the grownups were talking about demonstrations and guns. 'Don't speak in front of the children,' someone would say when they noticed us. This is a life that I never wanted for myself."

EDUCATION

Zulfikar Bhutto was the first individual in his family to attend college in the West. He and his wife prized education and determined that each of their children should attend the best possible schools. In 1969, 16-year-old Benazir was sent off to Radcliffe College in Massachusetts. Her father gave her a mother-of-pearl-bound copy of the Holy Koran and admonished her: "Very few in Pakistan have the opportunity you now have and you must take advantage of it. Never forget that the money it is costing to send you comes from the land, from the people who sweat and toil on those lands. You will owe a debt to them, a debt you can repay with God's blessing by using your education to better their lives."

It was the first time in her life that she had to wash her own clothes, walk to classes, answer her own phone. "At first I had to ask directions to the library, to the lecture halls, the dorms. I couldn't afford to be tongue-tied. I had been thrown into the deep end of a strange and foreign pool. If I were to get to the surface, I had to get there by myself." Though she cried often during those first few months, she said later that the experience forced her to grow up. Eventually, she made many friends and exchanged her *shalwar khameez* (the pants and long tunics that are the predominant attire of Pakistani women) for jeans and sweatshirts. She played squash (always in sweat pants; Islamic custom forbids women to show their legs), attended rock concerts, and ate "unconscionable numbers of peppermint stick ice-cream cones."

Benazir majored in comparative government after abandoning her plan to study psychology; she changed her mind when she discovered she would have to dissect animals. While she was at school, the PPP won the 1971 elections and her father became prime minister of Pakistan. Eventually, at Radcliffe, the politically oriented public speaker and activist began to emerge. Benazir marched in anti-Vietnam War demonstrations, at the risk of being deported. Civil war between East and West Pakistan—out of which the new state of Bangladesh would declare independence from Pakistan—was on the minds of her professors and colleagues. They would argue about her father's handling of the conflict, and many found themselves on the receiving end of Benazir's passionate defense of her father's actions in that volatile situation.

Zulfikar encouraged his daughter's interest in international affairs and fully supported her desire to enter Pakistan's Foreign Service after finishing college. Toward that end, Zulfikar had Benazir spend some school vacations accompanying him on various diplomatic jaunts. She joined him for his address to the United Nations, where she met future U.S. President George Bush. He took her to India, where she met Prime Minister Indira Gandhi, to China for his meeting with Chairman Mao Zedung, and to the White House for his meeting with President Richard Nixon.

In 1973, she graduated *cum laude* (with honors) from Radcliffe College. When she returned home, Benazir very much wanted to stay and work for the government. But, at Zulfikar's urging, she went off to England instead to follow his footsteps at Oxford University. There she joined the Oxford Union Debating Society, as have many future politicians. In 1976 she became the first Asian woman to be named president of the Society. Her father had been the first Asian to hold that position. Benazir earned a master's degree in politics, philosophy, and economics. She stayed on for an additional year to take a course in international law and diplomacy.

CAREER HIGHLIGHTS

In 1979, two weeks after Benazir returned home after graduating from Oxford, the PPP won new elections. Zulfikar's victory was challenged by the opposition, which led to riots by his supporters. Pakistan's army chief of staff, General Zia ul-Haq, overthrew Zulfikar Bhutto's government and imposed martial law.

Zulfikar was a charismatic leader, popular with the poor people of Pakistan who had long been oppressed by the feudal system. He was given to drinking alcohol (forbidden by Islamic law) and doling out snappy retorts to criticism. His campaign slogan was "bread, clothing, shelter." And while the elder Bhutto made gains toward a democratic Pakistan and instituted many positive reforms—including more equality for women, a minimum wage, and redistribution of land—the country was still racked with poverty when he was overthrown. He did not tolerate political opposition. Many independent accounts describe the imprisonment and torture of his political opponents while he was prime minister.

On September 3, 1977, Zulfikar was arrested, imprisoned, and charged with conspiracy to murder a political opponent. His wife, Nusrat, then became the official leader of the PPP, but Benazir was its real leader. She would run errands for her father, and he would continue her political education. "He would tell me, do this, do that, contact so-and-so—the nuts, the bolts, how to have patience." During a visit to her father in prison, Zulfikar told Benazir to continue his mission if anything happened to him. But Benazir too was placed under arrest by the end of the month, for holding demonstrations, organizing members of the PPP, and speaking out against Zia and her father's imprisonment. Benazir and Nusrat were followed and harassed by military police. They were often imprisoned in their house to prevent them from visiting Zulfikar.

Zulfikar Bhutto went to trial in October. He was convicted in March 1978 and sentenced to death. Former Attorney General of the U.S. Ramsey Clark attended the trial and observed that Bhutto had not been allowed to speak on his own behalf and that the evidence did not support the verdict. Leaders of many governments around the world, including U.S. President Jimmy Carter, implored Zia to reduce the sentence. The Bhutto family appealed to the Supreme Court of Pakistan, which upheld the decision.

THE DEATH OF ZULFIKAR BHUTTO

Zulfikar Bhutto was hanged on April 4, 1979, at 2:00 A.M., three hours earlier than scheduled and shortly after a final brief visit with Benazir and Nusrat. The family had sent the other children out of the country the morning Zulfikar was arrested. Benazir later told the *New Yorker* magazine that this was the worst memory she had of the years following her return from Oxford: "The martyrdom of my father, and my own feeling of helplessness. I knew that morning that he was going to be killed, but there was nothing—nothing—I could do. That's my starkest image, the one that comes back to haunt me, over and over again." For many nights after, she slept with the shirt he'd been wearing under her pillow. Zia did not allow the Bhuttos to attend Zulfikar's funeral, and Benazir and Nusrat were not released from jail until seven weeks after his death. People in Pakistan responded to news of the execution with outrage and demonstrations that ended in violent confrontations with the military.

Elections were to be held in November 1979. Zia canceled them, outlawed participation in political parties, and again arrested Benazir and Nusrat, holding them under house arrest for six months. By February 1981, their PPP joined forces with other factions against Zia to form a coalition—the Movement to Restore Democracy (MRD).

IMPRISONMENT

Benazir and her mother were repeatedly arrested and imprisoned during most of the next several years. On March 8, 1981, Benazir was put in solitary confinement at Sukkar Jail. Nusrat was held at Karachi Central Jail. That month some 6,000 people were arrested for political reasons. What prompted the mass arrest was the hijacking of a Pakistani International Airlines jet on March 2. The condition for the jet's release was Zia's release of some political prisoners who supported Bhutto and the PPP. Out of the country, Benazir's brothers had formed Al-Zulfikar, a group against the Zia regime, which took responsibility for the hijacking.

As the years of imprisonment wore on, they took their toll on Benazir's mental and physical health. She suffered a chronic ear infection, was unable to eat, and was once told by prison doctors that she had uterine cancer, for which reason she underwent an operation in April 1981. Bottles of poison would be left in her cell. "Sounds became so important in solitary confinement," she has said. "Like the sounds of dead bats falling on the roof of my cell." To pass the time, she tried to keep a diary, exercise, and maintain her gradually failing memory. Asked by an interviewer what sustained her most, she replied, "Anger." She prayed often and wrote in her autobiography that "I have coped. Each moment has dragged, but it has also passed. God alone has helped me in this ordeal. Without Him, I would have perished." Her old college friend Peter Galbraith (son of former U.S. ambassador to India John Kenneth Galbraith, and later a member of the U.S. Senate Foreign Relations Committee) later remarked: "Benazir got her B.A. from Radcliffe, her M.A. from Oxford, and her Ph.D. from Sukkar jail."

By the end of 1983 Benazir was losing her hearing and needed medical attention that was not available in Pakistan. In January 1984, she was finally permitted to leave the country for an ear operation in London. After the operation, she stayed on in London and there initiated a campaign for the PPP. She found support among the 400,000 Pakistanis who live in England, many of whom fled into exile from Zia's regime. She and others went to work on the behalf of the people held in prison in Pakistan for political reasons, writing appeals, publishing a magazine, and spreading their message to the U.S.

In July 1985, more tragedy struck the Bhutto family when, during a family reunion on the French Riviera, Benazir's brother, Shah Nawaz, was found dead in his apartment. The Bhuttos filed murder charges with French authorities, but no one was ever charged with the murder. Shah Nawaz's wife was eventually charged with failing to aid a person in danger, when she revealed to police that it had taken him some time to die. Both brothers carried vials of poison with them in case of capture, and doctors theorized that he had ingested a diluted dose. The Bhutto family returned to Pakistan to bury him and were greeted at the airport by 10,000 mourners. After the funeral, Benazir was again arrested and held until November 1985, when she was allowed to return to France for hearings investigating the death of her brother.

Benazir then traveled to the U.S. and spoke to the Senate Foreign Relations Committee while it was deciding whether to continue aid to Pakistan. Members of Congress grew more critical of Zia. This was the time of the war in Afghanistan between the Afghan rebels and the U.S.S.R. The U.S. was sending financial assistance to the rebels through the Pakistan government. At the same time, the U.S. government was also supporting Zia for his promise to protect U.S.interests. Zia ended martial law on December 30, 1985, and set a 1990 date for national elections.

BECOMING PRIME MINISTER

In April 1986, after making the obligatory Muslim pilgrimage to Mecca, Benazir Bhutto returned to Pakistan a national hero. An estimated 500,000 Pakistanis turned out to hear her call for fair elections. In mid 1986 she rallied for a program called "Doves for Democracy" that would have commandeered thousands of volunteers to perform such acts of passive resistance as sit-ins and hunger strikes. That initiative failed, but the PPP and MRD grew stronger. In 1987 when Benazir married, she and her husband held an enormous reception for the public at a sports stadium in a poor area of Karachi. More than 100,000 people showed up.

Although Bhutto, like her father, had survived attempts on her life, the threats became more frequent around this time. In January 1987, gunmen shot at a caravan in which Benazir was expected to be traveling. Nusrat, still co-chairman of the PPP, was shot at while campaigning in 1988. Recently, she identified one would-be assassin as Ramzi Yousef, who currently stands accused of masterminding the 1993 World Trade Center bombing in New York. During her campaign in the autumn of 1993, he was injured when explosives he was carrying went off near her home in Karachi.

Demonstrations for free elections continued, spawning violent clashes between police and protesters. Zia buckled under the pressure, but decreed that they would be held on November 16, 1988, the same day Benazir's first child was rumored to be due. The rumors were incorrect, and Benazir was on the campaign trail within two weeks after she gave birth in September. When some questioned how her 1987 marriage would affect her career, she said that "ending Zia's dictatorship is the goal I have chosen to single-mindedly pursue because I believe in democracy. . . . Marriage doesn't change my belief or affect the pursuit of that primary goal."

On August 16, 1988, a plane crashed carrying Zia, several high-ranking military officers, and Arnold Raphael, the U.S. ambassador to Pakistan. Everyone on board was killed. Investigations have not determined what caused the mysterious crash.

With Zia dead, many feared the military would again rule. But an interim prime minister was appointed instead. On November 16, the PPP won 92 of the 217 seats in the National Assembly election. It then rallied enough support within the Assembly to gather a clear majority of votes, and interim Prime Minister Ghulam Ishaq Khan called on Benazir to become Prime Minister. Benazir Bhutto became the first woman democratically elected to head an Islamic state.

Among the problems Bhutto faced upon taking office were a financially bankrupt country, the Russian presence in Afghanistan and resulting U.S. pressure, a tense history with India, a rampant heroin trade, and a military that resented her party. Her first act was to release political prisoners. While in office, she created a freer atmosphere in Pakistan, but was criticized for appointing relatives and friends to important government positions. *Time* magazine reported that, after 14 months in office, her government had passed no legislation and, further, that there was a PPP campaign to overthrow Bhutto's strongest opponent, Nawaz Sharif, chief minister of Punjab province.

On August 6, 1990, President Ishaq Khan dismissed her from office, accused her of corruption and nepotism, and began investigating her. Her trial began in October. Ultimately, Benazir Bhutto was acquitted of six out of eight charges of corruption and mismanagement. In addition, her husband was arrested on charges of being involved in kidnapping, as well as taking kickbacks from government contracts. He was released from prison in February 1993.

Pakistan gave a vote of no-confidence to the PPP when it was defeated in the October 1990 election. Bhutto won her seat in the National Assembly, but Nawaz Sharif became prime minister. She charged vote fraud, but international poll-watchers detected no evidence that elections were rigged. Benazir Bhutto was arrested in November 1992, after she held a demonstration calling for the removal of Sharif's government. She continued opposing the new government and ran for reelection in 1993.

During the 1993 campaign, family problems ensued with Bhutto's mother and brother, Murtaza. Facing arrest upon his return to Pakistan on terrorist charges for his involvement in Al-Zulfikar, Murtaza came home to run for National Assembly and provincial assembly seats as an independent candidate, with Nusrat's support. Benazir refused to back him because he would be running against the PPP. She would not allow him to run as part of the PPP because "He should first clear himself of the charges of terrorism, before he can be rehabilitated in the party." Benazir's PPP removed her mother from her position as co-chairman of the party, and Nusrat, in turn, released statements implying that her daughter is a dictator. Despite these family conflicts, Benazir Bhutto was reelected as prime minister in October 1993.

Depsite her reelection, problems remain. As before, critics have complained that her government is accomplishing nothing. And opposition party members have accused her of arresting thousands of political opponents in October 1994 during a general strike that turned violent.

Pakistan continues to struggle with terrible poverty, crime, ethnic violence, the long-term dispute with India over Kashmir, one of the lowest literacy rates in the world, and a steadily growing drug problem. Clearly, there are many challenges remaining for Benazir Bhutto as prime minister of Pakistan.

MARRIAGE AND FAMILY

Benazir Bhutto and Asif Zardari, a Karachi businessman who also comes from a landowning family, were married on December 19, 1987, at her home in Karachi. The marriage was arranged by their elder relatives, but Benazir had the final say on the matter. Zardari had admired Bhutto from afar for several years, but they met only a few days before the wedding.

Benazir had expected to marry for love, but, she wrote in *Daughter of Destiny*, "an arranged marriage was the price in personal choice I had to pay for the political path my life had taken. My high profile in Pakistan precluded the possibility of my meeting a man in the normal course of events. . . . Even the most discreet relationship would have fueled the gossip and rumor that circulated around my every move." Indeed, Bhutto considered the possibility of remaining unmarried; her public image was nearly that of a saint. However, she realized that she was living in a world in which many believe something is wrong with a single woman, and journalists were always asking her why she wasn't married. She decided in the end that the political goals of the PPP would be more easily achieved by a married Muslim woman. In a 1994 interview, she said that she thought her marriage "would be, more or less, a loveless marriage, a marriage of convenience. The surprising part is that we are very close and that it's been a very good match."

Their first child was a son, born on September 21, 1988—less than one month before she was elected prime minister. Bhutto and her husband named him Bilawal, which means "one without equal." They have gone on to have two more children, both daughters: Bakhtawar was born in 1990 and Asifa in 1993.

AWARDS AND HONORS

Bruno Kreisky Award for Human Rights: 1989
Honorary Phi Beta Kappa Award (Radcliffe College): 1989

WRITINGS

Foreign Policy in Perspective, 1978
Daughter of Destiny: An Autobiography, 1989

FURTHER READING

BOOKS

Doherty, Katherine M., and Craig A. Doherty. *Benazir Bhutto,* 1990
Encyclopedia Brittanica, 1993
Opfell, Olga S. *Women Prime Ministers and Presidents,* 1993
Sansevere-Dreher, Diane. *Benazir Bhutto,* 1991 (juvenile)
World Book Encyclopedia, 1993

PERIODICALS

Current Biography Yearbook 1986
Economist, Dec. 26, 1987, p.46; Sep. 18, 1993, p.42; Oct. 23, 1993, p.41;
    Apr. 2, 1994, p.36
Interview, Feb. 1989, p.68
Life, Oct. 1986, p.50; Feb. 1988, p.58
Maclean's, Sep. 1, 1986, p.24
Newsweek, July 7, 1986, p.33; Aug. 8, 1987, p.47; Jan. 24, 1994, p.43
New Yorker, Oct. 4, 1993, p.82
New York Times, Oct. 10, 1994, p.A9; Oct. 12, 1994, p.A4
New York Times Biographical Service, Sep. 1986, p.1160
New York Times Book Review, Mar. 19, 1989, p.6
New York Times Magazine, Jan. 15, 1989, p.27; May 15, 1994, p.36
Time, Jan. 29, 1990, p.56; Aug. 27, 1990, p.44; Oct. 15, 1990, p.66; Nov. 5,
    1990, p.45
U.S. News & World Report, Oct. 22, 1990, p.22; Nov. 1, 1993, p.58
Vogue, Apr. 1989, p.416

ADDRESS

Pakistani Embassy
2315 Massachusetts Ave., NW
Washington, D.C., 20008

Jonathan Brandis   1976-
American Actor
Stars on "seaQuest DSV"

BIRTH

Jonathan Gregory Brandis was born in Danbury, Connecticut, on April 13, 1976. His father, Greg Brandis, a former firefighter, is an independent businessman, while his mother, Mary Brandis, a former teacher, manages Jonathan's career and handles his fan mail. Jonathan has no brothers or sisters.

YOUTH

Brandis started working when he was still very young. He spent his early years in Danbury, commuting about 60 miles several days each week to work in New York. He had his first professional job at the age of two, modeling for an advertising campaign for Buster Brown children's clothing. By the age of five, he was doing commercials for Kix cereal and Fisher-Price toys. At six, he earned a recurring role on the daytime soap opera "One Life to Live."

By the time he was nine, Brandis had already appeared in about 100 TV commercials. He had proved how serious he was about acting. The family decided to move to the San Fernando Valley, near Los Angeles, so he could work in Hollywood. That move led the way to roles in a variety of formats, including TV series, mini-series, and movies. This early work experience, Brandis says, "taught me behavior, failure, success, discipline. When I was a little kid, always getting in trouble in class, the teachers would say, 'Do you act this way on the set?' And I'd say, 'No, that's a job.'"

EDUCATION

Brandis completed his education in two ways. When he was working, he would receive tutoring on the set; between parts, he would attend public school. In addition to his regular classes, he also took private acting lessons for his first two years in Los Angeles. "I was probably the only kid in L.A. who didn't have a series," he now jokes. In 1993, he graduated from Valley Professional High School. Currently, Brandis has delayed plans to attend college, preferring instead to continue building on his success as an actor.

FIRST JOBS

After moving to California, Brandis continued his steady climb up the career ladder, earning better and better acting roles. He started out in a TV mini-series, winning his first dramatic role in *Poor Little Rich Girl: The Barbara Hutton Story* (1987), playing the son of the wealthy heiress Barbara Hutton (played by Farrah Fawcett). Next, he appeared in the horror mini-series *Stephen King's "IT"* (1990) as the child stutterer. In feature films, he starred in *The NeverEnding Story II: The Next Chapter* (1990), in which he stars as Bastian Balthazar Bux in this fantasy/adventure about the importance of reading, a sequel to the original 1984 film. In *Ladybugs* (1992) he played a boy who dresses up as a girl to play on a girls' soccer team, which is coached by Rodney Dangerfield. *Sidekicks* (1993) features Jonathan as a scrawny, awkward, asthmatic kid who learns martial arts and becomes the sidekick of his hero, martial-arts movie star Chuck Norris. Brandis also appeared in guest-starring roles on a variety of TV shows, including "L.A. Law," "Murder, She Wrote," "Gabriel's Fire," "Blossom," "Who's the Boss?," "Full House," "The Flash," "Pros and Cons," "Webster," "Alien Nation," and "Saved by the Bell: The College Years."

CAREER HIGHLIGHTS

"SEAQUEST DSV"

Brandis's big break came in 1993, when he was cast in the NBC series "seaQuest DSV." Set in the early 21st century, this fantasy/adventure show details the explorations of the seaQuest Deep Submergence Vehicle (DSV) in its mission to patrol the underwater world, with its colonies, mining bases, scientific endeavors, and frontier mentality. Echoing the comments of many early reviewers, Brandis himself described it as "'Star Trek' on a submarine." The ship is staffed with a top-notch team of scientific and naval personnel: Nathan Bridger (Roy Scheider), the captain of this technologically advanced submarine; Comdr. Jonathan Ford (Don Franklin), the captain's second-in-command; Lt. James Brody (Edward Kerr), a special weapons expert; Dr. Wendy Smith (Rosalind Allen), a psychologist with ESP (extra-sensory perception); and many others.

Brandis plays Lucas Wolenczak, a cocky, young computer genius whose parents sent him to the seaQuest as a disciplinary measure. As the actor explains, "Lucas is a normal, extremely bright person who tries to prove he is more than just a computer expert. I especially admire his ability to stand up to criticism and overcome the barrier of being younger than the other crew members."

Produced by Amblin Entertainment, the company of noted filmmaker Steven Spielberg, "seaQuest DSV" was created with high expectations for success. But when the series debuted in September 1993, the critics panned it. Early ratings were poor, although the show was immensely popular with teenage viewers. Many wondered whether the show would be canceled after its first season. It was renewed and filming was moved from a studio lot in southern California to Universal Studios in Orlando, Florida, which allowed for more outdoor scenes. The show's popularity with its teen viewers has continued ever since, and Brandis is currently one of the hottest stars among teens. He receives about 8,000 letters from his fans each month, his mother reports, and sometimes as many as 4,000 letters in a single week.

In 1995, Brandis expanded his list of credits when he wrote the script for the "seaQuest DSV" episode entitled "The Siamese Dream." He also helped produce that episode, hoping that it will help him make the move into directing. In "The Siamese Dream," a psychic tries to take over the ship by creating nightmares in the crew. Commenting on the direction of the series and his own character, Brandis said, "I got so tired of creature shows with man-eating plants and 200-foot crocodiles. I'd like to see Lucas grow up a little—wear a uniform maybe, have a little more command—and get a girl for once."

In addition to his work on "seaQuest DSV," Brandis appeared in the cable film *The Good King* (1994). He co-starred with Joan Fontaine and Stefanie Powers. Filmed in Czechoslovakia and set in about 1350, *The Good King* is a medieval story about King Wenceslas, a Czech national folk hero who actually lived in the mid-1700s.

FUTURE PLANS

At this stage in his career, Brandis is looking for roles that are both appealing to and suitable for his teenage fans. "I want fun, spunky roles that kids like and that I have a good time shooting as well," he explains. "That's not to say

I wouldn't do a big dramatic movie about street kids or something, or an adult comedy. I'm just saying that I'm attracted to films that I would watch myself and that I'd have fun making. It's entertainment. It's the reason we're all here."

MAJOR INFLUENCES

Brandis gives credit to his parents as his greatest influence. He also mentions Steven Spielberg, who has been a hero to Brandis since he first saw *E.T.: The Extra-Terrestrial*.

HOME AND FAMILY

When he is not filming "seaQuest DSV" in Florida, Brandis lives in Los Angeles with his parents and his pets: a dog named Megan, a blue parakeet named Ernie, and a cat named Marbles. Despite his success, Brandis still has to do chores at home, including cleaning his room, doing his laundry, and clearing the table after dinner.

HOBBIES AND OTHER INTERESTS

Brandis enjoys playing pool and basketball, reading and writing, and listening to music by Nirvana, Lenny Kravitz, U2, Guns N' Roses, and Snoop Doggy Dogg. He also supports several charities, including the Make-A-Wish Foundation, Famous Fone Friends, the Spina Bifida Foundation, and Superstar Kids Challenge for Cystic Fibrosis.

FURTHER READING

PERIODICALS

Chicago Tribune, Sep. 14, 1993, Kidnews Section, p.7
New York Times, Oct. 10, 1993, Section 2, p.1
People, Aug. 29, 1994, p.63
Sun Sentinel, Nov. 27, 1994, Sunshine Magazine, p.5
Teen, May 1994, p.p.106
Toronto Star, May 30, 1994, p.E7
USA Today, Feb. 7, 1994, p.D3

ADDRESS

Jonathan Brandis Fan Club
11684 Ventura Blvd., Suite 909
Studio City, CA 91604

OBITUARY

Warren E. Burger   1907-1995
American Jurist
Former Chief Justice, United States
Supreme Court

BIRTH

Warren Earl Burger was born on September 17, 1907, in St. Paul, Minnesota. He was the fourth child born to German-Swiss parents, Charles Joseph Burger, a farmer, railroad cargo inspector, and traveling salesman, and Katherine (Schnittger) Burger, a homemaker. There were seven children in the family, five boys and two girls.

60

YOUTH

Burger grew up in Dayton's Bluff, a lower-middle class neighborhood in St. Paul on the banks of the Mississippi River. The family lived on a 20-acre farm there. The family struggled financially. By about age nine, Burger had gone to work delivering newspapers to help out with the family finances.

In fourth grade, Burger contracted a mysterious illness that doctors now believe was polio. It kept him out of school for a year and left him with a deformed spine that bothered him over the years as a sore back. Stuck at home, he began reading the law books and biographies of American historical figures that had belonged to his grandfather, Joe Burger. A Swiss-born immigrant who at the age of 14 joined the Union Army in the Civil War, Joe Burger went on to become a lawyer and to serve in the legislature. He also served as an inspiration for his young grandson.

EDUCATION

Burger attended public schools in St. Paul. He started out at Van Buren Elementary School, where he met Harry A. Blackmun, a life- long friend with whom he would later serve on the Supreme Court. At John A. Johnson High School, Burger was president of the student council and editor of the school newspaper. In addition to playing cornet and bugle, he earned letters in football, hockey, swimming, and track and field. He also held down jobs during the school year and during summer vacations, working as a track coach, lifeguard, truck driver, and camp counselor. He graduated from high school in 1925.

Because he was such an outstanding student, Burger earned a scholarship to Princeton University. But the amount of the scholarship was too small to cover his expenses and to help out his family, so he was forced to turn it down. Instead, he took a day job selling insurance for the Mutual Life Insurance Company and enrolled in night classes at the University of Minnesota. After two years, he enrolled in night-school at the St. Paul College of Law (now the William Mitchell College of Law). At that time, it was not necessary to earn a B.A. before attending law school. Burger earned his law degree in 1931 with high honors.

MARRIAGE AND FAMILY

Burger married Elvera Stromberg, a fellow student at the University of Minnesota, on November 8, 1933. They made their home for many years in Minnesota before moving to Arlington, Virginia, outside Washington, D.C., for Burger's judicial career. They had one son, Wade Allen, and one daughter, Margaret Elizabeth, as well as two grandchildren. Elvera Burger died in May 1994.

CAREER HIGHLIGHTS

PRACTICING LAW

For over 20 years, Burger practiced law in his home town in Minnesota. After graduating in 1931 from law school, he joined the faculty there, teaching contract law part-time for 12 years. He also joined a St. Paul law firm, Boyesen, Otis & Faricy (later Faricy, Burger, Moore & Costello). His successful handling of criminal, corporate, and probate cases earned him a partnership four years later. He remained with the firm until 1953.

In addition to practicing and teaching law, Burger became active in community affairs. He was president of the Junior Chamber of Commerce and the first president of the St. Paul Council on Human Relations, a group that he helped to establish. As president of that group, he organized a training program for police officers to improve relations between the police and the city's minority groups. Later, his interest in civil rights later led to his appointment to the Governor's Interracial Commission (1948-1953).

Burger was active in local Republican politics as well. In 1934, he organized the Young Republicans in Minnesota. A few years later he hooked up with veteran Republican Harold Stassen, working in his successful 1938 campaign to be governor of Minnesota. In 1942, Burger was rejected for service during World War II because of his back trouble, but he served as a member of the Minnesota Emergency War Labor Board from 1942 to 1947.

Burger entered national politics in 1948, when he went to the Republican National Convention as the manager of Harold Stassen's unsuccessful campaign for the Republican nomination for president. He attended the convention again in 1952, where he was a delegate to the credentials committee and, again, the manager of Stassen's campaign. While Stassen was again unsuccessful, the convention proved to be pivotal for Burger. On the last day, General Dwight D. Eisenhower was 9 votes short of winning the Republican nomination for president. At a crucial moment, Burger threw the Stassen votes over to Eisenhower, winning him the nomination. Eisenhower was elected president in 1952.

JOINING THE FEDERAL JUSTICE SYSTEM

In 1953, President Eisenhower rewarded Burger with a position as an Assistant Attorney General. In that job, Burger led the Civil Division of the U.S. Justice Department, supervising a staff of 180 lawyers and overseeing the federal government's civil and international lawsuits. He became an expert, in particular, in arguing cases involving maritime and labor law. Three years later, in 1956, President Eisenhower appointed Burger to the U.S. Court of Appeals for the District of Columbia.

The judicial system in the United States is divided into two separate systems, the federal and state courts. The state courts have responsibility for all matters involving state law, while the federal courts cover those involving federal law. The federal courts, where Burger served, are composed of three levels. The lower courts, the level at which most cases are originally tried, are the 92 District Courts. If one party wants to appeal the decision of the District Court, the case would go to the next level, the Court of Appeals. There are 11 Courts of Appeals covering the 50 states, plus one more for the District of Columbia. The appeals (or appellate) court judge reviews the lower court's decision and either sustains it or overturns it. After that step, the case could be taken to the Supreme Court, the highest court in the land. At all levels, federal judges are nominated by the president, confirmed by the U.S. Senate, and serve for life.

Beginning in 1956, Burger served for 13 years on the Court of Appeals for the District of Columbia. That is considered one of the most important appeals courts because it covers not only local cases for the District of Columbia, but also those arising from government agencies in our nation's capital. Burger served on the Court of Appeals during the 1960s, a very liberal period in the history of the Supreme Court. Yet Burger was known as a law-and-order judge because of his conservative approach to criminal cases. He deplored the breakdown of law and order in the nation's cities and denounced those who, in his opinion, unduly favored

the rights of criminal defendants over lawful government authority. In particular, he opposed overturning guilty verdicts because of what he considered legal technicalities.

THE SUPREME COURT

The selection of Warren Burger for the Supreme Court came about through a string of events that began in 1968. Earl Warren, then Chief Justice of the Supreme Court, announced his decision to retire in June 1968, prior to the presidential election held later that year. Democratic President Lyndon B. Johnson nominated Abe Fortas, an Associate Justice on the Court, to become the Chief Justice. But Fortas's nomination was quashed by the Senate, leaving no time for President Johnson to select another candidate before the November presidential election. Instead, his successor, Republican President Richard Nixon, would select the next Chief Justice.

Faced with selecting a Supreme Court justice, each president reviews the legal decisions and published opinions of potential nominees, hoping to find a candidate who will uphold his political and judicial philosophy. President Nixon was no exception. He had been elected, in the midst of the social and political turmoil of 1968, on a strict law-and-order platform. In Warren Burger, Nixon was sure that he had found his man. On May 21, 1969, President Nixon nominated Warren Burger to be the next Chief Justice of the Supreme Court. Burger was confirmed by the Senate and sworn in on June 23, 1969.

The selection of a Supreme Court justice is one of the most important decisions a president can make. As the highest court in the land, the Supreme Court is the final arbiter in all legal disputes, as well as the group charged with interpreting and upholding the U.S. Constitution. The justices' decisions have a profound and lasting impact on the direction of American law. These decisions, which are handed down in written opinions, are closely examined to understand the basis of their reasoning and the effect on current laws.

The Chief Justice of the court plays several roles. Like the other justices, the Chief hears cases, votes on their outcome, and writes legal opinions. But often, the Chief Justice is able to lead the discussions of individual cases and influence the ideas of other justices. When assigning which justices will write the legal opinions that summarize the Court's decision, the Chief Justice can often assign the justice whose opinion most closely reflects the Chief's. In addition, the Chief Justice is the top administrator of the entire American judicial system.

BURGER'S LEGACY AS CHIEF JUSTICE

Burger served as Chief Justice of the Supreme Court for 17 years, from 1969 through 1986. His legacy as Chief Justice can be found in two areas: as an administrator and as a jurist.

As an administrator of the court system, Burger received high marks for his many improvements. He organized and updated the court offices, bringing them into the computer age; lobbied Congress to increase pay and to add many new positions to make the work load more manageable throughout the justice system; eliminated and streamlined many federal court procedures; and created programs to provide alternative means, besides the courtroom, for settling disputes. One of his greatest achievements as an administrator was the creation of several different institutions, including the National Center for State Courts, the Institute for Court Management, and the National Institute for Corrections. Their purpose is to educate and train individuals from all areas of the American justice system, from prison guards, to court clerks, to judges. As explained by Federal Appeals Court Judge Frank M. Johnson, Jr., "Warren Burger has redefined the nature of his office. He has concentrated his energy not simply on exploring the subtleties of constitutional doctrine but on reforming the mechanics of American justice. More than any of his 14 predecessors, he has invested the prestige of the Chief Justiceship in efforts to make the American judicial system function more efficiently."

Many periods in the history of the Supreme Court, under a given Chief Justice, have come to be known for the unanimity of their opinions. This was not true of the Burger Court. The Warren Court, presided over by Burger's predecessor, Earl Warren, was known for its liberal, activist decisions. Many expected the Burger Court to be more conservative and to represent a retrenchment from these earlier decisions. Yet observers typically find the decisions of the Burger Court to be marked by philosophical ambiguity and unpredictability. As described by Aaron Epstein in the *San Jose Mercury News*, "Critics called the Burger Court rootless, leaderless, rudderless, fragmented, an enigma, nine justices in search of a theme." Some say that Burger presided during a transitional period from a more liberal to the current, more conservative court, presided over by his successor as Chief Justice, William H. Rehnquist. Burger's own comments on his tenure were more philosophical. "It's always been somewhat comforting to know," Burger said just after he retired in 1986, "that I have been castigated by so-called liberals for being too conservative and castigated by so-called conservatives for being too liberal. Pretty safe position to be in."

On the issue of criminal law, the Burger Court was fairly consistent. They voted to limit the rights of the accused in several ways. They limited the exclusionary rule, which banned evidence that was obtained through illegal means; they weakened the protections of the *Miranda* ruling, which said that suspects had to be advised of their rights before being questioned by the police; they extended the rights of police to conduct searches and seize evidence; and they reduced the appeals by death row prisoners and upheld the death penalty.

On other issues facing the Burger Court there was an overall lack of philosophical coherence. Still, certain opinions stand out. In the area of women's rights, the court affirmed the right of women to choose abortion in *Roe* v. *Wade*. That ruling has proven to be one of the most controversial and important decisions the Court has made this century. In the area of racial equality, the Court upheld the principles of affirmative action and also upheld the validity of busing students as a means to desegregate public schools. In the area of free speech, the Court changed the legal meaning of obscenity by redefining it in terms of "contemporary community standards"; protected the rights of the public and the press to obtain information about trials; and defined the clause prohibiting the establishment of a national religion. In the area of the separation of powers of the three branches of government, in a case with far-reaching consequences, the Court forced President Richard Nixon to turn over White House tape recordings to the investigators of the Watergate scandal. That decision ultimately forced Nixon to resign from the presidency.

RETIREMENT

In June 1986, Burger announced that he planned to retire from the Court. He had recently become Chairman of the Commission of the Bicentennial of the U.S. Constitution. With those responsibilities added to his administrative and legal duties on the Court, he was working three full-time jobs, he said. He felt he was too old to be working over 100 hours per week. He left the Court to devote more time to the Constitution, which had long been one of his special interests. Burger spent the next several years working with the Commission, overseeing the planning of both public celebrations and education projects to mark the 200th anniversary of our nation's Constitution and Bill of Rights. What Burger envisioned, he said, was "a history and civics lesson for us all."

Warren Earl Burger, 15th Chief Justice of the United States, died on June 25, 1995, in Washington, D.C., of congestive heart failure. He was 87.

HOBBIES AND OTHER INTERESTS

Burger was a confirmed workaholic who often logged 80 hours or more at the Court each week. In his rare time off, he was a connoisseur of fine wines, a knowledgeable collector of antiques, a talented sculptor and watercolor painter, and an avid history buff.

WRITINGS

It Is So Ordered, 1995

HONORS AND AWARDS

Smithson Medal (Smithsonian Institution): 1986
American Bar Association Medal: 1987

Charles Evans Hughes Gold Medal Award (National Conference of Christians and Jews): 1988
Presidential Medal of Freedom: 1988
Silver Buffalo Award (Boy Scouts of America): 1988

FURTHER READING

BOOKS

Barnes, Catherine A. *Men of the Supreme Court: Profiles of the Justices,* 1978
Encyclopedia Brittanica 1992
Schoenebaum, Eleanora W., editor. *Political Profiles: The Nixon/Ford Years,* 1979
Who's Who in America 1995
World Book Encyclopedia 1995

PERIODICALS

Atlanta Constitution, June 26, 1995, p.A4
Chicago Tribune, News Section, pp.1 and 4
Current Biography 1969
Los Angeles Times, June 26, 1995, p.A1
Miami Herald, May 8, 1985, pp.A1 and A16; June 18, 1986, p.A14; June 26, 1995, p.A1
Nation, Sep. 19, 1984 (Special Issue, "Fifteen Years of the Burger Court")
New York Times, June 18, 1986, pp.A1, A30, A31, and A32; June 26, 1995, pp.A1, C10, and C11
Newsweek, June 30, 1986, p.21
Reader's Digest, Apr. 1975, p.121
San Jose Mercury News, July 13, 1986, p.A14
Time, June 30, 1986, p.35
U.S. News & World Report, June 30, 1986, p.22
Washington Post, June 18, 1986, p.A1; June 26, 1995, p.A1

Ken Burns   1953-
American Documentary Filmmaker
Creator of the Acclaimed PBS Series
The Civil War and *Baseball*

BIRTH

Kenneth Lauren Burns was born in Brooklyn, New York, on July 29, 1953, to Robert Kyle Burns and Lyla Smith (Tupper) Burns. Robert Burns, a graduate student in anthropology at Columbia University at the time of his son's birth, went on to become an anthropology professor; Lyla Burns was a homemaker. Ken has one brother, Ric, who is 18 months younger than him; the two have worked closely together on several of Burns's films.

YOUTH

Robert Burns's job changes caused the family to move around quite a bit while Ken was young. He was three months old when they moved briefly to St. Veran, France, and soon afterward to Baltimore, Maryland. In 1955, his father took a job at the University of Delaware and the family moved to Newark, Delaware. Eight years later, in 1963, he took a new job at the University of Michigan, and the family moved to Ann Arbor, Michigan, where they remained.

By that time, Ken's mother, Lyla Burns, was already very sick. She developed cancer when he was only three; he doesn't remember her ever being well. "Her cancer was the great forming force in my life," he now says. Lyla Burns died when Ken was eleven, "permanently influencing all that I would become."

EARLY MEMORIES

Throughout those early years, there was one antidote to the pain of his mother's illness: baseball. During a recent discussion of his PBS series *Baseball*, Burns explained his emotional ties to the game. "I grew up with it. It was a way to abolish the horror that was overtaking my life. My mother was sick every moment of my life and . . . I found a refuge. I played Pony League and Little League and found in it, I won't say an escape, but a kind of an oasis." As he has said, "I played baseball all the time. Baseball was the beginning and end of having a real childhood."

EDUCATION

Burns attended high school in Ann Arbor. The late 1960s-early 1970s in Ann Arbor was an interesting time and place to be a teenager. At that time, the University of Michigan and the surrounding town of Ann Arbor were a hotbed of anti-war sentiment and leftist activities. "I remember getting gassed at an anti-Vietnam demonstration with [my father]," Burns recalls with a smile.

Burns graduated from high school one year early and started looking into Hampshire College in Amherst, Massachusetts, a small, progressive liberal arts school that had no grades and that encouraged students to design their own course of study. He soon decided to go there, even though it meant turning down free tuition at the University of Michigan. But Burns was determined. He worked at a record store for a year, during what would have been his senior year of high school, and saved enough money to attend Hampshire. After his first year at Hampshire he took another year off, working in the school bookstore to earn money to continue his studies.

Hampshire College was, for Burns, an excellent choice. He studied there under the still photographers Jerome Liebling and Elaine Mayes. Both are celebrated and well-known still photographers, and Liebling, whom Burns calls his mentor, proved to be a great influence on him. As a writer for the *Journal of Popular Film and Television* explains, "One distinctive aspect of Liebling's technique is its almost cinematic quality, revealing a sense of drama and movement within the frame"—a quality that many critics have admired in Burns's work as well.

While at Hampshire Burns also met Amy Stechler, who became his collaborator and later his wife. Stechler helped Burns with his senior year project, directing a film about nineteenth-century worklife in Old Sturbridge Village, Massachusetts. Burns graduated from Hampshire in 1975 with a B.A. degree in film study and design.

FIRST JOBS

After graduation, Burns moved to New York City and set up an independent film production company, Florentine Films. He and Amy collaborated on freelance assignments for several years before undertaking what would become his first film, *The Brooklyn Bridge* (1981). It took four years to complete, and they were broke and hungry the whole time. It was hard to raise grant money, he says, because of his youthful appearance—"I looked about twelve and I was trying to sell the Brooklyn Bridge," he jokes. "I got thousands of turndowns." Even to this day, reviewers routinely comment on how young he looks.

By 1979 all the filming for the movie had been completed, and Ken and Amy moved to Walpole, New Hampshire, where they could live inexpensively while working on the writing and editing. When it was finished, the film earned several awards, including an Academy Award nomination, and Burns was on his way.

MARRIAGE AND FAMILY

Burns married Amy Stechler, his college sweetheart, on July 10, 1982. They have two daughters, Sarah and Lilly. Ken and Amy have since separated. They both continue to live in Walpole and share custody of their children.

CAREER HIGHLIGHTS

For almost twenty years, Burns has been making highly acclaimed, award-winning documentary films that chronicle the American experience. As Burns has explained it, "The one question that has animated all my works has been a deceptively simple one. Who are we as a people?" Searching for the things that define and unite the American people, he has used a variety of devices to address that issue, from national landmarks (the Brooklyn Bridge and the Statue of Liberty), to important individuals (Huey Long and Thomas Hart Benton), to a major war (the Civil War), to "the national pastime" (baseball). Yet his films illuminate more than just historical facts, as *Premiere* magazine explains: "[It] is his uncanny awareness and understanding of . . . feelings that has made Burns the remarkable filmmaker he is. Burns likes to think of himself as a kind of emotional archaeologist, unearthing the passions that give meaning to the dates, facts, and events of the past."

EARLY FILMS

Burns found the inspiration for his first film, *The Brooklyn Bridge* (1981), in a book entitled *The Great Bridge* (1972) by the noted historian David McCullough. With McCullough's cooperation, Burns told the story of the construction of what was then the longest suspension bridge in the world, bringing to life a potentially arcane subject. McCullough narrated that film, as he has for many of Burns's works. Next, Burns went to work on *The Shakers: Hands to Work, Hearts to God* (1984), an exposition on the Shakers, a nearly extinct religious sect that is best known today for its architecture and furniture. From there, Burns turned to *Huey Long* (1985), a documentary on the controversial Louisiana governor who was assassinated in 1935. Burns's film *The Statue of Liberty* (1985), whose release was timed to coincide with its 100-year anniversary, explores the building of the statue, its restoration, and evolving ideas about liberty. During the next few years he started work on *The Civil War* and completed two shorter films: *Thomas Hart Benton* (1988), a biography of the American painter, and *The Congress* (1988), a history of the U.S. Capitol building.

THE CIVIL WAR

Until this point all of Burns's films were fairly standard length for documentaries, running approximately one to two hours. But his epic *The Civil War* (1990) changed all that. This five-part, eleven-hour series, "a feat of archival reconstruction, interwoven narrative, and anecdotal lore," according to *The New Yorker*, took Burns and his colleagues five years to make. But for Burns, it was crucial that he take the time. "I'm a historian of emotions," he reveals, "and the Civil War is about emotions much more than it is facts or battles. . . . The Civil War defines us—who we are as a people. It's a window into ourselves." As he further explains, "If we look at the history of a country the way we would an individual," Burns says, "then the Civil War is the traumatic event of our childhood."

In *The Civil War*, Burns refined and improved the cinematic techniques that he had used in his earlier films. There are three major components of the work: sound, words, and visual images. For sound, Burns provided a mix, including the sounds of wind and rain, battlefield artillery, and birds singing, and mixed in folk music of the era and melancholy contemporary music. The words of the series included narration mixed with excerpts from letters, diaries, and speeches from the era, read by an eclectic cast of voices. The first-person accounts from the war's participants were particularly moving and eloquent. In addition, these texts were supported by the on-screen commentary of several historians, including Shelby Foote and Barbara J. Fields of Columbia University.

The visuals for the film posed a particular problem. Of course, there are no "motion pictures" from the Civil War era, so Burns and his team had to use imaginative camera work to enliven the still photographs. The selection process was awesome: Burns personally examined almost 100,000 photographs for the series, eventually choosing 16,000 to film; of those, about 3,000 survived the editing process to appear in the final film. He used inventive camera work to make the still photos come alive, panning across a shot, then zooming in for a close up. In addition, Burns incorporated maps, period paintings, handbills, and modern film footage of Civil War battlefields, to great effect. As *Newsweek* magazine explains, "[By] having his cameras gallop over a ridge or lurch in terror through a woods—and then flash to photographic evidence of the carnage—he plunges us directly inside the horror."

The editing process was incredibly complex and difficult: first they worked on all these parts independently—sound, words, and visual imagery—and then had to go back, mixing and matching to find a good fit. They might take a narrative piece from a diary, then look for a compelling visual image, and then try to find a sound effect to strengthen it. Ultimately, it worked: the resulting montage of all these elements was, by all accounts, riveting, intense, emotionally compelling television.

When the series aired in September 1990, the response was overwhelming. The first documentary ever to earn over $100 million, it was loved by almost everyone: academics, television critics, viewers, and teachers, who made the series required viewing for their students and snapped up the study guides for classroom use. While historians were able to point to a few factual errors, they were, by and large, impressed with Burns's ability to bring the past to life in a way that so thoroughly engaged the American public. The publication of a lavishly illustrated, well-written companion volume to the series (as later with the series *Baseball*) further added to the acclaim.

BASEBALL

After that film, Burns completed work on his two-hour film *Empire of the Air: The Men Who Made Radio* (1991), a documentary about the early pioneers in the creation of the radio broadcast system, before going on to his most recent film, *Baseball* (1994). For Burns, the game that has been called "America's pastime" echoes many of the same themes as his earlier work: "Baseball is the story of race, labor, immigration. It's the story of the exclusion of women and the rise and decay of great cities. It's the story of popular media: newspapers, magazines, radio, and television. It's the story of the nature of heroes and villains and fools—all of these things that offer a window on the American soul. . . . I think anybody who's curious about what it is to be an American will find in this series an emotional continuation of what we began in *The Civil War.* This is a study of who we are."

The series runs to about 18 1/2 hours, structured in nine episodes, or innings, of about two hours each. It's an historical overview of the game, with particular emphasis on critical events and people in the game's past, like the Black Sox scandal, Babe Ruth, Ty Cobb, Jackie Robinson, and the New York Yankees dynasty of the 1960s. It relies on 4,000 still photographs, film footage, and extensive interviews with "witnesses" who testify to the game's importance in their lives. Perhaps the most eloquent is Buck O'Neil, first baseman and manager of the Kansas City Monarchs, who tells riveting stories about his experiences with segregated teams and the Negro League. Race relations is a dominant theme throughout the series, and the integration of the major leagues in 1947 by Jackie Robinson is handled with grace and poignancy. In fact, Burns often cites Robinson as one of his personal heroes.

Response to the series was mixed. While many viewers and commentators found the series fascinating, portions were said to drag. Some felt that 18 1/2 hours was simply too much baseball, while others faulted the tone of the work as overly reverential and pretentious for an account of a game. Despite such reservations, critics universally look forward to Burns's upcoming projects, which include a miniseries on the American West and a series of biographies on great Americans, including Thomas Jefferson, Lewis and Clark, Mark Twain, Elizabeth Cady Stanton, Frederick Douglass, and Sitting Bull.

MAJOR INFLUENCES

Burns lists several influences as key to his development as a filmmaker. The earliest influence was the films of John Ford, which he watched on late-night television. As he says, "I had always wanted to be a Hollywood director. . . . [As] I look back now in retrospect, I realize how influential Ford was in that if you look at sort of my whole body of work, it's a kind of documentary version of Ford that is a real love for biography, a real love for American mythology, a real love for the music of the period, a real love for ordinary characters who . . . remind us that the best history is not just from the top down, but from the bottom up."

Later, his photography professor and mentor Jerry Liebling and the historian David McCullough also proved tremendously influential: "As I got to know McCullough, he became very helpful in refining a story and how you tell a story. And I think if you combine this great visual and sort of honorable teaching of Jerry Liebling with McCullough's sense of narrative, that's a pretty potent combination, and two influences, the shoulders of two giants on whom I stand."

FILMS

(Dates listed after each title below reflect the year of release as a film; the date in parentheses reflects the year of broadcast on PBS television.)

The Brooklyn Bridge, 1981 (PBS, 1982)
The Shakers: Hands to Work, Hearts to God, 1984 (PBS, 1985)
The Statue of Liberty, 1985 (PBS, 1985)
Huey Long, 1985 (PBS, 1986)
Thomas Hart Benton, 1988 (PBS, 1989)
The Congress, 1988 (PBS, 1989)
The Civil War, 1990 (PBS, 1990)
Empire of the Air: The Men Who Made Radio, 1991 (PBS, 1992)
Baseball, 1994 (PBS, 1994)

WRITINGS

Centennial, 1986 (contributor)
The Shakers: Hands to Work, Hearts to God, 1987 (with Amy Stechler Burns)
The Civil War: An Illustrated History, 1990 (with Geoffrey C. Ward and Ric Burns)
Baseball: An Illustrated History, 1994 (with Geoffrey C. Ward)

HONORS AND AWARDS

Christopher Award: 1983, for *The Brooklyn Bridge*; 1987, for *The Statue of Liberty*; 1991, for *The Civil War*
Erik Barnouw Prize (Organization of American Historians): 1983, for *The Brooklyn Bridge*; 1986, for *Huey Long*
CINE Golden Eagle Award (Council on International Non-Theatrical Events): 1981, for *The Brooklyn Bridge*; 1984; for *The Shakers: Hands to Work, Hearts to God*; 1984, for *The Statue of Liberty*; 1985, for *Huey Long*; 1988, for *Thomas Hart Benton*; 1989, for *The Congress*; 1990, for *The Civil War*; 1992, for *Empire of the Air: The Men Who Made Radio*; 1994, for *Baseball*
Silver Baton (DuPont-Columbia Journalism Awards): 1988, for *Huey Long*; 1992, for *The Civil War*
George Foster Peabody Broadcasting Award (University of Georgia, Henry W. Grady School of Journalism and Mass Communication): 1990, for *The Civil War*
Lincoln Prize (Gettysburg College, Lincoln and Soldiers Institute): 1990, for *The Civil War*

Producer of the Year (Producer's Guild of America): 1990, for *The Civil War*

Emmy Awards: 1991, for outstanding informational series, for *The Civil War*; 1991, outstanding individual achievement—writing, for *The Civil War*

Bell I. Wiley Award (Civil War Round Table): 1991, for *The Civil War*

Charles Frankel Prize (National Endowment for the Humanities): 1991, for *The Civil War*

People's Choice Award: 1991, for best mini-series, for *The Civil War*

Grammy Awards: 1992 (two), Best Traditional Folk Album and Best Spoken Word Album

FURTHER READING

BOOKS

Who's Who in America, 1994

PERIODICALS

American Heritage, Sep./Oct. 1990, p.96
Current Biography Yearbook 1992
GQ, Sep. 1990, p.216
Journal of Popular Film and Television, Summer 1993, p.50
Life, Sep. 1994, p.40
Los Angeles Times Calendar, July 11, 1993, p.6
New York Times, Sep. 16, 1990, Section II, p.1
People, Sep. 24, 1990, p.95; Sep. 19, 1994, p.205
Premiere, Sep. 1994, p.76
Smithsonian, July 1994, p.38
USA Today Baseball Weekly, Jan. 26 - Feb. 8, 1994, p.6
Washington Post, Sep. 23, 1990, TV Section, p.Y8

ADDRESS

Florentine Films
P.O. Box 613
Walpole, NH 03608

Candace Cameron   1976-
American Television Actress
Plays D.J. on ABC's "Full House"

BIRTH

Candace Cameron is a native Californian. The year of her birth is 1976, but the exact date is unavailable; press releases circulated during her long stint with the popular ABC sitcom "Full House" indicate that she has a late-fall birthday. Candace is the youngest child of Robert Cameron, a junior high school physical education teacher, and his wife, Barbara, who owns a Los Angeles talent agency.

The other children in the family are Kirk Cameron, who starred for several years as Mike Seaver on another well-known ABC sitcom, "Growing Pains." In between Kirk and Candace in age are two sisters, Bridget and Melissa.

EDUCATION

Candace attended regular school in the earliest years of her fledgling career, but with the daily demands of taping episodes of "Full House" she eventually needed to be tutored on the set. She attended private school for two years in her teens but, again, had to turn to tutoring. Candace managed to keep up with her class, and graduated from high school in 1994. She has no immediate plans for college.

CAREER HIGHLIGHTS

Candace started her acting career when she was five years old. "My mom had a friend who had a son in the business," she reveals. "She asked us [Kirk and Candace] if we wanted to try it, and I was like, 'Sure, that's fine,' so I started doing commercials and I did a few movies, and then I got 'Full House' at ten." Candace admits that having a brother already in show business was a definite plus, saying that he landed his role in "Growing Pains" two years before her own TV debut (in a starring role) in 1987. She adds that he made all the adjustments first, so when her turn came, the family knew how to avoid the pitfalls.

Before she joined the cast of her current, long-running show, Candace had small feature roles in two movies, *Some Kind of Wonderful*, and *Punchline*. Her first television appearance was as a guest star in the 1980s show, "St. Elsewhere." But it was "Full House" that brought her to the public's attention. For eight seasons, she has played D.J. (Donna Jo) in the situation comedy about a widowed San Francisco television host raising his young daughters with the help of his brother-in-law Jesse (John Stamos) and best friend Joey (Dave Coulier). Bob Saget plays Danny Tanner, the dad; Jodie Sweetin is Stephanie; and appealing twins Mary Kate and Ashley Olsen share the role of Michelle. The "Full House" family also includes Becky (Lori Loughlin) Jesse's wife and Danny's co-host, and their twins Alex and Nicky (Blake and Dylan Tuomy-Wilhoit). Each week the show explores the problems and joys of growing up in this large, unusual, but always happy household.

Critics were not kind to the show when it debuted in the 1987-88 season. As writer-producer Jeff Franklin told the *San Jose Mercury News* it was "word of mouth" and audience interest that slowly built "Full House" into a megahit. "There was no clue [at the beginning] that it was going to turn into what it has." What it became was the most popular TV program with young viewers. "Kids love to watch kids," Franklin said in the *Mercury News*. "They found the show first and brought their big brothers and sisters to it, then their parents and grandparents . . . and now it has wide demographic appeal."

One California mother with two young children explained the show's appeal this way: "Kids never get enough of their father; he's always at work or napping. What you get with 'Full House' is a big dose of daddy love."

Most young-family situations have been explored during the show's eight-year run, though, and after this season, "Full House" is scheduled to go off the air. All of the actors have other avenues to explore. Both Saget and Coulier already have their own ABC programs: Saget hosts "America's Funniest Videos," and comedian-impressionist Coulier is host of "America's Funniest People"; both appear in other venues as well. The cute and popular Olsen twins have become hot commodities in the business. John Stamos and Lorie Loughlin have branched out successfully into other acting jobs, and Jodie Sweetin's special appeal has brought her several offers, too. Cameron plans to explore new territory, hoping that her eight-year success on "Full House" will pay off for her. She has been happy working on the show, for, as she says, "There are so many advantages to having a job." She adds, however, that she would love to do movies in the future. She's also interested in directing.

FAMILY LIFE

Candace still lives with her parents in California's San Fernando Valley.

She has a loving relationship with them both, but hopes to be out on her own soon, now that she is nearly nineteen. When her parents separated briefly several years ago, she found the rift in the family especially hard, and says that she is sure that those unsettling months helped her to mature.

MAJOR INFLUENCES

Candace is quick to say that her father is her best buddy. "He's fun to be with [and] he's always interested in helping me. . . . Whenever I have a problem, he really listens. I think that's neat." Barbara Cameron is given credit, too. She has been Candace and Kirk's agent from the beginning of their young careers, spending long hours with them on the sets of their shows.

HONORS AND AWARDS

Favorite TV Actress (Nickolodeon's Kid's Choice Awards): 1994

TV CREDITS

"Full House," 1987-1995
"Seventh Annual Kid's Choice Awards," 1994 (co-host)
"Mr. Foster's Field Trip," 1995

FURTHER READING

PERIODICALS

Chicago Tribune, Sep. 14, 1993, KIDNEWS section, p.5
Cleveland Plain Dealer, Nov. 9, 1993, p.1D
San Francisco Examiner, Aug. 10, 1990, Weekend section, p.C18
Woman's Day, June 19, 1990, p.30

ADDRESS

"Full House"
Lorimar Television
10202 West Washington Boulevard
Culver City, CA 90232

Jimmy Carter 1924-
American Peace Negotiator, Former Navy
Officer, and Former Governor of Georgia
Former President of the United States

BIRTH

James Earl Carter, Jr., better known to the world as Jimmy Carter, was born October 1, 1924, in the small farming town of Plains, Georgia. He lived there the first few years of his life before moving to a farm in the nearby community of Archery. His father, James Earl Carter, Sr., was a farmer and businessman; his mother, (Bessie) Lillian Gordy Carter, was a registered nurse.

The first of his parents' four children, he is, today, the only surviving sibling. Ruth Carter Stapleton, the third child in the family, died in 1983; William Alton (Billy), the youngest by eight years, in 1988; and Gloria Carter Spann, who was closest in age to her eldest brother, in 1990. All died of cancer in middle age.

YOUTH

The rural Georgia of Jimmy Carter's childhood was a simple world of family life, farm chores, church, school, and Saturday trips into town to mingle with neighbors and friends. It was the 1930s, and the country was in the midst of the Great Depression. This was a time of national economic crisis when up to one-third of Americans were out of work, creating widespread poverty and hardships. The Carters, while not rich, were also never destitute. They made a decent living in peanut farming and in the business they conducted in town selling seed and farm supplies. They were prominent in civic activities and respected by both blacks and whites in a time and place where racial segregation still went virtually unchallenged.

This was the environment where Jimmy Carter spent his youth. His life was centered on the farm in Archery and in the schoolhouse in Plains. At home, he was expected to share in the chores, gathering eggs and chopping wood. As he grew, he started picking cotton and peanuts side by side with the hired hands. At school, he was eager to learn and quick to progress in his studies. Friends from those years remember him as a bookworm.

Many amusing stories have circulated about Carter's childhood on the farm. Jimmy is always remembered as obedient to a stern father who accepted no nonsense from his children, especially from the two oldest. But he was also a normal boy who loved to tease his sister. Once he paid Gloria a nickel to pick peanuts for him, writes biographer Betty Glad in *Jimmy Carter: In Search of the Great White House*, "then got her to plant the nickel in a flower-bed—telling her that it would become a 'money tree'." Of course, he then dug up the nickel himself. Gloria, though, was not above taking revenge, and on more than one occasion she set her brother up for whippings from his exasperated father. "I remember once she threw a wrench and hit me," he says, "and I retaliated by shooting her in the rear with my B.B. gun. For several hours she re-burst into tears every time the sound of a car was heard. When Daddy finally drove into our yard, she was sobbing uncontrollably, and after she [gave her side of the story], Daddy whipped me without further comment."

Life in the Carter family was far from grim, however. The children were expected to perform their chores, but there was always time for play. Jimmy hunted and fished with his father and participated in other sports, although he was always expected to excel. His mother, known all of her life as Miss Lillian, had a balancing effect on young Jimmy's life—a political liberal in contrast to her conservative husband, and a Southern white

81

woman who was years ahead of her time in racial attitudes and community involvement. When her children were raised, and just before her 70th birthday, the widowed Miss Lillian left the comfort of her home to join the Peace Corps and do volunteer work in India.

EDUCATION

Carter graduated at the top of his class from Plains High School in 1941. He wanted to attend the U.S. Naval Academy at Annapolis, but he needed to take a chemistry course that was not offered at Plains High. So he enrolled at Georgia Southwestern, a junior college in nearby Americus.

It was a year of transition for Jimmy, when he could live at home and still get a taste of college life and an introduction to a broader social setting than Plains had to offer. He worked part-time in the chemistry laboratory, played some intramural basketball, and joined a fraternity. At the end of his year at Southwestern, still waiting for his appointment to the Naval Academy, Carter entered the Naval ROTC program at Georgia Tech (Georgia Institute of Technology) in Atlanta. The country had entered World War II, and he was anxious to be involved in an officer training program that would prepare him for acceptance by the Naval Academy.

Finally, in 1943, Jimmy Carter became a midshipman at Annapolis, and embarked upon a program condensed to three years from the traditional four because of the demands of World War II. He received his bachelor of science degree in June 1946—59th in a class of 820. Because of the accelerated studies, he is formally listed as a member of the class of 1947.

A few years later, Carter attended Union College in Schenectady, New York, for graduate work in nuclear physics and reactor technology.

MARRIAGE

Jimmy Carter was married on July 7, 1946, to the former Rosalynn (ROSE-a-lynn) Eleanor Smith. He was then a newly commissioned ensign from the U.S. Naval Academy, and she was a not-quite-19-year-old hometown girl whom he had known first as a close friend of his sister Ruth. Within months after the couple became romantically involved, Jimmy asked Rosalynn to marry him as soon as he graduated. She refused because she had promised her late father that she would go to college. Jimmy persisted, though, and she finally accepted his proposal just before Valentine's Day in 1946. They were wed the following summer in the Baptist Church in Plains, and left for Norfolk, Virginia, for Carter to begin what they thought would be a lifetime Navy career.

CHOOSING A CAREER

The professional career in the Navy that Carter had worked for during most of his early adulthood lasted only for seven years. During that time, he served in both the Pacific and Atlantic fleets under Admiral Hyman Rickover, developing the nuclear submarine program. He attained the rank of lieutenant (second grade). But when his father died in 1953, Carter felt it was his family duty to resign his commission and take over the family business. His younger brother Billy Carter went off to military service deeply resentful at being passed over. Jimmy and Rosalynn rebuilt the floundering business, but Billy eventually returned home to take over the farm and warehouse as his brother's interests turned toward civic affairs and politics.

CAREER HIGHLIGHTS

Carter became increasingly active in community affairs as the 1950s drew to a close. He held several district offices, among them the chairmanship of the county school board and the presidency of the Plains Development Corporation. He also was district governor of Lions International and first president of the Georgia Planning Association. With his small family business now grown into a profitable warehouse operation, Carter ventured into state politics. In 1962, he was elected to the Georgia Senate, where he served two consecutive terms. He lost his first campaign to become governor in 1966, but was successful in the next election, becoming Georgia's 76th governor on January 12, 1971.

Quickly gaining recognition as a symbol of leadership in the New South, Carter rose to national attention with his advocacy of, and his policies toward, equal opportunity for all. Two years into his state-mandated single term, he was chosen campaign manager by the Democratic National Committee for the upcoming (1974) congressional elections.

THE PRESIDENCY

At the end of 1974, Jimmy Carter—peanut farmer, low-key southern governor, and born-again Christian—declared himself a candidate for the United States presidency. Those who asked incredulously "Jimmy Who?" were to learn a valuable lesson on how contacts, power bases, and strategy could take a relatively obscure governor to the highest office in the land. Carter won his party's nomination on the first ballot at the 1976 Democratic Convention. With liberal Minnesotan Walter Mondale as his running mate, Carter pulled off a narrow victory over the incumbent president, Republican Gerald Ford.

Carter was president from 1977 to 1981. Although he developed a reputation as weak and ineffective in the handling of foreign policy, he is credited with several major accomplishments during his administration. Perhaps his greatest was in mediating the 1978 Camp David accords, the tricky negotiations between Egypt and Israel that resulted in the first peace treaty between Israel and an Arab country. He was also instrumental in advancing SALT II (the Strategic Arms Limitations Treaty) with what was then the Soviet Union. During his first year in office, his administration negotiated a treaty returning control of the Canal Zone to Panama by the year 2000, with that country agreeing to neutral operation of the canal. In addition, Carter championed human rights throughout the world, a mission he has sustained in the 15 years since his presidency came to an end.

Domestic programs of the Carter administration included a sweeping energy plan conducted by a new Department of Energy, major educational programs under the Department of Education, deregulation in transportation, communications, and finance, and major environmental protection legislation, including the Alaska Lands Act.

As his term progressed, however, many viewed his style as naive, even amateurish, in a political climate of shrewdness. Intelligent, methodical, and intense, Carter also projected an image that *Time* would later describe as "preachy and subtly vain." He suffered severe criticism in the final year of his term for his handling of the Iran hostage crisis. Fifty-five American citizens working in the American Embassy were taken hostage by Iranian students and imprisoned there for over one year. A botched attempt to rescue the hostages was also widely criticized. Even his own constituency began to fade. Carter lost his bid for reelection to Ronald Reagan, who won in a landslide. Although beleaguered, Carter was able to negotiate the hostage release in the final weeks of his presidency, but was further humiliated when announcement of the agreement was delayed until minutes after the inauguration of his successor.

Jimmy Carter, stunned by Reagan's sweeping victory, went home to Plains and a self-imposed exile.

TACKLING HUMANITY'S PROBLEMS

The transition to ex-president was painful at first, but Carter eventually returned to public life. He began work on his memoirs and became a visiting professor at Emory University in Atlanta in 1982. In partnership with the university, he founded the Carter Center, a think tank that concentrates on promoting democracy, resolving conflict, and protecting human rights. The center, which includes a presidential library and museum, sponsors Global 2000, an international aid organization that advances health and agriculture in the developing world. "It is," wrote Kai Bird a few years ago in *The Nation*, "as if Carter decided to take the most liberal and successful policies of his failed Administration—human rights, peacemaking, and concerns for the poor—and make them the centerpiece of a campaign for his own political resurrection. . . . His most ambitious goal, probably related to Camp David, [his] greatest foreign-policy success, is literally to serve as world peacemaker."

Carter most recently captured the public eye with his last-minute mediation in September 1994 in Haiti. A dictatorship led by Haitian military leaders had overthrown the democratically elected president, Jean-Bertrand Aristide. U.S. forces were ready to invade Haiti and oust the dictatorship—in fact, U.S. planes were already in the air, ready to launch the invasion. At the last minute, Carter and fellow negotiators Senator Sam Nunn and former Chairman of the Joint Chiefs of Staff Colin Powell were able to reach an agreement with the Haitian military leaders. They stepped down, Aristide returned to power, and the country erupted in celebration.

The former president's most publicized activity in recent years, other than his peace negotiations, has been the volunteer work he does for Habitat for Humanity. This innovative, nonprofit organization helps low-income families finance and build their own homes. The volunteers, including the Carters, do the actual construction work alongside the families. The publication *Workbench* tells how seriously the Carters take their responsibilities during their annual stint on a Habitat job site: "[They] ask for, and receive, the same treatment as the other volunteers. They sleep and

eat in the same dormitory and mess tent as the rest of the crew. And except for brief time-outs for media interviews, Carter puts in the same hours as every other volunteer."

Carter's activities in recent years have brought both praise and skepticism. While there have been critics who have challenged the efficacy of his peace initiatives and have questioned his motives, "the consensus view," says *Time* magazine, "is that [Jimmy Carter] has been a superb ex-president."

HOME AND FAMILY

Jimmy and Rosalynn live an unpretentious, small-town life when they are at home in Plains. Although their house is behind an iron fence and protected by the Secret Service, they personally are at ease as they wander around town or bicycle together on country roads they have known since childhood. However, with the former president adjusting to a renewed public image, the couple's busy schedule often keeps them in their modest apartment at the Carter Center in Atlanta.

The Carters have four children, all now grown: John William (Jack), James Earl III (Chip), Donnel Jeffrey (Jeff), and the youngest, Amy Lynn, who was reluctantly thrust into the public eye when she moved to the White House when her father became president. The Carter sons are businessmen pursuing their own interests, and Amy, now 27, is also on her own after graduating from the Memphis (Tennessee) School of Art.

The Carters have nine grandchildren.

MAJOR INFLUENCES

Political scientist and Carter biographer Edwin Diamond noted that Carter's father was a powerful influence on his son's development. When Diamond and Bruce Mazlish began collecting material for their 1979 Carter biography, "we quickly found," writes Diamond, "that . . . the real shaping figure in Carter's life was his father. . . . Jimmy Carter, we concluded, never forgot the authority that Mr. Earl embodied; it helped set his feelings toward all later authority, his own and others'."

Another person who made a lasting impression on the former president was Hyman Rickover, the controversial admiral under whom he served in the Navy's nuclear submarine program. Carter held the demanding and irascible officer in such high regard that he would admit later that Rickover had "a profound effect on my life, perhaps more than anyone except my own parents."

HOBBIES AND OTHER INTERESTS

For recreation, Carter jogs, cycles, fly-fishes, skis, plays tennis, and is a skilled woodworker who has handcrafted much of the furniture in his home. His wife confirms that this latter activity reached a peak and was a "form of therapy" for him when they moved back to Plains in 1981 after his defeat in his bid for reelection. She told *Woman's Day* that "when he was frustrated, he could step into his woodworking shop and bang on something."

Carter's quieter pleasures include reading, writing, and listening to music—mostly classical and soft rock. When they are at home in Plains, he and his wife teach adult Sunday school classes at the Marantha Baptist Church, where the former president is also a deacon.

WRITINGS

Why Not the Best? 1975
A Government as Good as Its People, 1977
Keeping Faith: Memoirs of a President, 1982
Negotiation: The Alternative to Hostility, 1984
The Blood of Abraham, 1985
Everything to Gain: Making the Most of the Rest of Your Life (with Rosalynn Carter), 1987
An Outdoor Journal, 1988
Turning Point: A Candidate, A State, and A Nation Come of Age, 1992
Talking Peace: A Vision for the Next Generation, 1993
Always a Reckoning and Other Poems, 1995

HONORS AND AWARDS

Gold Medal (International Institute of Human Rights): 1979
International Mediation Medal (American Arbitration Association): 1979
Martin Luther King, Jr., Nonviolent Peace Prize: 1979
International Human Rights Award (Synagogue Council of America): 1979
Conservationist of the Year Award: 1979
Harry S. Truman Public Service Award: 1981
Ansel Adams Conservation Award (Wilderness Society): 1982
Distinctive Service Award (Southern Baptist Convention): 1982
Human Rights Award (International League for Human Rights): 1983
World Methodist Peace Award: 1985
Albert Schweitzer Prize for Humanitarianism: 1987
Edwin C. Whithead Award (National Center for Health Education): 1989
Jefferson Award (American Institute for Public Service): 1990
Philadelphia Liberty Medal: 1990
Spirit of America Award (National Council for Social Studies): 1990
Physicians for Social Responsibility Award: 1991
Aristotle Prize (Alexander S. Onassis Foundation): 1991

FURTHER READING

BOOKS

Glad, Betty. *Jimmy Carter: In Search of the Great White House,* 1980
Hyatt, Richard. *The Carters of Plains,* 1977
Kucharsky, David. *The Man From Plains: The Mind and Spirit of Jimmy Carter,* 1976
Mazlish, Bruce, and Edwin Diamond. *Jimmy Carter: A Character Portrait,* 1979
Slavin, Ed. *Jimmy Carter,* 1989 (juvenile)
Wade, Linda R. *James Carter,* 1989 (juvenile)
Who's Who in America, 1995

PERIODICALS

American Spectator, Nov. 1994, p.14
Good Housekeeping, Jan. 1992, p.100
Maclean's, Dec. 17, 1990, p.9; Aug. 2, 1993, p.38
Mother Earth News, Nov./Dec., 1987, p.42
Newsweek, May 22, 1989, p.40; Oct. 3, 1994, p.36
New York Review of Books, Oct. 20, 1994, p.71
New York Times, June 20, 1994, p.A1; June 23, 1994, p.A6; Sep. 21, 1994, p.A1
New York Times Book Review, Sep. 25, 1994, p.1
People, Jan. 5, 1987, p.36; Oct. 3, 1994, p.44
Time, Sep. 11, 1989, p.60; Oct. 3, 1994, p.30

ADDRESS

Carter Center
1 Copenhill Avenue, NE
Atlanta, GA 30307-1498

OBITUARY

Agnes de Mille   1905-1993
American Choreographer, Dancer, and Author

BIRTH

Agnes George de Mille, one of the greatest choreographers of the twentieth century, was born in New York City on September 18, 1905. She and her younger sister, Margaret, were the two daughters of William and Anna de Mille. Born into a distinguished family of writers and academics, Agnes later referred to her famous kin as "compulsive achievers." Her father, William de Mille, was a well-known playwright and screenwriter, whose father had also been a successful dramatist. Agnes's mother, Anna Angela

George de Mille, a homemaker, was the daughter of the famous economist Henry George. When Agnes was nine, the family moved to California. They were lured there in part by her uncle, film director Cecil B. de Mille, who would go on to create some of the greatest screen spectacles Hollywood had ever seen.

EARLY MEMORIES

Agnes's first plan as a child of Hollywood was to be an actress in one of her Uncle Cecil's movies. Sometimes she was able to take off from school to witness the filming of one of her uncle's productions. One request to her teacher read: "Gloria Swanson is being thrown to the lions and Agnes has to be excused from her classes."

But it was when she saw the famous Russian ballerina Anna Pavlova perform that her fate was set. "I sat with the blood beating in my throat. She jumped, and we broke bonds with reality. We flew. We hung over the earth, spread in the air as we do in dreams, our hands turning in the air as in water. . . . All things were possible, even to us, the ordinary people." But both her parents were strongly opposed to her dancing. They didn't see it as a proper occupation for a young woman.

Even though her parents limited her dancing classes to one per week, Agnes practiced every day. She was told early on in her dancing career that she didn't have the classic ballerina's body. "I had a long torso and shortish legs. They are pretty legs, but very short. What I did have was a real acting ability and inventive, creative thought." And those were the qualities that drove both her choreography and her career.

EDUCATION

De Mille attended the Hollywood School for Girls and continued to dance. She was an outstanding student, and after she finished high school she attended UCLA (the University of California at Los Angeles). She majored in English and graduated with honors at the age of 19.

FIRST JOBS

De Mille's parents decided to divorce right after Agnes finished college. It was an unexpected and devastating blow to de Mille, who had been very close to both of her parents.

She moved to New York with her mother, and tried for several years to make a living as a dancer. She danced anywhere she could: in shows, nightclubs, even taking up Greek belly dancing to keep money coming in. She had her first dance concert in Santa Fe, New Mexico. She got rave reviews and made $364. In 1928, she gave a concert in New York, where she was hailed by the *New York Times* as "undoubtedly one of the brightest stars now rising about our native horizon." But the review didn't create any call for her work, so she decided to move to England to study and choreograph.

In 1934, she got a call from her Uncle Cecil to create dances for his upcoming film, *Cleopatra*. But Agnes was fired when she refused to "dance naked on the back of a live bull." She returned to London.

While in England, she studied classical ballet and created dances with such choreographers as Marie Rambert and Anthony Tudor. She developed the dances in *Nymph Errant*, a musical starring Gertrude Lawrence, a famous British star of the time.

Through all those early years of trial and disappointment, de Mille's unflagging spirit drove her on, and she learned how to do nearly everything involved with producing a performance. "When I was beginning my career, I had no endowment and was very poor," she recalled. "I felt sorry for myself, naturally, and as it turns out, quite foolishly, for in many ways the hardships were beneficial. I played the piano for rehearsal, I arranged and copied music, I designed costumes, shopped for material, cut and stitched, packed, pressed and hung. I learned lighting, lit and ran performances, I rehearsed groups myself, I took charge of printing, wrote copy and advertisement, organized photographic sessions, signed leases, devised and signed contracts, made up the payroll and kept the books." All these skills would stand her in good stead for the meteoric rise her career would take.

MARTHA GRAHAM

De Mille began her autobiography, *Dance to the Piper*, like this: "This is the story of an American dancer, a spoiled ego-centric wealthy girl, who learned with difficulty to become a worker, to set and meet standards, to brace a Victorian sensibility to contemporary rough-housing, and who, with happy good fortune, participated by the side of great colleagues in a renaissance of the most ancient and magical of all the arts." One of those colleagues was Martha Graham, one of the greatest choreographers of the twentieth century.

Graham, like de Mille, was forging a new statement in dance. Some called this new technique "modern dance," a term that both creators disliked. "As Martha Graham says, and has said often, there are two kinds of dancing: good and bad," said de Mille.

Graham and de Mille were exploring a new aspect of movement, of expression that took a different look at the material out of which a dance can be made. For Graham, it was often stories drawn from myth. De Mille saw herself as creating dances that fit in with her natural mode of story-telling, in a distinctly American voice, with the movements of American

91

folk dance. The two were close friends and creative spirits, but not col-
laborators, In fact, Graham, refused to work with de Mille. When she
begged, "Martha, let me work with you," Graham replied, "Certainly not.
I won't let you lean on me. Find your own way." That's exactly what
she did.

CAREER HIGHLIGHTS

RODEO

In 1941, after years of hard work and very little money, de Mille wrote:
"Youth gone. No husband. No child. No achievement in working. Time
was passing. Prospects ceased to be bright." But all that was about to
change. The Ballet Russe de Monte Carlo was looking for an American
choreographer to develop an American theme ballet. They hired de Mille
to create what would become her first triumph and a classic of the
twentieth-century ballet repertoire: *Rodeo.* De Mille insisted on a virtually
unknown American composer to create the music: Aaron Copland.

Rodeo announced a major, refreshing change in American dance. The male
dancers were dressed like cowboys; their movements mimicked horseback
riding. The story was of a feisty cowgirl—danced in the premier by de
Mille herself—out to win the heart of a young cowboy. De Mille took her
movements from folk dances, rather than from the academic, stylized

vocabulary of classical ballet. She had a hard time trying to teach the Russian male dancers, who had been taught, in her words, "to move like wind-blown petals." So she told them to pretend they were playing tennis, using stroking movements.

There was another inspiration for *Rodeo*. She had just met and fallen in love with a young man named Walter Prude. He was from Texas, and like almost all the young men of their generation, had just been sent to fight in World War II. While the pattern of the dance came to her, she thought "of the men leaving, leaving everywhere. . . . And what was left of any of them but a folk tune and a way of joining hands in a ring? And I searched my heart for the clues to remembering."

OKLAHOMA!

Opening night of *Rodeo* found Agnes de Mille a star, receiving 22 curtain calls. Two men sitting in the audience that night were to solidify de Mille's name as the preeminent choreographer of the Broadway musical. Richard Rogers and Oscar Hammerstein sent her a telegram saying: "We think your work is enchanting. Come and talk to us on Monday." They hired de Mille to choreograph *Oklahoma!*, one of the most enduring and often-performed musicals of the American stage. The show was an instant hit with audiences. And one of the most important aspects of the show was the dancing, particularly the dream ballet. Up to this point, the dancing in stage shows often had little to do with moving the story along. But in this scene, de Mille created a dance that told the story of the two characters, one that complemented and enhanced the narrative.

De Mille had to fight for recognition and decent pay for her efforts. "I was starving when I signed up to do the choreography for *Oklahoma!* The Theatre Guild said, 'Sign this, fifteen hundred dollars, no royalties, or don't sign it.'" It wasn't until the 1980s that de Mille, after years of negotiating, won a percentage of the royalties garnered by one of the most successful musicals of the American stage.

She went on to choreograph some of the most popular Broadway musicals of all time, including *Carousel*, *Brigadoon*, *Gentleman Prefer Blondes*, and her own favorite, *Paint Your Wagon*. In 1944, she became the first woman to have three hit musicals playing on Broadway at the same time, joining three other giants of the American musical theater, Irving Berlin, George Gershwin, and Cole Porter. She did more than make the dance for *Briga-doon*, she directed it, too, and she won a Tony award for the choreography. After several more hits, including *Out of this World*, *The Girl in the Pink Tights*, and *Goldilocks*, de Mille won another Tony for *Kwamina*.

At the same time, de Mille continued to create ballets, often for the American Ballet Theater, which she was involved with for fifty years.

An early work was *Three Virgins and a Devil*, in which she performed herself. Perhaps her most famous ballet after *Rodeo* is *Fall River Legend*, in which she tells the story of ax murderer Lizzie Borden.

In the late 1940s, de Mille began a second career of sorts as a writer. Her teachers had often encouraged her writing talent when she was growing up, and she had come from a distinguished line of authors. So when her son was born, she began to write, often scribbling down phrases and paragraphs on scraps of paper as she waited for appointments or to meet someone in a restaurant. Her first book, *Dance to the Piper*, became a best-seller. In this and later books, she wrote sensitively and knowledgeably about dance history and about the people involved in dance. Throughout the 1950s and 1960s, de Mille continued to choreograph, direct, and write, often overseeing new productions of her hits of the 1940s. She also founded her own dance company, the Heritage Dance Theater in NY, for which she continued to produce both old and new works.

A STROKE

In May 1975, while overseeing the opening night preparations for her own company, de Mille suffered a massive stroke. "Suddenly I discovered that half of my body was dead," she recalled. Her entire right side was paralyzed, and she was near death for days. She suffered from a number of embolisms over the next months, and even after years of therapy, the neurological damage was extensive. "The nurse said it's as though all the telephone lines had been dragged out of a switchboard and just left on the floor," de Mille said of the damage done to her neurological system. "I give the signals and nothing happens."

De Mille chronicled her illness and recovery in another book, *Reprieve*, published in 1981. She told of teaching herself to write again, this time with her left hand. She also wrote of learning to walk again, of forcing herself to do a daily set of ballet exercises at a barre in her Greenwich Village apartment. A heart attack in 1976 slowed her down again, but it could not stop her. In the late 1970s and early 1980s, she developed several television specials, including *Conversations About the Dance*, in which she gave her lecture-demonstrations on dance to a national audience.

De Mille continued to bring humor to her perspective on her life after the stroke: "I used to have to go out there and yell at people to dance. Now I just sit here, and everybody treats me as if I were some kind of holy relic. It does have its advantages."

De Mille was a vociferous and staunch defender of the importance of the arts in America. She served on the first board of the National Endowment for the Arts, lobbied Congress for arts organizations, and worked with dance and performing arts groups to improve wages and working conditions.

Agnes de Mille died October 7, 1993, at the age of 88. She had been in failing health for some time, yet her indomitable spirit sustained her to the end. She once said that she wanted one word on her tombstone: "Dancer." She will be cherished as a dancer, as well as a ground-breaking choreographer and a tireless champion of art and artists for generations to come.

MARRIAGE AND FAMILY

Agnes de Mille married Walter F. Prude on June 14, 1943, while he was an officer in World War II and she was a busy choreographer. After the War, Walter worked for Sol Hurok, the arts impresario who handled the careers of many famous international artists. Their only child, Jonathan, was born in 1946. Jonathan was a sickly child, and de Mille would often have the time off she needed to care for him written into her contracts. Jonathan is now a professor of history at Emory University. Walter Prude died in 1992.

HONORS AND AWARDS

Donaldson Award: 1943, 1945, 1947
New York Critics Prize: 1945, 1947
Woman of the Year (American Newspaper Woman's Guild): 1946
Antoinette Perry Award ("Tony"): 1947, for *Brigadoon*; 1962, for *Kwamina*
Dancing Masters Award of Merit: 1950
Dance Magazine Award: 1957
Theatre Hall of Fame: 1973
Handel Award (New York City): 1975
Kennedy Center Career Achievement Award: 1980
Commonwealth Award in Dramatic Arts: 1980
White House National Medal of Arts: 1986

SELECTED WORKS

MUSICALS

The Black Crook, 1929
Oklahoma!, 1943
Bloomer Girl, 1944
Carousel, 1945
Brigadoon, 1947
Gentlemen Prefer Blondes, 1949
Paint your Wagon, 1951
The Girl in the Pink Tights, 1954
Kwamina, 1962
110 in the Shade, 1963

BALLETS

Three Virgins and a Devil, 1941
Rodeo, 1942
Fall River Legend, 1948
The Other, 1992

SELECTED WRITINGS

Dance to the Piper, 1952
And Promenade Home, 1958
To a Young Dancer, 1962
Dance in America, 1970
Speak to Me, Dance with Me, 1974
Reprieve: A Memoir, 1981
Martha: The Life and Work of Martha Graham, 1991

FURTHER READING

BOOKS

De Mille, Agnes. *Dance to the Piper,* 1952
-----. *And Promenade Home,* 1958
-----. *Reprieve: A Memoir,* 1981
Fowler, Carol. *Contributions of Women: Dance,* 1979
Gilbert, Lynn, and Gaylen Moore. *Particular Passions: Talks with Women Who Have Shaped Our Times,* 1981
Robinson, Alice M., et al. *Notable Women in the American Theatre,* 1989
Who's Who in America, 1994

PERIODICALS

Current Biography Yearbook 1985
Horizons, Sep. 1980, p. 29
Los Angeles Times, Oct. 8, 1993, p.A1; Oct. 9, 1993, p. F1
New York Times Biographical Service, Dec. 1976, p.1709; May 1988, p.518
New Yorker, Oct. 14, 1991, p.119
Newsweek, Apr. 20, 1992, p.76
People, Sep. 21, 1981, p.71
Philadelphia Enquirer, Oct. 8, 1993, C18
San Francisco Examiner, Oct. 8, 1993, p.A21
Washington Post, Oct. 8, 1993, p.B6

Placido Domingo 1941-
Spanish Opera Star

BIRTH

Placido Domingo was born January 21, 1941, in Madrid, Spain. His parents are Placido and Pepita Domingo. Domingo has one sister, Mari Pepa, who is one year younger.

YOUTH

Domingo's parents were stars of the *zarzuela* (zar-ZWA-la), a form of Spanish light opera. It is, according to Domingo, "to Spain what operetta is to Vienna—a popular theatrical form that mixes musical numbers with spoken dialogue." The Domingos' work often took them away from home for long periods. While they were touring,

Domingo and his sister stayed with their Aunt Agustina, one of many close relatives in Madrid. Even though he missed his parents, Domingo remembers a warm and happy childhood in Spain. He loved school, playing in the park after school, and going home to his sister and aunt at the end of the day. "I remember the comfortable feeling of that constant rotation in my life—home, school, park, home, school, park, day after day."

When Placido was six, his parents were away from home for two years while they toured in Puerto Rico, Mexico, and Cuba. They loved Mexico and decided to stay to form their own *zarzuela* company. They sent for Placido, Mari Pepa, and Aunt Agustina, who arrived in Mexico in January 1949. The family settled in Mexico City.

Placido started performing early. As a child, he played small parts in his parents' productions. He loved to perform. Once, in a singing competition, he sang a flamenco song and won first prize—some books and a new soccer ball. He quickly gave these away to another contestant, who had dissolved into tears because he had not won.

Growing up in the theater exposed Domino to the basics of performing. He remembers that he "attended orchestra and stage rehearsals, watched the set and costume makers at work, and placed the music on the orchestra's music stands." At the age of eight, he began taking piano lessons. His teacher was a fine musician, and young Domingo worked hard. After his teacher's death, Domingo attended the National Conservatory. Although he felt the musical training was not as rigorous as with his former teacher, he did receive formal instruction in composition, harmony, and sight-reading, all of which helped him later in his opera career and inspired him to study conducting.

EDUCATION

Placido first attended an American school in Mexico City, then went to the Instituto Mexico. He remembers that at school, "for purely non-academic reasons, I had a great time." His teacher loved soccer, and the students practiced two hours a day. Placido, the goalie of the school team, developed a lifelong passion for the game. He has not-so-fond memories of another sport—bullfighting. According to Domingo, the "two standard ambitions of Spanish boys are to be soccer goalkeepers and to be bullfighters." Once, when he was 14, he and a friend went to a bullfighting training ring to try out the sport. The bull, which was "only the size of a large dog," chased him and tossed him to the ground. That was enough for Domingo, who went back to soccer. When Domingo was 14, he entered the National Conservatory, where he studied music and academic subjects.

During Domingo's adolescence, his parents continued to travel with their company, leaving Placido and his sister under the care of their Aunt

Agustina. While his parents were gone on an extended tour, Placido fell in love with a fellow student. Even though he was only 16, he and his girlfriend ran away and were secretly married. When his parents found out, they tried to end the relationship, but Placido stayed with his wife. Soon they had a son, Jose. The couple was young, and the marriage did not last. "It did not take long for us to realize that the situation was completely impossible," Domingo says in his autobiography, *My First Forty Years*. After a year together, he and his wife separated and later divorced.

In order to support his ex-wife and child, Domingo left the conservatory and began a life of freelance music making. He continued to sing parts in his parents' productions and took on roles in musicals, like the Mexican staging of *My Fair Lady*, as well as work in bars and nightclubs.

NATIONAL OPERA OF MEXICO

In 1959, at the age of 18, Domingo auditioned with the National Opera of Mexico and landed his first opera job. Up until that point, he had never had any formal training as a singer and had always sung baritone parts (the middle range of the male bass voice). At his audition, the committee told him he was a tenor (the upper range of the male voice) and asked for a tenor aria. He didn't know one, but sight-read through a part. He did so well that they offered him a contract, as a tenor.

Domingo made his opera debut in 1959 as Borsa in *Rigoletto*. His U.S. debut soon followed, in the role of Arturo in *Lucia di Lammermoor* with the Dallas Civic Opera., singing opposite the great opera diva Joan Sutherland. While he was developing his opera career, he was still active in *zarzuela*, musical comedy, television, and recording. Many commentators have noted Domingo's tremendous capacity for work, which he attributes to the demands of his early years. "When people ask me how I manage to hold up under my extremely heavy work load, I answer that I became accustomed to intense activity very early in my life and that I love it now as I loved it then."

MARRIAGE AND FAMILY

While performing with the National Opera, Domingo met the woman who would become his second wife, Marta Ornelas. She was an outstanding soprano and one of the company's rising stars. It was definitely not love at first sight. Marta's family wasn't too sure of the young man, either, and once, when he came to their apartment to serenade the family, they called the police. One of the policeman told them that they were "getting a beautiful performance, free, by a member of the National Opera." Eventually, Domingo charmed both Marta and her parents, and the couple was married August 1, 1962. They later had two sons, Placido and Alvaro.

CAREER HIGHLIGHTS

HEBREW NATIONAL OPERA

Shortly after their marriage, the Domingos were offered full-time positions with the Hebrew National Opera in Tel Aviv, Israel. In just over two years, they appeared in 280 performances. It was demanding but excellent training. "We learned our craft the best way—without a prompter and with no proper facilities to speak of," remembers Domingo. Sometimes the cast included people who could only sing in their native language. One memorable performance of *La Traviata* featured a baritone singing Hungarian, a soprano singing in German, Domingo singing in Italian, and the chorus performing in Hebrew. "Fortunately," says Domingo, "the conductor was leading in Esperanto."

While in Israel, Domingo undertook his first intensive training in voice, focusing on his breathing. He studied hard to learn how to support the voice by properly using the muscles of the diaphragm. Both his range and his ability increased.

Although they were asked to stay, Marta and Placido decided they wanted to leave Israel and expand their experience elsewhere. They also wanted to start a family. By the time they left Israel in 1965 to return to Mexico City, Marta was pregnant with their first child.

NEW YORK DEBUT

In 1966, Domingo made his New York debut in the New York City Opera's production of Alberto Ginastera's *Don Rodrigo*. His debut with New York's Metropolitan Opera came in 1968, when he sang the role of Maruizio in *Adriana Lecouvreur*. His career was off like a shot: within a few years, he had performed at all the major opera houses in the world. He debuted in Hamburg and Vienna in 1967, La Scala in Italy in 1969, and Covent Garden in England in 1972.

THE VOICE AND THE PERFORMER

Today, after starring in the major tenor roles for over 20 years, Domingo is considered the finest tenor of his generation. Unlike many opera singers, he is a highly trained musician who has studied instrumental performance, theory, and conducting. Different tenor voices have different qualities; Domingo's is dark and powerful. His voice lends itself to a wide variety of operas, and he has performed more than 100 different roles to date. His range spans the entire operatic repertory for tenor, encompassing light-lyric, lyric, *spinto* (a combination of lyric and dramatic qualities), and dramatic parts. Some of his most famous portrayals include the lead in Verdi's *Otello*, Cavaradossi in Puccini's *Tosca*, Radames in Verdi's *Aida*, the lead in Offenbach's *Tales of Hoffman*, Rodolfo in Puccini's *La Boheme*, Ricardo in *Un Ballo in Maschera*, and Calaf in Puccini's *Turandot*. Even though he has sung many of these roles dozens of times, he continues to learn from them. "I never feel I really possess a role until I have sung it at least 20 times," he says. "For although, in our profession, one can score a 'success' the first time one attempts a role, *really* worthwhile results are achieved only through a process of constantly maturing performances."

Domingo has a deep reverence for the great opera composers whose music he performs. "Being a singer is not enough. In order to serve the composers properly, you have to be a musician as well. Because to *really* sing, you have to delve into a score deeply and meticulously and seek to unravel all the secrets it contains, all the little things behind the notes and between the lines. For example, whenever there is a change of key, usually there is also a change of mood—from bliss to wistfulness or whatever—and you should modulate your voice accordingly."

This thoughtful, articulate opera star is known as one of the most gracious and cooperative of singers. Teresa Stratas called him a "dream partner." Kiri Te Kanawa says, "He loves his family, he loves his wife, he loves all his friends, he's good to his colleagues. It's quite difficult to talk about someone who's perfect, isn't it?"

In the past ten years, Domingo has ventured into the realm of Wagnerian opera, which is notoriously difficult for the voice. In 1985, he performed the lead in Wagner's *Lohengrin*, to critical acclaim. One of the most difficult and beautiful parts for the tenor voice is the lead in *Parsifal*, which Domingo tried for the first time in 1991. Again, his efforts were a great success.

In the mid-1980s, Domingo began to appear in film versions of some of his more famous roles, including *La Traviata* and *Carmen*, which reached a larger audience than his stage performances and continued to broaden his appeal. In yet another departure, Domingo ventured into the area of popular music, making records with such pop stars as John Denver. Their recording, "Perhaps Love," has sold more than one million copies. Domingo has continued to record non-opera works, including folk songs, popular ballads, and other music that some "purists" feel is beneath him. But Domingo loves all music, and he finds such thinking snobbish.

A TRAGIC EARTHQUAKE

In September 1985, while preparing for a performance in Chicago, Domingo heard of an earthquake that had devastated Mexico City. He soon heard that his parents had not been harmed, but that an aunt, uncle, cousin, and the cousin's infant son were among the missing. He flew to Mexico City, where he spent eight days digging in the rubble of his relatives' apartment house. Working with neighbors and friends in the rescue squad, Domingo finally uncovered the bodies of his relatives, who had perished in the disaster. Domingo and his family were grief stricken. As a way to deal with the pain of his loss, and to give something back to the city of his youth, Domingo began a series of benefit concerts that went on for six months and raised more than half a million dollars for the survivors of the earthquake.

"THE THREE TENORS"

In 1990, Domingo performed with two other tenor superstars, Luciano Pavarotti and Jose Carreras, at the Baths of Caracall in Italy. The three singers took turns singing favorite tenor arias from the classical repertoire, along with pop hits and ballads. The crowd's favorite piece was the aria "Nessun Dorma" from Puccini's *Turandot*. While the concert was going on, the World Cup soccer championship was taking place in Italy, and the Italian team took the song as their theme.

Much to everyone's surprise, "The Three Tenors" was a hit in three media: television, recording, and video. The televised show was watched by 800 million viewers world wide. The recording of the concert has sold 10 million copies, making it the best selling classical recording in history. And the video, *The Three Tenors in Concert*, made Billboard's Top 10 video chart, becoming one of the hottest selling videos for its label, PolyGram.

In 1994, the Three Tenors decided to try to bring back the magic. This time, the venue was Los Angeles's Dodger's Stadium, during the final games of the 1994 World Cup soccer championship. The show was again a spectacle and great crowd pleaser, as 56,000 attended, including American music legend Frank Sinatra, for whom the tenors sang "My Way," while close to one billion people watched on television.

CURRENT PROJECTS

Even at the age of 54, Domingo is full of energy and eager to take on new challenges. In the past year, he has added five new roles to his ever-growing repertoire, and he continues to thrive on his demanding schedule. On one day in May of this year, he performed Wagner's *Parsifal* in the afternoon and conducted a performance of Puccini's *Madama Butterfly* in the evening, an indication both of his stamina and of another direction his career is taking. He is developing his skills as a conductor and thoroughly enjoying the view from the orchestra pit. He has served as musical consultant to the Music Center Opera in Los Angeles for nine years and was recently named director of the Washington Opera. Domingo loves conducting, and he feels he brings a special quality to his direction. He has performed with the world's best opera conductors, including Herbert von Karajan, Claudio Abbado, Riccardo Muti, James Levine, Zubin Mehta, and Lorin Maazel.

Domingo's future plans also include a reunion of the Three Tenors at the 1998 World Cup in France. "We are all full of enthusiasm to do it again," he says.

HOMES, HOBBIES, AND OTHER INTERESTS

To accommodate his hectic schedule, Domingo has homes in London, Los Angeles, New York, Vienna, and Monaco. To relax, he and Marta go to a spa to swim, walk, and rest. Domingo is also involved in charity work. He founded a charity for handicapped and terminally ill children in Los Angeles, and he takes his young fans to rehearsals with him.

SELECTED RECORDINGS

Verdi: *Trovatore*, 1969
Verdi: *Don Carlo*, 1970
Leoncavallo: *I Pagliacci*, 1971
Offenbach: *Les Contes d'Hoffman*, 1971
Puccini: *Manon Lescaut*, 1972
Puccini: *Tosca*, 1972
Puccini: *La Boheme*, 1973
Bizet: *Carmen*, 1975
Giordano: *Andrea Chenier*, 1976
Wagner: *Die Meistersinger*, 1976
Cilea: *Adriana Lecouvreur*, 1977
Puccini: *Madama Butterfly*, 1978
Verdi: *Otello*, 1978
Mascagni: *Cavalleria Rusticana*, 1979
Verdi: *Luisa Miller*, 1979
Puccini: *Turandot*, 1981
Perhaps Love, 1981 [with John Denver]
Verdi: *Aida*, 1982
Verdi: *La Traviata*, 1983

Always in My Heart, 1984
Wagner: *Lohengrin*, 1988
Carreras, Doming, Pavarotti: In Concert, 1990
Saint-Saens: *Samson et Dalila*, 1993
Strauss: *Die Frau ohne Schatten*, 1992
De Mi Alma Latina, 1994

WRITINGS

My First Forty Years, 1983

HONORS AND AWARDS

Grammy Award: 1983, for *La Traviata*; 1984, for *Always in My Heart*; 1984, for *Carmen*; 1988, for *Lohengrin*; 1990, for *Carreras, Domingo, Pavarotti: In Concert*; 1992, for *Die Frau ohne Schatten*
Emmy Award: 1984, for "Great Performances: Placido Domingo Celebrates Seville"; 1992, for "Metropolitan Opera Silver Gala"

FURTHER READING

BOOKS

Domingo, Placido. *My First Forty Years*, 1983
Hines, Jerome. *Great Singers on Great Singing*, 1982
Matheopoulos, Helena. *Divo: Great Tenors, Baritones, and Basses Discuss Their Roles*, 1986
Snowman, Daniel. *The World of Placido Domingo*, 1985
Who's Who in America 1995

PERIODICALS

Current Biography 1972
Daily News of Los Angeles, Sep. 2, 1993, p.L6
Los Angeles Times, July 17, 1994, p.A1; May 9, 1995, p.F1
Montreal Gazette, July 18, 1994, p.C5
Newsweek, Mar. 8, 1982, p.56
New York, Mar. 1, 1992, p.56
Opera News, Mar. 27, 1982, p.11; Mar. 30, 1991, p.9; Sep. 1993, p.8; Sep. 1994, p.74
People, Mar. 29, 1982, p.102
San Francisco Chronicle, Nov. 6, 1994, p.D1
Time, July 18, 1994, p.52

ADDRESS

Metropolitan Opera Company
Lincoln Center
New York, NY 10023

Janet Evans 1971-
American Swimmer
Olympic Gold Medalist and World Champion

BIRTH

Janet Beth Evans was born August 28, 1971, in Fullerton, California. She is the youngest of three children born to Paul Evans, a veterinarian, and Barbara Evans, a homemaker. Janet has two older brothers, David and John.

EARLY MEMORIES—IN THE POOL

Janet started to swim around the time she started to walk. When she was 13 months old, she tried to get in the YMCA pool to join her older brothers in their swimming lessons. "Janet used to just throw a fit to get in the water," recalls Barbara Evans. "She loved the water." Her mom talked the instructor into letting Janet take lessons, and by the time she was two, Janet could swim the width of the pool. When she was three, she could swim all the competitive strokes: freestyle, backstroke, breaststroke, even butterfly. She began to compete at four, and by the time she was 10, she had broken national records.

TRAINING TO BE A CHAMPION

While she was a teenager, Janet began the kind of rigorous training required of swimming champions. She swam four hours a day, seven days a week, putting in 15,000 to 18,000 meters a day (that's roughly 10 miles a day). To this she added weight training, to increase muscle mass and endurance. Swimmers need alot of sleep, so Janet regularly went to bed at 8:00 or 9:00 to make her early morning workouts.

Evans has always been a tenacious competitor and has never complained about the sacrifices made for her sport. She once went two years without missing a single practice. "A lot of swimmers try to have their cake and eat it, too. You can't do that if you want to be the best. You can't let anything stand in your way." For Evans, the sacrifices always seemed to be balanced by what she got out of her sport. "When I was little, swimming was something I did, and I didn't know better. Now I know there are so many things a high school kid can do, and I don't get to do most of them. When I finally realized it, I was into swimming and enjoying it. And I think I've done alot more than most high school kids have ever done."

EDUCATION

Janet's education was organized to fit around her demanding swimming workouts. She would get up at 5:00 a.m., swim for two hours before school, go to school for five hours, then get back in the pool for another two hours. She attended the public schools in Placentia, California, and, despite the demands of her sport, was an honors student at El Dorado High School.

CAREER HIGHLIGHTS

Early on it became clear that Evans was a great distance swimmer, and her premiere events became the 400-meter freestyle, the 800-meter free, and the 1,500-meter free. Later, she added the 400-meter individual medley, or IM, 100 meters each of backstroke, breaststroke, butterfly, and freestyle.

EVANS'S STROKE

Much has been written about Evans's swimming ability. Her small, lightweight body rides high in the water, creating little water resistance.

Her stoke is powerful and incredibly swift: in the early years of her swimming career, she would take 55 stokes per lap (two lengths of the pool); most swimmers go the same distance in 40 strokes. Observers noted that she looked like a windmill, yet she didn't seem to tire. "Once she gets those arms going a millions miles per hour, she never slows down," said her high school coach, Tom Milich. Evans also has a highly efficient stroke: "Janet is the most economical swimmer in the world in terms of maximum uptake and velocity generated in the water," says John Troup of the U.S. Swimming Federation. "She is about the closest thing to a fish you're likely to find in a human being."

In 1986, while still in high school, Evans attended her first international meet, the Goodwill Games in Moscow. She was 15, and at 5'2" and 85 pounds, a tiny swimmer, especially in comparison to her competition. In an anecdote that has become legendary, the swimmers from the Soviet Union snickered as Janet got up on the starting block. They didn't laugh for long, as Evans posted her personal best times in two events.

In 1987, Evans really came into her own. She broke the three oldest records in women's swimming: the 400-, 800-, and 1,500-freestyle records. She began to attract all kinds of media attention, and as the 1988 Olympics in Seoul, Korea, approached, all the major networks, newspapers, and magazines descended on Placentia to follow her around. One film crew taped her while she brushed her teeth, another followed her through a "typical" day at her high school. "It's a pain, really," she said. "I mean, it's embarrassing."

Throughout it all, Janet stayed relatively cool and unaffected, a fact that many attributed to her upbringing. Her parents raised her to think of herself as "Just Janet," and she brought a measure of good humor and level-headedness not often seen in an athlete so young and so gifted. "Sometimes I do stop and think about what it means to hold a world record, to be able to do something better than anyone else in the world has ever done it, and I wonder, why me? It boggles my mind. But I'm still the same person I was before I swam that fast. I'm the student at El Dorado High School with a French test the next day." And despite her hectic training and competing schedule, Janet made time for typical high school activities, too. In her junior year, after she set two national records in a meet, she pulled on a formal gown in the locker room and went to the prom at her high school.

Just before the Olympics, in July 1988, Evans swam to three new world records, in the 400-, 800-, and 1,500-freestyle. She became the first woman to hold three world records since 1976. She trained hard, and she knew she was ready.

1988 OLYMPICS

With the cameras rolling and the eyes of the world on her, Evans swept her events at the 1988 Olympics, taking gold in the 400-free, 800-free, and the 400-IM (the 1,500-free is not an Olympic event for women). Nicknamed "Princess" by her teammates, Evans loved the competition. "I'm not merely happy, I'm ecstatic," she said after winning her first gold medal. She was toasted as "America's Newest Sweetheart," all giggles and with her signature smile.

After the 1988 Olympics, Janet continued to live in the public eye. She was named Grand Marshall of the Macy's Thanksgiving Parade and appeared on TV with Bob Hope and Tom Selleck. There was speculation that Evans might skip college and take advantage of the lucrative offers of endorsements that could earn her up to one million dollars. But Janet wasn't even tempted. "They say I could be set for life, but I believe all that will still be there after college. I want to major in communications. I want to enjoy college."

COLLEGE

When Evans graduated from El Dorado High in 1989, she was the most heavily recruited swimmer in U.S. history. Many schools wanted her: she was the best female swimmer in the world, and she had a 3.8 grade point average, too. She decided on Stanford University, in nearby Palo Alto, where she could be with other high-achieving kids and still train with some of the best swimmers in the country. Her new coach, Richard Quick, was delighted to have Evans. "Janet is a once-in-lifetime athlete, he said. "Her strength-per-pound is incredible . . . and she has a tremendous desire to do well. Janet is the hardest working swimmer I've ever seen or heard about."

At Stanford, she studied communications and continued her practice schedule of 5-6 hours of swimming a day. She carried a full academic load and enjoyed college life as a rather anonymous student. "One of the reasons I like it here is that there are no other swimmers in my dorm. I can talk about things besides swimming." But one night while she was studying, one of her friends knocked on her door to tell her that she had just been featured as a "Final Jeopardy" question on the popular game show.

In her first competition as a college student, and while studying for finals, Evans won three events—the 400-free, 400-IM, and 800-free—at the U.S. Open Swim Championships.

In 1990, Evans won the Sullivan Award, given to the top amateur athlete in the U.S. She was the first swimmer to win the award since Tracy Culkins received it in 1978, and she was thrilled. "It's kind of like the Olympics, she said. "You realize that your name will be a part of history." Later that year, Evans competed in her first NCAA (National Collegiate Athletic Association) finals. She swam the 500-free, the 1,650-free, and the 400-IM, and she also shared in Stanford's first-place victory in the 800-freestyle relay. In addition, 1990 proved to be the year that Evans showed she wasn't invincible. In the Goodwill Games that year, she won the 800-free, but lost the 400-IM to Summer Sanders, a young, up-and-coming swimmer. Evans hadn't lost the IM since 1986, and she was disappointed, but she was also a bit angry at the media, whom she believed focused on her loss, instead of Sander's win.

In 1991, Evans left Stanford because of changes in the NCAA rules regarding practice. The new regulations restricted college athletes to 20 hours of practice per week. Many college athletes, coaches, and commentators thought the decision was misguided and arbitrary. The policy was created to help football and basketball players, who as a group had a low graduation rate, improve their chances of graduating by limiting the hours they were required to practice. But it didn't take into consideration either the many athletes, like Evans, who were able to keep their grades up while competing, or the specific requirements of swimmers, who need to swim 30 hours a week or more to remain competitive. Evans was angry and wrote an eloquent rebuttal to the new policy in *Sporting News*, where she said: "By managing my time wisely, I was able to train 30-35 hours a week, travel with my team, maintain a full academic load, and enjoy a social life as part of my wonderful college experience. I never felt I needed to cut hours from my training in order to have time for the other aspects of college life."

Evans gave up her NCAA eligibility and her scholarship, and focused on training for the 1992 Olympics. She was now able to accept money from the U.S. Olympic Committee and the U.S. Swimming Federation. In the fall of 1991, Evans transferred to the University of Texas to train, but not to compete, on the college level, and to continue her studies. She worked with a new coach, Mark Schubert, whose specialty—distance training—matched her needs. Because she had declined to continue as a NCAA athlete, she was able to take advantage of endorsement offers and soon appeared in ads for swim suits, sunglasses, cereal, soda pop, and running shoes.

1992 OLYMPICS

Evans received far less media attention as the 1992 Olympics in Barcelona, Spain, approached. That was fine with her. "It's been kind of nice," she said. She entered the Olympics "less darling and more wild card," in the words of one sportswriter. Evans qualified for the 400- and 800-free for the '92 Olympics, but she didn't make the cut for the 400 IM. Her qualifying times were significantly slower than her world-record pace of 1988, and many commentators noted that she had lost the pixie look of 1988, and was older, heavier, slower. When it came to the finals of the competition, Evans won a gold in the 800-freestyle and a silver in the 400-free. She was happy with her win, but rather stunned by the media response. "I went to the press room and it was like, 'What happened? You lost.' And I said, 'I didn't lose, I won a silver medal.'" She couldn't understand why they couldn't see what she had done: she was now the only U.S. woman in history to win four Olympic Gold medals in swimming.

When she returned to the U.S. after the Olympics, Evans decided to take four months off to think about her future. "Coming into '92 as the Olympic champion was a lot of pressure to do this and do that and people telling you you've won 20 races in a row. For a while, I wasn't having as much fun. So now it's like I have nothing to lose in the sport. They can't put that much pressure on me, they just can't because I've done everything in the sport."

In the fall of 1992, Evans transferred to the University of Southern California (USC), to follow her coach, Mark Schubert, who had accepted the job as head coach of the USC swim team. After her four months off, Evans got back into shape quickly, and her times improved. She added running to her routine, and it helped her strength. Evans was also involved in promotional touring as part of her many endorsement agreements.

Evans graduated from USC in May of 1994, with a bachelor's degree (B.A.) in communications. In the fall of 1994, she competed in the World Championships, placing first in the 800-free and fifth in the 400-free. Also in 1994, she won her 37th national title, surpassing swimming great and Tarzan star Johnny Weismuller to become the number two all-time U.S. title-holder. (Only Tracy Culkins has more.)

Evans is focusing now on the 1996 Summer Olympics games, to be held in Atlanta, after which she plans to retire. She hopes to begin a career as a sports commentator, not in swimming, but in football! She loves the game, and claims to have an encyclopedic knowledge of the sport.

But it is her own sport that will forever bear her imprint: "Before she's done," predicts former coach Bud McAllister, "she will be considered the greatest female swimmer ever. It's a tribute to her dedication, consistency, and attitude."

HOME AND FAMILY

Evans lives at home with her family in California, in the house she grew up in. Her two brothers have graduated from college and are off on their own, and Janet shares the house with her mom, dad, and a new golden retriever.

HOBBIES AND OTHER INTERESTS

When she isn't in the pool, Janet likes to go shopping and to listen to the music of U2 and Garth Brooks.

HONORS AND AWARDS

U.S. Swimmer of the Year: 1987
World Swimmer of the Year (*Swimming Magazine*): 1987, 1989, 1990
Olympic Swimming, 400 meter freestyle: 1988, gold medal; 1992, silver medal
Olympic Swimming, 800 meter freestyle: 1988, gold medal; 1992, gold medal
Olympic Swimming, 400 individual medley: 1988, gold medal
Sullivan Award: 1989
USOC Sportswoman of the Year: 1989

FURTHER READING

BOOKS

Who's Who of American Women, 1993-94

PERIODICALS

Chicago Tribune, Aug. 28, 1988, p.C1; Aug. 17, 1994, p.C3
Philadelphia Inquirer, Sep. 19, 1988, p.F1
Los Angeles Times, Jul. 12, 1986, p.C13; Jul. 5, 1988, p.C1; Jan. 1, 1989, p.C1
San Francisco Chronicle, Mar. 13, 1990, p.D1; Apr. 4, 1991, p.B14
San Francisco Examiner, Sep. 5, 1993, p.C11
Sporting News, Apr. 29, 1991, p.5
Sports Illustrated, Aug. 10, 1987, p.29; Sep. 14, 1988, p.140; Sep. 26, 1988, p.64; Apr. 15, 1991, p.28
Time, Oct. 3, 1988, p.58
USA Today, Aug. 16, 1989, p.C1

ADDRESS

U.S. Olympic Committee
1750 E. Boulder St.
Colorado Springs, CO 80909

Patrick Ewing 1962-
American Professional Basketball Player
All-Star Center for the New York Knicks;
Gold Medal Winner in 1984 and 1992
Summer Olympics

BIRTH

Patrick Aloysius (al-o-ISH-us) Ewing was born in Kingston, Jamaica, on August 5, 1962, to Carl and Dorothy (Phipps) Ewing. He came to the United States at the age of 13 to live in Cambridge, Massachusetts, a few miles northwest of Boston, where his parents were establishing a home so that their seven children would have access to a better life. Dorothy Ewing arrived in this country first, in 1971, found work in the dietary department of Massachusetts General Hospital, and started to save money. She then sent for her husband, a mechanic, who was hired here by a rubber company. Their eldest daughter immigrated with her father, and the rest of the children joined them over the next few years.

Patrick is the fifth of the Ewing siblings, preceded by Lastina, Carl Jr., Pauline, and Rosemarie, and followed by Barbara and Karlene.

YOUTH

Ewing played soccer and cricket as a boy in Jamaica, but had never seen or heard of basketball until he arrived in Cambridge. He spoke about his introduction to the game in a conversation with filmmaker and Knicks fan Spike Lee in a 1990 article in *Interview* magazine. As Ewing recalled, the kids on the playground said it made no difference that he didn't know how to play, they just "needed an extra body. So I played . . . I messed up, I blanked up. But I liked it, so I kept on playing, kept on getting better." Friends from those days remember the quiet, tall, skinny kid with the "strange" accent (in Jamaica, Ewing grew up speaking a dialect of English that would be difficult for many Americans to understand). He was hard to forget: when he started playing organized basketball in seventh grade, he was already a six-footer; he would stretch to a full seven feet and fill out to 230 pounds by the time he entered his senior year.

The awkwardness that came with his towering height, his continuing difficulty in making his speech understood, as well as a considerable learning disability that required special tutoring, set Ewing up as a target of merciless taunts. He was ridiculed by basketball fans from other schools, even to the point of being called an ape and having banana peels thrown at him on the court. The appalling indignities followed him through his high school and college playing days. Today, even those who note his chilly arrogance and unapproachability with the media concede that his attitude most likely stems from the ridicule he suffered as a youth.

Ewing's early experiences in the U.S. were not all grim. He was always a little less outgoing than most boys, but he managed to make friends in the neighborhood fairly quickly. A teacher who met him "when he was right off the boat" told a *Sports Illustrated* writer in 1993 that he [the teacher] and his wife used to take Patrick and his buddies "up in the woods for a week, play football, go to movies, fun stuff. Patrick showed me how to fish with my hands, like they do in Jamaica. He'd just get in the water and snap 'em up. . . . Me? Nah, I couldn't catch 'em. I was too slow."

EDUCATION

To help ease his difficult transition into a new educational system, Ewing was sent to a remedial center in Cambridge to work on his reading and speaking skills. From there, he went on to that city's Rindge and Latin

High School. He played basketball there under the tutelage of coach Mike Jarvis, eventually leading his team to three consecutive Massachusetts state championships. Patrick became a naturalized citizen when he was a junior and, during summer breaks, went to Upward Bound programs at nearby Wellesley College to prepare himself for each academic year ahead. If his studies did not come easily to him, it was not for lack of trying, say those who remember him from high school days. His mother wanted more than anything for him to be educated, and she instilled in him that same desire. The disgraceful remarks hurled at him during games only made Ewing more determined to prove himself.

Ewing's superb performance as a center for Rindge and Latin's basketball team had major colleges across the country scrambling to recruit him. He accepted a four-year full scholarship from Georgetown University in Washington, D.C. Although his award-filled college career could have given him an early and lucrative entry into the NBA (National Basketball Association), he chose to stay in school and graduate as his mother would have wished. Dorothy Ewing died in 1983, still insisting that her son's education was more important than any monetary benefits he could provide for his needy family. Patrick, who had once thought his boyhood interest in drawing might lead to his life's work, received a B.A. degree in fine arts from Georgetown in 1985. "Getting that degree meant more to me than an NCAA title, being named All-America, or winning an Olympic gold medal," Ewing once said. "I promised my mother before she died that I would graduate on time, and I'm proud to have fulfilled that promise."

MAJOR INFLUENCES

Coach Jarvis of Rindge and Latin is the man whose efforts set Ewing on the path to his legendary career. Concerned about Patrick as colleges vied for the talented player, Jarvis took the unusual step of writing to 150 schools "the so-called Ewing Letter," says *Current Biography*, "which detailed the rules for recruiting Patrick and listed his academic and athletic requirements." The letter explained his disadvantaged background and his special educational needs. Eighty schools responded, but after visiting the five that most appealed to him, Ewing chose Georgetown. There he would be guided by the renowned coach, John Thompson, himself a former backup center to the Boston Celtics' great Bill Russell.

Ewing accepted Georgetown's scholarship offer mainly because of its coach. He concedes that he would have had access to a good education at any number of universities, but says it was Thompson who "knew the position, and was better equipped to teach me." Thompson also kept the media away from his star athlete during troubled times when Ewing was being harassed on court and off. Some of the most vocal (and racist)

115

critics saw the big center as a threatening presence, and would have drawn an aggressive response from him had it not been for Thompson's steadying and protective hand.

CAREER HIGHLIGHTS

THE SPECTACULAR YEARS AT GEORGETOWN

In his freshman year (1981-82), Patrick Ewing took Georgetown by storm. Intimidating by size and strength, if not by finesse, his impact was unmistakable. He led his team, the "Hoyas," to a 30-7 record and to a Big East Conference championship in his first year. The post-season NCAA (National Collegiate Athletic Association) loss to mighty North Carolina was by a single point, 63-62. The following year, the team made the regionals with a 22-10 record, but it was in Ewing's junior year that Georgetown triumphed in the Big East tournament, 34-3, beating Houston 84-75 for its first-ever NCAA championship and rejoicing when Ewing was named the tournament's most valuable player. The following summer, 1984, between his junior and senior years, Ewing played with the winning U.S. team in the Summer Olympics in Los Angeles, and collected his first of two Olympic gold medals.

In his senior year (1984-85), Ewing was the outstanding contributor to Georgetown's 35-3 season and to its Big East and post-season titles. The anticipated NCAA title was snatched away that year, though, in a heart-breaking loss to Villanova, 66-64. Ewing left Georgetown as the Hoyas' all-time leading rebounder (1,316) and shot-blocker (493), while ranking second in all-time scoring (2,184) to guard Sleepy Floyd's 2,304. That season, Patrick was honored as Player of the Year in a shared award with Chris Mullin of St. John University.

Georgetown University's athletic teams are known as the "Hoyas," a name that needs more explanation than most. A long-ago team at Georgetown was called the "Stonewalls," and it is believed that Greek and Latin terms were applied in dubbing the players "hoia saxa," or "what rocks!", implying that they were hard as rocks. From this obscure beginning was born the college yell ("Hoya, Hoya, Saxa," substituting a "y" for the original "i") and the widely used phrases that came into use during Patrick Ewing's playing days—"Hoya Paranoia," denoting the team's combative style and its distrust of others, and "Hoya Destroya," an expression coined specifically for the intense and intimidating Ewing.

THE BIG WARRIOR SIGNS WITH THE KNICKS

In 1985, the NBA changed its recruiting rules—and Ewing, a powerful center who has been compared to Bill Russell, Kareem Abdul-Jabbar, and Wilt Chamberlain, was said to be the foremost reason. A lottery was introduced that year, giving the seven lowest-ranked teams equal shots at the best player, and the New York Knickerbockers won the right to draft Ewing. They signed him to the most lucrative contract ever offered a rookie (reportedly $31.2 million for 10 years), and placed in him their hopes for a return to their glory days of the early 1970s. Ewing played well during his first year (1985-86), although a knee injury kept him out of 32 games and prevented him from taking his place on the all-star team, to which he had been named. He was, nevertheless, chosen NBA Rookie of the Year, the first Knick to win the honor since Willis Reed in the 1964-65 season. The team record was a discouraging 23- 59 that year, followed by an equally wretched 24-58 the next season.

Coaches were hired and fired, first Hubie Brown and then Bob Hill, but it was not until Rick Pitino took over the team in the 1987-88 season that Ewing began to perform up to his potential. Pitino gave Patrick the encouragement he needed and the opportunity to play the pressing style he had learned under John Thompson at Georgetown. He started in all 82 games in the first injury-free season of his pro career, averaging 20.2 points and 8.2 rebounds. He helped lead the Knicks to the NBA playoffs for the first time in four years, where they lost to the Boston Celtics.

By 1989-90, Ewing was into a great year, which sportswriters were calling his "all-everything season." He was the only player in the league to be in the top six in scoring, rebounding, blocking, and shooting; he was named to the All-Star team for the fourth time, his first as a starter; he scored a career-high 51 points in a regular season game against Boston; and he continued his heroics in the playoffs with a high of 45 points against the Detroit Pistons. The next season he finished among the NBA Top Ten in scoring, rebounding, and blocked shots, joining the San Antonio Spurs' David Robinson as the only top-ten player in all of those categories. He was again a leading scorer during regular season play the following two seasons, with some extra court

time as well: in 1993, he played a major role in the All-Star Classic in Utah; and in 1992, he played with the USA Dream Team at the Summer Olympics in Barcelona, Spain. There, in sparkling performances averaging 9.5 points and 5.3 rebounds per game, and with a field goal average of .623, he scored an Olympic-high 15 points in the victory over Croatia, winning a gold medal.

In the 1993-94 season, with the able direction of the renowned coach Pat Riley, Ewing led the Knicks to their first Eastern Conference championship in more than two decades. It was Patrick's first finals appearance, in a duel with another all-star center and longtime rival, Hakeem Olajuwon. "There is an NBA championship trophy to be had," wrote Phil Taylor in *Sports Illustrated*, "but . . . Ewing and Olajuwon cannot share it." Ultimately, the Knicks lost the NBA finals to the Rockets in the riveting seven-game series.

In the 1994-95 season, with the Knicks hovering near the top of the league, Ewing remains committed to helping his teammates win championship rings. Coming into the season, his 23.8 points-per-game average was third among active players, behind Boston's Dominique Wilkins and Karl Malone of Utah. This could be the year he has waited for, and he is doing his part to make it happen. As the legendary Larry Bird of the Boston Celtics told *Sports Illustrated*: "What I like about him is that he gives a champion's effort every time out. Every time."

MARRIAGE AND FAMILY

Ewing has been married since July 27, 1990, to Rita Williams, a Georgetown University law student. They live in Potomac, Maryland (suburban Washington, D.C.), with their daughter, Randi Dorothy, who will be four years old in April and whose middle name honors Patrick's late mother. He also has another child, 11-year-old Patrick Ewing, Jr., his son from a former relationship. Patrick Jr. lives with his mother, Sharon Stanford, but shares also in his famous dad's home life and has appeared with him in TV endorsements.

HOBBIES AND OTHER INTERESTS

At age 32, Ewing feels that, barring injury, he has about five more years left before retirement from professional basketball. He has considered the possibility of buying a car dealership, and perhaps a radio station in the Boston area because, he told Spike Lee a few years ago, "there really is no black [FM] radio station there. . . . My friends from Boston, man, they're like dying! NO MUSIC." Ewing is especially fond of reggae and the blues.

Ewing fiercely guards his life off the court, denying interviews and, often, autograph requests, but he has relaxed enough to be seen occasionally in TV or movie guest roles. He made cameo appearances several years ago in two films, *Funny about Love* and *The Exorcist 1990*. He also donates time to the Special Olympics and the Children's Health Fund, as well as to a number of other charities.

Described by the press as standoffish—even arrogant—Patrick Ewing is basically the same reserved person he was as a boy. Friends spring to his defense when he is attacked in print for his brusqueness, explaining that, in private, he is anything *but* the fierce warrior of the basketball court.

HONORS AND AWARDS

All-American Teams (*Sporting News*): 1983-84, Second Team; 1985, First Team; 1986, 1988-93, All-Star
Most Valuable Player (NCAA Big East Tournament): 1984
Olympic Gold Medals: 1984, 1992
College Player of the Year (*Sporting News*): 1985 (shared with Chris Mullen)
Kodak Award: 1985
NBA First Draft Choice: 1985
Rupp Trophy (named for Adolph Rupp, legendary Kentucky coach): 1985
NBA Rookie of the Year: 1986
All-NBA First Team: 1990

FURTHER READING

BOOKS

Newman, Matthew. *Patrick Ewing*, 1986 (juvenile)
Reiser, Howard. *Patrick Ewing: Center of Attention*, 1994 (juvenile)

PERIODICALS

Current Biography Yearbook 1991
Ebony, Feb. 1986, p.59
Interview, May 1990, p.136
Jet, Jan. 12, 1986, p.49; Dec. 16, 1991, p.52
New York, Sep. 16, 1985, p.126
Sport, June 1990, p.23; May 1994, p.30
Sporting News, Dec. 16, 1991, p.52; July 4, 1994, p.8
Sports Illustrated, Jan. 7, 1985, p.44; Oct. 28, 1985, p.44; Jan. 22, 1990, p.30; Oct. 11, 1993, p.74; Jan. 17, 1994, p.52; June 13, 1994, p.26
Time, Mar. 14, 1983, p.80

ADDRESS

New York Knickerbockers
2 Penn Plaza
New York, NY 10121-0091

Newt Gingrich 1943-
American Politician, Former History Professor
Speaker of the U.S. House of Representatives

BIRTH

Newton Leroy McPherson Gingrich (GING-rich), the first
Republican in nearly four decades to rise to the powerful post of
Speaker of the House of Representatives, was born on June 17,
1943, in Harrisburg, Pennsylvania. Kathleen (Kit) Daugherty,
only 16, had wed 19-year-old Newton McPherson, Sr., the
previous September, but their marriage was short-lived. They
divorced within a year, and Kit and her infant son moved in with
Kit's widowed mother in a neighboring Pennsylvania town. The
young father, Newton McPherson, Sr., left town and joined the
Navy. He has been dead now for 20 years.

YOUTH

Newt's early childhood was spent almost entirely with adults. He was the focus of his mother's attention in the first difficult years after her marriage broke up. In that time, they forged an especially close and lasting relationship. His grandmother, a teacher, helped to care for him and taught him to read when he was still a preschooler, thus introducing him to what would become a lifelong fascination with words. He was made to feel important, and his self-confidence was so deeply rooted that he was always comfortable talking about what he read and what he thought. One family story from Newt's young boyhood tells of his giving a little speech at a children's program in church. When he finished, he moved to another spot in the chancel and enthusiastically started to speak again. He had to be stopped by the minister.

A NEW STEPFATHER

In 1946, Kit married Robert Bruce Gingrich, a career Army infantry officer. He immediately filed to adopt little "Newtie" (the affectionate nickname his mother uses to this day). In adopting Newt, the elder Gingrich explains that he wished to give the child not only his name, but a sense of belonging as well. Bob and Kit Gingrich eventually also had three daughters: Susan, Roberta, and Candace.

At first, his mother's remarriage had little impact on young Newt. But when Bob Gingrich returned from active service in the Korean conflict in the early 1950s, life changed dramatically. The growing family moved around from one army base to another, in this country and in Europe, during Bob's subsequent tours of duty. Susan and Roberta had been born by this time (Candace came along many years later), and the young boy who had once been the center of his extended family's universe had to learn to share his parents' affection and attention. Newt admits to having had mixed feelings about his place in the family. He felt different from the others because he was adopted, and defiant in the more structured household headed by a military man. Yet he also felt "enormous admiration," developed during the Korean war years, for a parent who was away from home "doing something very important."

EARLY MEMORIES

As a small boy, Newt was conspicuously indulged by an aunt and uncle, the sister and brother-in-law of his biological father. The childless couple "turned their home," says a *Washington Post* feature story, "into a child's wonderland, their closets brimming with toys and books for Newtie." It was in that same home, where he continued to visit Aunt Loma and Uncle Cal Troutman, that nine-year-old Newt was prompted to become a Republican. "Uncle Cal," he remembers, "taught me to smile when

[Gen. Dwight D.] Eisenhower's image was on the television screen, and to turn [his opponent] Adlai Stevenson off."

EDUCATION

Gingrich received much of his elementary and secondary education at army base schools in the United States and abroad. His adoptive father was reassigned from a post at Stuttgart, Germany, to Fort Benning in Georgia when Newt was 16, and he joined the junior class at Newton D. Baker High School in nearby Columbus. Gingrich was only marginally involved in sports at Baker, having been ordered off the football team by his doctor because of recurring headaches. Instead, academics became his passion. A serious student with a curious and incisive mind, he was named a National Merit Scholar in his senior year. Republican politics had become one of Gingrich's great passions by this time, as had his developing crush on Jacqueline Battley, his high school geometry teacher, who was seven years his senior. He pursued her relentlessly. Their subsequent marriage, when he was a 19-year-old college freshman, startled friends and strained family relations.

After graduating from high school, Gingrich attended Emory University in Atlanta, Georgia, where he earned a bachelor's degree in history in 1965. As an undergraduate he balanced academics, campus activities, marriage, and fatherhood—he and his wife had two daughters within four years. Former classmates who remember him from those busy days say that he was already acquiring a thirst for political crusades. He founded Emory's Young Republicans chapter and even stretched an already busy schedule to include managing an unsuccessful Republican congressional campaign.

After his college graduation, Gingrich and his young family moved on to New Orleans, Louisiana, where he enrolled at Tulane University to pursue advanced degrees in history. He was awarded a master's degree in 1968 and a Ph.D. in modern European history in 1971. His doctoral thesis was on education in Zaire (then the Belgian Congo). Some of his experiences at Tulane might seem surprising, considering his later political conservatism. He became involved with the student protest movement, defended the student newspaper's right to freedom of speech, tried smoking marijuana, and accepted a deferment to avoid being drafted to serve in the Vietnam war.

CHOOSING A CAREER

At one point in his young life, Gingrich had dreams of becoming a paleontologist, a scientist who studies fossils from past geological ages. When he was ten years old he hopped a bus to Harrisburg, without his mother's knowledge, to try to sell officials on his plans for establishing a zoo. Soon though, he became interested in history and politics. He was curious about many subjects, as he had been since childhood, but now he questioned things in terms of their political value. "I have an enormous personal ambition," he has said. "I want to shift the entire planet." Confrontational and supremely self-confident, he has engineered his career from stage to stage with few hitches in between. As disgruntled former congressional staffer and Republican Dot Crews once said of him: "He never had a philosophy, he had an agenda: to get where he is now."

CAREER HIGHLIGHTS

While preparing his doctoral thesis, Gingrich joined the faculty of West Georgia College in Carrollton. As Nolan Walters of the *Philadelphia Inquirer* writes of this first academic appointment, "it didn't take long to discover that the new hire was a volcano disguised as a 27-year-old assistant professor. One year after arriving, Gingrich ran for chairman of the history department. Then, trumping his own audacity, he made a ridiculously improbable effort to become president of the 5,000-student college."

The West Georgia campus, where Gingrich taught history and environmental classes and founded a future-studies program, was merely a stepping-off spot toward his ultimate goal. While on the faculty, he made his first political bid in 1974 by challenging, and nearly upsetting, the longtime Democratic incumbent, John J. Flynt, Jr., for the seat representing Georgia's Sixth Congressional District. He tried again for Congress in 1976, but lost again to Flynt. Two years later, after the incumbent retired, he staged a rough battle against his Democratic opponent, smearing her with the kind of innuendo that was fast becoming his trademark. He mounted a sophisticated campaign as an anti-tax, ethics-in-government, anti-welfare conservative—and went to Washington vowing reform. "I intend to go up there and kick the system over, not try and change it," had been his promise since he first ran for Congress in 1974, and he was determined to keep his word.

ARRIVAL ON CAPITOL HILL

Gingrich's bombastic style was apparent from his first moments as a freshman congressman in 1979. Political writer Walters tells how he "cast about for a theme, trying such things as the environment and military reform. . . . He proposed little legislation, instead preaching a new form of conservatism based on authors Alvin and Heidi Toffler's theories of a Third Wave of postindustrial development." Gingrich's own 1984 book on that theme is titled *Window of Opportunity: A Blueprint for the Future.*

Gingrich began to cultivate the press, which he would later condemn as a tool of the liberal left. He quickly grasped the power of television in swaying public opinion. He jumped at the chance to publicize himself and his theories on C-Span, the independent cable network that broadcasts the proceedings of the U.S. Congress. He saw the new House television coverage as a rare opportunity to gain national recognition, and it is widely conceded that C-Span "made" Newt Gingrich. Gingrich would deliver after-hours tirades before a virtually empty chamber, giving the impression on camera that he was "a brave young crusader taking on the opposition in heated floor encounters," wrote *Vanity Fair*. Thomas P. (Tip) O'Neill, at that time Speaker of the House, was provoked into admonishing Gingrich for these tirades. The reprimand backfired, and it was O'Neill who was considered out-of-order. Gingrich reveled in the exchange, boasting about the TV air time he got out of it: "The minute Tip O'Neill attacked me, he and I got 90 seconds at the close of all three network news shows."

In his confrontational style, Gingrich concentrated on challenging corruption in government. He and his growing legion of young Republican followers, called the Conservative Opportunity Society, talked about their vision of the future. Others criticized his agenda as strident posturing, not ideology. But Gingrich saw himself as a Republican revolutionary, striking out at corrupt administrative practices.

In the late 1980s, he took on Washington's most powerful Democrat, Jim Wright of Texas, who had succeeded O'Neill as Speaker of the House. Gingrich charged Wright with unethical financial dealings, focusing specifically on a book contract that violated House rules on outside income. The investigation was taken up by Common Cause, the nonpartisan organization that keeps watch over government activities, and Wright resigned in the wake of the scandal. His toppling, wrote William Sternberg in the *Atlantic*, "made Gingrich a hero among his long-suffering Republican colleagues, who were anxious for more confrontation and less cooperation with the Democrats. In an almost tribal ritual, they rewarded him with the whip's position [second in leadership of the House minority] in 1989." Ironically, Gingrich himself soon came under scrutiny by the ethics committee for questionable book deals of his own. Nevertheless, he was cleared of wrongdoing.

THE "CONTRACT WITH AMERICA" AND THE SWEEP TO POWER

Gingrich set out to transform Congress. He formed an interest group called GOPAC (an acronym combining GOP, the abbreviation for Grand Old Party—the Republicans—and PAC, for Political Action Committee). Most PACs simply funnel money to various candidates, but Gingrich conceived of GOPAC as a different type of funding group. GOPAC recruited candidates that reflected the group's beliefs and provided tapes, booklets, and training sessions as part of a grand plan to capture the House of

Representatives with fresh political talent. Opponents asserted that GOPAC was just a new way to raise money for his personal mission. Gingrich survived the worst of his opponents' attacks, from charges of misuse of the perks of office to a near defeat in the primary election in his own district in 1992. The Democratic Party presidential victory that year brought Bill Clinton to office, but barely slowed Gingrich's agenda.

With confidence in a Republican takeover of Congress and the influential post as Speaker of the House for himself, Gingrich's vision of changing the way America works was taking concrete form. With a small group of fellow Republicans, Gingrich devised a wide-ranging "Contract With America," a ten-point legislative plan for change that tapped into the anger and discontent many Americans felt. The Contract includes provisions on the following issues: balancing the federal budget and limiting taxes; enacting new, comprehensive measures to fight crime; radically overhauling the welfare system; strengthening laws that support families, particularly those governing child support payments; creating tax cuts for families; restoring funding for defense; modifying laws that affect the earnings and insurance costs of senior citizens; establishing financial initiatives for business to create jobs and raise wages; reforming the legal system to limit litigation; and setting term limites for how long individuals can serve in Congress. Many of these ideas found widespread support among Americans. With this agenda, Republicans made a sweep of the midterm elections, reversing the balance of power in the House for the first time in 40 years.

On January 4, 1995, Newt Gingrich replaced Representative Thomas Foley, the Democratic leader from Washington State, as the Speaker of the House. In that role, his influence is powerful, probably more so than that of any speaker since the turn of the century, mainly because of his intensity of purpose and his dramatic fire. He is the presiding officer of the House, running the proceedings of debate and voting, while functioning, also, as chief spokesman for his own party. The position is unique: in the case of disability or death of both the president and vice president, the speaker becomes next in line for the presidency.

"Right now," notes *Time* magazine, "Americans are divided three ways on Gingrich: they love him, loathe him, or can't figure out who he is." It is difficult to predict how many parts of his ambitious legislative agenda will become law. At the end of the projected timetable of 100 days, some promises on institutional reform had been met. Others were pending in committee or awaiting Senate action, including hotly contested welfare and legal reforms, tax credits, an anticrime bill, a national security restoration act, and child-support enforcement. The controversial proposal for a balanced-budget amendment failed by two votes in the Senate in

March of 1995, with a surprised Republican membership vowing to bring it up repeatedly until it is passed. The bill's defeat prompted analysis and a call for restraint in adding another legislative clause to the U.S. Constitution, which outlines the nation's fundamental laws. "We must not destroy the Constitution with a badly written amendment," wrote editor Joe Stroud in the *Detroit Free Press*, "and we must find a more sensible way to get the deficit under control."

THE CHALLENGES AHEAD

For the "Contract" to make its way through Congress, three significant challenges remain. First, say observers, Gingrich must stay clear of any taint of unethical behavior. This may be difficult considering the recent accusations that he gained questionable financial rewards from his position in Congress (a new book deal and promotion of his tapes and TV lecture). Next, he must do what Ronald Reagan did in the 1980s: hold together a political coalition that includes individuals who support a broad spectrum of beliefs on social issues.

But most significantly, according to knowledgeable observers, Newt Gingrich wants to be seen as more than a right-wing agitator. He is promoting an ambitious agenda to move the American economy into a new era. Gingrich is a futurist who says that he wants to change the traditional workplace and is an agressive champion of new technologies.

Should Gingrich clear his first two hurdles, say analysts, he will retain his politicial significance. If he clears the third, he could become the seminal public figure of a generation.

MARRIAGE AND FAMILY

Newt Gingrich's private life has been the subject of widespread speculation for more than three decades. It started with the unconventional marriage to his high school math teacher, Jacqueline Battley. They secretly dated while he was still a high school senior and wed on June 17, 1962, at the end of his freshman year at Emory University. Although his parents were distraught at his decision, he could not be dissuaded. He and Jacqueline divorced in 1981 amidst a swirl of negative publicity that focused on Gingrich's alleged insensitivity and cavalier attitude. There are two adult daughters from that union, Linda Kathleen (Kathy) Lubbers and Jacqueline Sue Zyla, who remain in frequent contact with both parents.

In 1980, Gingrich met Marianne Ginther, chair of a county planning commission, while he was in Ohio campaigning for a fellow congressman. They married in August 1981, about six months after his divorce became final. The press has reported on trouble spots in this marriage as well, but the relationship has survived. The second Mrs. Gingrich has been described by her husband as his "best friend and closest adviser." Marianne Gingrich once explained to *People* magazine that she functions as Newt's "reality tester by keeping her mind-set outside [Washington, D.C.]," reminding him what people outside Washington's power circles really think.

There are no children from this second marriage. The Gingriches divide their time between a Washington apartment and their recently purchased home in Marietta, Georgia, close to Atlanta.

Marianne Gingrich stays away from making public disclosures, a policy that his mother may now wish that she had followed as carefully. In an interview on CBS's "Eye to Eye with Connie Chung," a day after her son became Speaker of the House, Kit Gingrich was coaxed into whispering to the newswoman (on camera) that Newt had referred to First Lady Hillary Clinton in a crude, unflattering manner. She claimed afterward that she thought her remarks had been made in confidence. The public flap that followed the interview did little to enhance either her son's or Chung's professional image, but the Gingriches and the Clintons managed to handle the ensuing controversy diplomatically.

MAJOR INFLUENCES

Many of the experiences of Gingrich's early life have helped to define him. He often speaks of a particular episode, one that made a lasting, and transforming, impression. He was a teenager living at an army post in France with his family when he visited the World War I battlefield at Verdun, the scene of the longest and bloodiest offensive of the Western Front. Half of the two million soldiers who fought at Verdun during 1916 died, and thousands of those victims are still unidentified. Gingrich relates that he was so moved by the sight of the skeletal remains of that bloodbath that his life literally was changed forever. "I came to the conclusion then that threats to civilization are real, that the quality of leadership is a major factor in whether civilization survives. So I sort of changed my vocational goal from zoo director or vertebrate paleontologist to being a leader." He emphasizes in *Window of Opportunity* that his visit to Verdun "is the driving force which pushed me into history and politics and molded my life."

HOBBIES AND OTHER INTERESTS

Gingrich's childhood interest in paleontology has never waned. His fascination with this subject endures today as a nonprofessional activity, adding color to his already complex personality. He keeps the skull of a

Tyrannosaurus rex (on loan from the Smithsonian Museum) in his office to remind him, suggests Jeanne Cummings in a recent issue of the *Atlanta Constitution*, of "how quickly power and dynasties can pass."

Books, especially those on history and the technology of the future, are also a big part of his life, filling many hours outside his busy schedule. His mother says that from the time he learned to read he has always had a book close at hand.

For exercise, Gingrich walks whenever possible, and tries to swim every morning before heading to his office. He jokes about his round physique, but is concerned enough to make time for physical activity.

WRITINGS

Window of Opportunity: A Blueprint for the Future, 1984 (with Marianne Gingrich and David Drake)
To Renew America, 1995 (forthcoming)

FURTHER READING

BOOKS

Bernstein, Amy, and Peter W. Bernstein (editors). *Quotations From Speaker Newt: The Little Red, White, and Blue Book of the Republican Revolution*, 1995
Connor, Tom, and Associates. *Newt Wit: The Wit and Wisdom of Newt Gingrich*, 1995
Gingrich, Newt, and Marianne Gingrich (with David Drake). *Window of Opportunity: A Blueprint for the Future*, 1984

PERIODICALS

Atlantic, June 1993, p.26
Current Biography Yearbook 1989
Los Angeles Times, Nov. 28, 1994, p.1; Jan. 17, 1995, Life and Style section, p.1
Mother Jones, Nov. 1984, p.14; Oct. 1989, p.29
New Republic, Nov. 7, 1994, p.28
Newsday, Jan. 9, 1995, p.A14
Newsweek, Oct. 17, 1994, p.36; Nov. 21, 1994, p.37
New York Times Magazine, Aug. 23, 1992, p.47
Philadelphia Inquirer, Jan. 3, 1995, p.F1; Jan. 4, 1995, p.H1; Jan. 5, 1995, p.G1 (3-part series)
Time, Jan. 9, 1995, p.23; Feb. 13, 1995, p.28
Vanity Fair, July 1989, p.32
Wall Street Journal, Nov. 1, 1994, p.A20

Washington Post, Dec. 18, 19, 20, and 21, 1994, all p.A1

ADDRESS

Office of the Speaker
U.S. House of Representatives
1201 Longworth Building
Washington, DC 20515-4705

John Goodman   1952-
American Television, Film, and Stage Actor
Co-Star of "Roseanne"

BIRTH

John Goodman was born June 20, 1952, in the small town of
Affton, Missouri, just southwest of St. Louis. His mail-carrier
father, Leslie, died of a heart attack in his middle 30s, leaving
his wife, Virginia Goodman, to raise their three children—older
brother Les Jr., then 16; John, almost two; and Elizabeth Ann, not
yet born at the time of her father's death. Virginia struggled for
years to make a living by taking in ironing, babysitting, waitress-
ing, clerking in a drugstore, and other jobs. Les Jr., older than
his little siblings, went to work at an early age to help his mother
with the family finances.

YOUTH

Goodman grew up relatively poor in a working-class neighborhood. There were few extras in their home, yet he does not remember feeling deprived. Looking back at the sacrifices his mother made to keep the family fed and clothed, he realizes how difficult those times must have been for her, "but we didn't know we were bad off, so we didn't care," he says. Goodman talks about doing typical small-town things as a boy, although he has remarked that he was unable to play Little League baseball because he couldn't afford the fees. He says that he was a misfit for a while—a skinny, bespectacled kid who sat in his room reading *Mad* magazine. A great fan of the public library throughout his school days, Goodman confirms now, as an adult, that his library card was his key to knowledge. "He thinks he started reading," says a profile in *GQ* magazine, "because every time he wouldn't get one of the references in the *Mad* parodies, he'd go look it up and end up reading the original."

EDUCATION

By the time he reached high school, the once-skinny youngster had bulked up enough to play starting offensive and defensive lineman on the Affton High School football team. Sports gave him an outlet for his newfound physical strength, but academics were not his long suit. His former teachers remember him as an indifferent student, but the self-effacing Goodman paints a more accurate picture of those years. "I was just a nerd," he says. "I spent most of my time staring out the window or playing 'drop the pencil.'" He admits that he felt insecure and that he showed off to get attention. He also started acting in high school productions, and his drama teacher, Judy Rethwisch, fostered his developing interest in the stage. Goodman graduated from Affton High in 1970.

Goodman attended Meramac Community College for one year before enrolling at Southwest Missouri State University in Springfield. He wanted to play college football, but a knee injury (combined with his failure to take the SAT [Standardized Aptitude Test], which was required of football players) dashed his hopes. He then turned to the theater department —"blazing through," says *GQ* magazine, "seizing leads, shining in character parts." Goodman studied acting theory, dance, movement, and singing, and appeared in four college productions per year. He loved the whole process surrounding acting—the rehearsing, the experimenting, the punishing hours. "I don't know why," he once said, trying to explain this new passion. "I just found it immensely satisfying to put on someone else's skin for a while." At Southwest Missouri, he found a mentor in Howard Orms, a drama professor with experience in the New York theater, who remains a friend and staunch supporter. Actresses Kathleen Turner and Tess Harper were Goodman's classmates at Southwest Missouri, and they recall the certainty they felt even then about his eventual success. During his college years Goodman also tried to break into repertory theater in St. Louis, but he was unsuccessful. In 1975 he earned his BFA (bachelor of fine arts) in theater production from Southwest Missouri with one thought in mind—a life on the stage.

CHOOSING A CAREER

Determined to become an actor, Goodman left for New York the summer of 1975 with the reluctant blessing of his brother. Les questioned his choice but gave him $1000 that he had saved for John to attend graduate school. Goodman found an apartment in a seamy section of Manhattan once known as Hell's Kitchen and started making the rounds looking for odd jobs. He often had to supplement his meager income with food stamps and offerings from family and friends, but he was never tempted to abandon his dream.

CAREER HIGHLIGHTS

It took 10 years of hard work and dedication before Goodman got a break as an actor. In the early days, he received fairly regular calls for work in dinner theater and children's theater, in off-Broadway plays, and in television commercials. Goodman hated doing commercials. "I thought I'd just get trapped in them," he recalls. "The people were nice, the money was nice, but I just kept telling myself, 'I'm drowning here. This is not what I want.' I started to develop this snotty attitude so I wouldn't get cast. Sometimes I'd show up hung over. I was drinking a lot back then." But all these small parts finally led to better roles on stage and in a few films. As his finances improved, he joined the boisterous party scene at New York's Cafe Central, where he made friends with other aspiring actors, including Dennis Quaid and Bruce Willis. Life was "a blast," Goodman says of those days, but the all-night carousing had ruined other careers just as promising as his. His hard partying interrupted a regimen of dieting and exercising, and he gained 100 pounds—weight he has since lost and regained several times over.

His professional luck held, though, and he continued to be cast for off-Broadway and regional theater productions. He toured for nine months in the late 1970s with a road show, *The Robber Bridegroom*. He eventually won supporting parts, and good notices, on Broadway in *Loose Ends* (1979). His big break came in 1985, when he won the role of Pap, Huck Finn's drunken father, in the Broadway musical *Big River*. His first major role in a film came the following year, when he appeared in David Byrne's *True Stories* (1986) in the part of the lovelorn bachelor. "A succession of film roles followed," wrote Jay Mathews in a *Washington Post* article, "many exploiting Goodman's unusual physique and wide dramatic range, from a goofy escaped convict in *Raising Arizona* (1987) to a crooked cop in *The Big Easy* (1987)." A growing roster of character parts began to draw acclaim from critics and to make Goodman's face familiar to movie and TV audiences. Still, few viewers would recognize him before he was tapped for "Roseanne," the show that would make him famous.

"ROSEANNE"

The producers of a promising new TV sitcom, "Roseanne," spotted Goodman in a Los Angeles stage production of *Antony and Cleopatra*. They asked him to audition for one of the upcoming program's leading parts—that of Dan Conner, the beefy and lovable husband of the show's star. His audition was so impressive that "Roseanne" was delayed until Goodman could finish shooting *Everybody's All-American* (1988), a film in which he was playing a sidekick to his old friend Dennis Quaid.

The casting of Goodman as Roseanne Barr's partner proved to be an inspiration. When "Roseanne" debuted in the fall of 1988, the sitcom quickly soared to the top of the weekly charts and Goodman became one of Hollywood's hottest character actors. Borrowing from his own roots, he brought to "Roseanne" a believability that instantly connected with middle America. Two years into the show, *Time* warmly praised his talent: "He has created a full-blooded portrait of a working-class lug, equally

credible whether giving advice to a teenage daughter or doing boisterous pirouettes in a bowling alley. He seems to mesh perfectly with Barr; Goodman can be deferential while he is stealing the show."

Goodman managed to stay clear of controversy in the early years of "Roseanne," when negative publicity swirled around Barr and co-creator Matt Williams over staffing and storyline control. Always a journeyman actor focused on the project at hand, Goodman was personally supportive of Barr, but he looked upon the show as his "day job" and continued to pursue other roles on stage and screen.

After his start on "Roseanne," Goodman scored in a number of character roles, appearing with such established stars as Sally Field and Tom Hanks (in *Punchline*, 1988), Holly Hunter and Richard Dreyfuss (in *Always*, 1989), Al Pacino (in *Sea of Love*, 1989), and Bette Midler (in *Stella*, 1990). "In film after film," said *Entertainment Weekly*, "he has entered the movie as if from a side door and walked away with the audience. Goodman has made such an impact in [what was then] such limited screen time that he has virtually redefined the term 'character actor.'" He turned in a chilling performance as a salesman/serial killer in *Barton Fink* (1991), which earned wide critical acclaim as well as a coveted Golden Globe nomination. That same year, he had his first title role in a comedy, *King Ralph* (1991), in which he played a Las Vegas lounge-singer who becomes the king of England. The movie did only moderate business.

RECENT PROJECTS

Goodman made his debut in a dramatic starring role in *The Babe* in 1992. He played George Herman "Babe" Ruth, America's most enduring sports legend, whose incredible career as a New York Yankee in the 1920s and 1930s gave rise to the stadium's nickname of "The House That Ruth Built." Goodman learned to pitch and hit left-handed, to mimic mannerisms and speech patterns, and to perfect Ruth's characteristic home-run trot. Just as difficult was having to shed 60 pounds to get down to the baseball hero's already ample size. Goodman gave more than a physical resemblance to the daunting role. In what *Us* magazine spoke of as a "textured performance," he *became* the character. Despite widespread critical acclaim, box-office receipts were disappointing. Goodman learned, as have many other actors, that success on TV does not always carry over to the big screen.

In the three years since *The Babe*, other projects have kept Goodman juggling a busy shooting schedule around his work on the "Roseanne" set. He has appeared in *Matinee* (1993), in a remake of *Born Yesterday* (1993), and as Fred in *The Flintstones* (1994), Steven Spielberg's hit movie patterned after the original television cartoon. In March 1995, Goodman produced and starred in *Kingfish: A Story of Huey P. Long*, a made-for-television movie about Louisiana's inflammatory politician of the 1930s. He followed this project with a return to the stage at the San Diego Globe Theater as Falstaff in *Henry IV*, a drama that combined two of Shakespeare's plays, *Henry IV, Part I* and *Henry IV, Part II*. Goodman has also been at work filming his most recent role in another made-for-TV movie, *A Streetcar Named Desire*, which is currently in production.

For the near future, Goodman plans to work for his own production company while continuing his role in the final seasons of "Roseanne," which is currently scheduled to end in 1997.

MAJOR INFLUENCES

As a seasoned performer, Goodman is often asked now who his role models have been. He mentions the late and accomplished actors Spencer Tracy and John Wayne, as well as such present-day performers as Al Pacino, Ed Harris, John Hurt, John Turturro, and Peter O'Toole. But there is one in particular he speaks of with something bordering on hero worship: "I always dreamed of being Marlon Brando. Of the many actors I really look up to, first and foremost will always be Brando. He seemed so effortlessly real . . . and the more I got to know about acting, the more I realized he was really a poet. He condenses things and crystallizes them and brings them to a head. And the little things he does—my God, I think he's a genius."

MARRIAGE AND FAMILY

Goodman met his wife, the former Anna Elizabeth (Annabeth) Hartzog, during the 1988 Mardi Gras in New Orleans, while he was taking a break from the filming of *Everybody's All-American*. Annabeth was a 19-year-old fine arts student at the University of New Orleans when she first introduced herself, and the unpretentious Goodman thought then, "What could this lovely young woman possibly want with me?" Romance soon blossomed, and the couple married in October 1989 in a lavish ceremony in New Orleans.

The Goodmans and their five-year-old daughter, Molly

Evangeline, live in California's San Fernando Valley and also spend a substantial part of the summer months in a house near Annabeth's parents in Louisiana. John Goodman has long talked of going home to St. Louis, though, and reportedly will build a home somewhere in the suburban area when "Roseanne" ends.

HOBBIES AND OTHER INTERESTS

Goodman's hectic schedule leaves him little time for relaxation. When a rare free week appears on his calendar, he prefers going either to New Orleans to "hang," or back to Affton, Missouri, to spend time with family and old friends. Watching sports is another favorite pastime. He has been a baseball fan since his sandlot days as a child, but still considers football his favorite sport.

SELECTED PERFORMANCE CREDITS

TELEVISION

"The Paper Chase," 1978-79 (guest appearance)
"Heart of Steel," 1983
"Face of Rage," 1983
"Chief," 1983 (guest appearance)
"Murder Ordained," 1987
"Roseanne," 1987-
Kingfish: A Story of Huey P. Long, 1995 (TV movie)

FILMS

The Survivors, 1983
Eddie Macon's Run, 1983
Revenge of the Nerds, 1984
C.H.U.D, 1984
Sweet Dreams, 1985
True Stories, 1986
The Big Easy, 1987
Raising Arizona, 1987
Everybody's All American, 1988
Punchline, 1988
Always, 1989
Sea of Love, 1989
Arachnophobia, 1990
Stella, 1990
Barton Fink, 1991
King Ralph, 1991
The Babe, 1992
Matinee, 1993

Born Yesterday, 1993
The Flintstones, 1994

STAGE

The Robber Bridegroom
Loose Ends, 1979
Big River, 1985
Antony and Cleopatra, 1987
Henry IV, 1995

HONORS AND AWARDS

Golden Globe Award: 1993, best performance in a TV comedy or musical, for "Roseanne"

FURTHER READING

PERIODICALS

Entertainment Weekly, May 1, 1992, p.14
GQ, Apr. 1992, p.170
Ladies Home Journal, May 1989, p.136; Feb. 1991, p.66
Life, Apr. 1992, p.52
New York Times Magazine, Feb. 10, 1991, p.47
People, Nov. 28, 1988, p. 83; Nov. 13, 1989, p.70
Premiere, Feb. 1990, p.74
St. Louis Post-Dispatch, Mar. 1, 1991, Everyday (magazine section), p.F1; Apr. 17, 1992, Everyday, p.F1; Mar. 2, 1995, Everyday, p.G1
Sports Illustrated, Sep. 30, 1991, p.44
TV Guide, Feb. 18, 1989, p.32; Dec. 28, 1991, p.4; Mar. 18, 1995, p.21
Us, Apr. 1992, p.50

ADDRESS

Casey Werner
4024 Radford Avenue, Building 3
Studio City, CA 91604

Amy Grant   1960-
American Singer and Songwriter

BIRTH

Amy Grant was born in Augusta, Georgia, on November 25, 1960. Her parents are Gloria Grant and Burton Grant, who is a physician who specializes in oncology and radiation. Amy has three older sisters, Mimi, Carol, and Kathy.

YOUTH

When Grant was six months old, the family moved to Nashville, Tennessee. The Grants had many ties to that area: Amy's father, Burton Grant, was the grandson of A.M. Burton, one of the founders of the city of Nashville. A.M. Burton also founded Life & Casualty Insurance, still a successful company, and he was a generous philanthropist as well, donating millions to local charitable organizations.

Family, music, and religion—these were the foundations of Amy Grant's early life, just as they are today. She grew up in a socially prominent, well-to-do family. Along with many of the Burton relatives, they lived on a street adjacent to the 109-acre family farm, at one time a local landmark. "I grew up on that farm," Amy says. "We rode horses there, and our whole family had a street on the back of the farm that my great-grandparents gave us. It was all cousins. It was fun!"

Amy always loved music. She started taking piano lessons in the third grade, picked up the guitar when she was 13, and started writing songs when she was 15. She loved to sing along with all the pop records her older sisters brought home—like James Taylor, Elton John, and Carole King.

And, of course, she also sang in church. Religion in the Grant household included services at the Church of Christ each Sunday, afternoon and evening, as well as Wednesday nights. Her family always stressed Christian faith and values, and for Amy, it was a living faith—even as a child she tried to live according to the Bible's teachings. But despite the family's strong religious beliefs, her parents were not rigid or strict about it. As she recalls, "Somebody might think, *Christian parents! Strict rules! No singing or dancing!* But my parents were wonderful. I grew up with healthy values; my parents encouraged doing things in moderation, whether it was the speed at which I drove a car or the songs I chose to sing."

EDUCATION—MUSIC AND SCHOOL

Amy attended Harpeth Hall, an exclusive private girls' school in Nashville. It was during her years there that her feelings about religion and music started to come together. She was going through "a time of searching," as she calls it, "to figure out where my life was going." When she was about 14, she had a life-changing experience when she joined Bible-study classes at Belmont Church. At first, she started going because her older sister's cute boyfriend asked her: "I was invited to a Bible-study meeting. The guy who invited me was dating my older sister, and he was so cute that I thought, 'I'm gonna go to this Bible study and make this guy fall in love with me.' So I went, and an amazing thing happened to me. I encountered the Bible in a way that really affected me."

At the same time, she began to feel that the pop music that she had long enjoyed simply didn't speak to her spiritual needs. As she tells it, "There were a lot of things happening in my life then. I went through all the usual growing-up pain: severe acne, braces on my teeth, Coke-bottle eyeglasses, crushes—I even fell in love with my sister's boyfriend. Pop music dealt with all that, and it was a big part of my life. But nobody was putting out music about the Christian experience I was going through, so I wrote songs to fill in that gap."

She started writing songs and singing them to her classmates at Harpeth Hall. When she was 15, she made a tape of those songs for her parents. One of the guys in her Bible study group worked in a recording studio, so she asked him to make a copy of the tape. While he was making the copy, a record producer overheard it. He liked it so much that he called his record label and played the tape over the phone. Myrrh Records, a Christian record label that is a division of the Christian record and book company Word, offered Amy a contract right over the phone. "They called me and said, 'We want you to do an album,'" she recalls. "And I thought it was a practical joke. We never thought it would go anywhere. We were probably five or six albums into it when I realized, hey, you know, I'd kind of like to do this as my life." Without ever really planning it, she was on her way to becoming a recording star.

Her first album, *Amy Grant* (1977), which was released before she even finished high school, sold over 50,000 copies—minor sales for a pop record, but a huge success for Christian music. Amy started touring and released her next album, *My Father's Eyes* (1979), which was even more successful. After graduating with honors from Harpeth Hall, she enrolled at Furman University in South Carolina. But the traveling back and forth to recording studios in Nashville soon became too much, and Grant quit Furman to attend Vanderbilt University in Nashville. She combined recording albums, touring, and attending classes until 1982, when she dropped out of Vanderbilt, just a few classes short of earning her degree in English literature.

CAREER HIGHLIGHTS

Since she started recording, Grant's approach to her music has gone through a number of transitions. She has grown from a sheltered teenager to a married woman with her own children, and her music and image reflect those changes.

During the first years of her career, Amy was still a very young woman. Her early recordings primarily feature soft folk/pop ballads, with just Amy's beautiful voice and her guitar testifying to her strong Christian beliefs. Distributed by Word, her records were sold primarily in Christian bookstores, and she was largely unknown outside the rather insular Christian community. Then in the early 1980s, as she tells it, "I realized that kids were listening to Van Halen and Billy Joel, and I sounded like Mickey Mouse. Kids like music they can jam to."

CHRISTIAN CONTEMPORARY MUSIC

She decided it was time for a change. Traditionally, gospel music included two types: black church music, which featured the rhythms and harmonies of the blues and soul music; and white church music, which included Amy Grant's recordings. But in the early 1980s, a new gospel sound called Christian contemporary music came onto the scene. As *Rolling Stone* magazine explained in 1985, "Amy Grant is at the forefront of a boom in a new kind of Christian music called 'Christian contemporary music.' It's modern gospel that fuses spiritual lyrics to various types of pop and rock." Today, Christian contemporary music is broad enough to encompass everything from soft folk music to rap to heavy metal. But in the mid-1980s, it was Amy Grant who led the trend away from the traditional sound to harder rock. It was a move guaranteed to earn her many new fans, especially when Amy's company, Word Records, signed a distribution deal with the industry giant A & M Records, putting her recordings into mainstream music stores. Yet that move alienated some fans of her earlier records, who worried that she was abandoning her Christian roots.

With the release of *Age to Age* (1982), *Straight Ahead* (1984), and *Unguarded* (1985), she began to update both her music and her image. Her music took on more of a rock sound, and she started touring with a seven-piece band, three back-up singers, and 20 tons of lighting and sound equipment. Although she retained her religious message, she updated her image—"a Christian message combined with sultry rock-star looks," as *Mademoiselle* magazine described it. As Grant explained at the time, "I think we've reached a point where we feel it's okay to be Christian and have fun too." And obviously, the new approach worked: *Age to Age* was the first gospel record to go platinum (sales of one million copies). Her subsequent records have also sold in the millions.

CROSSOVER INTO POP

Grant's career underwent a further transformation with her later records, particularly with the song "Baby Baby" from her 1991 release *Heart in Motion*. Many critics date her crossover into pop music to that point. Although Grant wrote the song for her new daughter Millie, many fans of her earlier work believed the song glorified romantic love. They particularly objected to the video, which featured Grant, a married woman, flirting with a male actor who was not her husband. Yet the song went to No. 1 on the music charts for pop, adult contemporary, and Christian music—a first—and the album went quadruple platinum, selling four million copies to date.

For Grant, the opportunity to stretch was a welcome change. "I'd recorded more than 120 songs that were about spiritual things. From the songwriting standpoint, I'd probably given my absolutely best years to

141

gospel music. And I thought I'd love the freedom to sing a song about being in love. Or about dancing." According to reviewers, both *Heart in Motion* and her newest release, *House of Love* (1994), feature catchy melodies and insightful lyrics about secular topics, like friendships and romantic relationships. While most of the lyrics are not specifically religious, they are described as wholesome and generally supportive of traditional Christian values. Some critics have accused Grant of abandoning her musical ministry, yet she is unconcerned. "If somebody tells me, 'You're trying to go secular,' I answer, 'Of course I am. That's the whole point.' If I'm going to impact my culture, I need to come in on a different stage, not keep doing what people expect me to do."

For Grant, it seems, that is the whole point—to reach out and spread her message to a broad new audience. And with sales of four million copies for *Heart in Motion*, and sales for her new release, *House of Love*, continuing to climb, it's clear that she is poised to do just that.

MARRIAGE AND FAMILY

Grant is married to Gary Chapman, a musician, songwriter, and record producer who at one time was also a guitarist in her band. They met when Amy was just 17, after she had recorded a song he wrote, "My Father's Eyes." It was the first time one of his songs had been recorded, and he was elated. "I was extremely happy I was going to be able to pay the rent," Chapman explains. "And then when I met her, like all guys, I was immediately taken with her as a girl. I felt, the heck with the song—I want to get to know her." They dated for a while, split up, then got back together. As she explains it, "[We] became kind of consumed with each other, which often happens to younger kids. It became an unhealthy thing, so we broke up. We started dating again the summer after my junior year at Vanderbilt University, and five weeks later he asked me to marry him." After a yearlong engagement, they were married on June 19, 1982.

But they were in for several rocky years. In the mid-1980s, while Grant was at the height of success as a Christian singer, Chapman was becoming dependent on cocaine and marijuana. Their marital problems became so severe that Amy, who has never used drugs, was ready to end the marriage. Chapman kicked his drug addiction, the two went into counseling, and their marriage survived. Today they have three children, Matthew Garrison, born in 1987; Gloria Mills (called Millie), born in 1989; and Sarah Cannon, born in 1992.

Grant and her family live on a farm in Franklin, Tennessee, just south of Nashville. They have 200 acres there, where they grow crops and raise animals. They also have a recording studio on the farm, where Amy recorded her most recent album, *House of Love*. For Grant, living a low-key, family-oriented lifestyle outside the musical mainstream keeps her well grounded.

HOBBIES AND OTHER INTERESTS

In addition to spending time with her music and her family, Grant supports a variety of charities. She participates in Nashville's Leadership Music Program and works with the "Make-a-Wish" Foundation, which grants the wishes of children who are terminally ill. She has played in celebrity softball and golf outings and has hosted benefit performances for the American Cancer Society, the American Heart Association, and the Nashville Symphony. She has also worked with Habitat for Humanity, a volunteer organization that raises money and then builds new houses for families in need.

RECORDINGS

Amy Grant, 1977
My Father's Eyes, 1979
Never Alone, 1980
Amy Grant in Concert, 1981
Amy Grant in Concert II, 1981
Age to Age, 1982
A Christmas Album, 1983
Straight Ahead, 1984
Unguarded, 1985
Lead Me On, 1988
Heart in Motion, 1991
Home for Christmas, 1992
House of Love, 1994

HONORS AND AWARDS

Dove Awards (Gospel Music Association): 17 awards, including 4 awards as Artist of the Year
Grammy Awards (National Academy of Recording Arts and Sciences): 1982, Best Gospel Performance, Contemporary or Inspirational, for *Age to Age*; 1983, Best Gospel Performance, Female, for "Ageless Melody"; 1984, Best Gospel Performance, Female, for "Angels"; 1985, Best Gospel Performance, Female, for *Unguarded*; 1988, Best Gospel Performance, Female, for *Lead Me On*
Pax Christi Award (Benedictine Order of St John's University): 1994

FURTHER READING

BOOKS

Who's Who in America, 1994

PERIODICALS

Ladies Home Journal, Dec. 1985, p.96

Life, Nov. 1984, p.186
New York Times, Apr. 8, 1984, Section II, p.25
People, Apr. 18, 1983, p.106; July 15, 1991, p.71
Rolling Stone, June 6, 1985, p.9
Saturday Evening Post, May/June, 1986, p.43; Nov./Dec., 1991, p.39
Woman's Day, Dec. 22, 1992, p.32

ADDRESS

Friends of Amy
9 Music Square, Suite 214
Nashville, TN 37203-3203

Jesse Jackson 1941-
American Political and Social Activist
Civil Rights Leader

BIRTH

Jesse Louis Jackson was born Jesse Louis Burns on October 8, 1941, in Greenville, South Carolina. His mother was Helen Burns, who later became a hairdresser. His natural father was Noah Robinson, who worked in a cotton mill. His adoptive father was Charles Henry Jackson, a janitor who worked many years for the postal service.

YOUTH

The circumstances of Jackson's birth and his early life were pivotal in his emotional development. Jackson was illegitimate. His mother, Helen Burns, was a teenager who had not even finished high school when Jesse was born. She was a talented singer who had earned scholarships from five music colleges when she had to quit school to have her baby. His father, Noah Louis Robinson, lived next door to Helen and her mother, Matilda Burns. Noah Robinson was older than Helen, in his 30s, and already married to someone else. At that time, it was a tremendous disgrace to have a baby outside of marriage, and Helen endured gossip, dishonor, and shame. Her church congregation expelled her until she stood in front of the whole church, holding baby Jesse, and apologized.

When Jesse was about two, his mother married Charles Henry Jackson, who later adopted the boy and gave Jesse his last name. It was World War II at the time, and Charles Jackson left to serve in the Army. Jesse's mother told him that Jackson was his father and didn't explain the circumstances of his birth. But the neighbor kids knew all about it, and they would taunt him: "Your daddy ain't none of your daddy. You ain't nothin but a nobody." Soon enough, Jesse figured out the truth.

When Charles Jackson returned from the service after the war ended, he got a steady job as a janitor. The family was not rich but not poor, either. They lived in a ramshackle old house, as Jesse recalls: "Three rooms, tin-top roof, no hot or cold running water, slop jar by the bed, bathroom in the back yard in the wintertime. Wood over the windows. Wallpaper put up not for decoration but to keep the wind out." But Charles Jackson always had work, and they always had plenty to eat and clothes to wear.

The Robinson family, meanwhile, had done very well. Noah Robinson and his wife and children had moved to the nicest black neighborhood in town, where they lived in a fancy stone house on a large corner lot that even had a basketball court. Jesse longed to be part of his father's life. He would stand outside the fence for hours, watching the house and hoping to catch a glimpse of his father. Although Jesse and Noah Robinson did speak on occasion, and although Noah had acknowledged his son, they had little contact when Jesse was young.

LIFE IN THE SOUTH

When Jackson was growing up in the Deep South in the 1940s and 1950s, his town was completely segregated. Laws created separate facilities for whites and blacks—separate housing, schools, restaurants, movie theaters, even bathrooms and drinking fountains. African-Americans were treated as inferior to whites, and they were expected to act subservient. "I remember being taught my place," Jackson says—to sit at the back of the bus, to use the "colored" drinking fountain, to treat whites with fawning respect. All these things Jackson was expected to accept, simply because he had been born black.

The consequences of forgetting these rules could be disastrous. One day when he was about eight, Jackson went to the neighborhood store to buy some candy. The white shopkeeper, Jack, was busy with another customer, but Jesse was impatient and in a hurry. He whistled to get Jack's attention. Jack reached under a counter, took out a .45 revolver, and pointed it at Jesse's face. "You ever whistle at me again, little nigger, I'll blow your head off," Jackson remembers him saying. "Two things I remember about that, and neither one of 'em was fear. One was knowing immediately I couldn't tell my stepfather, because he'd come and probably kill the guy. But the other was how the other people in the store, who were black, pretended they hadn't even noticed it."

Despite—or perhaps, because of—this segregation, the African-American community in Greenville was very close. People looked after one another. Growing up, Jackson felt protected by what he now calls "a love triangle." As he explains it, "Mother, grand mother here, teacher over here, and preacher over here. Within that love triangle, I was protected, got a sense of security and worth. Even mean ole segregation couldn't break in on me and steal my soul. It protected me long enough until I was able to break out and survive on my own. When it's working, that's what that thing really does." Being watched over by his family, his school, and his church created a feeling of love and security. Much of Jackson's work in recent years has focused on encouraging families to work with schools and churches to create this sense of community to take care of their children.

EARLY MEMORIES

Jackson once recounted his first memory of starting school in a lengthy interview for the *New Yorker* magazine. From the front of his house, Jackson could see a school right down the street surrounded by lush green grass. When he and his mother started walking in that direction, he made a run for it. But his mama stopped him: "That's not the one. You can't go there. It's another one." They had to walk through a hostile white neighborhood, across busy streets, to get to the local black school. White kids would go by in school buses and yell at them—there were no buses for black children. Finally they arrived at Jesse's school. "This was it. The other school, the one for us. The one that didn't have any grass. They didn't plant any. Didn't mean for grass to grow here, or children to grow, either. Only place for recreation was sliding on the sand on the sidewalk along here. No grass to play on."

EDUCATION

EARLY EDUCATION

Certain values were important to the Jackson family when Jesse was growing up: family, education, hard work, and church. And Jesse learned early—he was a good student and a hard worker throughout his youth. As a young boy at Nicholtown School, he goofed off a little but earned good grades even though he held a number of jobs from the time he was six years old. He worked cutting firewood, shining shoes, caddying at the local country club, working at a bakery, ushering at a movie theater, waiting tables. The jobs changed as he got older, but he always worked hard. Life at church was important, too. At age nine, he presented a report that was so well done that he was elected a representative to the National Sunday School Convention, which earned him the chance, each month, to present a report to his church congregation.

At all-black Sterling High School, Jackson was outstanding both as a student and as an athlete. He continued to work hard in his classes and earned such good grades that he was selected for the National Honor Society. He was also an excellent all-around athlete. He made the varsity football team in his freshman year, playing with seniors, and went on to become the star quarterback of their state championship team. He earned letters in basketball and baseball as well. He was popular with students and was elected to leadership positions in many student organizations. In his freshman year and each year after that, he was elected president of class and later he became president of the Honor Society. Jackson graduated from Sterling High School in 1959.

That spring, some major-league baseball scouts came to town to check out the local talent. Jackson attended the try-outs along with Dicky Dietz, an excellent athlete from the town's white high school. Pitching that day, Jackson threw a real fireball with amazing control. Dietz had an off day and struck out. Jackson was elated, at first, when the San Francisco Giants offered him a $6,000 contract to join one of their minor-league teams— until he learned that Dietz had been offered a contract worth $95,000. Jackson turned down the Giants.

COLLEGE YEARS

Instead, Jackson accepted a football scholarship to the University of Illinois. He was excited to be heading north to play football, anticipating that he would play quarterback, as always. Instead, he discovered that that position was reserved for whites, while blacks could only play running backs, linemen, or ends. He also discovered that such segregation existed throughout the school in social affairs as well. Black and white students didn't mix at all on campus, and black students were barred from attending many campus-wide social events. Racism in the North, he felt, was just as pervasive than in the South, it was just more subtle. Jackson left the University of Illinois after just one year.

In the fall of 1960 Jackson enrolled at North Carolina Agricultural and Technical State University (A & T), a predominately black college in

Greensboro, North Carolina. His decision was influenced, in part, by the sit-ins that A & T students had begun to stage at a local lunch counter. Earlier that year, four A & T freshman sat down at a whites-only lunch counter, thereby breaking the law. When the waitress refused to serve them, they remained in their seats until closing time. The next day and the next, more students came. Sit-ins started to spread to other cities as well, until finally the lunch counters were desegregated. It was a major victory in the struggle for civil rights.

Jackson thrived at A & T. An honors student, he became quarterback of the football team, president of the student body, and an officer of his fraternity. He also joined the Congress of Racial Equality (CORE), which was leading the sit-ins. His dedication and commitment energized the group. Soon Jackson was leading marches and picket lines and extending the sit-ins to hotels, theaters, restaurants, and swimming pools. He also got involved with one of his fellow protesters, Jacqueline Lavinia Brown, whom he married in late 1962. In 1963, the first time Jesse when to jail for participating in non-violent protests, Jackie had their first baby. That same year, he was named field director for CORE. The demonstrations in Greensboro ultimately succeeded in integrating the downtown.

In 1964, Jackson graduated from North Carolina A & T with a B.A. degree in sociology and economics. For some time, he had been struggling with the decision of how best to use his talents in the civil-rights movement. He was drawn to law school, but ultimately decided to attend seminary school.

SEMINARY SCHOOL

That fall, Jackson accepted a Rockefeller grant to attend the Chicago Theological Seminary. He studied there for two-and-a-half years. He also joined the Chicago branch of the Southern Christian Leadership Conference (SCLC). That group, organized by Dr. Martin Luther King, Jr., had been leading the non-violent protest movement against all forms of segregation throughout the South.

One of the most difficult challenges facing the movement was ensuring African-Americans' right to vote. On March 7, 1965, the SCLC staged a march from Selma, Alabama, to Montgomery, the state capital, to support the voters' registration drive and to urge the U.S. Congress to pass the Voting Rights Act. The marchers got as far as the Edmund Pettus Bridge on the edge of Selma, where local and state police, sent by Alabama governor George Wallace, were waiting on horseback with clubs, cattle prods, and tear gas. It was a bloodbath. Jackson, along with much of the nation, watched the beatings that night on the news. When Dr. King announced that they would complete the march and asked for volunteers to join them, Jackson was ready. He mobilized a group of his fellow seminary students, plus five of their professors, and drove to Alabama.

Some 50,000 Americans, blacks and whites, answered Dr. King's call. President Lyndon Johnson sent federal troops to ensure their safety, and the march proceeded. The Voting Rights Act was passed. For Jackson, the Selma march was a watershed event. When he arrived in Alabama, he immediately took on a leadership role, and started organizing the marchers. Many of the SCLC staffers were startled and annoyed. But Jackson caught the eye of Rev. Ralph Abernathy, a civil rights leader and Dr. King's closest friend. "There was something about him that impressed me," Rev. Abernathy said. "I could see the leadership potential in him." He convinced Dr. King to hire Jackson as an SCLC staffer in Chicago.

Jackson continued his studies at the seminary while working part-time as an SCLC organizer in Chicago. Dr. King was bringing his campaign for racial equality to the North, and he came to Chicago for several months. There, Jackson worked closely with the revered leader in fighting economic injustice. In particular, they marched to protest the housing discrimination that kept blacks living in squalid slums and barred them from white neighborhoods. The SCLC was delighted when Chicago mayor Richard Daley offered many promises, but ultimately black residents saw no improvement. The tactics that had worked so well in protests in the South against overt segregation were less effective in the North against more subtle forms of discrimination. When Dr. King asked Jackson to run the new Chicago chapter of Operation Breadbasket in 1966, Jackson left the seminary just one semester short of graduation. Two years later, in June 1968, he was ordained a Baptist minister.

CAREER HIGHLIGHTS

OPERATION BREADBASKET

Operation Breadbasket was an SCLC program designed to improve economic conditions, to provide better services, and particularly to create more jobs, for African-Americans. To meet these goals, the group used pickets and boycotts (the mass refusal to purchase a company's goods or services until certain conditions are met). The group's strategy was as follows. First, they identified companies that did business in the African-American community but employed few blacks; second, they met with the company's executives and asked that they hire more blacks and purchase materials from black-owned businesses; and third, if that failed, they picketed the company's stores and asked black consumers to boycott them.

Jackson staged his first boycott against Country Delight, a local dairy. Ministers spread the word to their congregations, and black consumers quit buying Country Delight products. At first, the company refused to consider Jackson's demands. But after a week of watching their perishable products rot on the shelves, the company announced that it would hire

44 black workers. Under Jackson's dynamic leadership, Operation Bread-basket went on to target other dairies, then the bottlers for Pepsi, Coca-Cola, and 7-Up, and then many other large companies, each time winning jobs for community members. The group's greatest success was against the A & P supermarket chain. After a 16-week boycott, A & P agreed to hire 268 black workers and to stock 25 black-owned brands on their shelves.

A special feature of the Chicago group of Operation Breadbasket was their Saturday morning meetings. Each week, Jackson would lead an inspirational meeting that was part political rally, part church service, and part lecture on pride and self-help. After the choir and the jazz band would play, Jackson would step forward to preach, asking the audience to repeat after him: "I am Somebody!"

In August 1967, Jackson was named national director of Operation Breadbasket by the SCLC. He continued to be assertive and determined to follow his own agenda, even when the SCLC leadership disagreed with him. Many executive staff members wanted him to move his operation to the group's headquarters in Atlanta, but Jackson refused. His relationships with the staff, and even with Dr. King, were often stormy.

THE ASSASSINATION OF REV. MARTIN LUTHER KING

On April 4, 1968, the Rev. Martin Luther King, Jr., was in Memphis, Tennessee, preparing to lead a protest march. He was standing on the balcony outside his room at the Lorraine Motel, talking to Jackson and several other friends and co-workers down in the parking lot, when he was fatally shot. Escaped convict James Earl Ray later pled guilty to the murder and was sentenced to 99 years in prison.

King's death was a national tragedy. The immediate aftermath was grief, despair, and violence as rioting erupted in African-American communities throughout the country. Buildings were burned, neighborhoods were demolished, and 39 people died in the riots.

Jackson's behavior in the hours and days following King's murder has been widely analyzed. He advised other SCLC staffers to avoid the media and then told reporters that he had been the last person that King had spoken to and that he had cradled the dying man in his arms. Others at the scene said that it was King's friend, Rev. Ralph Abernathy, who did that. The next morning, Jackson appeared on national television on the "Today" show wearing a turtleneck that he said was stained with King's blood. Some witnesses have disputed these claims, and the ensuing controversy has had a tremendous influence on Jackson's reputation. Some observers believed that Jackson's behavior was a result of his ego and his attempts at self-promotion, while others believe that he was overwhelmed by shock and grief. The controversy damaged his relationships with SCLC staffers and damaged his credibility, causing observers, even to this day, to question his truthfulness.

PUSH AND PUSH-EXCEL

Jackson continued working for the SCLC over the next few years, organizing economic initiatives for the African-American community. His relationship with the organization continued to deteriorate due to his insistence on independence as well as the financial problems of some of his ventures. In late 1971, Jackson left the SCLC and Operation Breadbasket to form PUSH, or People United to Save (later Serve) Humanity. In Jackson's words, PUSH would be a "rainbow coalition of blacks and whites gathered together to push for a greater share of economic and political power for all poor people in America in the spirit of Martin Luther King, Jr." Emphasizing the goal of economic growth, Jackson called it a "civil economics movement."

In PUSH, Jackson continued the type of work that he had done with Operation Breadbasket, securing agreements with major corporations for more opportunities for blacks. The group also worked in the political arena, registering people to vote and campaigning for sympathetic politicians. And always, they stressed racial self-respect and pride. National attention for these efforts began to pour in, and reaction was mixed. A

1972 profile in the *New York Times Magazine* explained, "[There] are doubts and criticisms raised about this complex man, a man characterized by ambiguity and contradiction. He is a brilliant speaker, a skilled mobilizer. He is also vain and self-seeking, a star, a man of great ambition."

In the mid 1970s, Jackson began a program for young people called PUSH for Excellence, or PUSH-Excel. This program, based in Chicago, advocated self-help, traditional values, and education. It called for young people to stay off drugs, stay in school, and develop a sense of purpose and self-esteem. It also called for parents and schools to work together to support children. The program spread rapidly to schools throughout the country, and many students were motivated by Jackson's chant: "I am Somebody!" While Jackson's oratorical skills and ability to inspire students are legendary, there has been criticism of the group's lack of organizational structure to carry out its goals.

Jackson continued to work with PUSH and PUSH-Excel throughout the 1970s and into the 1980s. But he also became involved in international issues as well. He visited South Africa in 1979, urging blacks there to use civil disobedience to fight apartheid. He toured the Middle East that same year, making stops in Israel, the West Bank, Lebanon, Syria, Jordan, and Egypt. Jackson argued for recognition of the Palestine Liberation Organization (PLO) and offended many observers with what they saw as his pro-Arab bias, an issue that would recur in his 1984 run for the presidency.

RUNNING FOR PRESIDENT, 1984 AND 1988

Jackson first ran for U.S. president as a candidate for the Democratic nomination in the 1984 election. He entered the race, he said, to challenge the social and economic policies of Republican President Ronald Reagan. Once again he referred to a "rainbow coalition" of blacks, whites, Hispanics, and Native Americans—all those who had been ignored by Reagan's policies. He wanted to represent "the poor and dispossessed of this nation" and to focus attention on the problems faced by blacks and other minority groups.

Jackson came in for criticism on all sides. Observers called his campaign underfunded, understaffed, and disorganized. Many faulted his lack of experience because he had never won election to political office. Some considered his positions too extreme. Black leaders were ambivalent about his candidacy, fearing that he would divide the Democratic party and ensure Ronald Reagan's reelection. He won praise in January 1984 when he traveled to Syria and secured the release of a United States Navy pilot, Lieutenant Robert O. Goodman, Jr., whose plane had been shot down over Lebanon by Syrian gunners. Yet the next month, February 1984, he earned widespread censure for his anti-Semitic comments when it was reported that he had called Jews "Hymies" and New York "Hymietown" in a private conversation. Jackson apologized, but he also maintained a relationship with Louis Farrakhan, the head of the Black Muslim group Nation of Islam, who has repeatedly made anti-Semitic remarks. These facts, coupled with Jackson's earlier support for a Palestinian state in the Mideast, caused great concern in the Jewish community. Despite the many problems throughout the campaign, Jackson proved to be a gifted and moving speaker who inspired and gave hope to many African-Americans who had felt locked out of the political process. Although Jackson won primaries in four states plus the District of Columbia, Walter Mondale won an overwhelming majority and secured the Democratic nomination for president. In the November election, Reagan won reelection in a landslide.

Following that election, Jackson returned to his work with PUSH and continued to speak out on such issues as better housing, schools, and health care. He continued to travel abroad, touring Europe, South America, and Africa emphasizing not just civil rights, but human rights. He also rejoined the struggle against apartheid and the boycott of companies that did business in South Africa.

Jackson again ran for the Democratic nomination for president in the 1988 election, campaigning on the theme of economic justice. Although his campaign was clearly better organized than it was in 1984, the same concerns were raised regarding Jackson's ability to govern. As he won primaries throughout the country, the headlines rang out "What does Jesse want?" Many saw this as an intrinsically racist remark because a white candidate as successful as Jackson would be presumed to want to be president, whereas Jackson's motives were somehow suspect. Others saw this as a simple reflection of reality: national polls repeatedly showed that much of the country still would not vote for a black person for president. A poll conducted by the *New York Times* showed that 39% of those questioned would not vote for Jackson because of his lack of experience, while 32% said they would not vote for any black candidate. By the end of the long, tiring primary season, Jackson had won seven million votes, coming in second to Michael Dukakis. In the November election, Dukakis lost to Republican George Bush.

RECENT ACTIVITIES

In 1989, Jackson and his family moved from Chicago to Washington, D.C. The following year, he was elected to the position of shadow senator to lobby for statehood for the District of Columbia. By law, the District does not have a voting member in Congress. The shadow senator has the right to attend meetings and to speak out, but is unable to vote. Jackson also continued his various other concerns: working as host of a television show; serving as an intermediary with Saddam Hussein and helping to free

American hostages after Iraq invaded Kuwait; and speaking out on social issues, particularly the violence that plagues the black community. He works primarily with the National Rainbow Coalition, a multi-racial, multi-issue organization that he founded in Washington, D.C. "[By] forming a mighty coalition across ancient barriers of race, gender, and religion," according to its mission statement, this group fights for social, racial, and economic justice.

Jackson's plans for the future are unclear. Some political writers conjecture that he will make a run for the presidency again in 1996, possibly running as an independent and challenging Democratic incumbent Bill Clinton. Jackson avoids either confirming or denying it, but observers have already begun to question his motivations for running again. A *New York Times* profile written prior to the 1988 campaign summarizes the issues that still confront Jackson today. The writer poses "the central question about the self-inventing Presidential candidate: To what end will he use his growing influence? Will he use it to feed his substantial appetite for attention, or to advance the cause of blacks, the poor, the displaced, the disenfranchised—all those he says he represents. His successful, provocative, often controversial past has made him an American political phenomenon. But it has also led people to wonder whether Jesse Jackson is out for the principles he so eloquently espouses. Or whether Jesse Jackson is out for himself."

Regardless of his decision on future presidential campaigns, Jackson remains a strong and eloquent voice for economic justice and human rights. Jackson himself recently said, "When the curtain finally falls on me, all I want is for history to say, 'He was a part of the conscience of his time.' I'll rest then."

MARRIAGE AND FAMILY

Jackson met his future wife, Jacqueline Lavinia Brown, when they were both students at North Carolina A & T. Jackie had had a rough childhood: her mother was a farmworker in Florida, picking beans for 15 cents an hour. Jackie never knew her father. She and Jesse started dating in college, and after a few months they found out she was pregnant. While neither Jackie nor Jesse had planned to have children at that point, they also had no intention of having a baby outside of marriage and repeating the difficulties of their own childhoods. "We got married and established family security. We broke the cycle," Jesse has explained. They got married in late 1962 at Jesse's family home in Greenville, and went on to have five children: Santita, Jesse Louis, Jonathan, Luther, Yusef DuBois, and Jacqueline Lavinia.

In 1968, Jackson discovered that he suffered from sickle-cell anemia trait. This chronic blood disease, common among blacks of West African descent, is a natural protection against malaria that has the side effect of lowering a person's resistance to other common diseases. Those whose red blood cells are shaped like sickles can have either the disease or the trait. While those with the disease suffer from life-threatening complications, those with the trait, like Jackson, experience far less serious problems.

HOBBIES AND OTHER INTERESTS

Jackson is known as a workaholic who often manages on little sleep. He has devoted so much time to his work that he really hasn't developed other hobbies. In addition to spending time with his family, Jackson enjoys listening to blues, soul, and jazz and keeping up with current events.

WRITINGS

Straight from the Heart, 1987
Keep Hope Alive, 1989

HONORS AND AWARDS

Ten Outstanding Young Americans (United States Jaycees): 1969
Eugene V. Debs Award (Eugene V. Debs Foundation): 1978
Jefferson Awards (American Institute for Public Service): 1979, for Greatest
    Public Service Benefitting the Disadvantaged
Grammy Award (National Academy of Recording Arts and Sciences):
    1988, for *Speech by Rev. Jesse Jackson (July 27)*
SANE Education Fund/Consider the Alternatives Peace Award: 1989
Springarn Medal (National Association for the Advancement of Colored
    People): 1989, "for his accomplishments and in appreciation of his
    enduring advocacy of human and civil rights; his stature as a national
    leader in the political arena; his role as a national and international
    activist; [and] his inspiration for our youth"
Martin Luther King, Jr., Nonviolent Peace Prize (Martin Luther King,
    Jr., Center for Nonviolent Social Change): 1993

FURTHER READING

BOOKS

Celsi, Teresa. *Jesse Jackson and Political Power,* 1991 (juvenile)
Chaplik, Dorothy. *Up with Hope: A Biography of Jesse Jackson,* 1986 (juvenile)
Encyclopedia Brittanica, 1993
Haskins, James. *I Am Somebody!: A Biography of Jesse Jackson,* 1992
    (juvenile)
Jackson, Jesse. *A Time to Speak: The Autobiography of the Reverend Jesse
    Jackson,* 1988

Jakoubek, Robert. *Jesse Jackson: Civil Rights Leader and Politician,* 1991 (juvenile)

Kosof, Anna. *Jesse Jackson,* 1987

McKissack, Patricia C. *Jesse Jackson: A Biography,* 1989

Otfinoski, Steven. *Jesse Jackson: A Voice for Change,* 1989 (juvenile)

Reynolds, Barbara A. *Jesse Jackson: America's David,* 1985

Who's Who in America, 1995

Who's Who among Black Americans, 1994-1995

World Book Encyclopedia, 1995

PERIODICALS

Current Biography 1986

New York Times Biographical Service, Nov. 1987, p.1252

New York Times Magazine, Mar. 4, 1984, p.40

New Yorker, Feb. 3, 1992, p.36; Feb. 10, 1992, p.41; Feb. 17, 1992, p.39 (3-part article)

People, Apr. 11, 1994, p.97

Vanity Fair, Jan. 1988, p.46

ADDRESS

National Rainbow Coalition
P.O. Box 27385
Washington, DC 20005

James Earl Jones   1931-
American Actor
Voice of King Mufasa in *The Lion King* and
Darth Vader in *Star Wars*

BIRTH

James Earl Jones was born on January 17, 1931, in Arkabutla
Township, Mississippi. His parents, Robert Earl Jones and Ruth
(Connolly) Jones, had separated before his birth; their marriage
"was destroyed by the Depression," according to James Earl, their
only child. Robert Earl Jones was a boxer, and later an actor, who
only saw his son once while he was a baby. After that, they did
not see or speak to one another until James Earl was in high
school.

James Earl was born at Home House, the name of the home on the 40-acre farm where his mother, Ruth, had grown up. Jones can trace his family history back before the Civil War. James Earl's great-great-grandfather, Brice, had been abducted from Africa while still a child and sold into slavery on a cotton plantation in Mississippi. He was freed after the Civil War. He married Parthenia Connolly, an indentured Irish servant, who taught him to read, gave him her last name, and bore him nine children. Their third child, Wyatt, was James Earl's great-grandfather. During Reconstruction, the era just after the Civil War, Wyatt Connolly started to buy cheap land in Arkabutla Township, until he had amassed 300 acres. In the center of the farm he built Home House. The land was eventually divided up among his children, with 40 acres, plus Home House, going to his son, John Henry Connolly. He and his wife, Maggie Connolly, were Ruth's parents; they raised James Earl when he was a boy.

YOUTH

When he was very young, James Earl stayed at Home House with his grandfather and grandmother, whom he called Papa and Mama, and several aunts, uncles, and cousins. It was the Depression, and there was no work in Arkabutla Township for a young, uneducated, black single mother. So Ruth traveled around looking for jobs, working as a migrant worker in the Mississippi Delta, a domestic in Memphis, and a seamstress in the Midwest. She tried to persuade her son to come with her, but he insisted on staying with his grandparents. Life there was hard, with lots of work on the farm and no outward demonstrations of affection from his grandparents. But still he preferred that security to the uncertainty of life on the road with his mother. In his autobiography, *James Earl Jones: Voices and Silences*, he writes movingly about how much he missed her. "For weeks before she came, I would repeat the old habit of simultaneously anticipating her arrival and mourning her inevitable departure." He would count the days until she would come to visit, and as soon as she arrived, he would count the days, despairingly, until she would have to leave.

When James Earl was about six, the family started making plans to move to Michigan. At that time in Mississippi, there were only four high schools in the whole state that accepted black students. A few children were sent to those towns to board while attending high school, but most black children were forced to leave school after eight grade. John Henry and Maggie Connolly valued education. It was too late for their older children, but they wanted to provide a better education for the rest of the family. They decided to move north to Michigan, where they had heard there were good schools for blacks. They started packing for the move.

Most of the family planned to go by train, but James Earl was sent in the car with his grandfather, Papa, and his uncle, H.B. They loaded up the car with luggage and a mattress and drove to Memphis, Tennessee, where they stopped at the home of James Earl's other grandmother, his father's mother. Without a word of warning, they announced to the young boy, "This is your new home." As Jones writes, "I could not speak. There were no words exchanged between Papa and me. But I knew I could not live with this stranger. Instinctively, I did the only thing I could think to do. Silently, stubbornly, I hung onto the mattress, physically protesting this separation with all my strength. I wouldn't turn loose, no matter what. I refused to let go." He was taken back to stay with the rest of the family to take the train with them to Michigan. But for Jones, "[Everything] had changed for me, the safety of home, the sense of belonging in the family. Even before we moved to Michigan, a world ended for me, the safe world of childhood.

"There are questions not asked, words not spoken. I could not talk to Papa and Mama about their decision to leave me behind in Memphis, and then their reprieve. There was so much I could not ask or say. The move from Mississippi to Michigan was supposed to be a glorious event. For me it was heartbreak.

"And not long after, I began to stutter."

LIFE IN MICHIGAN

The stuttering began soon after the family arrived in Michigan, and Jones describes it as one of the defining experiences of his youth. They were living on a farm in Dublin, near Manistee in northwestern Michigan. He soon started first grade at the local one-room schoolhouse. At the same time, he started to stutter. The problem became so severe that he virtually stopped speaking. At home he would speak a little, but would clam up the minute anybody stopped by. At school, he would communicate only in writing. His teachers were tremendously helpful, adjusting his schoolwork so he could complete it in writing. He was a good student, despite his inability to speak. As he says, "For about eight years, from the time I was six until I was about fourteen, I was virtually mute." Jones describes the reason for the silence, as he came to terms with it as an adult: "I suppose part of it was my need to stay quiet, in the background, causing no trouble, giving no displeasure, so I would be allowed to stay."

EDUCATION

It was while in high school, at Norman Dickson High School in Brethren, Michigan, that Jones regained his voice. His whole life changed when he took a class from an English teacher named Donald Crouch. A former college English professor, Crouch had grown tired of retirement and had started teaching at the local high school. He was aware of Jones's ability to speak a little among his family, and he also knew that Jones had tried his hand at writing poetry. So he decided to try a little experiment.

Crouch gave an assignment to the class to write a poem. Jones turned in an ode to grapefruit loosely patterned after Henry Wadsworth Longfellow's "The Song of Hiawatha." Crouch pretended that he doubted that Jones had written the poem and challenged him to prove it by reciting it from memory before the class. As Jones recalls, Crouch took him aside and said, "This is good enough that I worry about plagiarism here. In order to prove that you wrote it, I want you to get up in front of the class and recite it by heart." Stung, Jones stood up and recited the complete poem, with a full voice and no stuttering.

After that, Crouch helped Jones by creating a demanding program of speech training to conquer his fear of speaking and develop his prodigious vocal talent. Crouch coached him through high school debates and oratorical contests. On one day during his senior year, Jones won both a public speaking contest and a scholarship to college. As a reward, the school paid for Jones to put a long-distance call through to his father to report his good news. It took him an hour to get up the courage to call his father and speak to him for the first time ever. Jones graduated from high school in 1949.

He went on to college at the University of Michigan in Ann Arbor, one of the first in his family to do so. Referring also to his cousin Randy, Jones explained, "We knew that as first-generation college students, we would have to choose practical professions. College was for serious business— engineering, doctoring, lawyering." Jones enrolled in pre-med courses, as well as the ROTC (Reserve Officers Training Corps), an officers' training program for the U.S. military. During his first year he also joined the drama club and appeared in various productions in both university theaters and community theaters around Ann Arbor. Drama, of course, eventually won out over medicine, and he pursued a degree in English. That interest was further fueled when he visited his father in New York during a school vacation, spending several days together seeing plays. In his senior year, just before finishing his degree, Jones left school before taking finals, convinced that he would be shipped overseas to fight in the Korean War. Several years later, he completed the work and earned his B.A.

FIRST JOBS

After leaving the University of Michigan in 1953, Jones first went back to his home town. Because he had worked as a carpenter and mason during high school and college, he was able to get a job working as a member of the stage crew at the Manistee Summer Theater. He also got up the courage to try out for some of the smaller roles, and he appeared in several productions that summer, using the stage name Todd Jones.

MILITARY SERVICE

After that summer, Jones served two years in the U.S. Army to complete his ROTC requirement. His Army stint started soon after a truce was declared in the Korean War in the summer of 1953. Rather than being shipped overseas, as he had expected, Jones started out at the Army Ranger training camp at Fort Benning, Georgia. The experience proved difficult when he encountered racist treatment from some of the white soldiers. He was sent next to the Cold Weather Training Command in Colorado. He enjoyed the solitude and the rigors of the cold weather and rugged terrain so much that he considered making the Army his career. Instead, he decided to try acting. He was discharged from the Army in 1955 with the rank of first lieutenant.

CHOOSING A CAREER

Jones first got an inkling of his future career when he was still in high school. Looking through an old copy of *Look* magazine, he came upon a picture of his father, Robert Earl Jones, from a Broadway production of the play *Strange Fruit*. "I just happened to open the magazine and see my father," Jones recalls. "I felt very proud of that. I had not realized that I looked like him, for I had never really seen him since that one moment when I was a baby. Out of that discovery, I spoke out loud for the first time about being an actor. 'Well' I said, 'I am going to be an actor on the stage.'" At the time, his grandfather overheard him and responded with a whack on the head—he wasn't fond of James Earl's father, and he didn't consider acting a steady profession. But the idea stuck with Jones through the rest of high school, through college, and through his stint in the Army, until finally he decided to give it a try.

CAREER HIGHLIGHTS

STARTING HIS CAREER

In 1955, after completing his army service, Jones decided to move to New York to pursue his dream of becoming an actor. He lived with his father, changed his stage name back to James Earl in his honor, and studied acting under the G.I. Bill, which pays to educate American service men and women after they complete their tours of duty. For Jones, that meant two years at the American Theatre Wing, where he earned a diploma in 1957.

He landed his first part in 1957, a small role in an off-Broadway production of *Wedding in Japan*. One night during that show the lead actor was out, so Jones took over his role. By a lucky coincidence, an important agent was in the audience. She was so impressed by his performance that she signed him up. From that time onward he worked steadily in the theater, both in New York and, for the first few years, back at the Manistee Summer Theater. While he appeared in many small roles at low pay, and often had to supplement his income by cleaning floors and working in a sandwich shop, he worked almost unceasingly.

Well known today for roles in a variety of media, including film and television, Jones first established himself as an actor throughout the 1960s and 1970s in the New York theater. His appearances since then, and his awards, are far too numerous to mention—a partial listing of his awards includes two Obies, four Emmys, two Tonys, two Grammies, three awards from the NAACP, two Golden Globes, the National Medal of the Arts, and many others. Still, certain productions stand out. Jones considers his breakthrough role to be that of Deodatus Village in the 1961 staging of Jean Genet's *The Blacks*. He joined the famed Shakespeare Festival directed by Joseph Papp in 1960, appearing in the Shakespeare in the Park series in New York's Central Park. In 1963 he gave an award-winning performance in the title role in Shakespeare's classic *Othello*.

ACHIEVING NATIONAL PROMINENCE

Jones first came to national prominence in 1968 in Howard Sackler's Pulitzer-Prize winning play, *The Great White Hope*. Jones gave an uncannily evocative performance as the prizefighter Jack Jefferson, a character that was based on the first black heavyweight boxing champion, Jack Johnson. Shortly afterward, Jones reprised the role in the film version of the same name. His major dramatic work, since that time, includes *Boesman and Lena, A Lesson from Aloes*, and *Master Harold . . . and the Boys*, important plays by South African dramatist Athol Fugard; *Paul Robeson*, a one-man touring show based on the life of this actor, singer, and athlete; *Fences*, the Pulitzer-Prize winning play by August Wilson, in which Jones depicted Troy Maxson, a garbage collector and former baseball player in the early Negro Leagues; and many appearances in productions of Shakespeare's works.

During the 1960s Jones began working in other mediums, mixing roles in the theater with "bread and butter" parts on TV and in movies. Typically, actors make very little money working in live drama, so over the years Jones often turned to TV and film work to augment his income. In television, he started out by making guest appearances on the series "East Side/West Side," "Channing," and "The Defenders"; in 1965, he was the first black man to earn an ongoing role in a soap opera when he took the part of Dr. Jerry Turner on "As the World Turns." A brief sampling of his TV work from recent years includes portraying Alex Haley in "Roots II: The Next Generation," narrating and hosting the children's show "Long Ago and Far Away," and starring roles in the series "Gabriel's Fire" and "Pros and Cons." His first big-screen appearance came in the 1963 satiric anti-war film, *Dr. Strangelove; or, How I Learned to Stop Worrying and Love the Bomb.* Since then, his lengthy list of movie credits includes the *Star Wars* trilogy, where he provided the voice of Darth Vader, *Coming to America, Field of Dreams, The Hunt for Red October, Patriot Games, Clear and Present Danger, The Vernon Jones Story,* and *The Lion King,* in which he supplis the voice for the character of King Mufasa.

THE VOICE

But brief listings such as these fail to do justice to Jones's extraordinary career. His work encompasses everything from avant-garde drama to animated children's films, from Shakespeare's plays to Tom Clancy's techno-thrillers. But the one unifying element in all Jones's work is his commanding, sonorous voice. As described by a writer for the *Tampa Tribune,* his voice is the voice of authority, as the announcer for CNN; the voice of reason, as CIA chief Admiral James Greer in the films based on the best-selling novels of Tom Clancy; the voice of vision, as the reclusive author Terrence Mann in *Field of Dreams;* and even the voice of darkness, as Darth Vader in the *Star Wars* trilogy. Throughout his varied work, audiences respond to Jones's voice, "that signature basso profondo that critics have associated with the moral authority that he can bring to a role," as a writer for the *Toronto Star* explained. With that distinctive, thundering voice, Jones is able to define and give life to the characters that he plays.

MARRIAGE AND FAMILY

Jones has been married twice, both times to an actress who played Desdemona to his Othello. In 1967 he was married to Julienne Marie Hendricks; they later divorced. On March 15, 1982, he was married to Cecilia Hart. Their son, Flynn Earl Jones, was born on December 13, 1982. The family has two homes, one in Los Angeles, where they usually live, and a retreat in rural upstate New York.

WRITINGS

James Earl Jones: Voices and Silences, 1993 (with Penelope Niven)

SELECTED CREDITS

ON STAGE

Wedding in Japan, 1957
Sunrise at Campobello, 1958
Henry V, 1960
The Apple, 1961
The Blacks, 1961

Clandestine on the Morning Line, 1961
Moon on a Rainbow Shawl, 1961
Othello, 1963, 1964, 1968, 1971, 1981, 1982
Emperor Jones, 1964, 1967
Baal, 1965
Macbeth, 1966
Of Mice and Men, 1967, 1974
The Great White Hope, 1967, 1968
Les Blancs, 1970
Boesman and Lena, 1970
Hamlet, 1972
The Cherry Orchard, 1973
The Iceman Cometh, 1973
King Lear, 1973
Paul Robeson, 1977, 1978
A Lesson from Aloes, 1980
Hedda Gabler, 1980
Master Harold . . . and the Boys, 1983
Fences, 1985, 1987, 1988

ON FILM

Dr. Strangelove; or, How I Learned to Stop Worrying and Love the Bomb, 1963
The Great White Hope, 1970
King: A Filmed Record . . . 1970
Montgomery to Memphis, 1970 (narrator)
Malcolm X, 1972 (narrator)
Claudine, 1974
The Bingo Long Traveling All-Stars and Motor Kings, 1976
Star Wars, 1977 (voice of Darth Vader)
The Empire Strikes Back, 1980 (voice of Darth Vader)
Return of the Jedi, 1983 (voice of Darth Vader)
Soul Man, 1986
Gardens of Stone, 1987
Matewan, 1987
Coming to America, 1988
Field of Dreams, 1989
The Hunt for Red October, 1990
Patriot Games, 1992
Sneakers, 1992
Meteor Man, 1993
Sommersby, 1993
The Vernon Jones Story, 1993
Clear and Present Danger, 1994
The Lion King, 1994 (voice of King Mufasa)

ON TELEVISION

"Beyond the Blues," 1965
"As the World Turns," 1965
"Black Omnibus," 1973 (series host)
"The Cay," 1974 (TV movie)
"Roots II: The Next Generation," 1979
"Paris," 1979-80
"Atlanta Child Murders," 1984 (TV movie)
"Long Ago and Far Away," 1989 (series host)
"Heat Wave," 1990
"Gabriel's Fire," 1990
"Pros and Cons," 1991
"Earthworks," 1992 (narrator)
"Lincoln," 1993 (narrator)

HONORS AND AWARDS

Obie Awards (*Village Voice* Off-Broadway Awards): 1961-62, for Best Actor in the Off-Broadway Theater, for *The Apple, Clandestine on the Morning Line,* and *Moon on a Rainbow Shawl*; 1964-65, for *Baal*

Theatre World Awards: 1962, as most promising personality

Drama Desk Awards: 1964-65, for outstanding performance, in *Othello*; 1968-69, for outstanding performance, in *The Great White Hope*; 1970-71, for outstanding performance, in *Les Blancs*; 1972-73, for outstanding performances, in *Hamlet* and *The Cherry Orchard*; 1986-87, for best actor, in *Fences*

Emmy Awards: 1965, for performance in the documentary *Beyond the Blues*; 1985, for outstanding children's programming; 1991, for Outstanding Supporting Actor in a Miniseries or Special, for "Heat Wave"; 1991, for Outstanding Lead Actor in a Dramatic Series, in "Gabriel's Fire"

Tony Awards (Antoinette Perry Awards): 1969, for Best Actor, in *The Great White Hope*; 1987, for Best Actor, in *Fences*

Grammy Awards: 1969, for recording of *The Great White Hope*; 1976, for recording of *Great American Documents*

Golden Globe Award: 1971, for New Male Star of the Year; 1974, for *Claudine*

NAACP Image Award: 1974, for Best Actor, in *Claudine*; 1992, for Best Actor

Golden Hugo Award: 1975

Gabriel Award: 1975

Medal for Spoken Language (American Academy of Arts and Letters): 1981

Theatre Hall of Fame: 1985

Drama Critics Award: 1987, for *Fences*

Drama League's Distinguished Performance Award: 1987, for *Fences*

Outer Critics Circle Award: 1987, for best actor, in *Fences*
ACE Award: 1990, for Best Actor in a Supporting Role, in "Heat Wave"
National Medal of the Arts: 1992, for outstanding contribution to the arts
NAACP Hall of Fame Image Award: 1992, for great contribution to the arts

FURTHER READING

BOOKS

Jones, James Earl, and Penelope Niven. *James Earl Jones: Voices and Silences,* 1993
Who's Who in America, 1994
Who's Who among Black Americans, 1994-1995

PERIODICALS

Boston Globe, Oct. 18, 1981
Current Biography 1994
Detroit Free Press, Aug. 29, 1993, p.G1
New York Times Biographical Service, Mar. 1987, p.254
Reader's Digest, July 1994, p.121
Tampa Tribune, Oct. 10, 1993
Toronto Star, Oct. 7, 1993, p.D6

ADDRESS

Dale C. Olson & Associates
6310 San Vicente Boulevard
Suite 340
Los Angeles, CA 90048

Julie Krone 1963-
American Jockey
First Woman Ever to Capture a Triple-Crown
Horse-Racing Title

BIRTH

Julieann Louise Krone was born July 24, 1963, in the southwestern Michigan city of Benton Harbor, to Donald Krone, an art teacher and photographer, and Judi Krone, an accomplished horseback rider. Julie and her older brother, Donnie (Donald), who now rides as an exercise trainer in Maryland, grew up on the family's ten-acre farm in Eau Claire, a town close to Benton Harbor. The elder Krones have been divorced since Julie's teen years.

YOUTH

Judi Krone is a retired horsewoman whose specialty was dressage, the execution of complex riding maneuvers. She had both her children on horseback before they could walk, and has commented in recent years on her famous daughter's early and uncanny skills on a horse. "When Julie was two," Judi Krone has said, "I had her on a pony and I was leading him around the farm with just a lead rope, no bridle. I dropped the rope for a moment and he really took off, bucking like crazy, but her little butt never left his back—and she was laughing" Don has similar memories of his child's spunk and has said that being around this bundle of energy was "like going to a rocket launch every day." He tells of how she was on her pony at every opportunity, never failing to have some trick to show her astonished parents. Julie often could be seen racing around the farm on horseback, jumping fences and riding while standing up. "She was fearless," says her dad. "One day she was up high in a tree. I said to her, 'Better look out. You'll fall.' She answered, 'I already did. Watch me climb.'"

Judi began entering her daughter in horse shows when Julie was only five years old. She repeatedly won ribbons in Berrien, her home county, for the next decade, even when competing with contestants up to the age of 21. Her skill in riding and handling horses grew out of an early and unflagging love for the animals. Just recently, she searched for a pony she had trained as a child by calling every 4-H club in Michigan. She found Filly and, twenty years later, the old pony still remembers the tricks Krone taught her.

Despite an interest in gymnastics and other sports, there was never much doubt about where Julie's life would lead. From the trick-or-treating on horseback, to the reins attached to her bedpost, to the 4 a.m. wake-up calls for practice before school, her entire childhood was about horses. "The rest," she still contends, "is wasted time."

CHOOSING A CAREER

The inspiration for Krone's remarkable career can be traced directly to jockey Steve Cauthen. In 1978, 14-year-old Julie watched Cauthen, only four years her senior, ride Affirmed to win racing's vaunted Triple Crown (wins at each of the three biggest horse races: the Kentucky Derby, the Preakness, and the Belmont Stakes). That was the season that she announced to Don and Judi her determination to become a jockey.

FIRST JOB

County horse fairs only whetted Julie's appetite for bigger and better things in horse racing. So in the spring of 1979, not yet 16, she persuaded her mother to alter her birth certificate to read April 1963 (instead of July) and take her to Churchill Downs in Louisville, Kentucky, home of America's most famous horse race, the Kentucky Derby. There at the track, with her not-quite-accurate document, she found a job as a morning-workout rider. Menial as that first job was, it marked her entry into the world of thoroughbred racing.

EDUCATION

At the end of her summer at Churchill Downs, Julie returned to home and Eau Claire High. But after juggling track jobs and classes, she dropped out during her senior year to pursue full-time race riding. She moved to Florida to live with her grandparents and ride at the Tampa Bay Downs racetrack.

Although Krone has never returned to school, she is a celebrity at Eau Claire High. The fans in her hometown are proud of her accomplishments, and even though she didn't finish high school, her former teachers are proud of her, too.

CAREER HIGHLIGHTS

When Krone's mother conspired to alter the birth certificate that enabled Julie to get a job at Churchill Downs, the first chapter was begun on one of the greatest careers—for male or female—in the history of horse racing. But when it came time to ride for a living, the then-4'8" teenager (who now measures 4'10 1/2") was refused admission to Tampa Bay Downs. The determination that still defines her persona showed even then, and she climbed a fence without hesitation and began begging mounts. Jerry Pace, a track trainer, was so impressed with the girl's spunk that he put her on a horse. It was only five weeks later, in her eleventh race as an apprentice jockey, that Julie found herself in the winner's circle. She went on to win nine times in 48 races, placing second four times, and third ten times. She then teamed up with agent Chuck Lang, who took her to live with his family in Baltimore so that she could race at Pimlico race track, home of the Preakness Stakes. At first, Julie had difficulty getting rides because she was female. She traveled around to different tracks and started proving herself to the owners and trainers, many of whom felt that the racetrack was no place for women.

In 1980 Krone suffered some serious setbacks. The generally clean-living 17-year-old, caught with marijuana in her car, was suspended for 60 days and ordered into one year of drug rehabilitation. "It was a once-in-a-lifetime thing," she says. "I genuinely contemplated suicide, that's how devastated I was. I thought everything I had worked for and wanted was gone. Now, I just scratch my head when I read about other jockeys and drugs. I just don't understand it."

Later that same year, she fell from her horse in a race and broke her back. Julie had a calmer take on that mishap than she had on her riding suspension. Her philosophy about riding accidents—and she has had several serious falls—is always the same. "If you're not ready for something bad to happen, then you won't be able to overcome things," she's said, adding, "It makes all the good stuff in your life seem all that much better." Although she accepted the accident, she couldn't accept her bad run when she returned to racing: she lost her first 80 races. It was a difficult and depressing time, and she even considered quitting racing before her luck changed in 1981, and she started winning again.

HOLDING HER OWN IN A MALE-DOMINATED SPORT

Krone's career really took off in the 1980s. In 1982, she captured the riding title at Atlantic City, logging 155 wins, with a total of more than a million dollars in prize money; her share of the winnings was ten percent. The following year, she won her second straight title at Atlantic City. The mid-eighties saw Krone become the dominant jockey at New Jersey's Monmouth Park and, in a moonlighting stint, at the Meadowlands, where there is racing at night. She became the first woman to win riding titles at both tracks. However, neither victories nor respect came easily in this male-dominated (and often unabashedly sexist) sport. One incident stands out above others, although for its nastiness rather than its uniqueness. Krone and Miguel Rujano got into close quarters during a 1986 race at Monmouth, and he hit Julie in the head with his whip. Julie punched him at the weigh-in after the race. Rujano then responded by throwing Krone into the jockeys' swimming pool, leading her to heave a chair at him. Rujano was suspended, Krone was fined. "The punch I got in was a real good one, though," announced the feisty young woman. Few male jockeys now mess with Julie Krone.

In the late 1980s, Julie moved to New York's racing circuit, the toughest on the east coast. Willing to ride up to 15 times a day, she still rode nights at Meadowlands. In 1988, she took her mount, Forty-Niner, to a fourth-place finish in the $3 million Breeders' Cup Classic, while becoming the first woman ever to ride on a Cup day. She also captured the riding titles at Monmouth and Meadowlands and finished that year as the fourth-leading rider in the country.

Just a year later, injury stalled Krone again when her left forearm was shattered in a fall at Meadowlands. It would be eight months before her return to racing. In typical fashion, and with undiminished spunk, she chose Saratoga, racing's most prestigious meeting, for her track reentry in late 1990. That was also the year that she became the first woman jockey to win in Japan. Krone came close to claiming the 1991 riding title at Saratoga, battling with jockeys Angel Cordero and Mike Smith, the eventual winner, throughout the five weeks of top-class competition. One year later, she had added Gulfstream Park and Belmont Park track titles to her roster of riding honors.

THE TRIPLE CROWN WIN, THE FALL, THE TRIUMPHANT RECOVERY

The best and worst moments came in 1993. In June, she rode longshot Colonial Affair to victory in the grueling, one-and-a-half-mile Belmont Stakes, becoming the first woman ever to capture a Triple Crown race. "As if to put an exclamation point on her most gratifying season," wrote Gene Guidi in the *Detroit Free Press*, "Krone became the third jockey in 126 years of thoroughbred racing at storied Saratoga to win five races in one day . . . she had never been riding better, had never been more in demand." Then, that August at Saratoga, the hundred-pound jockey was thrown from her mount, Seattle Way, mangling her ankle and puncturing her elbow. Even more horrifying, she suffered a cardiac contusion when kicked in the chest by another thoroughbred. She might have died had she not been wearing a protective vest. "I did a 180 [degree turn]," she says, "so I was sitting facing the oncoming horses. Pow! I got hit in my heart. My arm was cut so you could see the elbow socket. My ankle hurt so bad I kept thinking, 'Pass out. *Please* pass out.' But I didn't." It was the first time that Krone had known fear in the 13 years she had been a jockey, and she admits now that she even questioned whether something was wrong with her that she would want to ride racehorses.

Krone spent three weeks in the hospital, enduring two separate operations and the placement of fourteen screws in her shattered ankle. After that ordeal, she underwent months of painful rehabilitation. The surgeon who worked on her broken body predicted that it would be a full year before she could ride competitively again. Julie beat the odds when she returned to the saddle in May 1994, three months ahead of schedule, wearing a "Live to Ride, Ride to Live" T-shirt that expressed her renewed spirit. She felt more determined than ever to do well, explaining that coming so close to losing something she loved—the racing that defines her life— made it even more important to her.

Julie Krone's riding style depends on communication with horses. "[To] relax a horse," she comments, "you find out what he wants. . . . Does he like to keep pulling or have you let him go? . . . I can tell by feel, by what he does with his weight and his head and his mouth, so that, by the end of the post parades, I know what he likes." Still, she also knows that no jockey can make a slow horse win a race.

Krone has always had supporters, such as trainers Bud and Richard Delp and Scotty Schulhoffer and ace agent Larry "Snake" Cooper. She also has her share of detractors, who attribute her success to constant self-promotion. The gender factor that Krone tires of hearing about could be an element in discrediting her abilities, although many racetrack insiders note than she can be quite abrasive. One turf writer's quote in a *New York Times Magazine* feature sums it up this way: "Some jockeys don't like her much. They say everything she does is political; they say she's a prima donna. Would they say that if she was a he? Who knows? Who cares? All I know is, she wins."

Winning is what matters, and Julie Krone is one of the best at it, outdistancing all but a few of her male colleagues. She's won more than 2,000 races, bringing in nearly $50 million in purse money. At 31 years of age, that could be only the beginning for a woman who seems totally disinterested in early retirement from this perilous sport. "I know what I do is dangerous," she says, "and I know I might pay for it, physically, sometime in the future, but I'm willing to make the trade-off. I'm willing to take that risk."

"To be a great jockey," trainer Carl Nafzger once said, "you need five traits: riding ability, physical strength, mental soundness, a great immune system, and class. That's the big unknown, class. . . . [The riders] who can deliver when the pressure's on—that's class. That's Julie."

MEMORABLE EXPERIENCE

Krone has wanted to be the best jockey ever since she was a child, and she finally captured one of the great races—the Belmont Stakes—in June

1993. Unlike many who witnessed the superb performance of this "girl jockey," she wasn't thinking about gender when she punched her fist in the air after guiding Colonial Affair past the finish line. "It would feel great to anyone," she said later. "But whether you're a girl or a boy or a Martian, you still have to go out and prove youself every day."

MARRIAGE AND FAMILY

Krone lives with six companions, two horses and four cats, at the home she owns on four acres of horse country in New Jersey. She shared the house for a time with a fiance, but that relationship has ended. Her mother lives in Florida, and her father still resides in the western Michigan area where she grew up.

HOBBIES AND OTHER INTERESTS

Krone enjoys movies, nature programs on television, Broadway shows, and reading—particularly autobiographies. None of these activities, though, measure up to the recreational hours she spends with the jumping horses she keeps at home.

FURTHER READING

BOOKS

Callahan, Dorothy M. *Julie Krone: A Winning Jockey*, 1990 (juvenile)
Condon, Robert J. *Great Women Athletes of the 20th Century*, 1991
Who's Who in America, 1994

PERIODICALS

Arizona Republic, Feb. 10, 1991, p.D1
Current Biography Yearbook 1989
Detroit Free Press, May 26, 1944, p.C1
New York Newsday, Mar. 16, 1990, Section II, p.2
New York Times, May 26, 1994, p.B7
New York Times Biographical Service, Oct. 1991, p.1024
New York Times Magazine, July 25, 1993, p.20
Newsweek, June 6, 1994, p.84
People, May 2, 1988, p.111
Philadelphia Inquirer, Feb. 28, 1988, p.D16
Sports Illustrated, May 22, 1989, p.84

ADDRESS

The Jockeys' Guild
20 East 46th Street
New York, NY 10017-2417

David Letterman 1947-
American Comedian and Television Personality
CBS Late Night Talk-Show Host

BIRTH

David Michael Letterman was born April 12, 1947, in Indianapolis, Indiana, the middle child and only son of H.Joseph and Dorothy Letterman. His father, who died in 1974, was a florist in Broad Ripple, an Indianapolis suburb. His mother, now remarried, is a retired church secretary whose face and gentle demeanor became familiar to "Late Show" watchers in her low-key interview segments from Lillehammer, Norway, during the 1994 Olympic Winter Games.

Letterman's sisters are Janice, still an Indiana resident, and Gretchen, who lives in Florida.

YOUTH

Quiet and painfully shy as a child, Letterman nevertheless showed a natural talent for comedy (both his father and maternal grandfather were pranksters), and he admits to having been something of a joker himself even then. He was reared in what he describes as an average middle-class family, with parents who both worked to keep the family budget afloat. He was a typical mid-American kid who played baseball (he still does) and built a tree house, and his memories of those boyhood days are happy ones, in spite of the financial difficulties that arose just prior to his teens. "We still got to do stuff [though] and had clothes and took trips. There was just a sense of tightness," he once told an interviewer. Letterman regards those youthful years in Indiana as a stable way to grow up.

EDUCATION

After elementary and junior high school, where he concedes that he deserved his poor grades, Letterman went on to Broad Ripple High. Surprisingly, he was *not* the class clown, as he was always too shy to perform in public. Mostly, he goofed off, and spent much of his time "riding around in a 1938 Chevy with four other guys who couldn't get dates [either] . . . that was every Friday and Saturday night." Then, toward the end of his high school years, he found a speech class that he thought would give him an easy "C." What he discovered was an interest that would change his life.

Letterman enrolled at Ball State University in Muncie, Indiana, as a radio and television major, gaining valuable experience outside the classroom as a disc jockey on the student station, WBST. True to form, he continued to find time for partying with his fraternity brothers and to sharpen his wiseguy image. He received his B.A. in radio and TV broadcasting from Ball State in 1970.

FIRST JOBS

Letterman's first paychecks were from an after-school job at Atlas Supermarket in Indianapolis while he was still a student at Broad Ripple High. During his college years, he filled in at Muncie's WERK radio station and, for two summers between semesters, worked as a booth announcer at Channel 13, WLWI-TV, ABC's affiliate in Indianapolis. Channel 13 hired him full-time after graduation as weekend weatherman, occasional news anchor, and host of both a kiddie show and a late-night movie program. Bored, he was eventually out of a job because of his on-air shenanigans, like describing hail as "the size of canned hams" and congratulating a tropical storm when it was upgraded to a hurricane. Letterman stayed around Indianapolis only about another year, taking a short-term job at WNTS radio.

CHOOSING A CAREER

In late spring, 1975, Letterman and wife Michelle (they are now divorced), moved to Los Angeles, where he took the plunge into show business. His offbeat humor landed him a regular slot at the popular Comedy Store on Sunset Boulevard. There he met Jay Leno, who helped him find a job as a writer for Jimmie Walker, a popular television sitcom star of those years. Soon Letterman was writing for other comedians as well—Bob Hope and Paul Lynde among them—while continuing to polish his own routines in clubs and on TV shows.

CAREER HIGHLIGHTS

THE YEARS WITH NBC

Letterman had appeared in three airings of Mary Tyler Moore's short-lived variety hour in 1978 when his first real break came along. Talent scouts for the "Tonight Show" booked him for an appearance, and his shrewd satire was so well received that he soon began a long association as Johnny Carson's most frequent guest host. Within a year, he had filled in twenty times as late-night interviewer, and recognition began to flow. Letterman continued writing, storing up new material, and playing clubs as the bottom half of acts featuring more celebrated entertainers.

NBC gave the gap-toothed comic a daytime talk show that showcased his mocking wit and on-air stunts ("Stupid Pet Tricks" were born here), but the program failed in its inappropriate time slot and was canceled after only four months. Although ratings were poor, reviews were not, and Letterman's writing and hosting earned him two Emmys. NBC then put him on a lucrative one-year holding contract to keep him from signing with another network. At the beginning of 1982, the right opening came along with the cancelation of "The Tom Snyder Show" at 12:30 to 1:30 a.m. Both time and scheduling were perfect for Letterman's quirky humor. He had found his niche, and the new program, "Late Night With David Letterman," began a run that would energize television's stale rule book for talk-show structure. His audience was drawn, for the most part, from the college crowd and the baby-boomers, and their endorsement of his loopy tricks and flip interviews was quick and enthusiastic.

"It's only television, folks," Letterman would say hundreds of times over the next decade as he horsed around on the late-night screen. The "Stupid Pet Tricks" were only one facet of his subtle madness. Other items on the menu included silly stunts—elevator races, Dave in a Velcro suit bouncing onto a Velcro-clad wall, Dave dropping TV sets and watermelons off a multi-storied building or badgering passersby with a bullhorn. In listing his contributions to American culture, *Time* recently spelled out its own top-ten inventory of Letterman's best offerings, the first being Dave's famous Top Ten List, "the show's most breezily topical, consistently funny and, yes, frequently imitated feature." The magazine added to its rundown the "celebrity trashing . . . by TV's least fawning host" and "company bashing, with [Dave's] endless GE jokes," in which he tossed gibes at the network's boss, and got away with it.

Much of the appeal of "Late Night" was hard to explain. Being a fan often simply meant being in on the joke as Letterman provoked his guests, goaded Larry (Bud) Melman, the inept stooge played so convincingly by actor Calvert DeForest, or bantered with his sidekick, bandleader Paul Shaffer. Oddball, hip, irreverent, exuberant—these were only a few of the adjectives that tried to capture the essence of Letterman's seduction of his youthful audience, yet the entertainer himself was known to his staff as an elusive comedian beseiged with self-doubts. He found it hard to concede that everything was going well, and brooded each night over minor glitches in the production. He was, and is, a perfectionist with a touch of cranky smugness that gives edge to his onstage performances.

THE DEAL WITH A RIVAL NETWORK

By 1993, after a decade of waiting in the wings for Johnny Carson to retire from the "Tonight Show," his long-held hopes to inherit the Carson spot were dashed when the network chose Jay Leno instead. Letterman decided to look beyond NBC. He has said all along that he blamed the network and not Leno, although it was no secret that Leno's own career had been given a major boost through his many appearances on "Late Night."

When the time came to renegotiate Letterman's contract, the late-night wars began in earnest. Dave was courted by CBS, ABC, and Fox, and even NBC is said to have made an offer that would have given the spurned comedian the "Tonight Show" at the end of Leno's contract. *New York Times* television reporter Bill Carter, explains in his 1994 book, *The Late Shift: Letterman, Leno and the Network Battle for the Night*, what went on backstage in the struggle to be Johnny Carson's successor. It is a story of two comics, each with considerable skills but contrasting campaign styles--the eminently likable, mainstream Leno, always anxious to build friendly relationships, and the "withdrawn, even sullen by nature [Letterman], who could not stomach the schmoozing at which Mr. Leno excelled."

Eventually, the negotiations of a super-agent—and the advice of Carson to accept a fabulous offer in mid-1993 from CBS—brought David Letterman even more than the 11:30 time slot he had so long desired. An eye-opening salary reported to be somewhere between $10 and $14 million, was only part of the CBS deal: along with the money came ownership of the program, the name of which has been changed to the "Late

Show With David Letterman," and a stunning new venue—the lavishly refurbished Ed Sullivan Theater in the heart of Manhattan. The new network offered a number of other contract advantages, such as Letterman's right to produce the show that would follow his and, most recently, a spot for Dave's first prime-time special.

The new show is now in its second year, sometimes soaring in late-night ratings as it did when it left the gate in September 1993, sometimes running neck and neck with its NBC counterpart. The ratings scramble is said to have added zest to both programs as they compete for top honors in the network battle. "Late Show" drew wide acclaim for two particularly inspired stunts last year: first when Dave sent his mother to the Winter Olympics as his network correspondent, and later, when he featured a series of silly on-the-road interviews with Mujibur Rahman and Sirajul Islam, trinket sellers from the studio neighborhood.

Letterman seems at last to be content (if that description applies at all) with his current situation. He claims, though, that he does not plan to be a late-night host indefinitely. "After a period of time with this, I will leave and go on. I'll probably never be on television again on any kind of regular basis. This [is] my new and final project."

MAJOR INFLUENCES

While he often mentions Steve Allen and Jonathan Winters as early influences, it is Johnny Carson whose name comes up most often when Letterman speaks of which brand of comedy inspired him most. He remembers watching TV after school (his parents took a dim view of the time he spent in front of the screen) and especially admiring Carson's "handling of the world's loonies," says a *Los Angeles* magazine feature. Letterman remains a devoted fan of the man who gave him his first real break, and whose job as host of NBC's "Tonight Show" he coveted, but lost. In a revealing interview last year, Letterman admits, "There was a time when I was a kid when all I wanted to be was Johnny Carson. But now that I've been doing it [hosting a nightly show], I know every shortcoming I have that he never had. And this is not false modesty. . . .This guy could get a bigger laugh by raising an eyebrow than I could get telling eight jokes."

MARRIAGE AND FAMILY

Letterman was married while still in college to fellow-student Michelle Cook, and they were together for several years until their 1977 divorce in California. Normally guarded about his personal life, he has been candid enough to say that the marriage would have come apart regardless of career pursuits or geography. He acknowledges that the "basic problem was that we'd just gotten married too young." The couple had no children.

After his divorce, Letterman had a longtime relationship with Merrill Markoe, who was an instructor at the University of Southern California when they met while both were testing their material at Los Angeles' Comedy Store. Markoe later became Letterman's head writer and producer, and they shared an apartment in Manhattan and an oceanfront house at Malibu in California. They split up more than six years ago, but Letterman always credits her with being "largely responsible for the success of the show."

David Letterman lives in New Canaan, Connecticut, close to New York City, and recently bought an eighty-acre spread north of Manhattan, with plans to eventually build a home there. He is romantically involved with Regina Lasko, until recently a production manager for "Saturday Night Live" but, in keeping with his well-documented low profile, he offers no comments on their relationship.

Much has been written about a mentally disturbed woman who has plagued Letterman for years, breaking into his New Canaan house, writing him irrational letters, and even claiming to be his wife. The comedian once carried on running jokes about this woman, Margaret Ray, but he speaks of her now more out of frustration and compassion than out of anger at her invasion of his privacy. He says, "She is a woman who spends her days in deep confusion."

HOBBIES AND OTHER INTERESTS

The lanky talk-show host who strides into camera range each week night in impeccably tailored finery is more at home in his everyday leisure outfits of sweat pants, running shoes, and baseball cap. He loves sports--especially baseball and auto racing--and loud rock and roll. He jogs and swims, plays basketball, is careful of his diet, and no longer drinks alcohol in any form. The ever-present cigars, which defined so much of Letterman's earlier image, now seem to be set aside as concession to his new health regime, but occasionally he can be seen with an unlighted stogie clutched between his fingers.

Letterman has what he calls "a small but important collection of German, British and Italian cars," but demurs when asked about his heavy foot on the accelerator. He apparently has collected enough tickets to at last make him wary as he drives back and forth to the studio and around the open spaces near his suburban home. He once lost his license for speeding citations and, writes Bill Zehme in a December 1994 *Esquire* profile, "[He] is a car guy . . . he nearly lost the will to live."

HONORS AND AWARDS

Emmy Awards (National Academy of Television Arts and Sciences): 1981 and 1982, best host and best writing for daytime variety series; 1984,

1985, 1986, best writing for a variety show (with others); 1987, best writing for "Late Night With David Letterman" Fifth Anniversary Show (with others); 1994, for outstanding variety, comedy, or music series
Jack Benny Comedy Award (University of Southern California, 1984
American Comedy Award: 1989, funniest male comedian in a television special, for "Late Night With David Letterman" Sixth Anniversary Show

WRITINGS

The Late Night With David Letterman Book of Top Ten Lists (with writing staff), 1990
An Altogether New Book of Top Ten Lists: From ''Late Night With David Letterman, 1991

Letterman also has written comedy material for a number of series and specials since 1976.

FURTHER READING

BOOKS

Latham, Caroline. *The David Letterman Story*, 1987

PERIODICALS

Current Biography Yearbook 1980
Esquire, Nov. 1986, p.144; Dec. 1994, p.96
Gentlemen's Quarterly, June 1990, p.166; Oct. 1993, p.120
New York Times, Feb. 22, 1994, p.C20; Apr. 10, 1994, Sec. II, p.1; May 15, 1994, Sec.II, p.15
New Yorker, Feb. 1, 1993, p.38; Oct. 18, 1993, p.108
Newsweek, Feb. 3, 1986, p.46; Jan. 25, 1993, p.60
People, Feb. 8, 1994, p.42
Rolling Stone, June 20, 1985, p.24; Nov. 3, 1988, p.70; Feb. 18, 1993, p.32
Time, Feb. 6, 1989, p.66; Jan. 25, 1993, p.60; Aug. 2, 1993, p.55; Aug. 30, 1993, p.51
Vanity Fair, Feb. 1989, p.38

ADDRESS

"Late Show"
Ed Sullivan Theater
1697 Broadway
New York, NY 10019

Rush Limbaugh   1951-
American Political Commentator and Author
Radio and TV Broadcaster

BIRTH

Rush Hudson Limbaugh III (LIM-baw), currently the country's predominant right-wing talk-show host, was born January 12, 1951, at Cape Girardeau, Missouri. In that small industrial city, which lies on the Mississippi River in southeastern Missouri, his family has been prominent for decades in Republican and legal circles. The commentator's late father, Rush Hudson Limbaugh, Jr., was an attorney and longtime Republican county chairman. His mother, Millie Limbaugh, has been active in Republican party politics for much of her adult life. Rush's only sibling, his younger brother, David, is also a lawyer, like his father. An uncle,

Stephen N. Limbaugh, is a lawyer and a Reagan-appointed federal judge. Rush's paternal grandfather was ambassador to India during the Eisenhower administration in the 1950s and recently, at the advanced age of 103, was recognized as the oldest practicing attorney in Cape Girardeau.

YOUTH

The environment of Rush Limbaugh's childhood was typical of upper-middle-class, mid-America in the 1950s. The pace was unhurried. Kids played whiffle ball in fenced backyards, joined Scout troops, and participated in other community activities. Limbaugh was called Rusty then, and still answers to that nickname in his old neighborhood. Despite this seemingly perfect childhood, young Rush felt enormous pressure to live up to the image of his unusually successful family.

Limbaugh grew up feeling lonely, unpopular, and socially insecure. As a teenager he didn't date, didn't have a girlfriend, didn't hang out. He was heavy then, a problem that has plagued him throughout his life. Shy and awkward, he says now that he felt like a "dork." Then radio entered Limbaugh's life. Craig Valle, his best friend from high school, explains in a *Vanity Fair* profile that radio was an interest Rush could develop by himself. "You would find him in his dark bedroom playing with his tape recorder and radio." Despite his lack of social interaction, Rush wasn't somber. He showed signs of a quirky sense of humor and a budding self-confidence. He was a prankster who would "con people over the telephone," recounts *National Review*, "by pretending to be running the Baptist Church's 'Know Your Bible' or the Lions Club's 'Know Your American History' contests. (He and his brother were caught in the latter case because they called the wife of the Lions Club president)."

EDUCATION

Limbaugh attended Cape Girardeau public schools. His teen years were those of the 1960s—a period marked by rebellion against traditional values, antiwar demonstrations, rock festivals, casual sex, and an upsurge in experimentation with drugs. But Rush was different. In explaining how out of touch he was with his own generation, he reveals that he never even owned a pair of blue jeans.

Rush played football and excelled on the debating team during his freshman and sophomore years of high school. And yet Limbaugh has said that school "felt like a prison." As he explains, "I'd be sitting at the breakfast table, dreading school and meanwhile listening to some guy on the radio who sounded like he was having a great time." Eager to get a radio broadcasting license, he coaxed his reluctant father into letting him go to Dallas for a six-week course at Elkins Institute of Radio and Technology. The course completed, Limbaugh returned home to finish high school, although he abandoned his previous extracurricular activities. Instead, with the help of his influential father, he worked his way into KGMO in Cape Girardeau. He started with odd jobs at the station before and after classes and eventually became a disc jockey in 1967. He was just 16. He thought at the time that his patter and music would make him popular with his peers. "It didn't," he concedes. "All it did was make people think that I walked the halls of high school as a stuck-up snob."

After graduating from Central High School in 1969, Limbaugh desperately wanted to pursue a career in radio. But his parents insisted that he attend college, expecting him to become a lawyer like the rest of his family. Limbaugh enrolled at the local college, Southeast Missouri State University. The one year he spent there was unimpressive. "I was in love with radio," he says. "I was immersed in it . . . and, at the time nothing [that college offered] seemed worthwhile." The glib commentator of today's airwaves and television screens flunked freshman speech class for refusing to outline his work. Even now, Limbaugh performs without a script or teleprompter.

Undeterred by his parents' misgivings about his choice of career, Limbaugh dropped out of college after just one year. He later regretted his decision to quit college before earning a degree, so he committed himself to an ambitious, self-directed reading program to compensate for his lack of formal education.

CAREER HIGHLIGHTS

After dropping out of college, Limbaugh began what would be, for the next ten years or so, his first in a series of failed jobs. In 1971 he made his debut in big-city radio in Pittsburgh, Pennsylvania, earning a substantial (for that time) $25,000 a year spinning Top 40 records and dispensing lighthearted nonsense. He worked for two stations during the few years he spent in Pittsburgh, using the pseudonyms Jeff Christie and Rusty Sharpe. He was eventually fired from both—the first time for ignoring proper record rotation, the second time for making political comments on the air. He then moved to a station in Kansas City, where he lasted for three years before again losing his job.

In 1978 Limbaugh left radio and took a job as the director of group sales and special events for the Kansas City Royals baseball team. His annual earnings there were considerably lower than they had been in radio, and he lost all enthusiasm for what he came to consider a dead-end job. "I was going backward," he says. "Yet, through all that, I was never doubtful of my success," he adds with the same conviction and bluster that has marked his rapid rise to celebrity. "From the time I was six years old, I have known that I was going to do something, whatever it was, with fame and notoriety. I've never doubted that. It got me through a lot of the dark days."

After several years with the Royals, Limbaugh returned to radio in 1983, with KMBZ in Kansas City. There, he created a new routine that combined news reading with commentary. His irreverence annoyed his employer, but intrigued the management at KFBK in Sacramento, California. In 1984, Limbaugh became a mid-day host on KFBK, where he replaced an even more outrageous talk-show host, the flamboyant Morton Downey, Jr., who had been fired for making an ethnic slur.

Limbaugh finally had found a comfortable niche espousing, with bombastic and satirical humor, the political views he had learned from his father. In his new venue, he promptly declared himself to be the World Famous Talk-Show Host Rush Limbaugh, and *People* magazine would later refer to him in that rollicking persona as the "Sun King of right-wing beliefs." His show drew an ever-widening listening audience in the Sacramento area, and Limbaugh became a local celebrity. He eventually came to the attention of media tycoon and former ABC Radio president Edward F. McLaughlin, who made Limbaugh a partner in his syndication enterprise and took him to New York in 1988. This would prove to be Limbaugh's big break—his chance at a national show, broadcasting throughout the country on the affiliate stations in the ABC Radio network.

THE PROVOCATIVE VOICE OF THE AIRWAVES

Limbaugh's show for ABC Radio had a shaky start, with only 58 AM stations tuned in to what Limbaugh promoted as his "Excellence in

Broadcasting Network." By 1990, however, he started to connect. Each show became a spontaneous monologue that combined his frequent egotistical self-promotion with caustic satire and witty parodies, often punctuated with short bits from rock songs. Unlike other radio hosts, Limbaugh combined entertainment with sometimes humorous but always lethal political commentary, including attacks on feminists, the NAACP, environmentalists, homosexuals, animal-rights' advocates, gun-control supporters, welfare activists, and others. Underlying it all was his deep-seated suspicion and distrust of big cities, big government, the media, and other institutions. Even those infuriated by his scornful tirades admit to being amused by Limbaugh's witty sniping, although many detect an undercurrent of intolerance and bigotry in his remarks. While friends and foes alike might agree that he is funny, some critics have accused him of distorting numbers, abusing statistical information, failing to provide sources, ridiculing others, and name-calling. A small sampling of the labels he has pinned on his political opposition are "environmental wackos, feminazis [radical feminists], and long-haired maggot-infested dope-smoking peace pansies." "Love him or loathe him," *People* magazine once said, "he's the most provocative voice on the air."

Limbaugh's barbed mockery of the liberal left built an impassioned nationwide audience that soon numbered in the millions, bringing huge advertising revenues to the affiliates that scrambled to be part of the phenomenon. Currently, Limbaugh has about 20 million ardent listeners, mostly white males, who tune in to more than 650 stations. His fans are called "dittoheads" for their shorthand term "ditto," which they use to express agreement with his comments. These fans follow Rush in many medias. He hosts a live radio show from noon to 3 p.m. every weekday and a taped program on late-night TV; he has written two best-sellers, *The Way Things Ought To Be* (1992) and *See, I Told You So* (1993), that together have sold more than seven million copies; and he produces a monthly newsletter, *Limbaugh Letter*, with more than 450,000 subscribers. In addition, his personal appearances consistently attract packed audiences in the small towns and suburbs of the South and the Midwest, where the greatest concentration of his fans are found. "Indeed," says one *U.S. News & World Report*, "Limbaugh has gone beyond politics to become a popular icon, a part of the language . . . and a part of the culture: Several hundred restaurants have opened "Rush Rooms," where fans can eat lunch while listening to his radio show. He has reached that rarified celebrity where one name is sufficient to identify him, like Oprah or Madonna."

Few would argue that Rush Limbaugh is a potent political force who many believe was responsible for the sweeping conservative Republican congressional victory of 1994. Shortly after the election in November of that year, the newly elected Republican members of the 104th Congress voted him an honorary membership, crediting him with delivering to them control of Congress for the first time in 40 years. There has been wide speculation that Limbaugh may soon run for public office himself. Limbaugh insists that he is just an entertainer who simply wants to be "the best radio guy there is." And yet one writer, Stephen Talbot, suggests that the socially awkward young boy from Cape Girardeau still is too uncomfortable around people to risk a political campaign. "He is a radio personality, magically transformed by a microphone," says Talbot in *Mother Jones* magazine, "a man who prefers the security of his studio bubble to the uncontrolled environment of real life. Inside his bubble, Rush can make wild, unfounded assertions that would doom any politician. And he can avoid the debate that would deflate him in a campaign."

MAJOR INFLUENCES

Family members and old friends say that his father undeniably made the greatest impact on Rush Limbaugh's life. His mother, Millie Limbaugh, says that Rush idolized his dad. Boyhood pal Valle remembers the senior Limbaugh as a crusty, opinionated man who exuded strong right-wing politics, telling *Vanity Fair* in 1992, "I think of his father all the time when I hear him." Although he chose his own career instead of studying law, Rush has a mission to prove his own worth to the parent who had fostered his political views since an early and impressionable age. Limbaugh's father died in December 1990. Near the end of his life, he finally was satisfied that his eldest son had found success.

William F. Buckley, Jr., is another idol of Rush Limbaugh. He credits the prominent author, editor, and intellectual with nurturing and enhancing the conservatism that defines his present-day philosophy. It was Buckley, claims Rush, who was his model for learning "to form and frame my beliefs and express them verbally in a concise and understandable way."

MARRIAGE AND FAMILY

Rush Limbaugh has been married three times. His first (brief) marriage, in 1977, was to Roxie McNeely, a secretary at a Kansas City radio station; they were divorced in 18 months. His second wife was Michelle Sixta, whom he met when she was a Royals stadium usherette working her way through college. That union lasted from 1985 until 1990, after Limbaugh's move to New York and the early years of his national radio program.

Limbaugh met his current wife, the former Marta Fitzgerald, through a computer network. She had sought his political advice for a college history class. When he failed to reply, she wrote him a caustic letter that piqued his interest. They began an e-mail relationship that eventually led to courtship and marriage. Supreme Court Justice Clarence Thomas performed the surprise ceremony May 27, 1994, at his home in Fairfax, Virginia, with only ten guests in attendance. The couple now lives in an Upper West Side apartment in Manhattan.

HOBBIES AND OTHER INTERESTS

Reading, which he does avidly, and learning about new computer technology are Rush Limbaugh's favorite pastimes. He also enjoys watching televised sports, especially pro football. He is generous and friendly with his staff and acquaintances, but shies away from membership in clubs or organizations.

Weight gain is a problem that has plagued Limbaugh throughout his life. In recent years his weight has fluctuated between about 250 and well over 300 pounds. He has tried many diets, with little success. For Limbaugh, this is a serious health issue. He has a tendency toward diabetes, which he inherited from his father. Diabetes can be a very serious disease, but its effects can be mitigated by controlling one's diet.

WRITINGS

The Way Things Ought to Be, 1992
See, I Told You So, 1993

HONORS AND AWARDS

Marconi Award (National Association of Broadcasters): 1992
Radio Hall of Fame (Museum of Broadcast Communications): 1993
One of the Most Intriguing People of the Year (*People* magazine): 1993
Outstanding Speaker in Media (Toastmasters International): 1994
Talk Show Host of the Year (National Association of Radio Talk Show Hosts): 1995

FURTHER READING

BOOKS

Davis, J. Bradford. *The Rise of Rush Limbaugh: Toward the Presidency*, 1994
Mahurin, Cecil. *A Public Rebuttal to Rush Limbaugh*, 1993
Muckien, Bruce J. *Rush Limbaugh Said What?!* 1994
Seib, Philip. *Rush Hour: The Politics, Persona and Timing of the Rush Limbaugh Phenomenon*, 1993
Who's Who in America, 1995

PERIODICALS

Current Biography Yearbook 1993
Mother Jones, May/June 1995, p.37 and p.41
National Review, Sep. 6, 1993, p.44
New Republic, May 23, 1994, p.12; Aug. 8, 1994, p.9
New York Times, Mar. 24, 1993, p.C1; Nov. 3, 1994, p.A29
New York Times Book Review, Feb. 21, 1993, p.35

People, Oct. 19, 1992, p.109
Saturday Evening Post, May/June 1993, p.54
Time, Sep. 23, 1991, p.65; Oct. 26, 1992, p.76; Nov. 1, 1993, p.60; Jan. 23, 1995, p.22
U.S. News & World Report, Aug. 16, 1993, p.27
Vanity Fair, May 1992, p.157

ADDRESS

Station WABC
2 Penn Plaza, 17th Floor
New York, NY 10023

Heather Locklear   1961-
American Actress
Star of Fox TV's Hit Series "Melrose Place"

BIRTH

Heather Locklear was born on September 25, 1961, in Los Angeles, California. Her parents are Bill Locklear, the director of the career placement office at UCLA (University of California—Los Angeles), and Diane Locklear, formerly a homemaker and now an administrative assistant at Disney. Heather is the youngest of their four children, with two sisters, Laurie and Colleen, and one brother, Mark.

YOUTH

The Locklear family started out in Canoga Park, a suburb just 20 minutes north of Hollywood. When Heather was six, they moved to Westlake. She had a happy home life there, with loving parents who always encouraged her and her siblings to work hard in school. But she was also painfully shy and socially awkward. "I was always shy— somebody had to make the first move," Locklear now says. She was also physically graceless. She was stick-thin, with knock knees and crooked teeth (and later braces)—"all knees and elbows," she now laughs.

EDUCATION

Locklear attended Newbury Park High School in Ventura County. It's hard to imagine now, but the blond bombshell on "Melrose Place" was a wallflower as a teenager, not popular at all. "[The] closest I came to getting somewhere was when I tried out for cheerleader. I didn't make it, and it was a rejection that took me a long time to get over." Things started to change in her senior year, when she was elected to her school's homecoming court—but as one of the Princesses, not as Homecoming Queen.

After graduating from high school in 1979, Locklear enrolled at UCLA as a psychology student. She didn't last long there, though. She took a drama class, although she failed it when she was too shy to stand up in front of the whole room to do a monologue. She also posed as a model in a school catalog and was soon discovered. She hired an agent and started landing small parts, first in TV commercials and later in TV and movies.

Encouraged by her quick success and the good money, she was soon fed up with school. The turning point came early in her sophomore year when she had to stay up all night to work on an English paper. The next day she marched into her father's office and declared that she was dropping out of school to become an actress.

FIRST JOBS

Locklear's first acting jobs included commercials for the California Dairy Council, Sea & Ski sun lotion, Polaroid cameras, Tame hair products, Toyota trucks, and both Pepsi and Coke. From there, she went on to one-line, walk-on parts, starting with the feature film *240-Robert* and going on to such TV movies as *Return of the Beverly Hillbillies* and *Twirl.*

CAREER HIGHLIGHTS

After Locklear quit college, it took only nine months until she got her big break. In 1981, she answered a casting call for a part on the nighttime soap opera series "Dynasty," then in its first season. At the age of 20, with very little experience, Locklear beat out 450 actresses who auditioned for the part. She got a contract for 13 shows as Sammy Jo, the scheming, nasty wife of Steven Carrington. At the end of that season, she was out of a job.

She soon landed a part on another series, "T.J. Hooker," playing rookie cop Stacy Sheridan. In the meantime, though, the executives at "Dynasty" decided to write her character back into the story. Suddenly, Locklear was in the enviable position of appearing in two successful primetime series, co-starring with William Shatner in "T.J. Hooker" from 1982 through 1986 and with Joan Collins and Linda Evans in "Dynasty" from 1981 through 1989. With acting lessons added in between shooting her scenes on the two shows, Locklear kept very busy.

Following the demise of those two series, her career went through a bit of a dry spell. She appeared in commercials for a chain of fitness clubs, a mildly successful exercise video in 1990, several made-for-TV movies, the feature films *Firestarter* and *Return of the Swamp Thing*, and a short-lived TV sitcom called "Going Places." That dry spell lasted a few years, until she landed the role on "Melrose Place."

"MELROSE PLACE"

"Melrose Place" debuted in July 1992. Originally a spinoff from the successful Fox series "Beverly Hills, 90210," "Melrose Place" moved from teenagers to a group of twentysomething characters who lived in apartments in the same building, all grappling with living on their own and working at their first jobs. But critical response to the show was hostile and condescending and the ratings were abysmal, so the producers decided to change its format. They eliminated issues-oriented themes, shifting the focus to characters and their relationships. They also changed from closed-ended episodes that dealt with a single issue to an open-ended series, soap-opera style, that showcased many ongoing, interrelated plots and intrigues amongst the characters. And, perhaps most importantly, in January 1993 they added Heather Locklear, who brought romance and intrigue, along with a bit of wickedness, to the series. Originally slated for just a few episodes, she was an immediate success.

Locklear plays the sophisticated, manipulative, catty, and even malicious Amanda Woodward, "an advertising executive with a Barbie doll figure and a scratch-your-eyes-out attitude," as the *New York Times* described her. She quickly dominated the inhabitants of Melrose Place—even buying the apartment complex and becoming their live-in landlord. Playing the bad girl, Amanda brought tension, conflict, and sizzle to a series that had become dull. Her performance has been so convincing that reporters consistently marvel at how nice Locklear really is, and how utterly different she is from the character she plays. As the producer Aaron Spelling points out, "You would think everybody on the set would loathe Heather—she gets all the covers, all the publicity—but they adore her."

Since Locklear joined the show, critical response is still lukewarm, but fans love it. Ratings surged after the character of Amanda Woodward was introduced, and the show became "a compulsively watchable, high-trash hit with almost unbeatable demographics," according to *People* magazine. "Melrose Place" is currently the No. 2 dramatic series among viewers aged 18 to 34—after "Beverly Hills, 90210"—and all agree that Locklear deserves much of the credit. The show, in fact, has become something of a cult favorite, "one of TV's campiest, trashiest, guiltiest pleasures," as *TV Guide* described it. Hooked, fans stop everything to watch it— sometimes in groups, sometimes secretly, alone—eager to see just what sort of trouble Amanda and friends have cooked up that week.

MARRIAGE AND FAMILY

Locklear met Tommy Lee, her future husband and the drummer for the band Motley Crue, while backstage at an REO Speedwagon concert in Los Angeles. They were married on May 10, 1986. The couple separated in August 1993 amidst rumors of his infidelity while on the road touring with Motley Crue, and Locklear and Lee are now in the middle of a divorce. While Locklear has described the experience as painful, she has refused to discuss it with the press.

Following their breakup, Locklear began dating Richie Sambora, lead guitarist with Bon Jovi, in February 1994. At first, spending time together was a logistical nightmare. Locklear had to remain in southern California while filming "Melrose Place," and Sambora was on the East Coast recording Bon Jovi's newest album. They must have found some time together, though, because Locklear and Sambora became engaged in September 1994. At press time, no wedding plans had been announced.

HOBBIES AND OTHER INTERESTS

Locklear still lives outside Los Angeles, just minutes from her parents, and sees them often. She has two dogs, a Yorkie named Kitty and a Maltese named Harley. She enjoys lots of physical activity and working out.

CREDITS

"Dynasty," 1981-89
"T.J. Hooker," 1982-86
"Melrose Place," 1993-

HONORS AND AWARDS

Golden Apple Award (Hollywood Women's Press Club): 1983, as New
  Discovery of the Year

FURTHER READING

PERIODICALS

Details, Oct. 1994, p.138
Los Angeles Magazine, Feb. 1994, p.28
New York Times, Apr. 3, 1994, Section 9, p.1
People, Feb. 7, 1983, p.102; May 26, 1986, p.116; Feb. 21, 1994, p.65
Philadelphia Enquirer, June 4, 1989, p.L2
Rolling Stone, May 1994, p.48
TV Guide, Dec. 27, 1986, p.26; Apr. 3, 1993, p.22; Feb. 5, 1994, p.18
Us, Sep. 1993, p.70
Washington Post, May 3, 1994, p.B1 (2 articles)

ADDRESS

"Melrose Place"
P.O. Box 900
Beverly Hills, CA 90213

Reba McEntire   1955-
American Singer, Songwriter, Actress, and Businesswoman

BIRTH

Reba Nell McEntire was born on March 28, 1955, in McAlester, Oklahoma. She was the third of four children born to Clark Vincent McEntire, a rancher and rodeo rider, and Jacqueline Smith McEntire, a schoolteacher and singer who gave up a musical career to raise her family. Alice, the oldest of the McEntire siblings, was the only one of the four not to pursue a musical career. Reba's older brother, Pake, also embarked upon a career in country music. Her little sister, Susie, who married rodeo star Paul Luchsinger in 1981, has become one of the top female Christian vocalists in the United States.

YOUTH

The McEntire clan was not wealthy in terms of money, but they were supported by a rich family legacy. Reba's grandfather, John McEntire, was a world champion steer-roper in 1934, and her father won the title in 1957, 1958, and 1961. All the children inherited their dad's determination, grit, and competitive drive, working hard on the family's 7,000-acre cattle ranch near Kiowa, in southeastern Oklahoma. The McEntire kids would get up at 4 a.m. to help work the herds and worm and brand cattle. Taking after their father, they would play at holding mock rodeos, throwing lariats at their bicycles. Reba began entering rodeos on her own at the age of 11. One of her best events was the barrel race, in which contestants are timed as they weave through an obstacle course of barrels on horseback. But she never let performing in rodeos interfere with her first love— music—and she often sang the national anthem before her events.

Reba inherited her love of music from her mother, Jacqueline McEntire. During the long car rides from one of her husband's rodeos to the next, for example, she taught the kids three-part harmony. It was while travelling the summer rodeo circuit with her family that Reba realized that she could earn money with music. After watching Pake hoist a guitar and earn a quarter singing and strumming in a hotel lobby, the red-headed, five-year-old Reba chimed in and got a nickel from one of the onlookers. As a child, Reba sometimes pretended to be a singing star by singing into a hairbrush in front of the mirror. In the first grade, she finally performed for a real audience, singing "Away in a Manger" for her school Christmas show. During junior high school, Reba, Pake, and Susie formed "The Singing McEntires." They played at country fairs, rodeos, and at dance clubs in nearby Ardmore, Oklahoma, for 13 dollars a night.

EDUCATION

In school, McEntire excelled in athletics, music, and academics. A member of the cheerleading squad, she also played guard on the Kiowa High School basketball team and ran track. Still, singing remained the activity closest to her heart. In pursuing this interest, she first helped organize and later performed in the eight-member High School Cowboy Band. The band, which won contests and booked a number of paying jobs, would graduate several professional musicians from among its ranks. Remembering some of the dance halls they played in back then, McEntire said: "The club audiences could be rough, but they gave us good training in how to work a crowd. Some of those dances turned into fistfights set to music. More often than not, it was so dark in those clubs that we couldn't even see them fighting. We just thought they were all dancing, and we'd play right through it." McEntire was also a good student, and she graduated as co-salutatorian of her high school class. With money saved from band and rodeo appearances, she enrolled at Durant, Oklahoma's Southeastern State University, planning to follow her mother into a teaching career. Before she graduated from college, however, her career plans changed significantly.

CHOOSING A CAREER

During college, McEntire continued to compete in rodeo events and showed increasing promise as a horsewoman. However, her rodeo appearances eventually began showcasing her vocal talents more than her equestrian skills. In fact, it was through a rodeo appearance that McEntire got her first break as an aspiring songstress. Texas singer-songwriter Red Steagall heard the 19-year-old college student perform at Oklahoma City's National Finals Rodeo in December 1974. Impressed by her clear, powerful voice, Steagall encouraged McEntire to accelerate her college studies, go to Nashville, and make a demo tape. He circulated her tape around Music City until Mercury Records signed her in 1975. In 1976, at the age of 21, McEntire decided to give up rodeo competition for good and concentrate all her energy on her music. She graduated from college later that year with a major in elementary education and minor in music, and then immediately headed to Nashville.

CAREER HIGHLIGHTS

The year 1976 proved to be a good time to hit Nashville. Country music was going through a period of transition. Reigning country queens like Loretta Lynn and Tammy Wynette were leaving their thrones, while the rock-and-roll based singers of the following decades' "Young Country" movement had yet to arrive. Along with artists like Randy Travis and Ricky Skaggs, who began the move back to country music's traditional roots, McEntire would soon carve a deep niche in the country music market.

Success in the music business was slow in coming, however. The first single off McEntire's 1976 self-titled debut album, "I Don't Want to Be a One Night Stand," caused scarcely a ripple in country music's Top 100. Shuttled among several producers at Mercury, McEntire never clearly defined her own "sound," which meant that her songs were not easily identifiable to the country radio audience. "Three Sheets in the Wind," a duet with fellow Mercury artist Jacky Ward, finally made it to the Top 20. But it was not until her third album that McEntire scored a single in the Top 10, "(You Lift Me Up) to Heaven," and she had to wait until 1982 for her first Number One hit. "Can't Even Get the Blues No More" was the first of two chart toppers off her fifth album, *Unlimited*.

During the early 1980s McEntire worked hard at increasing her exposure, opening concerts for popular stars like the Statler Brothers, Conway Twitty, and Ronnie Milsap. Then McEntire ran into MCA-Nashville president

Jimmy Bowen, who encouraged the talented—but frustrated—vocalist to take charge of her own career. She switched record labels to MCA-Nashville in 1984 and scored her second Number One hit with "How Blue," a single off that year's *My Kind of Country.* That album, her seventh, marked McEntire as country music's first female "neo-traditionalist"—a label given to singers who returned to a more basic form of country music than was popular at the time. Rather than recording songs that were picked by a producer, McEntire took her career firmly by the reins and insisted on performing songs that went back to basics, that she considered "her kind of country." *My Kind of Country* quickly jumped to *Billboard* magazine's Top Ten album list, partly because McEntire decided to drop the lushly orchestrated background music of her previous releases. "I'm basically the only female artist doing traditional country music right now," she explained at the time. "I don't want to be drowned out by string sections and backup singers. I'm singin' my guts out and I want to be heard."

The shift toward tradition didn't end with McEntire's musical style. Where Mercury had packaged her in glamorous sequinned gowns, *My Kind of Country* showcased her wearing jeans, with a big silver belt buckle from the National Finals Rodeo. "It takes a long time to figure out who you are and what you are," she confided at the time. "And now I've found an image that's comfortable with me—finally, after I've grown up and matured and stopped listening to so many other people instead of just myself—and that is, just to be *me.*" While her image became more folksy, McEntire's stage shows grew more sophisticated with help from choreographers and lighting directors—an indication of things to come.

McEntire's switch to hard-core country paid off. From 1984 to 1987 she swept the Country Music Association (CMA) Female Vocalist of the Year awards, and in 1986 she became the 61st member of Nashville's traditional Grand Ole Opry. As Bob Allen noted in *Country Music,* "Reba has become, much as Loretta Lynn was in the 1960s and 1970s, the voice of America's silent female majority, the voice of the American woman of the 1980s." In an industry dominated by male artists whose staying power depends on their appeal to female country music fans—who buy the majority of albums and concert tickets—McEntire's ability to identify with and inspire women was crucial in her rise to the top.

The next few years saw a new, more subtle shift in her musical direction as Nashville was overrun with neo-traditional country artists. Working with MCA's Tony Brown, McEntire began to scout the fringes of pop music territory with *Whoever's in New England* (1986). It became her first Gold Album. Two years later, on *Reba,* she included the blues classic "Sunday Kind of Love," and she began opening her stage shows by wrapping her big voice around a cover of Aretha Franklin's Motown hit "Respect." As her musical style evolved, her image changed as well. "Musically and personally, Reba has come of age," proclaimed Allen. "[The] big, shiny 'REBA' belt buckle, the sunburnt Oklahoma squint, the leather cowgirl skirts and the twin fiddle/steel guitar sound—is gone. . . . The 'new' Reba . . . favors sequins, flowing gowns, big hair, carefully choreographed stage moves, flashy costume changes, blue lights and synthesizers. This girl has definitely moved uptown."

The hard-core honky-tonk audience that had embraced her traditional image now began to feel alienated by McEntire's push toward a more commercially viable sound. But the sales figures of each new, progressively more pop album told a different story. "They all say they want me to go back to traditional music," McEntire said of her more strident fans in 1990, "but the majority of people obviously don't want to hear me sing traditional, even though I love to sing it and could probably sit and do it all my life." The more urban appeal of her new approach was best illustrated by the standing ovation she received before a sold-out crowd at Carnegie Hall in 1987.

In 1989, McEntire took another giant step toward increasing her exposure and courting a mainstream audience. She served as guest host on TV's "Good Morning America," and she made her film acting debut in the comic science-fiction movie *Tremors* the following year. Musically, *Rumor Has It* (1990) was McEntire's first true crossover album. Co-produced with Tony Brown, the album featured synthesizers and complex background vocals. This slick, pop sound mirrored the change in her concert tours. Compared—sometimes unfavorably—to large-production Broadway or Las Vegas shows, her stage shows boasted numerous costume changes, dance crews, laser lights, special effects, and other multi-media elements.

BAND KILLED IN PLANE CRASH

Tragedy struck the singer in March of 1991. After a tour date in San Diego—while McEntire stayed behind to rest from a bout with bronchitis before moving on to a Saturday night concert in Fort Wayne, Indiana— the plane carrying seven members of her band and her tour manager crashed near the airport, killing everyone aboard. The tragedy deeply affected McEntire, who reacted by plunging into a new album and a new movie, Kenny Rogers's *The Luck of the Draw: The Gambler Returns* (1991). Although some fans criticized her for diving into her work so soon after the tragedy, McEntire was dealing with her pain in true rodeo fashion: by getting back up on the horse. Her 1992 album, *For My Broken Heart,* with its ballads of heartache and sadness, was her personal therapy. "The crew and the two band members who survived couldn't talk about it at first," she explained a year later. "We had to talk. We had to work. We had to get back on the road, back on the stage and back on the planes. It took us all a long time to get things into focus again, to get the hurt to go away. But it doesn't. It never really has."

Despite her personal loss and the changes in her musical focus, McEntire never broke her stride, continuing to tour nine months out of the year. Her 1992 tour was the third-highest grossing country tour in the United States. And her 1993 winter-spring concert tour was the fourth-highest grossing of any musical group touring the country, ranking behind only perennial tour favorites the Grateful Dead, Paul McCartney, and Neil Diamond. By 1994, McEntire had become the highest-grossing country act in the nation, netting almost $19 million from 71 shows. She had also sold more than 20 million records. *Read My Mind*, which topped the charts in 1994, found the singer moving away from her characteristic ballads. Songs like "She Thinks His Name Was John"—about a woman dying of AIDS as a result of a one-night stand—and the rollicking "Why Haven't I Heard from You" showed a more mature voice. McEntire capitalized on the album's success by producing and starring in the made-for-TV movie *Is There Life Out There?* based upon the sentiment of a 1991 hit single. She also published her autobiography, entitled *Reba: My Story*, which reached the number two position on the *New York Times* best-seller list two weeks after its 1994 publication.

THOUGHTS ON BEING A PERFORMER

"I love the immediate feedback you get from an audience," McEntire admits. "The applause lets you know immediately that they like what you're doing." That desire for recognition has continued to fuel her career as a performer. "There was a place for my music, but not for me," she recalls thinking when she first arrived in Nashville. "I was just a singer. I didn't have an image, I didn't have a style. I just sang. Heck, I felt like a fish out of water." Since then, she has expanded the role of female vocalists within a male-dominated music industry. "Deciding to go real country was a big gamble to take, 'cause I didn't know if the people would really like to hear me sing straight-ahead country or not," she remembers thinking in the mid-1980s. "But thank God they did, 'cause I just got tired of goin' the contemporary route. . . . And I knew that if I was ever gonna make it in this business and be successful, I had to be me."

McEntire began co-producing her albums in 1984, which gave her greater artistic control. By 1990, she could confidently exclaim: "I think I've grown up. I'm not so dead set on making everyone else happy and pleased. I don't listen to anybody's input as much as I listen to my own gut feeling." While recognizing the importance of tradition in country music, McEntire also finds satisfaction in challenging herself and expanding her achievements. "I am very curious, very driven," she explains. "I'm always wondering what I can do next; is there something I can do better? Tradition is great if it continues to work, but I want to be flexible to change as well."

Critics credit McEntire's success in part to her knack for finding good songs. Instead of planning an album around two or three hits, she makes sure all the cuts are potential singles. In addition, she has always been drawn to material that is socially relevant to women, including issues like spousal abuse, divorce, illegal imprisonment, and the AIDS crisis. "I tend to center my songs for women," she explains. But she rejects many songs that depict women as weak-willed victims of circumstance. "I know a song is right when I hear it, just like I know a dress is right when I put it on. The wonderful thing is that even though I look for songs that speak to women, I find that when women like them, the men like them too."

McEntire's position as the reigning queen of country music rests equally upon her talent and upon her personal credo: "I want to do so much more. I want my family life, my personal life, my public life. I want to have my cake and eat it too. I like to take challenges and gambles. I don't care to play it safe." But as a seasoned veteran, McEntire also recognizes that the demands of a career in country music today are much different than they were when she boarded a bus bound for Nashville as a 21-year-old ex-barrel racer from Oklahoma. "I never would have expected it to be this way," she admits. "It took me eight LPs to take charge of my career and my music and realize there's a better way of doing it. Nowadays the artists are so pushed, that after one Top Five record, they're working 200 dates a year. By the time the first year's over with, I've seen so many

of them be so burned out they don't even want to hear someone hum around them."

MAJOR INFLUENCES

Growing up, McEntire listened to singers like Anne Murray, Barbra Streisand, Dolly Parton, and Loretta Lynn. Her favorite performers are Barbara Mandrell, who has inspired her stage shows, and Patsy Cline, who has inspired her emotional delivery. In fact, McEntire consulted with Harlan Howard, Cline's former co-songwriter, when putting together 1984's *My Kind of Country*. "I get people who knew her to tell me about her, and I read everything I can get on her. Nobody yet has sung better," she says of her idol.

MARRIAGE AND FAMILY

McEntire met rancher Charlie Battles at the Oklahoma City National Rodeo Finals, where she sang the national anthem and won her big silver belt buckle, in 1974. They were married in 1976 and lived on Battles' 250-acre ranch in Stringtown, Oklahoma, until their marriage ended in 1987. They had no children. McEntire's divorce caused a rift between her and some of her fans, who had seen in her lyrics a belief in the strength of family ties and traditional institutions.

In 1989 McEntire married Narvel Blackstock, a pedal-steel player who had joined her band in 1980 and gone on to become her manager. The couple has one son, Shelby Steven McEntire Blackstock, born in February 1990. McEntire—as dedicated a mother as she is a performer—flies home each night to be with Shelby. If she is on the road for several days, he accompanies her on tour. McEntire and her family make their home outside Nashville, Tennessee, in a Victorian-style, four-story mansion on a 32-acre estate, located across the street from their 42-acre, 29-horse Thoroughbred farm.

HOBBIES AND OTHER INTERESTS

In her spare time, McEntire enjoys watching the soap operas "All My Children" and "One Life to Live," as well as golfing, shopping, being with her husband and son, and raising horses. She is also an avid movie fan. Some of her favorites include *Gone with the Wind, Forrest Gump,* and *Steel Magnolias.* Barbara Stanwyck is her favorite film actress; in fact, McEntire hopes one day to follow in Stanwyck's footsteps and win an Oscar.

In 1988 McEntire organized a small booking agency. Under the guidance of her second husband, "Reba's Business" became Starstruck Entertainment, a management company handling country talents like Linda Davis and Aaron Tippin. Starstruck now incorporates flight services—begun in the wake of the 1991 tragedy—a trucking company, a racehorse farm, a construction and land development company, an advertising agency, and three publishing firms.

Active in community causes, McEntire was the spokesperson for the Middle Tennessee United Way in 1988, and she was the national spokesperson for the American Lung Association from 1990 to 1991. She is actively involved in the Texoma Medical Center, a retreat for single, pregnant women without the financial means to take care of themselves and their unborn babies. "I've had a lot of good fortune come my way," says McEntire, "and to be able to help people less fortunate makes me happy." McEntire is also devout in her faith in God, although she doesn't belong to any organized church. "I am not a religious person, but I am a spiritual person," she explains. "I feel I have a very personal relationship with God." Her spirituality is reflected in her down-to-earth attitude: "No matter what you achieve in life, you're always wondering, 'Is there something I'm missing?' You may have all the money in the world and the fame and the glory, but the smallest, simplest things will bring you more pleasure."

CREDITS

RECORDINGS

Reba McEntire, 1978
Out of a Dream, 1979
Feel the Fire, 1980
Heart to Heart, 1981
Unlimited, 1982
Behind the Scenes, 1983
Just a Little Love, 1984
My Kind of Country, 1984
Have I Got a Deal for You, 1985
The Best of Reba McEntire, 1985
Whoever's in New England, 1986
What Am I Gonna Do about You, 1986
Reba McEntire's Greatest Hits, Volume 1, 1987
The Last One to Know, 1987
Merry Christmas to You, 1987
Reba, 1988
Sweet Sixteen, 1989
Reba Live, 1989
Rumor Has It, 1990
For My Broken Heart, 1991
It's Your Call, 1992
Greatest Hits, Volume II, 1993
Read My Mind, 1994

FILMS

Tremors, 1989
The Luck of the Draw: The Gambler Returns, 1991
Man from Left Field, 1993
Is There Life Out There? 1994
North, 1994
The Little Rascals, 1994
Buffalo Girls, 1995

WRITINGS

Reba: My Story (with Tom Carter), 1994

AWARDS AND HONORS

Country Music Association: 1984, 1985, 1986, 1987, Female Vocalist of the
  Year; 1986, Entertainer of the Year; 1994, Vocal Event of the Year
Academy of Country Music: 1985, 1986, 1987, 1988, 1991, 1992, 1995, Top
  Female Vocalist of the Year; 1987, 1992, Video of the Year; 1995, Enter-
  ainer of the Year
Music City News Awards: 1985, 1986, 1987, 1988, 1989, Female Artist of the
  Year; 1987, Country Music Video of the Year; 1994, Best Vocal Collabor-
  ation
Grammy Awards: 1987, Best Country Vocal Performance, Female; 1994,
  Best Country Vocal Collaboration (with Linda Davis)
American Music Awards: 1987, Favorite Female Country Video Artist; 1988,
  1989, 1990, 1991, 1992, 1993, 1994, Favorite Female Country Vocalist; 1991,
  1993, Best Album
TNN Viewers' Choice Awards: 1988, 1989, 1993, Favorite Female Vocalist;
  1994, Best Vocal Duet
People's Choice Awards: 1992, Favorite Female Vocalist; 1992, 1993, 1994,
  Favorite Female Country Vocalist
Country Radio Awards: 1994, Entertainer of the Year; 1994, Female Vocalist
  of the Year
Billboard Magazine Awards: 1994, Favorite Female Country Artist

FURTHER READING

BOOKS

Cusic, Don. *Reba: Country Music's Queen,* 1991
Leggett, Carol. *Reba McEntire: The Queen of Country,* 1992
McEntire, Reba, with Tom Carter. *Reba: My Story,* 1994
Stambler, Irwin, and Grelun Landon. *Encyclopedia of Folk, Country & Western
  Music,* 1983

PERIODICALS

Cosmopolitan, Aug. 1988, p.28
Country Music, Aug. 1986, p.26; July/Aug. 1989, p.33; Nov. 12, 1990, p.31;
    Jan./Feb. 1993, p.42
Current Biography Yearbook 1994
Ladies' Home Journal, Mar. 1993, p.137
Los Angeles Times, Feb. 29, 1985, section 6, p.3
Philadelphia Inquirer, Apr. 21, 1985, p.E11
Saturday Evening Post, Mar./Apr. 1995, p.39
Stereo Review, Aug. 1985, p.54
Woman's Day, Nov. 3, 1992, p.110

ADDRESS

REBA International Fan Club
P.O. Box 121996
Nashville, TN 37212

Joe Montana   1956-
American Professional Football Player with the
Kansas City Chiefs
Three-Time MVP of the Super Bowl

BIRTH

Joseph C. Montana, Jr., was born June 11, 1956, in New Eagle,
Pennsylvania, to Joseph Montana, Sr., and Theresa Montana. He
was their only child. Joe Sr. was a manager of a local finance company and Theresa was a secretary with the same firm in the city
of Monongahela, where Joe grew up.

EARLY MEMORIES

Joe Sr. used to come home from work and find his son sitting on
the steps waiting to play. Joe Jr. had received a bat and ball when

he was just a year old, and from his earliest memories, he loved to play ball, any kind of ball. Some of the people in Monongahela thought Joe's dad pushed him into sports, but Joe insists he has always just loved to play. Father and son would practice nearly every day, using a neighbor's yard, with Joe often throwing the football through a tire swing to improve his aim.

BECOMING A YOUNG SPORTS STAR

Joe played three major sports from grade school through high school. His dad got him into a pee wee football league when he was eight, even though the rules stated that the players had to be nine, by lying about his age. His coaches from his earliest experiences in football were astonished at his natural talent for the game. He had learned to read the defense, to anticipate plays, and to throw the ball with accuracy when he was still in elementary school. When Joe was 10, his dad organized a basketball league for Joe and the local kids, and it was the young Montana's favorite sport for years. Joe played Little League baseball in the spring and summer, pitching three perfect games by the time he was in junior high.

When he was 11, Joe thought he had burned out on sports, He saw his cousins going to Boy Scout meetings and other non-sport activities, and he thought maybe he was missing out on something. He thought about quitting, but his dad made him stick it out to the end of the season. Then, he decided to stay with it.

Montana is from the Monongahela Valley, or the "Mon Valley" as the locals call it. The people of this coal-mining region 20 miles south of Pittsburgh take their football very seriously. No one is exactly sure why, but this area has produced some of the finest quarterbacks of all time, including Johnny Unitas, Joe Namath, Dan Marino, George Blanda, Jim Kelly, and Terry Hanratty, a Notre Dame quarterback who was Joe Montana's idol growing up.

EDUCATION

Joe went to the local public schools, including Waverly Elementary, Finleyville Junior High, and Ringgold High School. He was a good student, a great sports star, and always rather shy.

In high school, Montana was a B-student who was involved in extracurriculars that weren't all sports: he was class vice president in his senior year, and he sang in the choir. But it was athletics that defined his future.

His high school football coach, Chuck Abramski, was tough, outspoken, and as Montana remembers, an "explosive" kind of guy. He built a high quality football program at Ringgold by demanding a lot from his players and from the community, whom he talked into buying new uniforms and equipment for the team. Montana was a tall, skinny kid, and Abramski nicknamed him "Joe Banana." Joe started as quarterback for Ringgold in the middle of his junior year, and his prowess on the field led him to the attention of every major college in the country—he was recruited by 50 schools.

When he graduated in 1974, *Parade Magazine* named him as an All-American quarterback. He also received a basketball scholarship from North Carolina State, and was also offered a major league tryout based on his baseball skills.

But Montana had his sights set on Notre Dame and football. It was the school of his idol, Terry Hanratty, and was known for academic and sports excellence. "I knew if I could do well at Notre Dame, I could fulfill a lifelong dream," says Montana in his autobiography, *Audibles*. "Also, because Notre Dame stressed academics, I would graduate with a significant degree."

CAREER HIGHLIGHTS

NOTRE DAME

Montana was one of seven freshman quarterbacks at Notre Dame. He played only a few minutes per game in his freshman year, and he got pummeled in practice. The adjustment to college was tough for Montana. He was very close to his folks, and he missed them a lot. The courses were hard, too, and Montana found himself on academic probation his sophomore year. Also in his sophomore year, the legendary football coach Ara Parsegian resigned, and Dan Devine became the head coach. Devine was a different kind of coach, and Montana had a hard time understanding him and what he wanted.

During his sophomore year at Notre Dame, Montana got a chance to play on the varsity squad, when starting quarterback Rick Slager got injured. Eager to show what he could do, Montana sat out his third year, 1976, because of a separated shoulder. He was "red-shirted" that year, meaning that he took the year off from sports, but was allowed to start the next year as a junior, effectively taking five years to graduate and playing four seasons of football.

Montana was plagued with injuries during his career at Notre Dame, and he never got to play an entire season. He was often frustrated when Coach Devine would bench him. It ruined his confidence in himself, and he just couldn't understand why he couldn't get out there and play.

While at Notre Dame, Montana gained the nickname the "Comeback Kid" for a chain of come-from-behind victories that wowed the fans. In Notre Dame wins over Tennessee, Pittsburgh, and Air Force, Montana rallied the Irish offense during the last minutes of the game and pulled his team to victory. In the 1977 Cotton Bowl, Montana solidified his reputation as the comeback champ in what became known as the "Chicken Soup Bowl." A freak snowstorm had created an icy, windy day in Dallas. Notre Dame was down by 22 points to Houston at halftime, with Montana in the locker room suffering from hypothermia (his body temperature had dropped to 96 degrees because of the cold). He begged the coaches to let him play, but they wouldn't until his temperature came up to normal. Montana drank cup after cup of chicken broth until his temp returned to 98.6 degrees, and he returned to the field. With seven minutes left to go in the game, Montana led Notre Dame to a 35-34 victory over Houston, astonishing and delighting fans all over the country.

Through it all Montana displayed his famous cool, calm, tough leadership, which had been noted from the time he was a kid playing pee wee ball. "Whenever he came on the field," said former Notre Dame teammate Bob Golic, "the players knew they had a friend coming in." "When the pressure came," said 49ers safety Dave Waymer, "we knew he was the guy who wouldn't overheat."

SAN FRANCISCO 49ERS

After graduating from Notre Dame in 1979 with a degree in marketing, Montana became eligible for the NFL draft. He was taken by the San Francisco 49ers at the end of the third round, signing a three-year contract with a salary of $50,000 the first year, and $70,000 and $85,000 for each of the next two years. Many thought that Montana was too short and too thin to make it in the pros, which at that time favored taller men with a high release point on the ball. But Bud Walsh, the legendary coach of the 49ers, wanted Joe Montana. He was looking for a quarterback who was fast, intelligent, able to move and think quickly. "As soon as I saw Joe's beautiful, gliding footwork—quick natural steps, just poetry in motion, I knew we could develop the disciplines in him that would have been difficult with someone slower or less athletic."

Walsh was the first NFL coach to script the first sequence of plays the offense was to use in a game. That means that he would design an order of up to 25 plays that the offense would use to drive down the field for a touchdown. The concept was relatively new in pro ball, and with it Walsh, Montana, and the 49ers became one of the powerhouses in the NFL.

Much has been written about Montana's uncanny ability to read the defense, to remain cool under pressure, and to bring an almost mystical sense to the game. He calls what he does "feeling the colors." "Feeling the color is how I'm able to tell when I'm getting pressured in the pocket," explains Montana in *Audibles*. "As the ball is snapped I picture the play. It's like a movie running through my mind." "When the defense puts on a strong rush I see the colors. I only see colors, not faces, helmets, arms, or legs. Just that wall. If the wall of colors quickly changes from red to white in the first two steps of my dropback, things register automatically."

Montana further explains: "I have recognition. The experience to see everything on the field. I'm not a great runner, but I feel that I can make something happen if the play breaks down. And while I'll make mistakes, I'm a safe thrower who doesn't take chances unless the situation calls for it."

Montana started in only one game and appeared in 13 others during his first year in the pros, but that was part of Walsh's plan. He wanted to bring his young quarterback along slowly, to develop him carefully and not put pressure on him too early.

In a game in the 1980 season, Montana led the 49ers to the biggest comeback in NFL history. Losing early in the game 35-7 to New Orleans, Montana guided the 49ers to a 38-35 victory in overtime. The comeback kid was doing his thing in the NFL. In 1981, Montana became part of sports history with a play now known simply as "The Catch." In a post season win over Dallas, he threw a pass in the closing seconds to Dwight Clark. Montana remembers it like this: "On the touchdown play my concentration level was never so high. I remember pump-faking to get those guys chasing me off the ground, just like when I was playing basketball with my dad. I remember trying to get the ball to Dwight high, so no one else could get it. I never saw the catch. I heard the crowd roar."

That win landed the 49ers in the Super Bowl, where they beat the Cincinnati Bengals, 26-21. Montana was named MVP, his first of three such honors. He negotiated a four-year, $1.7 million contract and began to receive offers for a flood of endorsements. The 1982 season proved to be a disappointment for the 49ers. They didn't play that well, and tensions were high on and off the field because of a players' strike. The year 1983 was better for the team, but the 49ers were unable to advance beyond the NFC title game.

Montana's 1984 season was terrific. He had the highest NFL quarterback rating, at 102.9, and he led the 49ers to another Super Bowl and Super Bowl victory, where they beat the Miami Dolphins, 38-16. Once again, Montana was named MVP.

In 1985, Montana negotiated a six-year, $6.3 million contract. He was being called the greatest quarterback of all time and was riding a crest of success and popularity, when, out of nowhere, rumors of drug use appeared. The stories were never verified, but, because they persisted, Montana felt he needed to make a public statement denying them. The quiet, private Montana did his best to deal with the negative publicity, but the accusations and the fact that some people believed them hurt him deeply. That year, the 49ers lost to the New York Giants in a bid for the playoffs.

In the first game of the 1986 season, Montana injured his back. The doctors discovered a ruptured disk and a congenital defect of the spine, requiring surgery and possibly spelling the end of his career. But Montana would hear none of it. After surgery, he missed only 55 days. He came back to lead the 49ers to the playoffs, where they again lost to the New York Giants.

In the 1987 season, Montana posted a record 31 touchdown passes. The 49ers lost in the playoffs to the Minnesota Vikings, in a game in which Walsh benched Montana in favor of backup quarterback Steve Young. The 1988 season was a tough one for Montana, as, hampered by injuries, he watched Young win the starting quarterback position. Montana was angry and started looking around at other teams. The 49ers made it to the Super Bowl again at the end of the season. Playing in that game, Montana provided the fans with another classic come-from-behind finish, leading the offense 92 yards in 34 seconds to win the game against Cincinnati, 20-16. The following season (1989), Montana posted the best record of any quarterback in history, receiving a 112.4 rating and a 70.2 completion percentage. Once again the 49ers were in the Super Bowl, where they beat the Denver Broncos, 55-10.

At the beginning of the 1991 season, Montana injured his elbow, tearing the tendon off the bone and requiring surgery. He missed most of that season, and nearly all of 1992. In 1993, Montana was traded to the Kansas City Chiefs, in a deal that angered both Montana and his many fans for the poor way it was handled by the 49ers management. Montana thought it was clear that Young had won the starting quarterback position, and he was looking at several teams. But the 49ers management kept waffling on who the starting quarterback would be, as well as the intent and the terms of the trade, which involved other players, draft picks, and money.

KANSAS CITY CHIEFS

Montana signed a three-year contract with the Chiefs, much to the delight of fans in Kansas City. He went to his new team believing he had a job to do, and the 1993 season showed that he still had the talent and determination to do it. He led the team to the AFC championship, where they lost to the Buffalo Bills in a game in which Montana suffered a concussion and had to leave the game.

Montana prepared for the 1994 season by lifting weight to improve his strength. In his 16 seasons, he had led his teams to 29 fourth-quarter victories. "He's like Lazarus," commented former teammate Tim McKyer. "you roll back the stone, Joe limps out—and throws for 300 yards." But after a great start, he was again plagued by injuries, spraining his foot in a game in late November. In December, a reporter with the *New York Daily News* leaked a story that said that Montana was planning to retire. An angry Montana called a press conference to refute the story and to give the sports writers a piece of his mind. "I think, first of all, you guys are going to have to start standing up to what you write. I think it hurts the credibility of your field. It's ridiculous to have to put everybody through this. Until you hear it from me, I wouldn't worry about it."

Montana led the Chiefs to the playoffs in 1994, where they lost to the Miami Dolphins. Whether he will come back to play in the 1995 season remains to be seen, but in the eyes of most observers, if Montana is healthy, it will be hard to stop him from coming back one more time to prove what most fans already know—that he is the finest quarterback the game has ever seen.

MARRIAGE AND FAMILY

Montana has been married three times. His first wife, Kim Monses, was his high school girlfriend. They were married in 1975, during his freshman year at Notre Dame. They were divorced in 1978. Montana's second wife was Cass Castillo, an airline flight attendant, whom he married in 1979 and divorced in 1983.

Montana's third wife is Jennifer Wallace, a fashion model whom he met while filming a Schick razor ad in 1983. They were married in 1985, and they now have four children, Alexandra, Elizabeth, Nathaniel, and Nicholas. The Montana family has homes in both Kansas City and San Francisco.

HOBBIES AND OTHER INTERESTS

Montana is completing the training for a pilot's license, which he began when he was injured and forced to sit out most of two seasons in the early 1990s. He and Jennifer are also considering starting a winery in California after he retires from football.

WRITINGS

Audibles: My Life in Football, 1986 (with Bob Raissman)

HONORS AND AWARDS

National Football League Pro Bowl: 1982, 1984-86, 1989
Super Bowl Most Valuable Player: 1982, 1985, 1990
National Football League Most Valuable Player: 1989
Man of the Year (*Sporting News*): 1990
Sportsman of the Year (*Sports Illustrated*): 1990

Montana's many NFL records include most seasons with 3,000 yards passing (7), the highest pass efficiency in a season (112.4, in 1989), most touchdown passes in a Super Bowl game (5, in 1990), and most yards passing in a Super Bowl game (357, in 1989).

FURTHER READING

BOOKS

Appleman, Marc. *Joe Montana*, 1991 (juvenile)
Kavanagh, Jack. *Sports Great Joe Montana*, 1992 (juvenile)
Montana, Joe, and Bob Raissman. *Audibles: My Life in Football*, 1986
Raber, Thomas R. *Joe Montana, Comeback Quarterback*, 1989 (juvenile)
Who's Who in America 1995

PERIODICALS

Boy's Life, Nov. 1982, p.29
Chicago Tribune, Dec. 3, 1994, p.C2
Current Biography Yearbook 1983
New York Times Biographical Service, Jan. 1982, p.96
New York Times Magazine, Dec. 17, 1989, p.27
Newsweek, Jan. 23, 1989, p.54
Sport, Sep. 1993, p.71
Sporting News, Jan. 1, 1990, p.9
Sports Illustrated, Aug. 6, 1990, p.62; Aug. 13, 1990, p.72; Dec. 24, 1990, p.90;
   Apr. 26, 1993, p.12; Sep. 13, 1993, p.20
Time, Jan. 25, 1982, p.62

ADDRESS

Kansas City Chiefs
1 Arrowhead Drive
Kansas City, MO 64129

Cosmas Ndeti   1971-
Kenyan Runner
Winner of the Boston Marathon in 1993, 1994, and 1995

BIRTH

Cosmas Ndeti (KOS-mas nin-DET-ee) was born November 24, 1971, in Machakos, Kenya, a small village about 40 miles southeast of the East African nation's capital, Nairobi. He grew up on a farm, where he lived with his father, his father's three wives, and 36 brothers and sisters. He was the third-oldest of ten children borne by his mother. Ndeti, who is five-feet-six-inches tall and weighs 126 pounds, is a member of the Kambu tribe.

YOUTH

Like many Kenyan children, Ndeti began running at an early age. "I used to wake up late, and I trained myself to run fast so I wouldn't be late to school," Ndeti explains. He ran the nine miles round-trip to school and back every day beginning at age seven, and he started racing during elementary school. He competed in various cross-country and track events, including the 5,000 and 10,000 meter runs. His first major success came in 1988, when he finished second at the World Junior Cross-Country Championships at the age of 17. He had a bad year in 1989, but then he rebounded to win the 20-kilometer race at the World Junior Track and Field Championships in 1990. After this victory, a Japanese corporate team recruited him and he left home to train in Japan. Ndeti missed his family and found the training regimen very difficult, however, so he returned to Kenya in 1992. "I did not see things being well," he says of his time in Japan. "Their training is so tough. Sometimes they would run 50 kilometers in a day. My body couldn't handle that. Doing all the mileage, I lost speed." Back home, Ndeti drew upon the long tradition of world-class Kenyan distance runners to develop into an international champion.

DISTANCE RUNNING IN KENYA

In the past 30 years, athletes from Kenya have come to dominate the world's premier distance running events. For example, Kenyan runners have earned 32 Olympic gold medals since 1964, as well as many track and cross-country world championships. In fact, the team from Kenya swept the distance events at the 1988 Olympics and set three world records. Ndeti's third consecutive victory in the Boston Marathon in 1995 meant that Kenyans had won the event for five straight years, as well as six of the last seven years (fellow Kenyan Ibrahim Hussein won in 1989, 1991, and 1992). Athletes and coaches from around the world visit the African nation looking for the secret to its success.

Experts think many factors contribute to the Kenyans' dominance in distance running. For example, the western half of the country lies at a high altitude, where the air contains less oxygen than at sea level. Many endurance athletes prefer to train at high altitudes in order to condition their bodies to perform well on less oxygen. They believe that this gives them an advantage when they compete at oxygen-rich lower altitudes. Kenyan runners also benefit from their diet, which is typically high in carbohydrates that provide fuel for muscles. Genetics also plays a role in the Kenyans' success, as does the nation's year-round nice weather, which provides athletes with lots of time for training. But "perhaps the most important factor," according to one expert, "is that running is a way of life" in Kenya. Instead of running merely for exercise, many Kenyans grow up using running as a form of transportation, just as Ndeti did on his way to school. Moreover, many Kenyans have never even seen the expensive equipment that is required for other sports, so the best athletes tend to concentrate on running.

These factors combined to help the relatively small nation, with a population of only about 26 million, produce a huge number of world-class runners. As these athletes began posting an impressive string of achievements in international competition, they also became the main cultural heroes for young Kenyans. "In the tiny villages and small subsistence farms that dot the landscape, nearly everyone knows an Olympic runner or a world champion," one coach claims. Kids can see the wealth and prestige that successful runners enjoy, and as a result many dedicate themselves to becoming great runners. "When I was running in high school," Ndeti confirms, "I'd say one day I want to be a world-famous runner like [two-time Olympic gold medalist Kip] Keino. That's why I would fight and train so hard." Unlike the United States, where famous athletes do not usually go out of their way to help young hopefuls, Kenya provides an environment where they train together regularly. The most famous track in Kenya is inside a rickety old stadium near the village of Iten. There, one observer notes, "Kenyan runners who dominate the sport's middle- and long-distance events pass the baton from one generation to the next. Young athletes run alongside champions who, just a few years before, jogged beside the heroes of their day." It was here that Ndeti developed the unusual training philosophy that has led to his success.

UNIQUE TRAINING PHILOSOPHY

After his disappointing experience training with professional coaches in Japan, Ndeti decided to do without a coach. "A coach can tell you to do something which your body is not willing or ready to do," he explains. "If you do that at the time, you are exhausting your body." Instead, in a somewhat unusual situation for such a high-caliber athlete, Ndeti coaches himself. "I train how my body feels," Ndeti says. "I don't have a schedule— today I will run such and such miles. I arrange my training in the morning after I wake up. If I'm tired, I'll rest. In the evening I'll go for a tough run." His favorite training run involves sprinting six miles up the side of a mountain near his home as fast as he can, and then running back down again as fast as he can. Experts find it strange that he sometimes takes long breaks from running—up to three months at a time—and that he rarely races more than two or three times per year. Most successful marathoners train with a coach on a pre-determined schedule and race regularly. However, no one can argue with Ndeti's recent success.

CAREER HIGHLIGHTS

After Ndeti returned to Kenya from Japan in 1992, he continued training for various cross-country and track events. His marathon career began later that year, when Benson Masya, his childhood friend and a respected Kenyan marathoner, convinced him to enter the Honolulu Marathon as a pacesetter. Even though he had only two weeks to prepare, Ndeti ended up finishing second, only nine seconds behind Masya, in this first attempt at the 26.2 mile event. "It's a long way, but easy. I feel my body can resist the fatigue. That's the time I made my mind up to switch to the marathon," Ndeti recalls.

1993 BOSTON MARATHON

When Ndeti entered the prestigious Boston Marathon for the first time in April 1993, he was virtually unknown. In fact, his name was mis-spelled "Cosmos N'Deti" in the race program. The weather conditions on race day were sunny and unseasonably hot, with temperatures reaching 77 degrees. For the first half of the race, the lead pack responded to the heat by setting a slow pace. Ndeti ran near the back of the group of about 20 leaders with his friend Masya. Around the 15 mile mark, however, a little-known runner from the African nation of Namibia, Lucketz Swart-booi, broke into the lead by setting an impressive pace of 4 minutes, 39 seconds per mile. The lead pack began to dissolve, as some runners attempted to keep up while others chose to conserve their energy.

As he watched the leaders disappear, Ndeti turned to Masya and said, "Those people are moving." Masya replied, "Go if you want," and Ndeti took off in pursuit. He steadily made up time on the leader, and he passed Swartbooi at the 24.5 mile mark, with less than two miles to go. The crowd went wild as Ndeti crossed the finish line with a time of 2 hours, 9 minutes, and 33 seconds (also written as 2:09:33), just 10 seconds ahead of Kim Jae-Yong of Korea, making it the sixth-closest margin of victory in the history of the Boston Marathon. Since Ndeti had never been mentioned among the favorites, race analysts were amazed by his perfor-mance. "At the time, Ndeti's victory seemed like a caddy winning the Masters [golf tournament]," one observer remembers. Experts were even more shocked to find that Ndeti had become the first runner in modern race history to post a "negative split," meaning that he finished the se-cond half of the course—which has many hills and is considered the most difficult—faster than the first half. In fact, his time of 1:04:10 was the best ever recorded for the second half of the Boston Marathon. Ndeti was so pleased with his performance that he named his son, who had been born two days earlier, "Gideon Boston" in honor of the event.

1994 BOSTON MARATHON

Despite his impressive victory in the 1993 Boston Marathon, many experts still did not view Ndeti as a serious contender the following year. They noted that he had not run well in earlier races, and they criticized his unusual training habits. Others felt that he did not take the race seriously because he brought his young son with him to all the pre-race press conferences. But Ndeti responded to doubters by saying, "If God let me win last year's race, if he allows me to wear number 1 on my jersey, then why not again be number 1 this year?"

The 1994 event featured ideal weather conditions: cloudy and mild, with temperatures in the 50-degree range, with a strong breeze blowing at the runners' backs. Still, the lead pack, headed by American Keith Brantly, traveled at a relatively slow pace for the first half of the race. Around mile 15, the pack caught Brantly and picked up the pace to a near world-record level. Then they came to the part of the course known as Heartbreak Hill, a mile-long series of three steep downhills that "presents both the greatest opportunity and the greatest difficulty" for competitors. Ndeti, putting all the hill training he did near his home in Kenya to use, ran a scorching 4:31 over this stretch and took the lead with four miles to go. Mexican Andres Espinosa closed in with half a mile left, but Ndeti held him off to win by a four-second margin. His time of 2:07:15 set a new course record, beating the old record by 36 seconds, and was the fifth-fastest marathon ever run. He also managed another negative split, covering the second half of the course in an incredible 1:02:15.

1995 BOSTON MARATHON

Even after Ndeti had won his second consecutive Boston Marathon, some race analysts still doubted his ability. "Ndeti's unusual training habits and erratic race history leave so much unsaid about him that tongues are prone to wag about how little chance he has to become the third man to three-peat as Boston champion," one observer explains. Critics pointed out that Ndeti had failed to complete the Chicago Marathon the previous fall due to blisters, and that he had run so slowly in a warmup half marathon that he finished only a few strides ahead of the top woman racer. They also remarked that his "crash-diet style of training, which packs everything into the final weeks before a race," made him prone to injury and burnout. Nevertheless, Ndeti claimed that his level of training was weeks ahead of the previous two years. "Many people thought it was an accident the first time," Ndeti says. "It put me on the world map of marathoners, but last year I came back and no one expected me to win. I won and set a course record. This year people are saying, 'You're not going to win.' I'm sure I will win, because my God is able." Ndeti even set a personal goal to break the world marathon record of 2:06:50, set by Ethiopian Belayneh Densimo in 1988.

Runners were greeted by cool temperatures and swirling winds at the start of the 1995 race. Using the same strategy as he had used in his two victories, Ndeti hung back initially and waited to make his move. He took the lead at mile 21 and fought off threats from four other runners before he picked up the pace to 4:39 per mile. He broke the tape with a time of 2:09:22, beating fellow Kenyan Moses Tanui by a comfortable one-minute margin. Ndeti thus became only the third person in the 99-year history of the Boston Marathon to win it in three consecutive years. The other two were Americans Clarence DeMar (1922-1924) and Bill Rodgers (1978-1980). In fact, only four other people had even won the race three times. For the first time, however, Ndeti did not record a negative split on his way to victory. During the celebration surrounding his three-peat, Ndeti predicted that he would win the 100th Boston Marathon in 1996.

REWARDS OF WINNING

Finally, after his remarkable three-peat, race analysts seemed ready to give Ndeti the praise he deserved. "He's a tactical genius," Bill Rodgers admits. "He has phenomenal focus and determination. I think he's great. He's a very exciting runner." Other experts commented on his patience and his smart race strategy. Ndeti explains that he is more comfortable running at the rear of the lead pack and making his move late in the race: "In the back, you can read the other guys. You can watch the way they're running. You can see the ones who are strong. It's a good advantage. You watch the others and let them lead you." He also likes to stare down his opponents as he takes over the lead.

Ndeti received $75,000 in prize money for his 1995 Boston Marathon win, while corporate sponsorships raised his annual income much higher. At home in Kenya, where the average person earns about $500 per year, he is a very wealthy man. He is also famous, and people call out his name when one of his two chauffeurs drive him through town. He has used some of his money to buy land and is planning to build a new house for his family. Another reward Ndeti received for winning the Boston Marathon was a trip to Washington, D.C., to meet and jog with President Clinton. After the president tried to out-sprint him toward the end of their mile run together, Ndeti laughed and told American reporters, "Your president, he breathes very hard."

MARRIAGE AND FAMILY

Ndeti is married to his high-school sweetheart, Jane. The couple lives in Machakos with their two children, son Gideon Boston, born in 1993, and daughter Serafina, born in 1995. "His wife takes a lot of responsibility off of him," Ndeti's agent, Mark Wetmore, says of his family life. "She lets him just train. He comes back beat from a workout and she brings food to him. He loves getting on the floor with his son." The Ndeti family also shares their home with Ndeti's mother and several of his training partners.

HOBBIES AND OTHER INTERESTS

When Ndeti is not training or playing with his children, he loves to watch boxing videos. He especially admires Mike Tyson for his toughness and conditioning. Ndeti is also deeply religious—he became a born-again Christian in 1993—and very active in his church. In fact, while he was in the United States he wanted to buy a tent that would be large enough to cover his 1,500-member congregation during the rainy season in Kenya. Ndeti credits his faith for much of his success in running. "If you trust in God," he explains, "everything is possible. Now I have peace of mind."

HONORS AND AWARDS

World Junior Cross-Country Championships: 1988, second place
World Junior Track and Field Championships, 20-kilometer run: 1990, first place
Honolulu Marathon: 1992, second place; 1993, second place
Tokyo Half Marathon: 1992, second place
Boston Marathon: 1993, first place; 1994, first place; 1995, first place
Track and Field News Rankings: 1993, fifth-best world marathoner; 1994, third-best world marathoner

FURTHER READING

PERIODICALS

Boston Marathon Official Program, Apr. 17, 1995, p.25
Chicago Tribune, Oct. 28, 1994, p.1; Apr. 17, 1995, p.3
Houston Post, Apr. 16, 1995, p.B1
New York Times, Apr. 17, 1995, p.C3
Philadelphia Inquirer, Apr. 18, 1995, p.DO1
Rocky Mountain News, Apr. 21, 1993, p.B1; May 21, 1995, p.B32
Runner's World, July 1993, p.64; July 1994, p.64
USA Today, Apr. 14, 1995, p.C1

ADDRESS

Cosmas Ndeti
Machakos, Kenya

Hakeem Olajuwon 1963-
Nigerian-Born American Professional
Basketball Player
All-Star Center for the Two-Time NBA
Champion Houston Rockets

BIRTH

Hakeem Abdul Olajuwon (ah-KEEM ahb-DUHL ah-LIE-zhu-wahn)
was born in Lagos, Nigeria, on January 21, 1963. His parents,
Salaam and Abike Olajuwon, are middle-class owners of a cement
business. He has four full siblings: sister Kudi and brothers
Akin, Taju, and Afis. He also has a half-brother, Adeyemi Kaka,
from his mother's first marriage. Athletic skills run in the Olajuwon family—Hakeem's grandfather was a noted equestrian in

neighboring Benin, and his younger brother, Afis, is a table-tennis champion. Although no one on either side of his family is short, Hakeem is by far the tallest of them, at an even seven feet.

Earlier, there was some confusion about Olajuwon's first name. When he first came to the United States, his first name was consistently misspelled in the news reports. Because the "H" was silent, his name was initially listed as "Akeem" when he arrived in this country. He corrected the error in 1991, explaining that the correct spelling, "Hakeem," means "wise one" or "doctor" in Arabic.

YOUTH

Lagos, where Olajuwon grew up, is the capital of Nigeria. Located in equatorial West Africa on the coast of the Gulf of Guinea, it is a large, hot, crowded, urban city whose metropolitan area numbers some six million people. People in the United States misunderstand what much of Africa is really like today, according to Olajuwon. His country has a reputation for violence and poverty that he feels is undeserved. He had to fight against this misperception when he first came to the United States to attend college. "I know some people think I was living in Nigeria naked in the jungle and swinging through the trees," he said defensively then. "I know what they think about Africa. I do not like it. They are stupid. Lagos is a big, vibrant city. Tall buildings. Offices. Civilization. Designer clothes . . . we have videos in Nigeria."

As a child, Olajuwon took to sports at a young age, especially soccer and team handball. He learned to play soccer on the sand fields across from his home, eventually becoming a star on his school team. He confirms matter-of-factly that he was an excellent goalkeeper, but that it was his height that drew him to basketball. He often was taunted when, at only 15, he had already grown to 6'9". "They would tease me all the time in Nigeria, and I would get into fights every day," he remembers. "Sometimes I would be ashamed of being so tall. I would wish I was normal height so I can be friendly, just like everyone else. Everywhere I went, people were looking. My parents knew why I was always fighting, and they tried to encourage me about my height."

EARLY MEMORIES

Growing up, Olajuwon had no idea that he would excel in such an unfamiliar sport as basketball—games were not televised then in his country. Still, he had a sense of his destiny. "In Nigeria, I had a special feeling inside of me," he revealed in later years. "Something was going to happen. I have something no one else has, and when it's time, I knew my road was going to be in sports."

EDUCATION

Olajuwon comes from a family of educated people, most of whom speak English, French, and four African dialects (Yoruba, Hausa, Ibo, and Ido), as he does. He attended Lagos's Baptist Academy and Moslem Teachers' College, which is roughly equivalent to a U.S. high school. After coming to the United States in 1980, at the age of 17, he enrolled at the University of Houston as a business major, but left school after his junior year to play professional basketball.

CHOOSING A CAREER

Olajuwon started playing basketball as a teenager in Lagos. He first picked up a basketball at the age of 15 and soon dropped his other sports to devote himself to this new game. As he explains here, "Basketball is a cool game. *Cool.* Also it is an American game and in Nigeria people admire those things. So I wanted to play. You know: 'I'm cool now!'" After only two years, Olajuwon was playing center for the Nigerian national team in the All-African games. He was spotted by Chris Pond, a U.S. State Department employee and a friend of the University of Houston coach Guy Lewis. Pond arranged to have Olajuwon visit several American college campuses through a program called Partners of America. The first stop was in New York, where the young Nigerian was scheduled to visit St. John's University, but the change in climate proved too great a shock to his system. "It was so cold, so I went on to Houston, where I was told it was warm," he explains simply.

Olajuwon's basketball skills were rough, but Houston coach Guy Lewis saw enough talent to offer the young man a scholarship. This talent, along with his physique and work ethic, set a career course for Hakeem that would ultimately grace basketball with one of its finest centers ever. It would be a long road, though. Olajuwon was clearly out of his element in college ball at that time. "We knew he'd get better," says Clyde Drexler, his teammate on the University of Houston Cougars and the Houston Rockets, "because he couldn't get any worse."

CAREER HIGHLIGHTS

COLLEGE PLAY WITH THE COUGARS

Olajuwon sat out during the 1980-81 season. Because NCAA (National College Athletic Association) rules limit a player's eligibility to four years of college basketball, Coach Lewis had Olajuwon sit out while he refined his game and adapted to his new culture. The next year, 1981-82, the young center began to astonish opponents with his shot-blocking ability, but he still didn't play much. Coach Lewis was largely concerned about a lack of conditioning in his future star. Exhausted after five or ten minutes of play and prone to foul trouble, Olajuwon had difficulty guarding fresh, quick players. But when he complained about lack of time on the court, Lewis was firm. "He actually hurt us in there," the coach said. "You can't play up-tempo when four guys are running and the other is dyin'." Olajuwon was especially angry with the coach for failing to start him against North Carolina in the NCAA semifinals of 1982. "They're coming down the lane shooting lay-ups! I am so mad," he recalled. "I am burning up." Lewis, who regularly criticized Olajuwon in the press, did not bend. The coach defended his decision by saying, "I don't care how you slice it, he flat out didn't know how to play." Still, in 29 games, Olajuwon had scored an average of 8.3 points, with 6.2 rebounds and 2.5 blocked shots.

Olajuwon's second year on the team, 1982-83, brought both the greatest triumphs and the biggest disappointment of his college career. The Cougars, who were nicknamed "Phi Slamma Jamma" for their dunking ability, won 25 straight games while holding the top national ranking for most of the year. Olajuwon averaged 13.9 points, 11.4 rebounds, and 5.1 blocks per game for the year. Moving into the NCAA final game by defeating Louisville, Lewis decided to slow down his team's game to match up against North Carolina State, a team that hadn't been favored to make it to the Final Four. In one of the greatest upsets ever, the Wolfpack edged Houston 54-52 on a last-second shot. Olajuwon retreated to the locker room in tears, unconsoled by the tournament MVP (Most Valuable Player) award, a rare honor for a player on a losing team.

The 1983-84 season also ended in disappointment. After leading the nation in rebounding and field-goal accuracy, Olajuwon once again brought the Cougars to the NCAA final game. Houston was defeated by Patrick Ewing and the Georgetown Hoyas, 84-75. Upset with his team-mates for failing to get the ball to him often enough and sure that he was ready to play basketball with the pros in the NBA (National Basketball Association), Olajuwon decided to forgo his final year of college eligibility to enter the NBA draft.

THE ROCKETS

The 1984 NBA draft offered a huge amount of talent. The Houston Rockets used the first pick in the draft to select Olajuwon above such stellar prospects as Michael Jordan, Charles Barkley, and John Stockton. With his quickness, strength, leaping ability, and speed, Olajuwon was just what the Rockets needed. All these came together in the 1984-85 season, as Olajuwon and the 7'4" Ralph Sampson brought the Rockets to the playoffs with a unique "twin towers" scheme. Olajuwon's 20.6 points per game helped offensively, but more important were his defensive skills, demonstrated with 974 rebounds, 220 blocks, and 99 steals. Olajuwon was named to the 1985 All-Star Team, but the Rockets lost to the Utah Jazz, 3-2, in the first round of the playoffs.

The 1985-86 season would be the Rockets' most successful for years to come. Hakeem chipped in with more than 23 points and 11 rebounds per game, leading his team to a 51-31 record overall and the Midwest Division title. Wins against the Sacramento Kings and the Denver Nuggets brought Houston into the conference finals against the NBA Champion Los Angeles Lakers. Although Olajuwon had been beaten by Kareem Abdul-Jabbar for the All-NBA first team, the Lakers also had Magic Johnson, and few gave the Rockets any chance of prevailing. Olajuwon dominated Abdul-Jabbar, though, and Houston won the series 4-1. "In terms of raw athletic ability," Johnson would say later, "Hakeem is the best I've ever seen." Despite a fabulous final series from Hakeem, who was double- and triple-teamed most of the time, the Boston Celtics proved to be too much for the Rockets, who fell 4-2 in the NBA finals that year. Olajuwon had come once more within a hairbreadth of a championship.

By the start of the 1986-87 season, the Rockets were regarded as the NBA team of the future, but that future was further away than observers imagined. Olajuwon improved with each succeeding season, averaging 20 points and 11 rebounds per game while increasing his defensive

domination. Nevertheless, the superior guard play of such teams as the Detroit Pistons and the Chicago Bulls was beginning to become the decisive factor in a changing sport. After a second- round elimination in the 1987 playoffs, the Rockets attempted to respond by trading Sampson, the other half of the twin towers. The move didn't help. When the Rockets lost to Dallas in the opening round of the 1988 playoffs, Olajuwon started to complain about team management.

An image as a malcontent, coupled perhaps with his failure to win a title at any level, prevented Olajuwon from cashing in on the endorsements and commercials peopled by the charismatic Jordan and Barkley. While Hakeem griped about the Houston front office's failure to bring in a talented supporting cast, analysts chided him for selfish play. First-round failures in the 1989 and 1990 playoffs did not help public perception. Then two events, both of which occurred when the sports world was watching the Chicago Bulls win three straight championships, turned the tide.

A CHANGE IN FOCUS

In 1991, Olajuwon suffered a career-threatening injury when the Bulls' Bill Cartwright fractured the bones around Hakeem's right eye with an accidental jab of his elbow. Sidelined for 25 games, Olajuwon worried with the rest of Houston that the Rockets would fall apart, but the team rallied around such utility players as Otis Thorpe, Larry Smith, and Vernon Maxwell. Then, when Olajuwon returned, the Rockets became, in the words of NBA coach Don Nelson, "the most feared team in the league." Even though Houston was eliminated by the Lakers in the first round of the playoffs, Olajuwon's focused play had helped to win new respect for his team.

The opening of the 1992-93 season was darkened as Olajuwon feuded with (then) Houston owner Charlie Thomas about a contract renegotiation. He was suspended for five games for allegedly faking a hamstring injury, and the Rockets failed to make the playoffs for the first time since 1984. But Olajuwon was vindicated when the injury in question proved to have been real. New coach Rudy Tomjanovich intervened in the owner/player dispute, and Hakeem and Thomas made peace in the off-season. Olajuwon had one of his best seasons in 1992-93, winning the Defensive Player of the Year award but finishing second to the Phoenix Suns' Barkley in MVP voting. The Rockets won the Midwest semifinals that year, but fell to the Seattle Supersonics in a tough seven-game series.

THE TURNING POINT

The next season, 1993-94, brought redemption. Houston reached the finals, where they faced the New York Knicks. And this time, the battle for the title would go Hakeem's way. Up against Patrick Ewing and the Knicks,

Olajuwon had his chance to avenge the college loss to Georgetown a decade earlier. The NBA sorely missed the recently retired Jordan, and few sports writers were enamored of the series. Nevertheless, each of the seven games came down to the last minute, and Houston prevailed in a series that is regarded as a classic. Olajuwon was outstanding, averaging 26.9 points, 9.1 rebounds, 3.6 assists, and 3.9 blocks per game. He finally had a championship. He also became the only player ever to be the regular-season MVP, finals MVP, Defensive Player of the Year, and All-NBA first-teamer. Remaining, though, was the nagging "Jordan factor," a feeling that this championship somehow meant less with Michael Jordan in retirement. Olajuwon had one more thing to prove.

Jordan returned to a struggling Bulls team in the 1994-95 season, shortly after the Rockets made a controversial trade of Otis Thorpe for Olajuwon's college teammate, Clyde Drexler. Houston accomplished something remarkable in that season's playoff. Without home-court advantage in a single series, they beat the Jazz, the Suns, and the Spurs—the teams with the three best records in the NBA—to reach the finals against the Orlando Magic. Olajuwon destroyed emerging superstar center Shaquille O'Neal, and the Rockets took the series in a four-game sweep that brought the team their second straight title. This time, Hakeem "The Dream" got to share it with former Cougar teammate Clyde "The Glide" Drexler. It was agreed that no team had ever taken such a hard road to the title, nor made it look so easy.

After a decade of racking up remarkable statistics, Olajuwon has finally established himself as one of the game's great champions. Some analysts dare to hint that he may be even better than Jordan was in his prime. Whatever his future, it will be here in the United States, where he became a citizen in 1993, and for whom he will play in Atlanta's 1996 Summer Olympics.

MEMORABLE EXPERIENCES

When Olajuwon tried to leave the stadium and go home after celebrating his first championship in 1994, he found himself in a major traffic jam. He happily sat in his car listening to honking horns, and then someone realized who he was. His fans swarmed around him. "That scene was history," he says. "It's a memory that's so special. I would like to really tell the fans of Houston how grateful I am for the way they embraced the team. Just beautiful. Houston, it's home."

MAJOR INFLUENCES

During the summers between his college seasons, Olajuwon worked out with renowned star center Moses Malone, then with the Houston Rockets, who helped him mold his game. It was Malone who convinced Hakeem to play more aggressively. "Moses always tells me to be hungry for rebounds and blocked shots," he said in those days. 'Eat 'em up.' I can always hear him saying that to me. Moses is a great man."

FAMILY LIFE

Olajuwon has a seven-year-old daughter, Alon Riskat Abisola Ajoke Olajuwon. He is not married to her mother, California attorney Lita Spencer, whom he met when both were students in Houston, and with whom he had a lengthy relationship during college and his early years with the Houston Rockets. Hakeem looks forward to his daughter's frequent visits to Houston, where he has a contemporary one-story house southwest of the city.

HOBBIES AND OTHER INTERESTS

Hakeem Olajuwon is an avid collector of modern abstract art, which he showcases in the gallery-like rooms of his Houston home. He likes to paint in oils, and also has a distinct interest in cooking. Drawing on credentials from his college business courses, he has established an import-export firm which sends sporting goods to Nigeria. The company, Barakat Holdings, Ltd., also markets bottled water in the United States.

The Islamic faith of his youth is of such importance to Olajuwon that the Rockets schedule their practices around his daily devotions. As a Muslim (a follower of Islam), Olajuwon prays five times each day, beginning at 5:30 A.M. When he travels, he carries a special prayer rug and a compass that points toward Mecca, the Muslim holy city in Saudi Arabia. For some years now, since re-embracing the tenets of his religion, he has kept his life very serene. "What's important to me," he says, "is God, my daughter, and basketball."

HONORS AND AWARDS

NCAA Tournament MVP: 1983
All-America Team: 1984
Jim Thorpe Pro Sports Award: 1984
NBA Rookie of the Year: 1984
NBA All-Star Team: 1985-90; 1992-95
NBA MVP: 1994
NBA Finals MVP: 1994-95

FURTHER READING

BOOKS

Harvey, Miles. *Hakeem Olajuwon: The Dream,* 1994 (juvenile)
Knapp, Ron. *Sports Great Hakeem Olajuwon,* 1992 (juvenile)

Lincoln Library of Sports Champions, Vol. 10, 1993
Rekela, George R. *Hakeem Olajuwon: Tower of Power,* 1993 (juvenile)

PERIODICALS

Boys' Life, Feb. 1995, p.8
Current Biography Yearbook 1993
Esquire, Feb. 1994, p.37
Houston Post, Oct. 30, 1994, p.N2
Sport, Jan. 1994, p.43
Sporting News, June 12, 1995, p.44
Sports Illustrated, Nov. 28, 1983, p.106; Apr. 8, 1991, p.54; Nov. 28, 1993, p.106; Mar. 13, 1995, p.18
Wall Street Journal, Feb. 24, 1995, p.B14

ADDRESS

Houston Rockets
The Summit
10 Greenway Place East
Houston, TX 77046

Mary-Kate and Ashley Olsen   1986-
American Actresses
Twin Stars of "Full House"

BIRTH

Mary-Kate and Ashley Olsen were born in 1986, in California. Because they are so popular, their parents do not want their exact birth date revealed. In the past, when their birthday was made public, overzealous fans have gone to their house in person, and the girls were frightened by all the attention.

Mary-Kate and Ashley are "fraternal" rather than "identical" twins. That means that even though they look very much alike, they are not mirror images of one another, physically and genetically, as are identical twins. Ashley is the oldest—by two minutes.

Mary-Kate and Ashley's parents are Dave and Jarnette Olsen. Dave is a mortgage banker and Jarnette is a full-time homemaker and former ballerina with the Los Angeles Ballet. The twins have one brother, Trent, who is two years older, and a sister, Elizabeth, who is three years younger.

"FULL HOUSE"

Mary-Kate and Ashley were only six months old when their mom took them to a tryout for "Full House." Because child labor laws limit the number of hours a child can work each day, TV shows or movies looking for a baby or child actor will usually choose identical twins. That way, one twin can work for a few hours, then the other can take over. And although Ashley and Mary-Kate aren't identical, they have always looked so much alike that they can share a role.

"We saw seven sets of twins," remembers "Full House" producer, Jeff Franklin. "There was no contest. The other kids were crying. Ashley and Mary-Kate had a great time. They were happy kids with these amazing big, blue eyes." Mary-Kate and Ashley won the part of Michelle Tanner in 1987, a part they played for eight years.

"Full House" ran on Tuesday nights on ABC from 1987 to 1995. As the many fans of the show know, "Full House" is the story of the Tanner family. The dad, Danny Tanner (played by Bob Saget), is raising his daughters—D.J.(Candace Cameron), Stephanie (Jodie Sweetin), and Michelle—without a mom, who died in a car accident. Instead, he has the help of his brother-in-law, Jesse (John Stamos), and his best friend, Joey (Dave Coulier). The "Full House" family also includes Jesse's wife, Becky (Lori Loughlin), and their twins, Alex and Nicky (Blake and Dylan Tuomy-Wilhoit). Together, the cast of "Full House" brings its loyal fans stories about life and growing up in a loving family. Although the show was very popular, many of the cast members were looking for a change after eight years on the air. The final episode of "Full House" was broadcast in May 1995. Even though the series stopped making new episodes, it continues to be shown in reruns in many areas.

WORK AND SCHOOL

While they worked on "Full House," Ashley and Mary-Kate went to a private school two days a week. On the days when they were working on the show, the twins took turns doing their scenes and studying with their private teacher. Mary-Kate is an early bird, so she did her scenes in the morning and spent the afternoon with her teacher. She also got the lines in the show that are more serious. Ashley is more of an afternoon person, so she worked with her teacher in the morning and acted in the afternoon. Ashley also acted in those scenes where Michelle is more rambunctious. Are they like Michelle? No, says their acting coach, Adria

Later. "The twins are more polite than Michelle in real life. They aren't as sassy as Michelle is on the series."

Even before they learned how to read, the twins would study with their acting coach to memorize all their lines. If they made a mistake, the rest of the cast was patient and understanding. The cast of adults, children, and everyone's favorite, Comet the dog, got along very well. Mary-Kate and Ashley named Jodie Sweetin as their favorite co-star, saying "she's like a sister to us."

DEALING WITH BEING A STAR

Mary-Kate and Ashley are very popular. They have one of the highest "Q" ratings of any entertainer in the U.S. ("Q" ratings are based on recognizability and popularity.) They were named the most popular people on TV with kids ages six to 11. When they go to special appearances in stores, up to 15,000 fans show up. Sometimes it's a bit overwhelming. "I get a little scared and a little bit nervous," says Ashley. Still, they do get to meet famous people. They were most impressed with magicians Siegfried and Roy, who have a live animal act that runs in Las Vegas.

Their parents try hard to maintain a regular life outside of the public eye for the girls. They almost pulled the twins off the show after the first year, "because we worried whether it would be too disruptive to them and to

the rest of the family," says Dave Olsen. But they enjoyed it so much, "we eventually decided that as long as they were having fun, we'd let them keep doing it." Mary-Kate and Ashley each have chores to do every week, and they each get an allowance of five dollars. They don't know how much they've made, which is fine with their parents. "They think they earn $10 a week," says Dave Olsen. "That's how it should be right now."

And, according to TV writer Joe Rhodes, they are just as normal and typical as they appear on TV. "They are shy around strangers, giggly when left to themselves. They share secrets. They like ice cream and ponies and swimming-pool slides. And, like most little girls, they fidget when they're sleepy and pout when they're angry."

BEING A TWIN

Although it's hard to spot on the screen, there are a few differences between the twins. Ashley has a freckle above her lip, and she's a little bit taller. And Ashley is right-handed, while Mary-Kate is left-handed. When Mary-Kate and Ashley were asked what's the best and worst thing about being a twin, they said: "We get to play with each other, and you always have a friend. There's nothing bad about being a twin."

FUTURE PLANS

Now that "Full House" has ended, Mary-Kate and Ashley plan to do another TV show for ABC, one that will be created just for them. It is scheduled to appear as part of ABC's 1996 fall season. The Olsen twins have their own company, "Dualstar," which was created to produce their records, videos, TV movies, and specials. Right now they are doing a mystery series for video, with several movies out so far.

When they grow up, the twins have separate plans. Mary-Kate wants to be an animal trainer. Ashley wants to be a ballet dancer.

HOME AND FAMILY

Ashley and Mary-Kate live with their family in a five-bedroom house in the San Fernando Valley in California. They have made a lot of money after being on a hit TV show for eight years. Their parents have put their money away for them so that they can use it for college. They've hired lawyers and bankers to handle the girls' money and do not take a percentage of it.

In their spare time, Ashley and Mary-Kate like to play with their friends. They also belong to a Brownie troop, play softball, and take ballet and horseback riding lessons. And they both love the Beach Boys.

TELEVISION, FILMS, AND RECORDING CREDITS

TELEVISION

"Full House," 1987-1995
"The Olsen Twins' Mother's Day Special," 1994

MADE-FOR-TV-MOVIES

To Grandmother's House We Go, 1994
Double, Double, Toil and Trouble, 1994
How the West Was Fun, 1994

RECORDINGS

Brother for Sale, 1991
I Am the Cute One, 1993
Give Us a Mystery, 1994

VIDEOS

Mary-Kate and Ashley Olsen: Our First Video, 1993
Logical I Ranch, 1994
Thorn Mansion, 1994
The Case of the Sea World Adventure, 1995
Mystery Cruise, 1995
The Case of the Christmas Caper, 1995
The Case of the Funhouse Mystery, 1995

FURTHER READING

PERIODICALS

Billboard, July 23, 1994, p.6
Detroit Free Press, Dec. 11, 1992, p.D11
Los Angeles Daily News, Dec. 6, 1992, p.L18
Newsday, Jan. 9, 1994, Section II, p.2
People, Aug. 31, 1992, p.107
St. Petersburg Times, Oct. 29, 1993, Weekend Section, p.5
TV Guide, Dec. 8, 1990. P.2; Aug. 7, 1993, p.7

ADDRESS

Warner Brothers Studios
4000 Warner Blvd.
Burbank, CA 91522

AUTOBIOGRAPHY

Jennifer Parkinson 1977-

[Editor's note: Jennifer Parkinson is a senior at Ward Melville High School in East Setauket, New York. As a student with learning disabilities, she has been in special education classes since grade school. This year she is graduating from high school and, despite the obstacles and challenges she discusses in this autobiography, will realize her dream of attending college. Her story, submitted to us by her Resource Room teacher, Lucrezia Iacomino, is one of courage and triumph. We are proud to bring it to the readers of Biography Today.*]*

GRADE SCHOOL

They hated me at my Catholic school. I was not like my brother or any one of my three older sisters. I was never able to sit still in class so I was made to stand. That was the reason my mother was given as to why I was not learning my ABC's. The real reason I was not able to learn was that no one helped me. Instead, I was made to sit at the back of the classroom with a coloring book and a few crayons.

Since the teacher did not pay attention to me none of the children did either. I ate lunch with my oldest sister Inga when I was in second and third grade, because she would not let anyone make fun of me. In the middle of second grade a black girl came into my school. Her name was Leda. No one talked to her either because at that time my school was basically white. I began to play with Leda most of the time. At last I had a friend; a good friend. Unfortunately, she moved away in third grade.

My mother was always at school because of me. They told my mom I was failing because of behavior problems, but truly it was because they just didn't care about me. Every year it was the same thing. First they would try to teach me for a month or so, then they would blame me for not learning, and finally out would come the coloring books.

One day my mom told me to do my homework. I told her I did not have any. I did, however, get very simple math homework occasionally, but never any writing or reading work. My mom called up my friend James. He would not talk to me in school because no one would talk to him if he did. He told my mom that he had homework. My mom was sure I was lying. My mom went nuts. She hit me with the buckle side of the belt on my back. I endured this beating because I could not learn and because I would not lie. My sister put cold towels on the welts to ease the pain and bring the swelling down. I'll never forget it.

The next week was rough because my mom went up to school and talked to the teachers about what I told her. The teachers denied everything. They told my mom that I got homework everyday. But I never did it. Well, my mom went through my desk and found the coloring books. Not one teacher could explain their presence. Well, my mom said Sorry to me, but I was still embarrassed. I accepted her apology and went on with my life. My mother never hit me again because of school. Actually, my mother then became my biggest supporter. When I did not do well on a test she would ask me, Did you try? I would say yes, then she would say, You did not fail, you just did not pass.

As soon as my mother realized what I had told her was true, she was very upset. She called P.S. [Public School] 66 to see what they could do to help me. They then brought me after school to be tested. I went to individual tutoring and speech class while still at my old school. I then went to P.S. 66 for third grade so I could have Resource Room help which was not available at my old school. It was so much easier, and I was so much happier.

Fourth grade was so different for me. I had friends, a great teacher, and a new Resource Room teacher. She was nice, but I did not trust her at first. Mrs. Levenson was her name. Her classroom was on the third floor. After testing me, she said I did not need to go to Resource Room twice a day, once a day would be enough. That made my mom happy. In this grade they started giving me spelling tests. On the first test I scored a O. I studied so very hard, but it just did not help. On the next test I scored 5%. I was so happy that I ran home and told my mom that I received a real number this time. Well eventually I got test scores in the two-digit numbers. I was thrilled. Although I never got a 100%, I was happy and proud of myself.

On the Standardized Reading tests I always scored in the 30th percentile. Eventually that got me down. In the fourth and fifth grade I started to hate myself because I did not feel normal. Everyone was smarter than me. In fifth grade, James, the boy from my old school, came to my school. He was no longer afraid to talk to me since all the other kids did. We became very good friends. Sixth grade was a good year. I was a senior and the class started a school business. I was elected Vice-President. That made me feel real good. I also had one more year to prove to myself that I could pass the state reading test. Well, I worked hard every day and on May of 1989 I passed my first reading test. I scored in the 56th percentile. I was so excited and happy.

JUNIOR HIGH SCHOOL

September 1990 I went to a new school. The junior high was so big and I really did not know where I belonged. I found my friends and did okay in seventh grade but lost the motivation to try.

In the eighth grade I just messed up. I lost what little motivation I had left. It just seemed like I didn't care anymore. I was sick of trying. I felt like I was disappointing my whole family over and over again. During this time I found out my family was going to move to a place called Stony Brook. I made a promise to myself that I would not embarrass any one of them there.

I promised myself that in ninth grade I was going to go to all of my classes and once again try hard. Once again, I had no friends and I felt like I did in the first grade. I managed to get over the fact that kids did not like me. Well, I worked hard on my grades and even made Honor Roll. I had never been that successful before. I even began to join clubs at school and made the ninth grade Volley Ball Team. I was in mixed classes, some Regent's and some non-Regent's. [Regent's classes, which prepare students for the New York Regent's exams, are more difficult courses.] At the end of the year, although I did very well in all my classes, my teacher told me I was not Regent's level material. As a result my high school schedule went through many changes.

HIGH SCHOOL

At Ward Melville High School the tenth grade Global Studies non-Regent's level class was too easy for me and I felt I was not learning much. I asked to switch into a higher level history class but was told I would not pass the class or the Regent's exam. However, with the help of my Resource Room teacher, Mrs. Iacomino, and my Global Studies teacher, I not only passed the class with a B+ but passed the Regent's exam with a "77" grade. I was so proud of myself.

In the eleventh grade I took two more Regent's level classes—English and U.S. History. Some of my old teachers from the year before told me not to be upset if I didn't pass. Well, Mrs. Iacomino always believed in me. She felt I could do it when everyone else thought it was impossible. Well, I did it again—I passed the English Regent's exam with a grade of "71" and the U.S. History Regent's with a grade of "81."

Back on the homefront, my family felt I should be out of the Resource Room. They felt that I never did anything on my own. Sometimes I wish everyone in my family could walk in my shoes for a day. They just don't understand how or why I have a hard time with reading, writing, and spelling. They don't believe the Resource Room helps me. They think it is damaging me as a person. I wish they could remember how I was in the first grade when all the children made fun of me. Now the only people making fun of me seem to be them. If I needed glasses they would buy them for me, but when it comes to asking someone to help me read a paper it's like I asked them to commit a sin. The reason I would like them to walk in my footsteps is because I know they would trip and fall when they tried. It's a good thing I had the Resource Room to support me when I needed it academically and emotionally.

It's not my fault that I was born three months premature. I weighed in at two and a half pounds. The doctors said if I made it through the first 48 hours I had a chance of surviving, but the doctors really didn't believe I would live, but here I am 5′ 5″ tall and at an appropriate weight.

I'm sure that my struggle to survive had a lot to do with my learning problems. It seemed as if I was always in the doctor's office. My ears were always infected. The medications never seemed to work. I wasn't able to tell the direction sound was coming from or what people were saying. I learned to read facial expressions well. At seven my left ear drum burst making problems worse. My hearing loss definitely contributed to my learning problems in my early years.

Today I still have a hard time reading and hearing; directionality is also a problem. I may need something repeated or I may need more time to read an assignment or an exam, but I get it done!

I feel I've made some great strides, but I'm only halfway there. I still have a lot to prove to myself and my family mainly. I want to prove that I can go to college and do well.

The idea of college is a big joke in my home at the present time. They don't believe I can make it. This is probably the biggest challenge my family has put me up to. They feel college is not for me. They think I'll fail out of any school I get into. However, they said they will let me go to a local community college, but I feel I can go to a four-year school and do well. My sisters are also opposed to my going to college. However, they have no right to keep me from fulfilling my dreams.

Even though my parents and my family have given me a hard time over the years, I have to admit that I wouldn't be where I am today if it wasn't for them. They protected me, supported me, and comforted me when I needed it. They also ridiculed me, but I'm a stronger and better person for it today.

I know I will have to work real hard but that's nothing new to me.

Someday, I will prove to them all that I am intelligent and that I will succeed. I know that I am able and willing to take on challenges.

I can tell you one thing, I really believe in myself even though I don't look good on paper and tests like the SAT and ACT. These tests do not measure my ability to survive in life and I am a survivor.

Well, here I am a senior in high school. It is a dream I never thought would come true in a million years. Right now I am trying to get into college— something else that was once just a dream but is now almost a reality.

My parents have become more supportive now that they have seen my determination has paid off. So far, I have been accepted to three of the five colleges I applied to. I'm still waiting to hear from my first choice.

ADDRESS

Jennifer Parkinson
c/o L. Iacomino—Special Education
Ward Melville High School
380 Old Town Road
East Setauket, NY 11733

OBITUARY

Linus Pauling   1901-1994
American Scientist and Social Activist
Two-Time Nobel Prize Winner
Only Person Ever to Win Two Unshared
Nobel Prizes

BIRTH

Linus Carl Pauling, distinguished scientist and social activist, was
born February 28, 1901, in Portland, Oregon. His mother, Lucy
Isabelle (Belle) Darling Pauling, was a descendant of an Oregon
pioneering family. His father, Herman Henry William Pauling, was
a pharmacist who soon moved his growing family eastward to
the small town of Condon, Oregon, where he established a drug

store. After his death in 1910, Lucy Pauling returned to Portland with Linus and his two younger sisters, Pauline and Frances Lucille, where she earned a living as proprietor of a boarding house.

YOUTH

A shy and curious child, Pauling showed an early interest in science as he wandered through the woods collecting insects and minerals. Chemistry became his particular passion by the time he was 11 or 12, and his teen years were filled with extensive reading, home-conducted experiments, and probing questions that brought him to the area of research he would one day help to transform. His elementary experimentation with chemicals "opened for him an incredibly complex and beautiful world," observed John Wintterle and Richard Cramer in their *Portraits of Nobel Laureates in Peace*, "a world of balance, proportion and symmetry which challenged his understanding and led him on to [a lifetime] of exploration and discovery."

Other more practical activities were part of Pauling's life as well. He delivered milk, washed dishes, worked in a machine shop, and did a variety of odd jobs to help support his mother and sisters. He held some of these jobs while still in high school and others he managed to fit in with his college schedule. At one point, he dropped out of college for a year to teach in order to relieve a financial crisis in the family.

Most accounts of Pauling's attitudes in those years point to the fierce independence that would drive and sustain him throughout his adult life. He left high school at the age of 16, before graduation, after refusing to take a required senior course that he viewed as pointless. *Current Biography* calls the act "an early instance of his legendary intellectual cockiness," but Pauling always stood firm in his beliefs and validated most of them with his remarkable achievements.

EDUCATION

Although he failed to receive a diploma from Portland's Washington High School, Pauling was accepted in 1917 by Oregon Agricultural College (now Oregon State University) in Corvallis, where he majored in chemical engineering. He was so academically advanced that he was given a teaching assistantship during his undergraduate years. A professor wrote then that he possessed "one of the best minds I have ever observed in a person of his age, and in many ways he is superior to his instructors."

The young prodigy received his B.S. in 1922 and began doctoral studies in chemistry at the prestigious California Institute of Technology (Caltech) at Pasadena. He spent three years there, first as a graduate assistant and then as a teaching fellow. His Ph.D in chemistry, with minors in physics and mathematics, was awarded summa cum laude (with highest distinction) in 1925. After a brief period as a National Research Fellow, Pauling went to Europe on a Guggenheim Fellowship for postdoctoral study with famed physicists Arnold Sommerfield in Munich, Erwin Schroedinger in Zurich, and Niels Bohr in Copenhagen. There, he was part of pioneering research in quantum mechanics, the theoretical framework used to explain the structure of the atom and the motion of atomic particles. As Wintterle and Cramer note in *Portraits of Nobel Laureates*: "It has been suggested that Pauling's great discoveries stem from the fact that, as a modern theoretical chemist, he took the trouble to learn physics and quantum mechanics, which led him to new areas of research."

CAREER HIGHLIGHTS

Dr. Pauling's first professional positions were back at Caltech as a teacher and researcher. He held assistant and associate faculty ranks in theoretical chemistry from 1927 until 1931, when he was elevated to full professorship, a position he would hold for more than three decades. Only 30 years old at the time, Pauling had already published 50 papers based on his original research. In 1931, he was honored by the American Chemical Society (ACS) with its Award in Pure Chemistry. He was admitted two years later to the National Academy of Sciences, "the Mount Olympus of American science," says writer Keay Davidson, "[and] a dazzling honor for one so young." Meanwhile, Pauling was gaining fame as a guest lecturer and, surprisingly, considering the weighty matter of his subject, as an exuberant speaker who entertained as well as informed his audience. His many years on the Caltech faculty were interrupted only by visiting professorships at Massachusetts Institute of Technology, Cornell, and Oxford.

In the early 1930s, Pauling was experimenting with determining crystal structure by X-ray and gas molecules by electron diffraction. In that process, beams of electrons and x-rays were shot at targets made of a specific gas or crystalline material, and the way the beams scattered allowed Pauling to understand important details of the atomic nuclei within the gas or crystalline targets. That research became the foundation for his influential theories on the force that binds atoms together in compounds, the force that gives atoms the cohesiveness to form molecules, which are the basis for all physical matter. He worked throughout the 1930s devising his quantum theory of chemical bonding, with the key element being "resonance," the circumstance in which atoms and molecules become cohesive by sharing electrons. In 1939, his landmark textbook, *The Nature of the Chemical Bond and the Structure of Molecules and Crystals*, was published. Pauling's official biographer, Professor Robert J. Paradowski of the Rochester Institute of Technology, asserts that the book "provided a unified summary of his experimental and theoretical studies and was responsible for the dominance that Pauling's ideas had on chemistry for several decades."

BIOCHEMISTRY AND WARTIME RESEARCH

Dr. Pauling became director of the Gates and Crellin Laboratories of Chemistry at Caltech during these years, a post he held from 1936 to 1958. His investigations were also turning to biochemistry because of his keen interest in proteins and particularly hemoglobin, a type of protein found in blood. He began to study the chemical structure of proteins and amino acids. By 1942, with the United States deep into World War II, he and his colleagues had succeeded in creating the first synthetic antibodies by changing the chemical structure of globulins (proteins). Pauling's talents were put to use as a consultant for the National Defense Research Committee and for the Office of Scientific Research and Development, working on such diverse projects as the creation of an artificial substitute for human blood serum, inks for secret writing, oxygen indicators for submarines and aircraft, and rocket fuel. He also was asked to work on the country's top-secret atomic bomb program, known as the Manhattan Project, but declined for two compelling reasons: he was suffering at the time from a severe kidney inflammation (nephritis, or Bright's Disease), and he was involved in too many other government projects. Pauling's wartime service was recognized in 1948 when President Harry S. Truman awarded him the prestigious Presidential Medal of Merit.

Pauling returned to academic life at the end of the war, and soon became interested in sickle cell anemia, a chronic, inherited disease occuring primarily among people of African ancestry. Pauling discovered that the red blood cells of patients with this disease became sickle-shaped in the venous blood but returned to their normal shape in the arterial blood, and he began to suspect that this change in shape was caused by a defect in the cell's hemoglobin. He and a colleague, Dr. Harvey Itano, were able to find the cause of the condition—a genetically transmitted defect in the protein portion of the red blood cells' hemoglobin molecule.

Throughout these years, the unrelenting researcher also was examining the physical structure of DNA (deoxyribonucleic acid), the blueprint for cellular reproduction. DNA, located in the nucleus of the cell in living things, contains a genetic blueprint for the organism, allowing the genetic code to be passed down through the generations. In 1953, he published his theory of a three-dimensional structure with three strands twisted together like a rope, but it was incorrect. However, when renowned British geneticists James Watson and Francis Crick proposed what was found to be the correct structure, the double helix, Watson acknowledged that it was Pauling's prior work that led to their discovery.

THE PEACE CRUSADE AND THE NOBEL PRIZES

In the aftermath of the first atomic explosion in 1945 and the arms race that followed World War II, Pauling had become a leading voice for world peace. He was one of a small group of scientists focusing their energies against the horrors of atmospheric nuclear testing, while vigorously crusading to support multinational disarmament. "He began the work that was to occupy most of his time for the next fifteen years," say Wintterle and Cramer in *Portraits of Nobel Laureates in Peace*, "[and] was everywhere—making speeches, debating, writing, arguing, fighting for a cause so great that his own illness [nephritis] . . . seemed trivial by comparison."

Pauling's peace activism became increasingly unpopular as cold-war tensions accelerated between the United States and the Soviet Union, and he came under attack from right-wing political groups. He was labeled a Communist by Senator Joseph R. McCarthy, chairman of a Senate subcommittee. McCarthy held Congressional hearings to accuse people of being Communists, playing on people's fear of Communism, destroying many reputations, and ruining many careers. In addition, Pauling was twice denied a passport by the State Department. In 1954, Pauling was awarded the Nobel Prize in Chemistry for his earlier research into the nature of the chemical bond. In a scramble by the State Department to cover their obvious embarrassment over their earlier treatment of the renowned scientist, an undersecretary of state overruled the Passport Office in 1954 so that Pauling could travel to Sweden to collect the Nobel Prize in Chemistry.

The maverick scientist's ideas benefited from the prestige of his first Nobel honor. As others began to note the genetic defects of radioactive fallout from atomic blasts, his influence spread quickly, and he became a leading participant in a series of international disarmament conferences. In January 1958, Pauling and his political activist wife, Ava, presented the United Nations with a test-ban petition signed by more than 13,000 scientists from 43 countries, but it was not until the summer of 1963 that the U.S. and the Soviets reached an agreement on a limited treaty to contain the development and deployment of nuclear weapons.

On the autumn day in 1962 that the treaty took effect, Pauling received the news that he had won the Nobel Peace Prize for 1962, thereby becoming the only recipient ever to win two individual Nobel awards. Pauling was cited for his work "not only against the testing of nuclear weapons, not only against the spread of these armaments, not only against their very use, but against all warfare as a means of solving international conflicts." The announcement was greeted without enthusiasm in the U.S., but Pauling emphasized the importance of the award, saying, "For many years it has not been respectable to work for peace. Perhaps the Norwegian Nobel Prize committee's action will help to make it respectable."

A number of administrators and colleagues at Caltech continued to look with disfavor on Pauling's activism, so late in 1963 he moved to the Center for the Study of Democratic Institutions in Santa Barbara. There, writes Professor Paradowski, "he divided his energies among the fields of chemistry, medicine, and world peace." He moved again, four years later, to the University of California at San Diego as "professor of chemistry in residence." In 1969, Pauling accepted what would be his final academic position, a professorship at Stanford University in Palo Alto.

THE FUROR OVER VITAMIN C

Pauling was forced to retire from Stanford at 70, still-vigorous and ready to set out on another venture. He founded the Linus Pauling Institute of Science and Medicine, a nonprofit research organization. "He thus began a phase of his life," said the *New York Times*, "that proved to be as controversial as his earlier periods of political activism." As an outgrowth of his interest in megavitamin therapy, Pauling had become convinced that large doses of Vitamin C could build up the human immune system and ward off infectious diseases—specifically, the common cold. The eventual outcome of his research was his bestselling and award-winning book published in 1970, *Vitamin C and the Common Cold*. Sales of the vitamin increased so dramatically across the country that pharmacies and health-food stores were unable to meet public demand. Nevertheless, his theories were viewed with skepticism in the biomedical community, and controversy over his beliefs became even more intense as he broadened his claims to include Vitamin C as a treatment for cancer. The furor continued throughout the 1970s and 1980s. When respected clinics and scientific journals began to publish the results of their experiments that refuted his research, Pauling responded with aggressive counterattacks in print.

Alexander Rich, an MIT biophysics professor who once studied with Pauling, entered the continuing controversy in 1992 in a comment to *People* magazine: "[Pauling] made a number of proposals that seemed outrageous, but there's been a great deal that's come out recently that lends strong support to the importance of Vitamin C." Pauling believed that his prostate cancer, diagnosed a year and a half before his death on August 19, 1994, may have been put off for 20 years by his own daily regimen of high Vitamin C intake. He also suggested then that the same vitamin therapy may have delayed his late wife's death from stomach cancer for as long as five years.

MARRIAGE AND FAMILY

Pauling and his wife, the former Ava Helen Miller, had been married nearly six decades when Ava died in December 1981. The couple met as undergraduates when Linus, only in his junior year, was allowed to teach chemistry to home economic students. *California* magazine tells that "the relationship began unromantically; the first thing he asked her was what she knew about ammonium hydroxide. She knew a lot, fortunately for her—and for him as history would show." Ava would become Pauling's lifelong inspiration and helpmate. Her outspoken ethical and political beliefs were the prime motivators for his growing social conscience and his eventual campaign against the dangers of nuclear testing. When Dr. Pauling won the 1962 Nobel Peace Prize, his only disappointment was that the award was not made to them jointly.

The Paulings had four children: Linus Carl, Jr., Peter Jeffress, Linda Pauling Kamb, and (Edward) Crellin Pauling. There are also 15 grandchildren and 19 great-grandchildren. Pauline Emmett is Dr. Pauling's only surviving sister.

HOBBIES AND OTHER INTERESTS

The curious child who collected insects and minerals grew into manhood with his thirst for knowledge intact. As an adult, his hobbies veered toward the study of words, and he became an avid collector and reader of dictionaries and encyclopedias. On a lighter note, one that portrays his love of life and his boundless energy, he loved to dance in the days before advancing age and waning health robbed his body of vigor. Daughter Linda remembers her parents dancing together at every opportunity and remembers being waltzed around the living room herself by her fun-loving father.

Linus and Ava Pauling had two California homes in the later years of their lives, one in Palo Alto, the other a small ranch house set on sixty acres at Big Sur, overlooking the Pacific Ocean. It was at Big Sur that Linus Pauling lived out his last days.

SELECTED HONORS AND AWARDS

National Research Fellow in Chemistry: 1925-26
Guggenheim Foundation Fellow: 1926-27
Irving Langmuir Prize (American Chemical Society [ACS]): 1931, Award in Pure Chemistry
William H. Nichols Medal (New York section of ACS): 1941
Willard Gibbs Medal (Chicago section of ACS): 1946
Davy Medal (Royal Society of London): 1947
Presidential Medal of Merit: 1948
Louis Pasteur Medal (Biochemical Society of France): 1952
Nobel Prize for Chemistry: 1954
Thomas Addis Medal (National Nephrosis Foundation): 1955, for reseach on kidney disease
John Phillips Memorial Medal (American College of Physicians): 1956

Avogadro Medal (Italian Academy of Sciences) 1956
Gold Medal (French Academy of Medicine): 1957
Humanist of the Year (American Humanist Association): 1961
Nobel Peace Prize: 1962
International Lenin Peace Prize: 1971
National Medal of Science (National Science Foundation): 1975
Lomonosov Gold Medal (Soviet Academy of Sciences): 1978
Award in Chemical Sciences (National Academy of Sciences): 1979
Vannevar Bush Award (National Science Board): 1979
Gold Medal (National Institute of Social Sciences): 1979
Arthur Sackler Foundation Chemistry Award: 1984
Priestly Medal (ACS): 1984

In addition to these and numerous other honors in science and medicine, Pauling was awarded the Order of Merit of the Italian Republic, the Medal of the Senate of the Republic of Chile, and l'Ordre du Merite Social del Belgique (Belgium).

WRITINGS

The Structure of Line Spectra (with Samuel Goudsmit), 1930, 1963
Introduction to Quantum Mechanics, With Applications to Chemistry (with E. Bright Wilson, Jr.), 1935, 1985
The Nature of the Chemical Bond and the Structure of Molecules and Crystals: An Introduction to Modern Structural Chemistry, 1939. Shortened edition, *The Chemical Bond: A Brief Introduction to Modern Structural Chemistry,* 1967
General Chemistry, 1947, 1953, 1970
College Chemistry: An Introductory Textbook of General Chemistry, 1950, 1964
Molecular Structure and Biological Specificity, 1957
No More War!, 1962, 1983
The Architecture of Molecules (with Roger Hayward), 1964
Science and World Peace, 1967
Structural Chemistry and Molecular Biology (editors, Alexander Rich and Norman Davidson), 1968
Centennial Lectures: 1968 to 1969 (editor), 1969
Vitamin C and the Common Cold, 1970
Orthomolecular Psychiatry: Treatment of Schizophrenia (editor with David Hawkins), 1973
Chemistry (with son, Peter J. Pauling), 1975
Vitamin C, the Common Cold, and the Flu, 1976
Cancer and Vitamin C: A Discussion of the Nature, Causes, Prevention, and Treatment of Cancer With Specific Reference to the Value of Vitamin C (with Ewan Cameron), 1979

Pauling also published hundreds of scientific papers and contributed scores of articles on social and political issues to periodicals. He was an associate editor of the *Journal of the American Chemical Society*, 1930-40; of the *Journal of Chemical Physics*, 1932-37; and of *Chemical Reviews*.

FURTHER READING

BOOKS

Aaseng, Nathan. *The Peace Seekers: The Nobel Peace Prize*, 1987
Newton, David E. *Linus Pauling: Scientist and Advocate* (Makers of Modern Science Series), 1994 (juvenile)
Serafini, Anthony. *Linus Pauling: A Man and His Science*, 1989
Wintterle, John, and Richard S. Cramer. *Portraits of Nobel Laureates in Peace*, 1971

PERIODICALS

California, Feb. 1991, p.58
Current Biography 1994
Harper's Bazaar, May 1983, p.154
Mother Earth News, Aug./Sep. 1992, p.74
Nature, Nov. 9, 1989, p.135
New York Times, Aug. 21, 1994, p.A1
Omni, June 1993, p.44
People, Aug. 31, 1992, p.101
Scientific American, Mar. 1993, p.36

Itzhak Perlman 1945-
Israeli-Born American Violinist

BIRTH

Itzhak (ITS-sock) Perlman was born August 31, 1945, in Tel Aviv, in what was then Palestine and is now Israel. He was the only child of Chaim and Shoshana Perlman. Chaim was a barber and Shoshana was a homemaker. They had immigrated to Palestine from Poland in the 1930s.

EARLY MEMORIES

Even though Chaim and Shoshana were not musicians, there home was full of music from the radio, and young Itzhak loved it. His parents boasted that he could sing operatic arias when he was only two-and-a-half. When he was three, Itzhak got a toy fiddle, but he couldn't play well, and, he remembers, he "threw it under the bed."

POLIO

When Itzhak was four, he came down with polio. Polio, short for poliomyelitis, is a viral disease that can cause crippling, paralysis, and death. Its victims are most often children, which is why it is sometimes called "infantile paralysis." In 1949, when Perlman got polio, there was not yet a vaccine to protect people against the disease. The vaccine was not developed until 1952.

Polio is caused by a virus that gets into the body through the intestines. Once there, it produces the aches and pains of the flu viruses we know today. In the majority of cases that is the extent of the disease, and the body develops an immunity because the system has built up defenses to fight the infection. But in some people, as in Itzhak Perlman, polio travels through veins or nerves to the spinal cord, where it attacks the nervous system and the brain. Polio destroys the muscles and paralyzes arms and legs, and often within 24 hours of the onset of the disease the patient is unable to walk.

When Perlman first recovered from the disease, he couldn't move his arms or his legs. His parents tried the only therapies known at the time for polio victims: they massaged his limbs everyday and applied warm water compresses. Slowly, feeling and movement returned to his arms and upper body, but his legs remained paralyzed. He had to learn to walk with crutches, and to live with his legs encased in steel braces. It was a long, exhausting effort, but Itzhak, with characteristic determination, never gave up.

BEGINNING THE VIOLIN

It was while convalescing that Itzhak asked his parents for a real violin and lessons. They thought it would be a good idea, both to strengthen his upper body and to offer a positive alternative to his difficult and often painful therapy. They bought him a used violin for six dollars, and Itzhak began his studies with enthusiasm—he practiced two to three hours a day! It wasn't easy, though. The violin is an extremely difficult instrument to play, but Itzhak persisted.

The family soon discovered that Itzhak had an extraordinary talent: by the time he was five, he was able to find the correct fingerings for the notes on the violin by instinct. He also has perfect pitch: the ability to identify a note—a "G" or an "A"—just by hearing it. Sometimes, he didn't practice willingly. "I didn't like to practice when I was a kid. I had to be reminded and forced to do it," he recalls. But he was determined to play like his idol, Jascha Heifetz. "Heifetz revolutionized fiddle playing by bringing it to the highest level ever of technical brilliance and strength," says the adult Perlman. "He was the most sizzling player who ever lived." And he provided the inspiration for the player who is considered by many to be Heifetz's successor as the greatest violinist of his generation.

EDUCATION—SCHOOL AND VIOLIN

When Perlman was growing up, "The tendency was to send handicapped kids away," Perlman remembers. "But my parents instinctively did things right. They treated me in a natural way." So when it came time for Itzhak to go to school, Chaim sold his barber shop and bought a laundry in an area where Itzhak could walk to the local elementary school. Despite the problems presented by his handicap, Perlman remembers his childhood as happy. The kids in school accepted him readily, and he even played soccer. "I was the goalie, he recalls. "With both my crutches and my legs, I could stop anything."

While still in grade school, he got a scholarship to the Tel Aviv Academy of Music, where he studied with Ryvka Goldgart. He played his first recital at age 10, and was soon performing with the Jerusalem Broadcasting Orchestra and the Tel Aviv Ramat-Gan Orchestra. His parents encouraged Itzhak to do anything he wished. While some felt that his disability meant he could never have a performing career, the Perlmans did not see their child's future determined by it. They recognized and nurtured his talent, and he worked hard.

As a young prodigy, Perlman came to the attention of two famous American musicians, violinist Isaac Stern and conductor Leonard Bernstein, during their travels in Israel. Stern, who has helped many of the most outstanding musicians of the current age, was and is both a mentor and friend to Perlman.

EARLY CAREER

Another famous American brought him to the attention of the American audience. Ed Sullivan heard Perlman play while on a search for new talent in Israel in 1958. He brought Perlman back to the United States, where he appeared on the "Ed Sullivan Show," a variety series that was one of the most popular shows on television in the 1950s and 1960s. Perlman was a sensation.

Only 13 years old, Perlman went on a concert tour of the U.S. and Canada, accompanied by his mother. They settled in New York after the tour. It was a depressing time for Itzhak and his mother, despite the promises it offered his career. Neither spoke English, they had very little money, and it was extremely difficult to keep Kosher—to follow the Jewish dietary laws. Chaim Perlman, still in Israel, had to wait another year before he could join them permanently. To support the family, Itzhak would play at local fund-raising dinners for Jewish organizations. "I would perform around 11:30 or midnight, after the fund-raising part, and I was up against the sound of the waiters collecting the forks. It was terrific training. My debut at Carnegie Hall was a breeze by comparison."

Perlman was accepted into the prestigious Julliard School at 13, where he studied with Dorothy DeLay and Ivan Galamian, another famous teacher. He took his high school courses at home, on the advice of this parents, then entered Julliard's college division.

DeLay, one of the greatest violin teachers in the U.S., remembers Perlman auditioning for her at this time. "I remember when I first heard Itzhak Perlman play. He was 14. He had just come here from Israel, and he was miserable. It was in an old, crummy hotel in downtown Manhattan, and it was raining. I know he looked at me and thought, 'Who is this horrible woman: I don't like her. Yuck!' I couldn't speak Hebrew, and he couldn't speak English. God, I never felt so sorry for anyone! And then he played, and I thought, 'I've never heard anyone like this in my life'." In addition to taking him on as a student, DeLay also taught him to drive a car, using hand controls, and introduced him to the culture of New York—its museums and artistic community.

CAREER HIGHLIGHTS

In 1963, at age 18, Perlman made his Carnegie Hall Debut. But because it took place during a newspaper strike in New York City, it was not the critical career move it might have been. His excitement over his Carnegie Hall debut was also marred by a commentator who said that he wasn't sure if Perlman received a standing ovation because of his playing or because of his disability. Once again, the stigma of being disabled appeared to be standing in his way. But once again he persevered.

The pivotal moment in Perlman's young career took place the following year, when he won the renowned Edgar M. Leventritt violin competition. The distinguished jury included Isaac Stern, composer Lukas Foss, and conductor George Szell. Perlman's victory was a bit overshadowed by the hubbub surrounding the disappearance of the violin Julliard had leant him for the competition. While he was on stage to receive the award, someone stole the $50,000 Guarneri violin, a story that made the front page of newspapers all over the country. Luckily, the thief "was not a musician," as Perlman recalls. The next day the priceless violin was found in a New York pawn shop, going for $15.

"Winning the Leventritt competition was the turning point," remembers Perlman. "I had 15 or 16 concerts the first year, 25 the next, 35 the next, and so on. And as I improved, people stopped bothering about my handicap—the doubts just disappeared." Many thought that the general audience would not accept a disabled violinist, one who must sit during performances, and who must enter the concert stage on crutches. But it proved to be a minor obstacle to his career, which took off like a meteor.

Now a seasoned veteran of concert stages all over the world, Perlman brings a unique and delightful personality to his music. In performance, his audiences are moved by his rich, warm tone and consummate musicianship. Of Perlman's musical gifts, critic Peter Davis says, "He seems to have just about everything, a fabulous technique, a string sound of ravishing tonal properties, a warm, romantic temperament, . . . a thoughtful musical intelligence, and an indefinable personal aura that makes audiences love him." He also charms audiences with his outgoing, funny personality. His irrepressible humor will often bubble to he surface, and he's been known to interrupt his recital with the scores of a local baseball game. He's never felt stagefright. "I've always loved to perform, right from the beginning,' he says. "It was always a comfortable thing for me—I just did it."

Perlman has a devoted following all over the world, and that includes other violinists. His friend and longtime mentor Isaac Stern says this: "His talent is utterly limitless. Nobody comes anywhere near him in what he can physically do with the violin. His hands are huge and he plays with incredible accuracy and dexterity."

Perlman performs and records solo recitals, concertos with large orchestras, and chamber music. Chamber music is a special love, especially the music of Brahms, which he claims "plays a very special part in my life. For me, there is no evening spent playing music for fun without playing one or two of the chamber works of Brahms." He has performed with a certain group of musicians and friends for many years. These include pianist Vladimir Ashkenazy, cellist Lynn Harrell, pianist and conductor Daniel Barenboim, and fellow violinist Pinchas Zuckerman. Zuckerman is also an Israeli, trained at the same academy as Perlman, and was also a prodigy. "We came out of the same ear, so to speak," says Zuckerman.

Perlman plays on a 1714 Stradivarius, valued at half a million dollars. The two greatest names in violins are Stradivarius and Guarneri, named for the eighteenth-century violin masters who made them. The Guarneri is noted for its deep, rich sound, the Strad for its sweet, melodic tone. Perlman plays the entire violin repertory, from the baroque masterpieces to modern works. He has also recorded jazz albums with his friend and fellow classical musician Andre Previn, as well as a recent album with jazz great Oscar Peterson. Perlman also played the violin solos on the soundtrack to Steven Spielberg's Academy-Award winning film *Schindler's List*.

Perlman finds his worldwide celebrity surprising, but he enjoys it nonetheless. He has appeared in American Express ads and on *Sesame Street*, where, he says, "I realized my dream—I got to play with Oscar the Grouch." He has become known to many people through his television appearances. "I suppose TV has always been my . . . call it my karma. I came to the United States from Israel to do [the Ed Sullivan] show, and TV has sort of followed me ever since."

Perlman is a teacher as well as a performer, giving master classes each year in New York and elsewhere. He is also an outspoken critic of the failure of schools to educate children properly in music. "I think music is one of the greatest, most inspired parts of an education. At least it should be." He claims that music education in the U.S. is "pathetic" because of the lack of good teachers and the way music is taught. "Very rarely do you find a teacher who is so inspired that the inspiration becomes infectious to the students. That's really what's needed."

PERLMAN ON MUSIC

Of his life in music, Perlman says this: "My music has nothing to do with the violin. It's what you have in your head, in your *personality*. When you play music, what you're really exploring is yourself. The big challenge is

to cleanse yourself of the 499 ways you played the Brahms or Beethoven concerto when you sit down to play it for the 500th time." When he was named "Top Fiddle" by *Newsweek*, he said, "It's a silly title. The most important thing to me is what my colleagues and audience think of my music. All the money, glamour, and glitter that have been associated with this is very, very, nice, but I feel I should not forget what I'm dedicated to. I'm a musician first, and I hope to grow nicely old with music."

MARRIAGE AND FAMILY

Perlman met the woman who would become his wife, Toby Friedlander, when he was a student at Julliard. He was playing a piece during the summer concert season at Meadowmount in New York, when Toby heard him play. "I heard the first phrase and said, 'This is for me.'" She ran backstage and asked him to marry her. Four years later, they finally did get married. Toby, also a concert violinist, has given up her career to raise the couple's five children, Noah, Navah, Leora, Rami, and Ariella, and to devote herself to her husband's career.

Perlman plays about 80 concerts each year, and often commands fees as high as $10,000 per concert. But he is also a devoted father who tries to commute to concerts as much as possible. He also refuses to play on any of his children's birthdays. "If you're not careful, the children will grow up on you and you'll miss the most glorious part of life." he says.

The Perlman family has an 11-room apartment overlooking the Hudson river on the Upper West Side of New York City. It is the former home of Babe Ruth, which pleases the Yankee-fan Perlman. They also have a country home in upstate New York that has been updated to include barrier-free access for Perlman.

ON BEING DISABLED

Perlman is a tireless supporter of the rights of the disabled and has been consulted by architects in the construction of schools and concert halls. "A lot of people think access means the ability to get into a building no matter where or how you can get into it, whether you get into it through a back alley, or through an elevator that usually carries garbage or food." And he has refused to play at certain concert halls in the U.S. until they improve their handicapped access. He also insists that he be shown on television entering the stage on his crutches, and not sitting down.

He spends a good deal of time with disabled kids. "Whenever I have the chance, I visit and play at hospitals for kids with severe disabilities. I do it to show them that a disability should not mean that you cannot do anything." Perlman encourages these kids to "separate their abilities from their disabilities. Youngsters especially, who are impressionable, are at the mercy of people around them, vulnerable to what people think they can or cannot do." He is on the board of Jean Kennedy Smith's Very Special Arts, an organization that helps bring the arts to the nearly half-million disabled Americans. Perlman appeared in a film on the organization with Barbara Walters.

HOBBIES AND OTHER INTERESTS

Perlman is a passionate fan of the Yankees and New York Knicks, and he also loves to fish. He is a gourmet cook, and especially enjoys cooking Chinese and Japanese dishes.

SELECTED RECORDINGS

Vivaldi: The Four Seasons, 1977
Beethoven: Sonatas for Violin and Piano, 1978
Brahms: Concerto for Violin in D Major, 1978
Berg: Concerto for Violin and Orchestra/Stravinsky: Concerto in D Major for Violin and Orchestra, 1980
Brahms: Concerto in A Minor for Vioin and Cello, 1980
The Spanish Album, 1980
Tchaikovsky: Piano Trio in A Minor, 1981
Elgar: Concerto for Violin in B Minor, 1982
Mozart: Violin Concertos Nos. 2 and 4, 1987
Beethoven: The Complete Piano Trios, 1987
Shostakovich: Violin Concerto No. 1 in A Minor/Glazunov: Violin Concerto in A Minor, 1990
Brahms: The Three Violin Sonatas, 1990
Beethoven: String Trios, 1992
Mendelssohn: Concerto in E Minor, 1993
Brahms: Piano Trios Nos. 1,2,3,4, 1994
Great Romantic Concertos, 1994

HONORS AND AWARDS

Eugene M. Leventritt Award: 1964
Grammy Award: 1977, for *Vivaldi: The Four Seasons;* 1978, for *Beethoven: Sonatas for Violin and Piano* (with Vladimir Ashkenazy); 1978, for *Brahms: Concerto for Violin in D Major;* 1980, for *The Spanish Album;* 1980, for *Brahms: Concerto in A Minor for Violin and Cello* (with Mstislav Rostoprovich); 1980, for *Berg: Concerto for Violin and Orchestra/Stravinsky: Concerto in D Major for Violin and Orchestra;* 1980, for *Music for Two Violins* (with Pinchas Zuckerman); 1981, for *Tchaikovsky: Piano Trio in A Minor* (with Lynn Harrell and Vladimir Ashkenazy); 1981, for *Isaac Stern: 60th Anniversary Celebration* (with Isaac Stern and Pinchas Zuckerman); 1982, for *Elgar: Concerto for Violin in B Minor;* 1987, for *Beethoven: The Complete Piano Trios* (with Lynn Harrell and Vladimir Ashkenazy); 1987, for *Mozart: Violin Concertos Nos. 2 in D and 4 in D;* 1990, for *Shostakovich: Violin Concerto No. 1 in A Minor/Glazunov: Violin Concerto in A Minor;* 1990, for *Brahms: The Three Violin Sonatas*
Musician of the Year (Musical America): 1981
Medal of Liberty (Statue of Liberty—Ellis Island Foundation): 1986
Lions of the Performing Arts (New York Public Library): 1989

FURTHER READING

BOOKS

Behrman, Carol H. *Fiddler to the World: The Inspiring Life of Itzhak Perlman,* 1992 (juvenile)

Ewen, David, ed. *Musicians Since 1900,* 1978

PERIODICALS

Boston Globe, Oct. 25, 1993, p.A39
Boy's Life, June 1980, p.9
Chicago Tribune, July 3, 1986, p.A3; June 19, 1988, p. B14
New York, Dec. 21-28, 1992, p.108
New York Times Biographical Service, Mar., 1979, p.367; Oct. 1981, p.1403
Newsweek, Apr. 14, 1980, p.62
People, June 8, 1981, p.55
Philadelphia Inquirer, May 25, 1983, p.E1
Time, Jan. 15, 1965, p.49

ADDRESS

IMG
22 E. 71st St.
New York, NY 10021

Cokie Roberts   1943-
American Broadcast Journalist
Reporter and Political Correspondent for ABC
News and National Public Radio's "All Things
Considered"

BIRTH

Mary Martha Corinne Morrison Claiborne Boggs Roberts, now
known as Cokie Roberts, was born on December 27, 1943, in New
Orleans, Louisiana. Cokie is the daughter of (Thomas) Hale Boggs,
a member of the U.S. House of Representatives from Louisiana
who died in a plane crash in Alaska, and Corinne Morrison
(Claiborne) Boggs, called Lindy, his helpmate, the organizer of
his political campaigns, and his successor in the House. Cokie
was the third of their four children. One brother died in infancy.

Her older sister, Barbara Boggs Sigmund, was the mayor of Princeton, New Jersey, before her death from cancer in 1990; her older brother, Thomas Hale Boggs, Jr., is considered one of the most powerful and financially successful lobbyists in Washington, D.C. Cokie earned her nickname as a baby, when her brother Tom, then just three, couldn't pronounce Corinne.

YOUTH

For Roberts, covering politics, and particularly the U.S. House, is the most natural job in the world. She grew up dividing her time between the family home in the Garden District of New Orleans and their second home in Bethesda, Maryland, outside Washington, where they lived when Congress was in session.

Roberts has often been called the consummate Washington insider, for a very good reason. In her words, "Politics is the family business." Politics was a constant part of life in the Boggs family, and the children were always included. "From the time I was born, my father was in politics. My parents knew that if they wanted to have any opportunity for a family life, they'd have to involve us in politics." She learned her love of debate and of good conversation early: political talk at the dinner table was an ongoing feature of family life, and the children participated even when guests came. "There was never a sense 'the children shouldn't be here.' Lyndon Johnson, Sam Rayburn [then Senate majority leader and speaker of the U.S. House, respectively] would come to the house and we'd argue with them about civil rights, Vietnam, everything."

With her father, Roberts practically grew up in the Capitol building, accompanying him to work. Even today, while covering the Capitol as a reporter, she meets with people who knew her as a child. Her mother taught her about another side of politics, too. Lindy Boggs worked full-time managing her husband's reelection campaigns as well as his Congressional office. She also planned the inaugural celebrations of John F. Kennedy and Lyndon B. Johnson.

With her mother's example, Cokie grew up believing that women's opinions mattered, at a time when that was rare. In the Boggs family, everybody loved to talk, especially the women. "I had women around me who had no shyness whatsoever, to put it mildly," she once said.

EDUCATION

That attitude was reinforced in her schooling. The Boggses were a deeply Catholic family, and Cokie attended Catholic schools run by Sacred Heart nuns both in Louisiana and Maryland. They were all-girls schools, with all female faculty, and the girls talked because "there's nobody else *to* talk."

By the time Roberts reached high school she showed a talent for journalism, acting as editor of the school newspaper. After graduation, she attended Wellesley College, a prestigious women's college in Wellesley, Massachusetts. In 1964, when she was only 20 years old, she earned a B.A. with distinction in political science from Wellesley.

During her years at Wellesley, Cokie attended a student political conference in the Midwest. Defying the early 1960s assumption that women should be seen but not heard, Cokie stood up to speak and caused a commotion. One person who was not upset by her audacity was Steven Roberts, another student attending the conference and the man who would become her husband. Here, Cokie describes Roberts, then the editor of *The Harvard Crimson*, the student newspaper at Harvard University: "He was cute. He was funny. He was smart. And I knew even then that he'd be a wonderful father." He was also Jewish, and the difference in religions upset both families.

MARRIAGE AND FAMILY

Cokie and Steven dated for about four years before getting married on September 10, 1966. They were married at Cokie's childhood home in Bethesda, Maryland, outdoors under an apple tree. Lindy Boggs, Cokie's mother, did all the cooking for their 1500 guests, including then-President Lyndon B. Johnson and most of Congress.

Today, Cokie and Steven Roberts live in that same house in Bethesda where she grew up. They have two children, Lee and Rebecca, who are both now grown.

CHOOSING A CAREER

When Cokie Roberts was young, most women devoted their work efforts to their homes and families. Here, Roberts explains what she and her sister Barbara anticipated for their own future careers: "Growing up, our expectation was to do what our mother did. We thought we would graduate from college, have an interesting job for a year or two, get married, have babies, and contribute to the community. It never occurred to us that we would have careers."

FIRST JOBS

And for a long time, that's pretty much what she did. After finishing college in 1964, Roberts spent two years working at WRC-TV in Washington, D.C. She was the host of "Meeting of the Minds," a weekly political show. When she married in 1966, she moved to New York, where her husband was working for the *New York Times*. After that point, her career took a back seat to her husband's and to her family responsibilities. "But that's what I wanted to do," Cokie says. "We had little kids. My career came second—in both my husband's and my mind." Ultimately, Roberts says that she became a journalist because it suited their lifestyle. "When we were married . . . I was not committed to journalism in any way. We kept moving around the country and the world, and it was by far the easiest thing to do—go out and report a story and come back and write it— because that is portable. That is how [my career] evolved."

Once in New York, she started looking for a job and soon encountered blatant sexism. Despite holding a degree with honors from a prestigious college, Roberts remembers repeatedly hearing "We don't hire women writers." As she recently explained, "For eight months I job-hunted at various New York magazines and television stations, and wherever I went I was asked how [fast] I could type." She eventually landed a job with Cowles Communications in 1967 as a reporter and editor on *Insider's Newsletter*; the following year, she worked as a producer at WNEW-TV in New York. Her husband was then transferred to Los Angeles, California, where Cokie worked as a producer for Altman Productions from 1969 to 1972. She then spent two years as a producer for KNBC-TV in Los Angeles, where she won an award for excellence in local programming.

HALE BOGGS DISAPPEARS

On October 16, 1972, when Roberts was 28 and living in California, her father disappeared. Hale Boggs was then Majority Leader of the House; it was widely expected that he would soon become Speaker of the House. His plane disappeared over Alaska on the 550-mile flight from Anchorage to Juneau. Cokie, along with her mother, sister, and other family and friends, flew up to Alaska to wait for word.

For a month, a search was conducted of the mountain ranges, glaciers, and deep, freezing waters of the Prince William Sound. Although the search continued until Thanksgiving, no trace of the plane or its occupants was ever found. For the whole family, the grief surrounding his death was made even harder by the lack of concrete proof that he was really gone. In fact, that lack of finality was one of the reasons that Lindy Boggs decided to run for his seat in Congress. As she explains, "[Even] when I was finally persuaded to run for his seat, I'm not sure it was because I really accepted the fact he was gone. I figured that if anybody was willing to give up the seat to him if he came back, it would be me." Ultimately, Lindy Boggs did decide to run for that seat, which she held until her retirement in 1990. Together, the Boggses represented their Congressional district for almost 50 years.

CAREER HIGHLIGHTS

Roberts's big break as a broadcaster came after she and her family moved to Athens, Greece, in 1974 for Steven's job. While there, she started working for CBS News radio as a stringer. (A stringer is a correspondent who works for a news agency part-time and who is paid only when his or her reports are aired.) And Cokie's reports were aired. At that time, Greece was in a state of political upheaval that resulted in the 1974 coup that overthrew the military junta. Roberts happened to be driving by the presidential palace on the day that the military junta was drummed out and the city erupted in joy. That day, her report was the lead story on the TV broadcast of the "CBS Evening News."

NATIONAL PUBLIC RADIO (NPR)

In 1977, Roberts and her family returned to the U.S. and moved into the old Boggs family home in Bethesda, just outside Washington, D.C., where they have lived ever since. In February 1978, she began working for the news division of National Public Radio (NPR), a public, non-commercial radio network that is funded by the government, businesses, charitable groups, and by its listeners. Its influential news programs, "Morning Edition" and "All Things Considered," mix solid hard news reports and feature stories, all covered in great depth. Then as now, NPR was known for having many talented female reporters. Roberts was recruited to work there by two of them, Linda Wertheimer and Nina Totenberg. As Roberts recalls, "When I came in for an interview, Linda and Nina were there, greeting me and encouraging me. And it just made all the difference in the world. NPR was a place where I wanted to work because they were there."

At NPR, Roberts was assigned to cover Congress. For Roberts, that proved to be the ideal assignment. Having grown up on Capitol Hill, she knew many of the Congressional leaders personally. Her contacts, and her reputation, quickly grew as she provided concise, insightful, and well-informed reports on the working of Congress. As Linda Wertheimer recalls from that time, "I had spent years trying to develop a beat in Congress, working really hard, trying to understand what the talk meant, how the monster actually worked. I thought I was good at it. Then Cokie arrived, after living in Greece for years, and I had the feeling that she was born to understand Congress."

Roberts has continued to analyze the activities of Congress on NPR since that time. But she soon started to supplement her work there with commentary in other media as well. In 1981, she and Linda Wertheimer joined the weekly PBS TV show "The Lawmakers" in what was the first joint effort between public radio and public television. From 1984 to 1987 she was the congressional correspondent on the PBS show "MacNeil/Lehrer NewsHour." In 1987 she received widespread national attention during the PBS coverage of the Iran-Contra hearings. And throughout all this time she was also juggling her work assignments with raising children, a job that she always makes clear was just as important as her paid work. "The greatest challenge of my life has been the one most women have . . . of doing it all," she once said. "There were really hard years raising kids and writing stories and trying to have a household that bore some resemblance to the one I grew up in, which I liked a lot."

ABC NEWS

In 1988, Roberts started appearing with regular panelists Sam Donaldson and George Will on "This Week with David Brinkley," a Sunday morning roundtable discussion show on ABC. Although Roberts started out as an occasional guest, viewer response was so positive that she soon joined on as a weekly regular. The ABC network took the unprecedented step of offering her a contract that would allow her to continue on NPR a few days a week while also working as the Washington correspondent for ABC. For the last few years, Roberts has been an ABC News special correspondent covering politics, Congress, and public policy. In addition to appearances on "This Week with David Brinkley," she has reported on the "ABC Nightly News" and has also acted as substitute anchor on "Nightline" for Ted Koppel. On NPR, Roberts continues to provide commentary on political life in Washington as a senior news analyst. In 1992, with the election campaign season in full swing and Roberts broadcasting reports on a variety of programs on radio and TV, she achieved widespread national prominence.

From her early days on radio to her recent appearances on TV, Roberts has developed the professional persona that has earned her the respect of other journalists and the affection of millions of viewers. After growing up on Capitol Hill, she has an easy familiarity with and comfortable access to many Congress members, making her one of the most well-informed observers on the Washington scene. Despite years spent in a Democratic household, she is objective in her work. In the words of Alison Cook in *Lear's* magazine, "Roberts seems resolutely apolitical—as apt to deflate liberal dogma as conservative cant." Her common sense, down-to-earth manner, and slightly bemused air have particularly appealed to viewers, who trust her honesty and directness. They enjoy her sense of humor, her ability to combine serious political analysis with a quick response to all that's funny about politics and politicians. And on the TV news, a format that can be rather dry and on which the commentators often sound rather self-important, her laugh—what Cook describes as "a five-part chuckle vaulting into glissades of cackles"—has endeared her to her fans. "Cokie is one of the most appealing newspeople anywhere," the writer for *New Choices* magazine says, "articulate, attractive, slightly amused by all the huffing and puffing, almost always making darn good sense, and exhibiting political savvy and broadcast cool."

With all her success, the only question that remains is how long Roberts will be able to keep it up. Television is a medium that prefers to showcase youth. While this is true for men also, it is particularly true for women. There have been several male silver-haired eminences on the news, but there are no older women who look their age. Women have only been appearing on the national news for about the last twenty years or so, and few have been allowed to age on-air. Barbara Walters is the one notable exception, and even she once observed that "Anchor women don't get older, they get blonder." For Roberts, who despite her years of other journalistic experience didn't start appearing on the network news until her 40s, it's unclear how long she'll be able to stay on the air. But no matter what happens, it's clear that Roberts will find a way to stay on top.

HOBBIES AND OTHER INTERESTS

In her rare spare time, Roberts enjoys many of the pleasures of the home. She enjoys needlepoint and cooking, especially using the produce from the family's large vegetable garden. She once picked and pitted 24 cups of cherries and then baked six cherry pies; another time, she put up 32 quarts of homemade tomato sauce.

WRITINGS

In addition to writing her own on-air commentary, Roberts also writes a weekly syndicated newspaper column with her husband, Steven R.

Roberts. Her opinion columns have appeared in the *New York Times* and the *Washington Post*; she has also written pieces for the *New York Times Magazine* and *The Atlantic*.

HONORS AND AWARDS

Broadcasting Award (National Organization of Working Women): 1984
Distinguished Alumnae Achievement Award (Wellesley College): 1985, in recognition of excellence and distinction in professional pursuits
Everett McKinley Dirksen Award (Everett McKinley Dirksen Congressional Leadership Research Center): 1986, for distinguished reporting of Congress
Edward Weintal Prize for Diplomatic Reporting (Georgetown University Institute for the Study of Diplomacy): 1988
Edward R. Murrow Award (Corporation for Public Broadcasting): 1990, for outstanding contributions to public radio
Exceptional Merit Media Award (National Women's Political Caucus): 1989
David Brinkley Communications Award: 1992
Mother of the Year Award (National Mother's Day Committee): 1992

FURTHER READING

BOOKS

Who's Who in America 1995

PERIODICALS

Current Biography Yearbook 1994
GQ, Dec. 1990, p.146
Lear's, Feb. 1993, p.54
McCall's, May 1991, p.23
New York Times Magazine, Jan. 2, 1994, p.1
Philadelphia Inquirer, Apr. 14, 1993, p.E1
TV Guide, June 19, 1993, p.23
USA Weekend, June 18-20, 1993, p.4
Washington Post Magazine, June 20, 1993, p.W8

ADDRESS

ABC News
1717 DeSales Street NW
Washington, DC 20036

OBITUARY

Wilma Rudolph   1940-1994
American Runner
First Women to Win Three Gold Medals in
Track and Field in a Single Olympics

BIRTH

Wilma Glodean Rudolph was born on June 23, 1940, in St. Bethlehem, Tennessee, a small, rural town about 50 miles southeast of Nashville. Her parents were Ed and Blanche Rudolph. Wilma was the 20th of 22 children in the family, including those from Ed's first marriage.

Soon after Wilma's birth, the family moved to the home where she would grow up. It was a small cottage in the town of

Clarksville, Tennessee, about 50 miles northwest of Nashville. Ed Rudolph worked as a railroad porter and also did odd jobs for families in town; Blanche Rudolph took in laundry and sewing and worked as a maid or domestic, cleaning homes for white families.

EARLY YEARS

For poor families in the South, life could be pretty tough. The tiny Rudolph home had no running water or bathrooms or electricity. The children never had new, store-bought clothes, just those their mother could sew from flour sacks. But as Rudolph wrote in her 1977 autobiography *Wilma*, "We didn't have too much money back then, but we had everything else, especially love."

Life was especially tough for black families. It was a time when racial prejudice was widespread and overt, and black people were routinely denied their civil rights. The South, in particular, was segregated by race. Blacks were limited in their choices of housing and jobs, were forced to attend segregated schools, and were prohibited from using many restaurants, movie theaters, and other public places. The facilities open to blacks were usually in poor condition. In every way, blacks were made to feel inferior.

In Rudolph's town, there was only one restaurant black patrons could go to, only one school black students could attend, only one doctor black patients could see. When she was about five, she realized that "there were a lot of white people in this world, and that they belonged to a world that was nothing at all like the world we black people lived in."

"My mother used to go out to these people's homes with all the latest electrical gadgets, with modern plumbing and fancy bathrooms and big white pillars in the front. She would get there on Saturday mornings, and the first thing she would have to do is to serve these people with all the latest conveniences their coffee in bed. I resented that right off, my mother having to do that. We didn't have electricity in my house, and when we had to go to the bathroom we went outside, in this little shed, the outhouse. The way my mother worked, somebody should have been serving her coffee in bed on Saturday mornings. Instead, she did the serving. . . . I said to myself, 'There's something not right about all this. White folks got all the luxury, and we black folks got the dirty work.' I made up my mind right then and there: 'Wilma,' I said to myself, 'you ain't never gonna be serving coffee to no white folks in bed on Saturday mornings.'"

ILLNESS

Rudolph's life story is an amazing one, filled with the determination to overcome overwhelming obstacles. She struggled with illness throughout her early life. She was born two months prematurely, after her mother suffered a fall, and weighed only four and a half pounds at birth. At the time, they weren't even sure if she would live. She later wrote, "Being a premature baby may explain why I was sick all of the time when I was growing up. I was so skinny, and I never had the strength the other kids had. I would get a common cold, and it would last for weeks, and then it would develop into something else. I was the most sickly kid in all of Clarksville."

As a young child, she had mumps, measles, chicken pox, and whooping cough—all serious illnesses that are treatable today with vaccines and medication. At about four, she became dangerously ill with double pneumonia followed by scarlet fever. There was only one black doctor in town, and the nearest hospital that would accept black patients was 50 miles away, in Nashville. The Rudolph family didn't have any insurance, or any money to pay for medical care. So Wilma's mother took care of her at home.

At some point during those early years she also had polio, a serious illness caused by a virus that attacks the nervous system and destroys muscle control. Then common in children, polio often caused paralysis in the arms and legs of its young victims; in the worst cases, the muscles that control breathing were affected. In 1952, the worst year of the polio epidemic, 57,000 cases were reported in the U.S. alone. The vaccine to prevent polio wasn't widely available until the early 1960s.

For Rudolph, the lasting effect of all her illnesses was paralysis in her left leg; the leg and foot were also crooked. At age five, she began wearing a heavy metal brace to correct it, along with heavy brown Oxford shoes. Each week, on her mother's one day off, she would take Wilma to Meharry Medical College in Nashville, which treated black patients. They would ride the Greyhound bus, sitting in the back, where blacks were allowed to sit. If the bus was crowded that day and any white people needed seats, the black people would be forced to leave their seats and stand in the aisle. The doctors at Meharry put Wilma through a rigorous physical therapy program to strengthen her leg muscles. They also taught her mother how to massage Rudolph's leg to keep working on her muscle strength between visits. Her older brothers and sisters pitched in to help, and between them all they would massage her leg four times a day.

EDUCATION

At first, Rudolph was too sick to start school. When the other kids went off to kindergarten, she was stuck at home. She hated it, and she was miserable. "Being left behind had a terrible effect of me. I was so lonely, and I felt rejected. I would drift off, close my eyes, and just drift off into a sinking feeling, going down, down, down. I cried a lot." The neighborhood kids teased her and taunted her and tried to make her cry. But after a while, she shifted from depression to determination. "I started to get mad about it all. I got angry. I went through the stage of asking myself, 'Wilma, what is this existence all about? Is it about being sick all the time? It can't be.' So I started getting angry about things, fighting back in a new way, with a vengeance. I think I started acquiring a competitive spirit right then and there, a spirit that would make me successful in sports later on. I was mad, and I was going to beat these illnesses no matter what. No more taking what comes, no more drifting off, no more wondering. Enough was enough."

When she was seven, Rudolph was finally well enough to start at Cobb Elementary, the local black school. Fortunately, she was put into the second grade, with the other children her age. "That first year of school was a big one for me," Rudolph once wrote; "it turned my life around. I went from being a sickly kid the other kids teased to a normal person accepted by her peer group, and that was the most important thing that could have happened to me at that point in my life. I needed to belong, and I finally did." Gradually, all the hard work was paying off—her leg was slowly getting better, and she was feeling better about her life.

LOSING THE BRACE—AND GAINING A LIFE

When she was almost ten, Rudolph first appeared in public without her brace. She went to church without the hated brace and walked right up the center aisle. Later, all the townspeople came to congratulate her. It took another two years, though, until she was twelve, before she was able to get rid of the brace for good. It was a great day for Wilma, and for her whole family, when her mother could pack it up and send it back to the hospital. Wilma had recovered. "My whole life suddenly changed just as I was ending my sixth-grade year in school. No more brace; I was healthy all over my body for the first time."

DISCOVERING SPORTS

That very same summer, Rudolph discovered sports. She started hanging around the playground, like the other kids, and was soon joining in their basketball games. Often they would play in someone's yard, using a bushel basket nailed up to a tree and any ball they could find. She had watched enough games while sidelined with her bad leg to learn all the rules and memorize all the plays, and now she was ready. Her mother worried that she would be injured and warned her not to play, but Rudolph couldn't be stopped. She spent that first summer without a brace learning the game.

That fall, she started seventh grade at Burt High School—in Clarksville, black students attended the segregated high school from seventh through twelfth grades. And the best part, for Rudolph, was that students from all grades were eligible to join the basketball team. She signed up right away. The first year, seventh grade, she spent the whole season on the bench, studying the game. She didn't get to play, but she did practice—every day, after school, and every other chance she got. In fact she was around so much that the coach, Clinton Gray, nicknamed her "Skeeter," for mosquito, because she was always "buzzing" around. The second year, eighth grade, she got in a few games, and even managed to score a basket. That spring Coach Gray started a track team when the basketball season ended. Rudolph joined, mostly just to have something to do after school. Her third year on the basketball team, in ninth grade, was the most frustrating. She felt ready to play, and the coach still virtually ignored her. That spring she joined the track team again. They held meets against the surrounding schools, and Rudolph ran in the 50-, 75-, 100-, and 200-meter races. She was winning consistently, with no formal training and no knowledge of the technical aspects of her sport, like warm ups, or starting techniques, or breathing control.

Rudolph finally earned a starting spot on the basketball team the next season, when she was a sophomore in tenth grade. She had worked really hard for that spot, and her perseverance paid off when she led the team to victory in the Middle East Tennessee Conference. During that first full season of play, she scored 803 points in 25 games, setting a new record for female high school players in Tennessee. The Burt team went on to the state tournament, the Tennessee High School Girls' Championships. The team did not play well and was soon defeated. Although she didn't know it at the time, that loss would later pay off for Rudolph.

She also suffered a crushing defeat that year in track. In 1956 she entered her first official track meet, the Amateur Athletic Union (AAU) contest held at Tuskegee Institute in Alabama. After her many wins in the informal meets at her school, she was cocky about her chances for success. But this time she was up against seasoned runners, and she lost every event she entered.

The losses were devastating for Rudolph, but they taught her a lesson. "It was the first time I had ever tasted defeat in track, and it left me a total wreck. . . . After so many easy victories, using natural ability alone, I got a false sense of being unbeatable. . . . [It] made me realize that I couldn't do it on natural ability alone, that there was more to track than just running fast. I also realized it was going to test me as a person—could I come back and win again after being so totally crushed by a defeat? . . . I learned a very big lesson for the rest of my life as well. The lesson was, winning is great, sure, but if you are really going to do something in life, the secret is learning how to lose. Nobody goes undefeated all the time. If you can pick up after a crushing defeat, and go on to win again, you are going to be a champion someday." Ultimately, Rudolph's loss in the AAU contest made her determined to go back the next year and beat them all.

HIGH SCHOOL ATHLETICS

Later that spring, Wilma's parents were approached by Ed Temple, the coach of the women's track team at Tennessee State University in Nashville. That team, the Tigerbelles, was one of the best in the nation. Coach Temple had been one of the referees at the basketball championships where Rudolph's team had fared so poorly—he often worked as a referee to scout out new talent. Impressed with the speed of the six-foot tall, ninety pound player, he invited Rudolph to spend the summer at Tennessee State University, training with other promising high school students. He explained to the Rudolphs that Wilma's running skills might win her a scholarship to college. Her parents were elated. As her mother told her, "You're the first one in this house that ever had the chance to go to college. If running's going to do that, I just want you to set your mind to be the best!"

She did. Rudolph spent that summer at Tennessee State, working out with other young track hopefuls. The girls ran up to 18 miles a day, five days a week, to build their endurance. They also did exercises to increase their muscle strength. Racing strategy, how to breathe properly, and how to use the starting blocks to get off to a fast start were also emphasized. Throughout these drills, it was clear that Rudolph was a sprinter, a runner who runs very fast for a short distance, as opposed to a long-distance runner, who runs slower to pace herself for the longer distance. She excelled in several short races as well as the relay—a race between teams of runners in which each member of the team runs one leg of the race before passing a baton, or cylinder, to the next runner. The final runner, usually the fastest member of the relay team, is called the anchor.

Rudolph's hard work soon paid off when Temple and his group went to the next AAU meet, late that summer of 1956 in Philadelphia, Pennsylvania. She was entered in three events—the 75-yard dash, the 100-yard dash, and the 440-yard relay, running as the anchor. There were many runners that day, so several qualifying rounds were held for each race, to determine which runners would be eliminated and which would move up to the final event. By the end of that day in Philadelphia, Rudolph had competed in nine separate races, including the qualifying rounds and the finals, and had won in every one. Her success that day earned her the chance to meet Jackie Robinson, who had battled racial prejudice to become the first black man to play major-league baseball. He gave her some advice she would always treasure. "You are a fascinating runner. Don't let anything or anybody keep you from running. Keep running." "[For] the first time in my life," she later wrote, "I had a black person I could look up to as a real hero."

Following those successes, Coach Temple invited Rudolph to join the Tigerbelles in traveling to Seattle, Washington, to try out for the U.S. team for the upcoming 1956 Olympic Games. Only 16 at the time, Rudolph was afraid to travel so far from home. She received a lot of support and encouragement from one of her team mates, two-time Olympic veteran Mae Faggs, so Rudolph joined the team on that long drive from Nashville to Seattle. She was so nervous before the qualifying round for the 200-meter race that Faggs told her "Concentrate on doing nothing else but sticking with me." Rudolph took her advice so seriously that she and Faggs reached the finish line at exactly the same time. Wilma Rudolph, a poor teenager from Tennessee who had been partially paralyzed ten years earlier and who had thrown away her leg brace only four years earlier, was on her way to the Olympics.

1956 OLYMPICS

After a two-week training camp in California, Rudolph traveled to Melbourne, Australia, site of the 1956 Olympics. It was exciting and fascinating for this small-town girl to be part of the Olympic village and meet athletes from all over the world.

Rudolph was entered in two events—the 200-meter and the 4 x 100-meter relay. In the 200-meter race, she only advanced to the semi-finals, the last heat before the finals. It was a devastating loss. "I felt terrible after," she later wrote in her autobiography. "I couldn't eat or sleep. I felt as if I had let down everybody back home and the whole United States of America. . . . Watching [Australian runner Betty Cuthbert win gold medals in the 100-, 200-, and 400-meter races] motivated me into making a commitment to do the very same thing someday. I was determined that four years from then, no matter where the Olympics were held, I was going to be there and I was going to win a gold medal or two for the United States. Meanwhile, I still had the chance to help win one for the United States in the relay. . . . I was determined to give my very best effort in the relay to salvage something, not only for the U.S. team but for myself." The relay team didn't take the gold, but they did bring home a bronze medal for third place.

RETURNING TO HOME AND SCHOOL

After the excitement of the Olympics, Rudolph returned home to her junior year in high school and to basketball season. On the day of her return, the school held a big assembly to cheer her victory. For Rudolph, Olympic athlete, the most important issue was whether she could play in the season-opening basketball game that night. That year, the team went on to win the state championships. But she soon had her first brush with real tragedy that spring. On prom night, her teammate and best friend Nancy Bowen was killed in a car accident. The driver, who had just gotten his license, was drag racing another car. Doing 90 miles an hour, he lost control of the car and hit a concrete pillar. He and Nancy died instantly. Soon afterward, Rudolph returned to Tennessee State to run track, but it was a tough and confusing time for her.

In fall 1957, she returned to her senior year of high school. She was looking forward to a great year. She had been dating Robert Eldridge, a longtime friend and a fellow high school student and athlete. As she later said, "Robert was the star of the school's football and basketball team, and I was the star of track and girl's basketball; we were like the King and Queen." That was all about to change. Soon after her annual physical before basketball season, she learned that she was pregnant.

She was afraid to tell anyone—her parents, her teachers, her coach. She finally told her sister, who told her parents. They were very supportive, but set down two rules: no more Robert, and no shame—everybody makes mistakes, they said. After facing her parents, Wilma's greatest fear was that it would jeopardize her future in athletics. But Coach Temple was also very supportive. After hearing a rumor that Rudolph was pregnant, he came to visit the family. On learning the truth, he told her that he still wanted her to come to Tennessee State after her baby was born. As Rudolph later wrote, "The people I loved were sticking by me, and that alone took a lot of pressure, and pain, and guilt, off my shoulders."

Although she missed the basketball and track seasons, Rudolph completed her schoolwork and graduated from high school in May 1958. She had a baby girl, Yolanda, in July. Robert wanted to get married, but Wilma's father absolutely forbid it—he blamed Robert for everything and even tried to prevent him from seeing his own daughter. But Wilma, too, was reluctant to marry and throw away her chances as a runner. Her family offered to take care of the baby, so six weeks after Yolanda's birth Rudolph left for Nashville and an athletic scholarship at Tennessee State.

TENNESSEE STATE UNIVERSITY

That first year of college was a real adjustment for Rudolph. She missed her baby, struggled to keep up with her schoolwork, and tried to focus on her running. But she was determined to let nothing interfere with her plan to attend the next Olympics. Now bulked up to 130 pounds on her six-foot frame, she made the college track team in her freshman year. At the beginning of the following year, the year of the trials for the 1960 Olympics, she started regularly losing races, and neither she nor Coach Temple could figure out why. Finally the doctor diagnosed a tonsil infection, which had been sapping her strength, and removed her tonsils.

After recovering from surgery, Rudolph returned to her old form. In May 1960, at the AAU indoor meet in Chicago, Illinois, she set record times in the 100-yard and 220-yard dashes of 10.7 and 25.7 seconds. In June, at the AAU outdoor meet in Cleveland, Ohio, she again set national records, running the 100-yard dash in 10.6 seconds and the 220-yard dash in 23.9 seconds. In July, at the AAU meet in Corpus Christi, Texas, the last major meet before the Olympic trials, Rudolph ran the 200-meters in 22.9 seconds, setting a new world record. In August, when the try-outs for the U.S. Olympic team were held in Abilene, Texas, she qualified in three events—the 100-meter, the 200-meter, and the 4 x 100-meter relay—winning a place on the U.S. team. The good news continued when three of her Tigerbelle teammates also made the team, and her mentor, Coach Temple, was named coach of the U.S. Olympic women's track team.

1960 OLYMPICS

After training at Kansas State University in Emporia, Kansas, the Olympic team flew on to Rome, Italy. It was miserably hot there, with temperatures climbing to 100 degrees. But Rudolph and her fellow Tigerbelles didn't mind—they were used to training in such heat every summer in Nashville. After training for two weeks, it was finally the day before Rudolph would run her first race. It was scorching. She and a few teammates were out having a light practice when they saw some sprinklers in an open field. They started running through the sprinklers, laughing, playing, and soaking themselves in the 100-degree heat. Suddenly Rudolph landed in a hole in the grass and twisted her ankle. She even heard it pop. She was sobbing from the pain and the fear that she had ruined her chances in the Olympics. The trainer ran out, put the ankle on ice to keep the swelling down, taped it up tight, and ordered her to stay in bed with her foot elevated. The next day, the day of her first race, she got up in the morning and discovered that she could put her weight on it. With her ankle tightly taped, she would be able to run.

After that, despite her injury, everything went smoothly. Rudolph was calm, focused, intense. She was the favorite of the fans, and 80,000 spectators chanted her name. But she tuned it all out, just concentrating on the race. She was so calm, in fact, that she fell asleep between races, amazing her fellow competitors. She won all of her trial heats for the 100-meter, her first race, and even ran a world-record time of 11.0 seconds in the final trial. (That record time was later disqualified because there was a strong wind at her back helping her.) With her smooth, fluid running style, she easily won first place, taking her first gold medal. In the trials for the 200-meter, she set an Olympic record time of 23.2 seconds. In the finals, she ran in a stiff wind and still won the gold with a race time of 24.0 seconds.

In her final event, the 4 x 100-meter relay, Rudolph was running the anchor position on a team with her three fellow Tigerbelles. The U.S. team was not favored to win. She was a bit concerned about her injured leg, because this race would be run on a curved track, which would place more stress on her ankle. On the day of the race, the first three runners, Martha Hudson, Barbara Jones, and Lucinda Williams, each ran a very fast leg. As Williams approached Rudolph, ready to pass the baton, she was two yards ahead of her closest competitor, from the West German team. Yet the pass was bobbled. Rudolph had to slow down to get a firm grip, losing valuable time and their two-yard lead. After that Rudolph had to run flat out to catch up, and then pass, the German runner. The U.S. team won the relay, and Rudolph took her third gold medal, becoming the first woman in Olympic history to win three gold medals in track in a single Olympics. Her only disappointment was that her family had not been there to see her win—they simply could not afford the trip, and at that time there was no funding available to help out the families of Olympic athletes.

After the Olympics, Rudolph was mobbed by her admirers, and by the press, who adored her. She and the U.S. Olympic team spent the next two months traveling to different track meets throughout Europe. Everywhere she went she drew crowds of devoted fans. On returning to the states, she was treated like royalty, with parades and celebrations, honors and awards, and invitations to meets all over the country. She was invited to several prestigious meets that had previously barred women, opening the door for future female runners. She even got to meet President John F. Kennedy. But perhaps the most important event took place in her home town of Clarksville. To celebrate her return, the town held its first ever integrated event, with both blacks and whites honoring Rudolph at a parade and banquet.

RETIREMENT FROM SPORTS

Within a year, Rudolph started thinking about retiring. She was determined to "go out early and on top," before she lost her edge and started losing. She thought about the 1964 Olympics, and worried that if she went and lost there, she would always be remembered for her losses, not for her wins. Complicating matters was the fact that there was no financial support at that time for amateur athletes. She made her retirement official in 1962, after a meet in California against Soviet athletes. After she had been signing autographs for a while, a small boy finally got his chance. She took off her running shoes, signed them both, and gave them to him. Her career in track was over.

A NEW CAREER

After graduating with a degree in education from Tennessee State on May 27, 1963, Rudolph returned to Clarksville and worked as a teacher and track coach. It was the first of several jobs that she would hold over the coming years that would combine her love for children and for athletics. She was soon discouraged, though, because there were few job opportunities that were well paying, and she changed jobs and cities often. After leaving Clarksville, Rudolph became the director of a community center in Evansville, Indiana, and then moved on to a physical education program at a Job Corps center in Poland Springs, Maine. In 1967, she was asked by Vice-President Hubert Humphrey to work on a new project called Operation Champ, bringing star athletes into inner-city ghettoes to teach sports to children.

She went on to work for a short time for the Job Corps in St. Louis, and then taught at a school in Detroit. Next she went to Los Angeles and worked at the Watts Community Action Committee, and then worked at UCLA as an administrator ·in the Afro-American Studies program. She did a brief stint in Chicago at the Youth Foundation, and then went to Charleston, West Virginia, as a fundraiser for a Track and Field Hall of Fame. She also worked as a goodwill ambassador in West Africa, acted as a corporate spokesperson, and coached at DePauw University.

In many of these positions she had felt frustrated because she was expected to act like a figurehead—she was given the title with no real power to do the work. She felt exploited. Eventually, in 1981, she set up the Wilma Rudolph Foundation, a non-profit group based in Indianapolis, Indiana, that trains young athletes in their chosen sport. The group provides coaching, encourages athletic and academic success, and prepares amateur athletes for meets and other events. Ultimately, the Foundation's goal is to teach children how to overcome the obstacles in their lives, just like Rudolph did.

RUDOLPH'S LEGACY

Rudolph died from brain cancer at her home in Nashville, Tennessee, on November 12, 1994. Before her death, she had said that "If I have anything to leave, the Foundation is my legacy." But for many, her greatest gift was the inspiration she provided to succeeding generations of athletes. According to Jackie Joyner-Kersee, considered the finest female athlete of this generation, "[Rudolph] laid the foundation for all of us women who wanted to aspire to be great athletes." Her husband and coach, Bob Kersee, concurs. "You don't mention Wilma in the same breath with any female athlete in track and field. Everybody else stands below her." According to Edwin Moses, two-time winner in the Olympic hurdles, "Everybody says she was a great role model for young women athletes. It wasn't only that. She was a hero to all of us in the sport." Sportswriter Fred Russell, who covered her wins in the 1960 Olympics, adds this: "[Rudolph] was more than the fastest woman of her time. She was a symbol of courage, the personification of the idealism of the Olympic Games."

MARRIAGE AND FAMILY

Rudolph was married and divorced twice. In 1961, she married William Ward, a fellow student and runner at Tennessee State; they divorced the next year. In 1963, she married Robert Eldridge, her high school sweetheart. They divorced in 1976.

Rudolph was survived by her four children: daughters Yolanda Eldridge-Jones and Djuana Rudolph-Bowers, and sons Robert Eldridge and Xurry Eldridge, and by seven grandchildren.

WRITINGS

Wilma, 1977 (autobiography)

HONORS AND AWARDS

Olympic Track and Field, 4 x 100 Meter Relay: 1956, bronze medal; 1960, gold medal
Olympic Track and Field, 100 Meters: 1960, gold medal

Olympic Track and Field, 200 Meters: 1960, gold medal

Associated Press Sports Award - Athlete of the Year, Women (Associated Press Sports Department): 1960, 1961

James E. Sullivan Memorial Award (Amateur Athletic Union of the United States): 1961, as top amateur athlete in the U.S.

Babe Didrikson Zaharias Award: 1962

Black Sports Hall of Fame: 1973

National Track and Field Hall of Fame (The Athletics Congress of the USA): 1974

International Women's Sports Hall of Fame - Contemporary (Women's Sports Foundation): 1980

U.S. Olympic Hall of Fame (United States Olympic Committee): 1983

Silver Anniversary Award (National Collegiate Athletic Association): 1990

National Sports Award: 1993, presented by President Bill Clinton

FURTHER READING

BOOKS

Biracree, Tom. *Wilma Rudolph*, 1988 (juvenile)
Coffey, Wayne. *Wilma Rudolph*, 1993 (juvenile)
Encyclopedia Brittanica, 1993
Great Athletes: The Twentieth Century, 1992
Jennings, Jay. *Long Shots: They Beat the Odds*, 1990
Notable Black American Women, 1991
Rudolph, Wilma. *Wilma*, 1977
World Book Encyclopedia, 1993

PERIODICALS

Current Biography 1961
Jet, Nov. 28, 1994, p.58
Newsday, Nov. 13, 1994, Sports section, p.2
New York Times, Nov. 13, 1994, Section 1, p.53; Nov. 13, 1994, Section 8, p.9; Nov. 19, 1994, p.33
Washington Post, Nov. 13, 1994, Sports section, p.D5

SALT 'N' PEPA

Cheryl James (Salt)
Sandi Denton (Pepa)
Dee Dee Roper (Spinderella)
American Rappers

EARLY YEARS

The hot hip-hop trio Salt 'N' Pepa is made up of three women: the rappers Cheryl James (Salt, born March 28) and Sandra Denton (Pepa, born November 9), and the DJ Deirdre Roper (Spinderella, born August 3). Roper joined the group in 1987 after the original DJ, Pamela Greene, left to get married. The birth years of all three women are unknown; they adamantly refuse to divulge their ages, but they are widely reported to be in their late 20s.

All three women grew up in New York City in strong black families that valued education. Cheryl James lived in Queens with her father, a subway conductor, her mother, a bank manager (now retired), and one brother and one sister. She attended Grover Cleveland High School. Sandi Denton was born in Kingston, Jamaica, but later moved to Queens with her parents and her eight brothers and sisters; her mother, a nurse, has supported the family since her father died in 1983. Dee Dee Roper grew up in Brooklyn with her five sisters and brothers. Her father was a steamfitter for Con Edison. Roper attended Franklin K. Lane High School; in fact, she was still a high school senior when she first hooked up with Salt 'N' Pepa.

FORMING THE GROUP

The group first got together in 1985. Both James and Denton were college students at Queensborough Community College. Although they weren't friends at first, they would watch each other across the college cafeteria—a clear case of opposites attract. James was quiet, sedate, and conservatively dressed. As she says, "I was a solemn child. I still am. I wore dresses and heels all the time. Not sexy dresses—frumpy dresses. I was like the old maid at my young age." Denton was different—outgoing and flashy. As James says, "She was so wild and so loud and so dressed and so popular. She just fascinated me." As Denton recalls, "I used to be punkin' out, with safety pins in my ears. Salt was so quiet and calm with her little outfits. . . . I'd be over there wilding and stuff, but I'd always look to see what she was up to."

As they became friends, the two began spending all their time together. James was working at the Sears store in Queens as a telephone customer-service representative. She helped Denton get a job there also. The two would sit in adjoining cubicles talking to each other on the phone. Each time the boss would come through, they would pretend to be speaking to a customer. Each of the customer-service reps had sales quotas to meet. James and Denton started lying about the number of sales they had made. Instead of getting caught, they kept getting raises. For a while, it was a great job. That Sears store in Queens was, at the time, filled with talent— other employees included the comedian Martin Lawrence, the star of the Fox series "Martin," and the rappers Chris Reid and Chris Martin, or Kid 'N Play, the stars of the *House Party* movies.

Another coworker and friend was record producer Hurby (Luv Bug) Azor. Then a music student at the Center for the Media Arts in Manhattan, Azor was behind in his classwork—in fact, he had skipped all of his classes and had completed none of his schoolwork. To graduate, he had to produce a demo record. At first, Azor planned to make the record with James—at that point the two were dating. They picked the name Salt 'N'

Pepa to go with their light and dark toned skins. But then he decided that the song would work better with two women—an audacious decision, considering that at that time rap was an all-male genre. Azor convinced James and Denton to be the rappers on his demo.

GETTING STARTED

At first, it was all run by Azor. He named the pair Supernature and wrote a rap song for them to record, "The Showstopper," a cocky, self-confident response to the popular hit "The Show" by Doug E. Fresh and Slick Rick. That first song earned Azor an "A" and started James and Denton on the road to their career. Their friends all liked the record's funky beat and lyrics so much that Azor decided to play it for DJ Marly Marl, the host of a radio rap show in New York. Marly Marl started playing it on his show, and listeners started calling in to request it. Soon, James and Denton quit school, changed their name to Salt 'N' Pepa, added a DJ (Pamela Greene), started performing at clubs around New York, and signed a recording contract with a small, independent record label.

THE BIG BREAKTHROUGH

Salt 'N' Pepa released their first album, *Hot Cool & Vicious,* in 1986. The first single, "My Mic Sounds Nice," reached the Top 40 on the black singles charts. Their next single, "Tramp," did even better. Then a California DJ checked out the other side and found "Push It." He remixed it, started playing the new version, and sent it on to the record company. They released the new version as a single. When it crossed over to the Top 20 of the Billboard pop charts, it pushed sales of the album to over one million copies and brought Salt 'N' Pepa to national attention. Writing in the *Los Angeles Times,* Connie Johnson described their appeal. "Salt 'N' Pepa mixes mildly salty language, a hot, peppery dance beat, and a heavy dose of attitude in a sound that sets the group miles ahead."

With *Hot Cool & Vicious,* Salt 'N' Pepa became the first million-selling female rap group, a landmark in the history of rap music. As Joy Duckett Cain explains in *Essence* magazine, "Lest we forget: Hip-hop in the eighties was—as it still is—a male-dominated genre, one where women rappers were routinely disregarded, dogged or dissed. Salt 'N' Pepa brought a whole new female flavor to the mix. With their sassy, sexy, bold, fun-loving, trash-talking, take-no-prisoners attitude, the group showed that they were *women,* damn it, and proud of it. They knew what women wanted to hear—and they weren't afraid to say it." It was a whole new approach to rap, according to Dinitia Smith in *New York* magazine. "Salt 'N' Pepa mock the macho posturing of male rappers. . . . [They] don't hesitate to put men down. . . . In Salt 'N' Pepa raps, the women are in control."

SUCCESS

They went on to great success with their next two albums. Dee Dee Roper (Spinderella) joined the group in 1987, before the release of *A Salt with a Deadly Pepa* (1988), which produced the hit song "Shake Your Thang." That album was followed up by *Blacks' Magic* in 1990. Both albums sent platinum, selling over one million copies each.

The group underwent some changes in both the style of their music and the tone of their lyrics during that time. They started out with a soul/rhythm & blues-based sound on *Hot Cool & Vicious,* and then tried more of a pop sound on *A Salt with a Deadly Weapon.* On *Blacks' Magic,* they combined a bit of both. Their lyrics underwent a change as well. On their first two albums, they boasted about themselves, rapped about partying, and put down men. With *Blacks' Magic,* they made the move into more serious issues, like teenage pregnancy, drugs, AIDS, sexual responsibility, and black pride. They also stressed empowerment, independence, and self respect for all women. They toured relentlessly to support these albums, and their stage shows were always crowd pleasers, with backup singers and dancers, choreographed numbers for each song, smooth moves, and flashy costumes.

HIATUS

After *Blacks' Magic,* the group took a three-year break before releasing their next album. During that time, all three women had babies, and all three are currently single parents. Denton was first. Her son, Tyran, was born in 1990. She refuses to discuss the father, except to say that he left her while she was pregnant. She is currently seeing Treach from Naughty by Nature. James's daughter, Corin, was born in 1991. Corin's father is Gavin Wray, a carpenter, whom James is still seeing. Roper's daughter, Christenese, was born in 1992. Her father is Kenny Anderson, a basketball player with the New Jersey Nets. He and Roper split up just after Christy was born. Roper is now seeing Kermit Holmes, a basketball player with the Oklahoma City Cavalry. Denton, James, and Roper have all praised the men now in their lives for being respectful, supportive, and helpful with their children.

Many commentators have remarked that the births of their children seemed to make the members of the group stronger and more focused. As James explains it, "[Having kids] totally changes your mind, your thinking. It makes you grow up. We changed record companies, took control over our money, and we changed our attitude. Basically, we became women. And that shows in our videos. It's a take-charge, take-control attitude."

First, they took control of their bodies. After having their babies, they all went on a serious exercise program. Since then, they've received many compliments on their new look. But as James and Denton make clear here, they didn't do it to please anyone but themselves. "We had babies, we lost weight, we've been working out," James says. "We feel very good about ourselves. We don't mind showing off, as long as you know that's not all we're about." Or as Denton says, "I did it for me. I'm showing off for me. . . . A girl can look good and still be respected."

Next, they took control of their finances. Although they had been selling millions of records, their earnings were low. They felt they had received bad advice from their lawyers on the terms of their first contract—they had signed an agreement for 50 cents per album sold, only half the going rate. They renegotiated to earn a larger share of the profits from their records.

Finally, they took creative control. Until this point, Hurby Azor had continued to be the primary creative force for the group. While he is still involved in producing their music, the members of Salt 'N' Pepa are now far more involved in writing, selecting, and producing their songs.

RETURN TO PERFORMING

Salt 'N' Pepa returned from their hiatus in 1993 with the release of *Very Necessary*, "soul-tinged R & B melodies [mixed] with teasing, street-savvy raps about maturity, independence from men, and sexual responsibility." As Denton explains, "We were involved in every stage of this album from songwriting to production— *everything*," and their involvement paid off. The album won glowing reviews and sold some three million copies, making them the best-selling female rap group ever. (To date, Salt 'N' Pepa is still the only female rap group to sell a million copies of its records.) The videos for two of the hits, "Shoop" and "Whatta Man," which features back-up vocals from the group En Vogue, were both huge hits on MTV, boosting sales of the records.

Despite the fun and the flash, there is a serious side to the album as well. Salt 'N' Pepa included a powerful and moving public service announcement about AIDS done by a teen group, and a forceful message about self-respect and independence for women. As James explains it, "This girl told me we inspired her to get out of an abusive relationship: 'Salt 'N' Pepa makes me strong.' That's what we stand for—being a woman and not being weak. Not being so strong that you act like a man, because I feel there's nothing wrong with being sexy and being feminine. But being strong." As Denton tells it, "Our message is 'Respect yourself. Raise yourself up.' If you treat yourself like a queen, you're going to attract a king."

RECORDINGS

Hot Cool & Vicious, 1986
A Salt with a Deadly Pepa, 1988
Blacks' Magic, 1990
Very Necessary, 1993

HONORS AND AWARDS

MTV Video Awards: 1994, 3 awards for "Whatta Man," with En Vogue—
  Best Dance Video, Best R & B Video, and Best Choreography in a Video
Grammy Award: 1995, Best Rap Performance by a Duo or Group, for
  "None of Your Business"

FURTHER READING

Essence, Sep. 1988, p.73; Oct. 1994, p.86
Mother Jones, Sep./Oct. 1990, p.34
New York, Jan. 17, 1994, p.32
People, Apr. 18, 1988, p.113
Rolling Stone, June 30, 1994, p.21
Us, Aug. 1994, p.54

ADDRESS

Island Records
825 Eighth Avenue
24th Floor
New York, NY 10019

Barry Sanders 1968-
American Professional Football Player with the Detroit Lions
1994 NFL Rushing Leader

BIRTH

Barry Sanders was born July 16, 1968, in Wichita, Kansas. He was the seventh of eleven children born to William and Shirley Sanders, and the youngest of three boys. Shirley and William, a roofer and carpenter, and Shirley raised their family in a modest three-bedroom house in Wichita.

YOUTH

Sanders grew up in a close-knit household that was marked by his mother's kindness and his father's strict sense of discipline.

286

"I had a very strong father figure, a wonderful mother, and those are the people I took instruction from. They looked after me and took care of me," recalls Sanders. While his family did not have a great deal of material wealth, Sanders and his brothers and sisters were taught to respect both themselves and others. "We were raised to use what you have and not go around looking for more," says Sanders. "We were taught not to be greedy or obsessed with what you couldn't have. It was instilled in us as kids. It's a trait that comes from not having very much outside and a lot inside."

Still, there was a period during his childhood when Sanders got into a fair amount of trouble. "When I was younger, people thought I was a bully. I got into fights and did a lot of wrong. My older brother Byron and I stole candy and got in a lot of fights at school. We'd throw rocks at cars. One time I started a fire on the floor of our bathroom at home." Worried that Barry and Byron were following in the footsteps of their oldest brother Boyd, who was heavily involved with drugs and alcohol at the time, Shirley Sanders sat her two youngest sons down. She pointed out that a number of Boyd's friends were in prison or had died of drug overdoses. The two boys realized that they had to straighten up or risk the same fate down the road. As time passed, the Sanders family was relieved to see Boyd turn away from the drug and alcohol abuse that had been ruining his life. He emerged as a strong positive influence in Barry's life and eventually became an ordained minister.

Years later, Sanders remains grateful for his mother's strong interest in guiding her sons and daughters to adulthood. She took all the children to services at Paradise Baptist Church and watched over them to make sure they did their schoolwork. "My mother is the backbone of our family. At the age of 43, she finished work on her nursing degree at Wichita State. Not many people have the strength to raise 11 children, work in the home and go to school, but my mother did it," says Sanders. "She would rather see other people happy than herself. I've never heard her curse. I've never seen her take a drink. She is a Christian woman. A real one."

As Byron and Barry grew older, they became known as the neighborhood's best athletes. "We played a lot of keep-away, you know, when one guy gets the ball and everybody tries to tackle him," Sanders later related. "Because I was smaller I had to learn real fast to avoid getting hit." But neither of the schools that Sanders attended as a youngster—Bryant Elementary School and Hadley Junior High School—offered organized football. Instead, he played in the Greater Wichita Youth Football League from sixth through ninth grade. Barry was a dazzling runner in the league, but he was so small that many people did not take his talent seriously. When he attended Wichita North High School in Wichita in 1983 as a freshman, Sanders was only 5'5" and weighed less than 140 pounds; his brother Byron, on the other hand, was a big strong runner who had become the star of the high school's football team.

EDUCATION

As a freshman, Sanders saw little playing time on the football field. A year later he saw some varsity action as a defensive safety, but his coaches remained convinced that he was too small to carry the ball and wondered among themselves whether he was afraid of contact. This attitude frustrated Sanders's father, who had seen how elusive his youngest son was on the playgrounds of their neighborhood and the fields of the Wichita Youth League. He encouraged Sanders and badgered the coaching staff to play Barry at running back. "I never knew how good I could be then because everyone was always telling me I was too small," recalls Sanders. "Everyone but my father. He told me I could be great. I know people think that was just a father talking, but he always told the truth."

By the time of Sanders's junior year in high school, his hard work in the weight room was showing results. Taking notice of how strong and muscular he had become, the Wichita North High School coaches played him at several different positions, including receiver, kick returner, and cornerback. His brother Byron, though, remained the team's primary running back.

In 1986 Sanders and his father thought he'd finally have the opportunity to show what he could do as a running back. Byron had graduated from high school and had received a scholarship to play football at Northwestern University. In addition, Wichita North High School's new head football coach, Dale Burkholder, was impressed with Sanders's speed. Still, Barry was not named the starting running back until the third game of his senior season. In his first game at tailback Sanders exploded for 274 yards rushing and four touchdowns. The opposing team had so much difficulty holding on to him that the game officials checked his uniform for Vaseline.

Sanders's darting, weaving running style proved impossible for opposing defenses to stop. One of his coaches noted much later that "I can still see him out there doing things that seem impossible. As fast as he was, he could stop on a dime and reverse his field before the defense could even react. He made some dazzling runs and was fabulous all year."

His success on the football field, though, never caused him to ignore his schoolwork. He remained a good student, especially in math, and retained his unassuming manner. "Barry was a quiet kid, never bragged about himself, or did anything to draw attention to himself," recalls one of his coaches. "He was very religious even then and popular with the other students. In fact, I had six members of his family in my classes over the years and they were all fine kids."

By the end of his senior season, Sanders had gained over 1,500 yards rushing and been selected to the All-City and All-State teams. He and his father thought that the University of Oklahoma might be interested in offering him a football scholarship, but they were scared off by his small size. Other schools voiced similar reservations, so Sanders received scholarship offers from only three schools. He eventually decided to attend Oklahoma State.

CAREER HIGHLIGHTS

COLLEGE—OKLAHOMA STATE COWBOYS

At Oklahoma State, Sanders spent his freshman year backing up Thurman Thomas, a talented running back who went on to enjoy a fine career with the Buffalo Bills. By mid-season, however, Sanders was the team's primary kick returner, a position he excelled at. In his sophomore year Sanders led the nation in kickoff returns with an average of 31.3 yards per return, including two amazing 100-yard touchdown sprints. He was also one of college football's leading punt returners in 1987.

As his junior year approached, Sanders was poised to prove what he could do as a running back in a major college football program. Thurman Thomas had moved on to the National Football League (NFL), a development that meant that Sanders would be the Cowboys' starting tailback at the beginning of the season. Sanders had also built his weight up to more than 200 pounds as a result of long hours in the team's weight room. In the summer months leading up to the season, however, rumors about recruiting violations and illegal payments to players began to swirl around the team. Sanders clearly was not one of the players suspected of receiving big cash payments to play for Oklahoma State. He drove an eight-year-old Pontiac and spent the summer bagging groceries at a local supermarket. Ignoring the

rumors about possible NCAA sanctions against the football program, Sanders kept his focus on the upcoming season.

The quiet young man from Wichita began the 1988 season against Texas A&M by running the opening kickoff back 100 yards for a touchdown. The return was a sign of things to come. He racked up big rushing totals in the first couple games of the season, but it was in the third game, against Tulsa, that Sanders suddenly emerged as a leading candidate for the Heisman Trophy, the award given each year to the nation's best college football player.

Against Tulsa the darting, slashing Sanders carried the ball 33 times for a startling 304 yards and five touchdowns in a 56-35 victory for Oklahoma State. Afterwards, Cowboys head coach Pat Jones marveled at Sanders's performance. "He's the most explosive guy I've ever seen. He sees an opening, and he can be at full-speed, bam, just like that. Plus he's so strong and tough that people just can't tackle him." Cowboys quarterback Mike Gundy agreed. "Guys will come up and take a stab at him, and he'll make one quick move and never slow down. They don't even touch him. It's the most amazing thing I've ever seen."

Even such traditional football powerhouses as Nebraska and Oklahoma found that they were unable to stop Sanders. The running back registered 189 yards and four touchdowns in a losing effort against the Nebraska Cornhuskers and 215 yards against Oklahoma in a near-upset of the favored Sooners. By the end of Sanders's remarkable season, he had tied or broken 24 different NCAA single-season records. He obliterated the previous single-season rushing record, tallying 2,628 yards, and led the nation with 39 touchdowns. Sanders finished his junior season by exploding for 332 yards to lead the Cowboys to victory against Texas Tech in the Coca-Cola Classic, which was played in Tokyo, Japan. When the dust of the season had settled, some observers called Sanders' year the greatest individual season in college football history.

Sanders was honored for his spectacular season with the Heisman Trophy, an award that brought with it a great deal of media attention that embarrassed the soft-spoken young man from Wichita. The acclaim and accolades initially disconcerted Sanders, who preferred his previous quiet lifestyle. But he was determined that his sudden celebrity status would not change him. "People always try to get you to change—like in junior high it was popping pills and booze and marijuana, and everybody calling you square if you didn't do it," Sanders said. "Well, I consider what's happening now another type of peer pressure. And I don't care what anybody says about me in all this. They don't know me."

In January 1989 the Oklahoma State football program was placed on probation by the NCAA as punishment for various recruiting violations. This penalty meant that the football team could not appear on television or in a bowl game for the 1989 season, which would be Sanders's last year of college. This factor, combined with the graduation of several of his best friends on the offensive line and the tough financial situation of his family, convinced him to leave college before his senior season and make himself available for the NFL draft. Sanders knew that a contract with a professional team would make him a rich young man, able to provide for his entire family. Still, the decision was a difficult one. His mother and several of his sisters wanted him to stay in school for his senior year and get his diploma. His father, though, argued that his son should join the professional ranks. He warned him that if he suffered a serious injury during his senior season, the millions of dollars available in the NFL might be lost forever.

After a long period of indecision, Sanders decided to go pro, although he promised his mother that he would someday return and earn his college diploma. The 1988 Heisman Trophy winner was the third selection in the NFL draft in 1989. He was selected by the Detroit Lions, a dull, mediocre team that desperately needed an injection of excitement.

THE PROS—DETROIT LIONS

Contract negotiations with the Lions proved rocky, however. Lions fans and newspaper reporters accused Sanders and his agents of being greedy, but when Sanders finally signed a five-year, $6.1 million contract three days before the beginning of the 1989 season, he promptly wrote out a check for more than $200,000 to the Paradise Baptist Church in Wichita that he and his family had long attended.

Sanders played sparingly in the first two games of the regular 1989 season; he had missed the entire training camp and exhibition season and knew only a few of the team's plays. In the third game of the season, however, the Lions' rookie running back showed the flash that had earned him the Heisman Trophy the year before, burning the Chicago Bears for 126 yards on 18 carries. By mid-season Detroit had won only one game and lost seven others, but players and coaches around the league noted that the team had a potential rookie of the year in their backfield. Several members of the Minnesota Vikings defense even insisted that Sanders was spraying himself and his uniform with silicone, a slippery substance that would have made him even more difficult to tackle. Game officials checked Sanders's uniform, then returned to give the Vikings the bad news: their inability to tackle the Lions back had nothing to do with silicone.

Sanders weaved his way to 184 yards against the Green Bay Packers in the eighth game of the season, then led a sudden surge by the Lions that put them in playoff contention as the season went on. Detroit won six of their last seven games to finish with a respectable 7-9 record for the year. Sanders finished 10 yards behind Christian Okoye in the battle for the NFL rushing title that year, but his coaches and teammates noted that he could have almost certainly won the title if he had decided to play in the fourth quarter of the season finale, a lopsided win over the Atlanta Falcons. But when Lions head coach Wayne Fontes asked Sanders if he wanted to return to the game to secure the rushing title, he declined. As he explained later, "when everyone is out for statistics—you know, individual fulfillment—that's when trouble starts. I don't want to ever fall victim to that."

Sanders finished his rookie season with a team single-season record 1,470 yards and 14 touchdowns on 280 carries, totals that earned him NFL Rookie of the Year honors, a trip to the Pro Bowl, and numerous other awards.

A year later Sanders proved that his rookie season was no fluke. He led the NFL in rushing in 1990 with 1,304 yards on 255 carries. In 1991 he continued his spectacular performance, sprinting for 1,548 yards and 16 touchdowns. Sanders's legs carried Detroit all the way to the National Football Conference Championship that year before they were vanquished by the eventual Super Bowl champion Washington Redskins.

By this time Sanders had become established as one of the game's great modern runners. Some onlookers felt that he had the capacity to be one of football's all-time greats. Walter Payton, the NFL's leading career rusher, once declared that "I don't know if I was ever *that* good" after watching Sanders destroy his old Chicago Bears team. *Sports Illustrated* writer Ed Hinton noted that a player of Sanders's ability could, "if he wished, be the trash-talkingest guy in the league, with the flashiest lifestyle. Sanders has never been heard to utter so much as a syllable of trash, and since arriving in the NFL in 1989 he has never spiked the ball after a touchdown." Such understated behavior has contributed immensely to his enduring reputation as one of the sports world's most modest and unassuming stars.

The year 1992 was a disappointment for Sanders and the Lions. After their success in 1991, the team had expressed high hopes of reaching the Super Bowl the following year. Instead, Detroit stumbled to a five-victory season. Sanders enjoyed a fine season individually, rushing for 1,352 yards and nine touchdowns, but he absorbed a great deal of punishment because of the Lions' poor blocking. He averaged 4.3 yards per carry in 1992, the lowest of his career.

In 1993 the Lions rebounded from their terrible showing the year before. Sanders again led the way, compiling a league-leading 1,115 yards rushing through 11 games. A knee injury suffered against the Bears, though, cut his season short. Sanders missed the rest of the regular season, although he was able to return for the opening round of the playoffs against the Packers. He was superb in that game, dodging and diving for 169 yards on 27 carries, but his heroics were not enough to save Detroit from defeat.

Sanders enjoyed his best season yet in 1994. Coaches and opponents around the league marveled at his talent as the little back scorched his foes for big yards in nearly every game. Dallas Cowboys safety Bill Bates says, "there have been many times when I *knew* I had him, when I *knew* it was about to be one of those tackles where the guy is just going to get his clock cleaned by me. And I tackled air." Veteran pro and college coach Dan Hennings adds that "he has the most unusual ability to stop and start that I've ever seen." Lions coach Wayne Fontes proclaimed that "you can't begin to pick out one favorite run that he's had this year. Why?

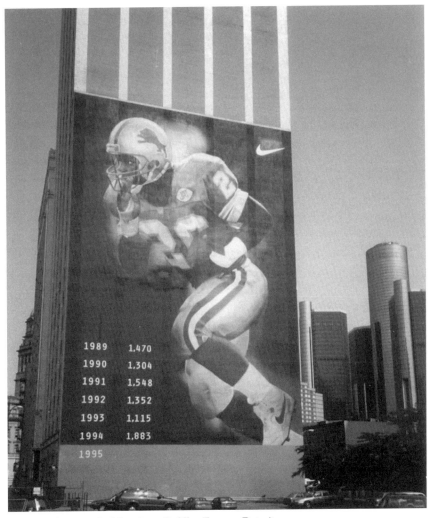

Photographic mural of Sanders, Cadillac Towers, Detroit.

Because he's had some three-yard runs that may have been the greatest three-yard runs in the history of the game. Those were even more exciting than his 20-yarders."

Throughout the year Sanders rode roughshod over other NFL teams. He torched defending Super Bowl champ Dallas for 194 yards, ripped the Packers for 188 yards, and overwhelmed Tampa Bay for 403 yards in two games. Of the nine rushes of more than 60 yards registered around the league in 1994, he accounted for six of them. By the end of the season he had tallied 1,883 yards, the fourth-highest single-season rushing total in NFL history. In recognition of his brilliant season, Sanders once again received numerous post-season honors, including Associated Press Offensive Player of the Year. With that type of outstanding performance in 1994, his fans are eager to see what he will accomplish next.

FUTURE PLANS

Sanders expects to go into business after he retires. "There are so many things besides football. Football is temporary. It could be over in a second, I guess. It's a ticket. I mean it's fun and I thank God for the chance to play, but I can't say I love the game. It's helped me, but when my last day comes I won't be that sorry."

HOME AND FAMILY

Sanders has a son named Barry James who was born in the spring of 1994. The child lives with his mother in Dallas, and Barry tries to visit when he can. Sanders does not plan to marry the child's mother, whose name he does not wish to reveal for privacy reasons. Sanders lives in suburban Detroit, although he often visits his parents in Wichita during the off-season. "As I get older, I realize that family was the biggest thing to me."

MAJOR INFLUENCES

Sanders counts his oldest brother Boyd and his parents as major influences in his life. These members of his family, he says, taught him the value of perseverance, discipline, and respect for others. His mother and father also helped him to keep his talent at carrying a football in perspective. "I hate to see athletes forget who they really are. People treat them differently, and they start thinking they're better than everybody else. They're not, and I know I'm not. I'm an average person."

HOBBIES AND OTHER INTERESTS

"It's pretty easy for me to relax and unwind," says Sanders. "I don't have to go fishing or anything to relax. But some of the things I do include movies, bowling, an occasional concert." Sanders also loves to play basketball, a sport that he has loved since he was a child. "When the football season is over, I just like to go back to my old neighborhood and play indoor or outdoor basketball."

HONORS AND AWARDS

All-American College Team *(Sporting News)*: 1987, 1988
Heisman Trophy: 1988
College Football Player of the Year *(Sporting News)*: 1988
NFL Rookie of the Year: 1989
NFC Rookie of the Year (United Press International): 1989
Pro Bowl: 1989, 1990, 1991, 1992, 1993, 1994
All-Pro Team(Associated Press): 1989, 1990, 1991, 1994
All-Pro Team *(Football Digest)*: 1989, 1991, 1994
All-Pro Team *(Sporting News)*: 1989, 1990, 1991, 1994
NFL Rushing Record: 1990, 1994
All-Pro Team (United Press International): 1990, 1991
Player of the Year *(Football Digest)*: 1991, 1994
Offensive Player of the Year (Associated Press): 1994
"Espy" Award for NFL Performer of the Year: 1994
All-NFC Team: 1994

FURTHER READING

BOOKS

Devaney, John. *Winners of the Heisman Trophy,* 1990
Gutman, Bill. *Barry Sanders: Football's Rushing Champ,* 1993 (juvenile)
Kavanagh, Jack. *Barry Sanders: Rocket Running Back,* 1994 (juvenile)
Knapp, Ron. *Sports Great Barry Sanders,* 1993 (juvenile)
Reiser, Howard. *Barry Sanders: Lion With a Quiet Roar,* 1993 (juvenile)

PERIODICALS

Boys' Life, Dec. 1990, p.50
Detroit Free Press, Dec. 17, 1989, p.D1; Aug. 26, 1994, p.C1; Sep. 24, 1994, p.B1
Detroit News, Dec. 17, 1989, p.C1; Oct. 15, 1991, p.D1; Dec. 9, 1994, p.F1
Los Angeles Times, Dec. 18, 1988, p.3
Sport, Nov. 1994, p.24
Sports Illustrated, Dec. 12, 1988, p.4; April 10, 1989, p.24; Sep. 10, 1990, p.61; Dec. 5, 1994, p.3
Washington Post, Nov. 8, 1988, p.E1

ADDRESS

Detroit Lions
1200 Featherstone Road
Pontiac, MI 48057

William Shatner   1931-
Canadian Actor, Director, Producer
and Writer
Starred as Captain James T. Kirk in
"Star Trek" Television Shows and Movies

BIRTH

William Shatner was born March 22, 1931, in Montreal, Canada,
to Joseph and Anne Shatner. His family owned a profitable
uniform and work clothes business, Admiration Clothing Company, which his parents assumed he would someday join. A close-
knit family, Bill and his two sisters grew up in comfort and security; in his words, "never wanting for anything."

EARLY MEMORIES

What Shatner remembers most about his childhood was getting into trouble. At the age of seven, he spent his time narrowly escaping one scrape after another. He was a creative and imaginative child, always dreaming up new types of mischief. Like the clean slice he made with his saw through the leg of his father's brand new dining room table. No one would notice, he must have thought. And they didn't until dinner, when the table crashed to the floor, spewing plates, food, and silverware all over the place. And the new carrots in the farmer's garden nearby, begging to be picked. There was no applause then, only the belt. His parents had to admit there were times when they didn't know what to do with him. His sisters considered him a nuisance.

YOUTH

Shatner first experienced the thrill of acting at a young age when he attended summer camp. He played the role of a Jewish boy in Nazi Germany so convincingly that "I found out I could make people cry," he recalled. "I was a lonely kid and the play and audience made up for that." Camp opened other vistas, too, by introducing Shatner to sports and the outdoors.

At the age of eight, Shatner made his professional acting debut as Tom Sawyer at the Montreal Children's Theatre. More roles followed. On weekends he read the parts of fairytale characters on a local radio show. By the time he enrolled in Montreal's West Hill High School, he was an accomplished actor and radio personality.

EDUCATION

Friction among family and friends continued as his appetite for acting grew. In addition to taking part in high school plays, he joined the football team, the wrestling team, and the ski club. His athletic friends teased him about acting, but he resisted. Even during senior year, his parents didn't take him seriously. They still believed that he would join the family business.

Shatner graduated from high school in 1948 and enrolled in the College of Commerce at McGill University in Montreal. No model student, he quit sports, barely attended classes, and did just enough work to get by. What he *did* do was devote his time and energy to writing, producing, and acting in college musicals and off-campus plays. At McGill, "all my waking hours were involved in drama courses," he once said. "I was very shy in those years. I withdrew into a world I loved." Also, he worked part-time as an announcer for the Canadian Broadcasting Corporation and served as president of the university's Radio Club.

By junior year he told his parents his true feelings. He and his father argued for weeks, until his father finally relented and made him a deal.

If Bill did not make it in acting after five years, he would join the family's clothing business.

In 1952, William Shatner received a Bachelor of Arts degree in Commerce and took a job as business manager for the Mountain Playhouse, a small summer stock theater in Montreal.

CAREER HIGHLIGHTS

A NEW INDEPENDENCE, 1952-1956

Shatner soon proved to be a poor business manager, but a promising actor. The producer was so impressed with Shatner's talents that he referred him to the Canadian National Repertory Theatre in Ottawa. There he lived alone for the first time, his meager wages covering only rent and meals. He continued to work at the Mountain Playhouse during the summer and toured with the Repertory Theatre the rest of the year. Despite good notices, this was a lonely time. He later told one of his daughters, "I learned all about how terrible, debilitating, and mind-numbing loneliness can be. Fear of that has always been with me." His father offered a place at home, but the determined young man never took him up on it.

His first break came in 1953 when he was invited to join the new Stratford Shakespearean Festival in Ontario. Sir Tyrone Guthrie, one of the most renowned directors at the time, chose Shatner as understudy for Christopher Plummer, who was playing King Henry in Shakespeare's *Henry V*. When Plummer fell ill, Shatner was asked to take the lead, even though he had not rehearsed the part. That night theater-goers were treated to the birth of a genuinely original style—the "halting, melodramatic speech"—that was to become his trademark. Reviewers raved, and the cast cheered. Shatner worked three summers at the Stratford Festival, ultimately mastering a wide range of roles.

Shatner made his New York debut with the Stratford Festival in 1956. He continued his work with the Stratford Festival and starred in a television drama, "Dreams," that he had written. By the fall of 1956, Shatner had become a well-known actor on Canadian television, had broken the ice in America, had met and married his first wife, Gloria Rand, and received the Tyrone Guthrie Award for most promising actor.

The young couple moved to New York. Shatner had the good fortune to enter television during its "Golden Age" when shows were broadcast live, and he found plenty of work. Over the next ten years he appeared in nearly one hundred dramatic television shows. He was described by critics as the "Canadian Wunderkind" and TV's "Golden Boy"; his performances were called "superb."

HOLLYWOOD: IN PURSUIT OF EXCELLENCE, 1957-1965

In 1957, MGM offered Shatner a two-movie contract. He made the first film, *The Brothers Karamazov* (1958), and earned good reviews for his portrayal of Alexi. But the second movie was not to be. Instead he heard about a stage role, that of Robert Lomax, an artist who falls in love with a Chinese prostitute, in the play *The World of Suzie Wong*. Shatner opted out of his movie contract. Unfortunately by the time the play opened in October 1958, the script had been altered so many times that it was completely different from the original. The play was a dismal failure. As described by Dennis Hauck, Shatner's biographer, "entire rows got up and walked out, and the reviewers were unanimous in condemning it." Production limped on, however, due to $1.5 million in pre-sold theater parties, so Shatner livened things up by turning the "dark drama" into a comedy. By the end of its 18-month run, the show boasted 508 performances and had became a commercial success. Shatner received the 1958 Theatre World Award for best actor, the play received several Drama Circle awards, and it was made into a movie in 1960.

Shatner continued appearing on television, in plays, and in movies, flying back and forth between New York and Hollywood, to support his growing family. He was turning down three out of every four scripts because he did not want to be "typecast," or cast repeatedly in similar roles. He began writing scripts, and in 1965 he founded his own film production company, Lemli Productions, named after his three daughters, Leslie, Melanie, and Lisabeth. Soon after his company was formed he received the phone call that would typecast him in the minds of millions anyway, and change his life forever.

STAR TREK — CAPTAIN'S LOG, STAR DATE: 1966-1969

Gene Roddenberry, the creator of the "Star Trek" series, was searching for the right actor to step into the Captain's shoes of the Federation Starship *Enterprise*. He knew what sort of man he wanted, "about 34, an Academy graduate, clearly the leading man and central character . . . (a hero)." He chose Shatner to be Captain James Tiberius Kirk, setting out on a five-year mission to explore the universe "Where No Man Has Gone Before." The series was slated to begin in the fall of 1966, and he moved permanently to Los Angeles. That same year his marriage broke up. "The hardest work in show business is having a lead in a series," he once said. "It's physically debilitating, marriage-wrecking, and mind-blowing."

Shatner and the other lead characters, Leonard Nimoy as Mr. Spock and DeForest Kelley as Dr. "Bones" McCoy, were given great creative freedom to develop their characters. "Captain Kirk behaved as the ideal William Shatner would behave in the face of danger, love, passion, or a social situation," Shatner later recalled. "So all of me was invested in him." Because the scripts were seldom finished, he had to be spontaneous. The leading trio, who became close friends, and the regular cast members were one big, happy family. Or so he thought. Only much later, when he began interviewing them for his memoirs, *Star Trek Memories*, did he learn the truth. He was stunned to discover that, in fact, they all resented the fact that their lines were repeatedly cut, minimizing their parts, so that Shatner could appear on the screen 90 percent of the time. Indeed, they considered him arrogant, insensitive, and patronizing.

Despite its later popularity, "Star Trek" had very low ratings when it was originally broadcast in 1966. By the middle of its second season, rumors began circulating that the show would be canceled. Fans mobilized, flooding NBC mail rooms with over a million letters. The strategy kept the show on the air one more year, but it was moved to ten o'clock on Friday nights, traditionally a slow night for TV viewing. The show was canceled at the end of its third year after 79 episodes. Shatner's world crumbled along with it when he became virtually penniless due to taxes, agent's fees, and divorce costs. He went back to working summer stock in New York and lived in a camper to defray expenses. The episodes were then syndicated and rebroadcast on independent stations in the U.S. and in over 100 foreign countries, which continues to this day. With the addition of the *Star Trek* films and an animated version of the series, the original crew did well. Shatner and Nimoy have become multimillionaires,

reported to command as much as $20,000 for a single appearance at a "Star Trek" convention.

But Shatner's career took a dip following the cancellation of the "Star Trek" series. While he continued to find work in television and movies, he began to accept roles in films of lesser quality, sometimes depicting him in love scenes that he is "not proud of." He could also be seen on game shows, talk shows, and commercials. That period came to an end when he resumed work on Star Trek.

STAR TREK MOVIES, 1979 TO THE PRESENT

In 1979, William Shatner returned as Kirk in *Star Trek: The Motion Picture*, the first of seven *Trek* films to date. Set in the 23rd century, the first *Star Trek* movie showcases Kirk, now an Admiral, piloting the *Enterprise* to save Earth from destruction by a massive machine/organism called V'Ger. In *Star Trek II: The Wrath of Khan* (1982), Kirk and the crew battle Khan and save the *Enterprise*, but Spock dies of severe radiation exposure. In *Star Trek III: The Search for Spock* (1984), Spock is revived by Vulcan mindmeld and returned safely to the planet Vulcan. In *Star Trek IV: The Voyage Home* (1986), the crew travels back in time to the 1980s to save a pair of humpback whales. Shatner directed *Star Trek V: The Final Frontier* (1988), an ambitious venture to find God, who turns out to be evil and destroys Spock's half-brother Sybok. *Star Trek VI: The Undiscovered Country* (1991) was made with a mixture of sadness and celebration: it was expected to be the original crew's final film, but also marked "Star Trek's" 25th anniversary. In the film, Kirk and Dr. McCoy are convicted of murdering the Klingon chancellor during a peace conference; the crimes become a crucial block to intergalactic peace.

Between *Star Trek* movies, Shatner continued to take on various creative projects. In the popular television series "T.J. Hooker," which ran from 1982 to 1987, he played a tough detective who gave up a desk job to work a street beat. In 1988 he began to write his science fiction *Tek* novels. The books follow the adventures of ex-policeman Jake Cardigan, who fights an addictive brain stimulant concealed in computer software that creates dangerous virtual-reality fantasies in the 22nd century. Although Shatner admitted that *Tek* is "no great American literature," reviews were generally favorable. Gene Roddenberry quipped when he read an earlier version, "I prepared to suffer, but the story flowed and it was so poetic I caught myself wishing I could write that well." "TekWar" premiered on television in a series of two-hour movies and a weekly syndicated show in January 1994. Shatner directs half the episodes and makes cameo appearances. Since 1990, he has also hosted one of the first real-life drama television series, "Rescue 911," which has received over 25 awards.

STAR TREK: GENERATIONS

The seventh *Trek* film, *Star Trek: Generations,* was released in 1994. The film introduces a new generation of crew members as Kirk "passed the baton" to Captain Jean-Luc Picard (Patrick Stewart). As captain of the Enterprise on "Star Trek: The Next Generation," the popular TV series that was a follow-up to the original "Star Trek" show, Picard is Kirk's successor. In *Star Trek: Generations,* a time-warp device has moved Kirk into the same era as Captain Picard. The two captains join forces to avert destruction of the universe by a murderous alien (Malcolm McDowell). While it packed plenty of action and special effects, it was also "about family and morality and growing old," said Brannon Braga, one of the film's writers. "It's the concern that all of us have about death, about what it means to die." Shatner's role in future installments of the ongoing *Star Trek* series remains unclear, but his legacy as Captain Kirk remains secure.

MARRIAGE AND FAMILY

Shatner met his first wife, actress Gloria Rand, when they were appearing in the television drama "Dreams." They were married in 1956 and had three daughters, all now grown: Leslie Carol, born August 13, 1958; Lisabeth Mary, born June 6, 1961; and Melanie Ann, born August 4, 1964. Bill and Gloria's marriage broke up in 1966.

Shatner met his second wife, Marcy Lafferty, in 1970 while filming "The Andersonville Trial" for public TV. Marcy said of their meeting, "I fell for him hook, line, and sinker. Bill had just been through a terrible divorce and a folded series. He didn't want to get involved. But I hung in there and wormed my way into his heart." They were married in Brentwood, California, on October 20, 1973. The couple splits their time between their house in Malibu, California, and "Belle Reve" (Beautiful Dream), their ranch in bluegrass country near Lexington, Kentucky.

HOBBIES AND OTHER INTERESTS

Shatner's main interests are fitness, horses, and the environment. Throughout his life he has tried to keep physically fit, maintaining that exercise "clears his head," and has performed many of his own movie stunts. His favorite sports are scuba diving, canoeing, skiing, golf, archery, motorcycling, and horseback riding. In answer to a teen-age dream of owning a horse ranch, he breeds American Saddlebred and quarter horses and often competes in world-class shows. He is the owner of the world champion Sultan's Great Day.

Pollution, recycling, and other environmental issues are also important to Shatner. "What really bugs me are smokers. And polluters. At home we rigorously divide our garbage so that the recyclable items can be carried away. It's the little things that make the difference. Little things snowball into big ones."

SELECTED CREDITS

ON STAGE

Henry V, 1956
Tamburlaine the Great, 1956
The World of Suzie Wong, 1958-59
A Shot in the Dark, 1961-63
Remote Asylum, 1970-71
An Evening with William Shatner, 1976-77
Symphony of the Stars, 1978
Cat on a Hot Tin Roof, 1981

ON FILM

The Brothers Karamazov, 1958
Judgment at Nuremburg, 1961
Alexander the Great, 1968
The Barbary Coast, 1975
Kingdom of the Spiders, 1977
The Bastard, 1978
Star Trek: The Motion Picture, 1979
Star Trek II: The Wrath of Khan, 1982
Airplane II: The Sequel, 1982
Star Trek III: The Search for Spock, 1984
Star Trek IV: The Voyage Home, 1986
Star Trek V: The Final Frontier, 1989 (director)
Star Trek VI: The Undiscovered Country, 1991
Star Trek: Generations, 1994

ON TELEVISION

"Star Trek," 1966-69
"The Andersonville Trial," 1970
"Star Trek" Animated Series, 1973-75 (voice of Captain Kirk)
"Benjamin Franklin: The Statesman," 1975
"T. J. Hooker," ABC 1982-85; CBS 1985-87
"The Search for Houdini," 1987
"Voice of the Planet," 1988
"Rescue 911," 1989 to present
"TekWar," 1994 to present

WRITINGS

Believe, 1992 (with Michael Tobias)
Star Trek Memories, 1994 (with Chris Kreski)

303

Star Trek Movie Memories, 1994 (with Chris Kreski)

TEK SERIES

TekLords, 1992
TekWorld, Marvel Comics, 1992-Present (with Ron Goulart)
TekLab, 1993
TekVengeance, 1993
TekWar, 1993
TekPower, 1994
TekSecret, 1994

HONORS AND AWARDS

Tyrone Guthrie Stratford Festival Scholarship Award: 1956
Theatre World Award for Best Actor: 1959
Theatre Guild Best Actor of the Year: 1959
Drama Circle Acting Awards: 1959
Best Actor Award: 1965
Star of the Year Award: 1967
Most Exciting Star of the Year: 1967
Annual Life Career Award: 1980
City of Hope Award: 1981
Star on Hollywood's Walk of Fame: 1983
People's Choice Award for Favorite New Television Dramatic Series: 1990
Award of Excellence (Banff Television Festival): 1994

FURTHER READING

BOOKS

Dillard, J.M. *Star Trek: 'Where No One Has Gone Before:' A History in Pictures,* 1994
Engel, Joel. *Gene Roddenberry: The Myth and the Man Behind Star Trek,* 1994
Foster, Alan. *Star Trek, Log Seven, Log Eight, Log Nine,* 1993
Hauck, Dennis William. *William Shatner:, A Bio-Bibliography,* 1994
Nichols, Nichele. *Beyond Uhura: Star Trek and Other Memories,* 1994
Okuda, Michael and Denise, and Mirek, Debbie. *The Star Trek Encyclopedia,* 1994
Shatner, Lisabeth. *Captain's Log: William Shatner's Personal Account of the Making of Star Trek V,* 1989
Takei, George. *To the Stars: Star Trek's Mr. Sulu,* 1994
Van Hise, James. *The Man Who Created Star Trek: Gene Roddenberry,* 1992
Who's Who in America, 1995

PERIODICALS

Booklist, Nov. 15, 1994, p.554

Current Biography Yearbook 1987
Los Angeles Magazine, Oct. 1989, p.24
Maclean's, Oct. 10, 1979, p.14; May 2, 1994, p.70
New York Times Book Review, Dec. 26, 1993, p.15
People, July 5, 1982, p.50; Nov. 11, 1991, p.54; July 20, 1992, p.40; Nov. 1, 1993, p.27
Publisher's Weekly, Oct. 25, 1993, p.25
Toronto Star, June 8, 1991, p. PS5; Jan. 11, 1994, p.PB5; Aug. 1994, p.PB3; Nov. 18, 1994, p.PD1
TV Guide, Aug. 14, 1982, p.18; Dec. 16, 1989, p.26; Oct. 13, 1990, p.10; Aug. 31, 1991, p.4; July 24, 1993, p.21; Jan. 15, 1994, p.16; Oct. 8, 1994, p.25; Jan. 14, 1995, p.13

ADDRESS

Lemli Productions
760 N. LaCienega Blvd.
Los Angeles, CA 90069

OBITUARY

Elizabeth George Speare   1908-1994
American Writer of Historical Fiction
for Children
Newbery Award Winner and Author of
The Witch of Blackbird Pond and *The Sign
of the Beaver*

BIRTH

Elizabeth George (later Elizabeth George Speare) was born on
November 21, 1908, in Melrose, Massachusetts. Her father was
Harry Allan George, an engineer, and her mother was Demetria
(Simmmons) George, about whom she once said, "My mother

was a very wonderful woman of great understanding." She had one younger brother.

YOUTH

"I remember my childhood as an exceptionally happy one," Speare once wrote. She grew up in Melrose, which she called "an ideal place in which to have grown up, close to fields and woods where we hiked and picnicked, and near to Boston where we frequently had family treats of theaters and concerts." Summer vacations were spent in Marshfield along the Massachusetts South Shore, about 30 miles south of Boston. "Every summer we went to the shore, where we stayed on a hill with a breathtaking view of the ocean, with fields and daisies and blueberries, and lovely secret paths through the woods, but, except for my small brother, not another young person anywhere. As I grew older I realized that those lonely summers had been a special gift for which I would always be grateful. I had endless golden days to read and think and dream, and it was then that I discovered the absorbing occupation of writing stories."

EARLY MEMORIES

Although she grew up in a small family, Speare was often surrounded by a large clan of aunts, uncles, and cousins. "They made my growing up immeasurably richer. Looking back on so many totally different personalities and talents and interests, I can see with gratitude how each one of them helped to stretch my mind and heart. Some of my best memories are of family reunions—big Christmas dinners and summer picnics under the sun."

"Whenever one branch of our family met, a favorite cousin just my own age and I, with barely a greeting to anyone else, used to rush into a corner clutching fat brown notebooks and breathlessly read out loud to each other the latest stories we had written. One summer day an aged uncle invaded our corner and to our dismay asked permission to listen. He sat for some time very gravely, and then got up and walked away shaking his head in bewilderment. But nothing ever discouraged us."

BEGINNING TO WRITE

Speare started writing when she was very young, as she explains here. "I believe I'm a very fortunate person because I discovered almost by accident the kind of work that I especially love to do. Young people always ask me, 'How old were you when you started to write? When did you decide you wanted to write? And I have to say that I can't remember a time when I didn't want to write. I think it was because I loved to read so much. I loved to read books, I loved to touch books and hold them and to collect them and to own my own. And I always knew that someday I was going to write one." She started out writing poetry and stories. When she was only eight, she wrote her first novel, about a girl named Dorothy Swain. It was to be the first in a series modeled on the Bobbsey Twins books. "After that," Speare said, "I always scribbled, all the way through school, all the way through college."

EDUCATION

In fact, her love of literature and of writing inspired her throughout her education. In high school she contributed to the school paper and performed in school plays, and in college she was on the editorial staff of the school literary magazine.

Speare attended Smith College in Northampton, Massachusetts, for one year. Her father died unexpectedly, so at the beginning of her sophomore year she transferred to Boston University, where she took an apartment with her mother. In 1930, she earned her B.A. in English.

Speare continued her studies at Boston University, pursuing her master's degree. At the same time, she taught English at Chamberlain School, a small private school, for two years. In 1932 she earned her M.A. degree in English and took a new job. From 1932 to 1935 she taught high school English in Rockland, Massachusetts, and then taught for one year, 1935 to 1936, in Auburn, Massachusetts. Teaching in a high school in the depths of the Great Depression, when millions of Americans were out of work, proved to be an eye-opening experience. "At the end of two years I had acquired a master's degree and the illusion that I could teach. Then, still shy and naive, in the midst of the Depression, I ventured into a high school and offered my Shakespeare and Browning to a volcanic classroom crowded to bursting with boys who were only biding their time till the closed factories would reopen. I don't suppose any of them has ever remembered a word of what I tried to teach them, but I have never forgotten what they taught me. Surprisingly, in that first toughening year I discovered that I really *liked* teaching."

MARRIAGE AND FAMILY

Elizabeth George met her future husband, Alden Speare, through her brother. The two men were working during a college vacation at the Boston University athletic field. George would see Speare when she went to borrow her brother's car, and soon they were dating. They were married on September 26, 1936. They settled in Wethersfield, Connecticut, near where Speare worked as an industrial engineer. They had two children: Alden, Jr., born in 1939, and Mary Elizabeth, born in 1942.

For many years, while her children were young, Elizabeth George Speare devoted her time to taking care of her family. They enjoyed a variety of activities together, like ski trips in the winter and fishing, hiking, and picnicking in the summer. Speare was involved in her children's school activities as well. As she says here, "Any family can fill in the record of the next 15 years, crowded with piano practice and dancing school and camping and orthodontists and PTA and Cub Scouts and Brownies—those familiar things which never seem dull and conventional when they happen to *you* and which leave little time for writing. Not till both children were in junior high school did I find time at last to sit down quietly with pencil and paper."

BECOMING A WRITER

As her children grew older, Speare was ready to return to writing. She hooked up with a local group of women who were also aspiring writers. "The Quill Drivers," as they called themselves, offered each other advice, support, inspiration, and encouragement to keep writing.

In the beginning, Speare followed the practical advice for new writers to write about what you know. For Speare, the obvious topic would be family living. Her first success came in a lighthearted but informative article about skiing with children that appeared in *Better Homes and Gardens* in December 1949. Other early articles during the 1950s were published in such magazines as *Woman's Day, Parents*, and *American Heritage.* Speare also wrote two one-act plays, and one, *The Anchor*, was produced in 1953 by a local amateur drama group. From 1953 to 1956 she also worked part-time at the University of Connecticut interviewing disabled home-makers and writing pamphlets on handicapped homemakers for the univer-sity's home economics pro-gram. She quit that job in 1956, when she learned that a publisher was interested in her first novel.

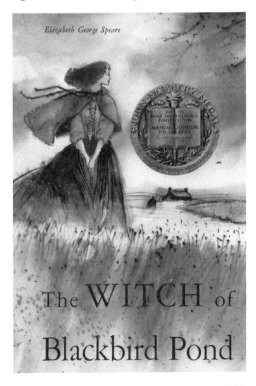

CAREER HIGHLIGHTS

Speare formed the idea for her first novel, *Calico Captive* (1957), when she came across a true story while reading a history of Connecticut. The author of the story, Susanna Johnson, along with her husband, their three children, and her younger sister, Miriam Willard, had been captured by Indians in 1794. They had been forced to march through the wilderness from Charlestown, New Hampshire, to Montreal, Quebec, where they were sold to the French for a ransom.

Speare was obsessed with the story after she read it. She kept returning to thoughts of the younger sister, Miriam, as explained here. "[One] day I stumbled on a true story from New England history with a character who seemed to me an ideal heroine. For a long time this girl haunted my imagination, and finally I began to write down her adventures, filling in the outlines of the actual events with new characters and scenes of my creation. It was like living a double life, stepping every day from my busy world into another time and place and into a family that came to seem as familiar as my own. . . . Though I had begun my first historical novel almost by accident it soon proved to be an absorbing hobby. I was no longer writing about what I knew best. In order to truly share the adventures of my imaginary people I had to know many things about them—the houses they lived in, the clothes they wore, the food they ate, how they made a living, what they did for fun, what things they talked about and cared about. You can call this research if you like but that seems to me a dull word for such a fascinating pursuit."

Speare's hard work soon paid off. After finishing three chapters, she wondered if she had any hope of getting it published. She started by sending it to publishing companies whose names she read off the books on her daughter's bookshelf, but it was rejected and returned by the first two places she sent it. At the third publishing house, the editor sent her back a note: "I would like to see the rest of this story." Speare was elated. *Calico Captive* was published in 1957 and was a huge success for a first novel by a new writer. Praised as vivid and harrowing, it was called "superior historical fiction."

Speare's next novel, *The Witch of Blackbird Pond* (1958), is, like *Calico Captive*, based on history but wholly imaginary. In reading about early New England history, Speare had found an account of English children from the Caribbean island of Barbados who were sent to Boston for an education. What would happen, she wondered, if a girl from that sunny island came instead to the dreary, narrow confines of the small Puritan town of Wethersfield, Connecticut? Speare created Kit, a 16-year-old orphan who arrives from Barbados in 1687 to stay with her stern and hard-working aunt, uncle, and two cousins. Kit's only refuge from her difficult life is in the marshes surrounding Blackbird Pond. There she befriends Hannah Tupper, a Quaker woman who the townspeople believe is a witch. With its accurate historical background, strong characterization, and believable plot, *The Witch of Blackbird Pond* earned a Newbery Award, a prestigious honor in children's literature.

Speare reached much farther back in history for her next novel, *The Bronze Bow* (1961). She wanted to teach her seventh-grade Sunday school class about ancient Palestine during the life of Jesus Christ. "[For] all of us the life and people of ancient Palestine about which we were studying seemed very dim and far away. Actually the first century [A.D.] was an exciting and colorful and violent age. To make the time come alive I began to imagine a group of young people who grew up learning to hate the Roman conquerors and to long for the freedom of their country and who would hear and come to know the great Teacher of Galilee." That group of young people was led by Daniel bar Jamin, an 18-year-old fugitive who is fighting for freedom for his people, the Jews. This exciting and moving story, full of excellent historical detail, won for Speare a second Newbery Award.

In her final historical novel, *The Sign of the Beaver* (1983), Speare returned to early New England. One day on a fishing trip in Maine with her husband, she grew bored and wandered into the town library. There she read a true story from local history. In 1804 a boy and his father had come from Massachusetts to make their home in the Maine wilderness. They had cleared some land, built a cabin, and planted some crops. Then the father had returned to their former home to get the rest of the family, leaving the boy to guard their new home. In the father's absence, a bear got into the cabin and consumed all their supplies. The boy survived through the help of local Native Americans. From this story, Speare created *The Sign of the Beaver*, a riveting tale of the fight for survival and the growing friendship between the boy, Matt, and his Indian protectors.

Speare wrote several additional pieces as well: *Child Life in New England, 1790-1840* (1961), a pamphlet; *Life in Colonial America* (1963), a nonfiction book that describes the homes, schools, army, trades, travel, and other aspect of early American life; and *The Prospering* (1967), a novel for adults about the founding of Stockbridge, Massachusetts.

But it is her historical novels for young readers for which Speare is remembered today. She was honored in 1989 with the Laura Ingalls Wilder Award, a major award given only once every three years by the American Library Association. They cited her "vitality and energy, grace of writing, historical accuracy, and tremendous feeling for place and character." These qualities, together with her gift for storytelling and her vivid and natural writing style, have made Speare a beloved author of books for children.

Elizabeth George Speare died of an aortic aneurysm on November 15, 1994, in Tucson, Arizona, just one week before her 86th birthday.

SPEARE'S APPROACH TO WRITING

"There is one piece of advice that is often given, especially to young writers, and that is that one should write about what one knows best," Speare says. "If you live in a small town in America, they say, do not try to write about London or Paris, or a desert or a mountain peak that you have never seen. But suppose, like me, that is exactly what you want to do! I have to admit that I have never been able to follow this wise advice. I wanted to write about the early days in colonial New England, or even about Palestine in the days of Jesus. And I found the answer. It is RESEARCH, a word that sounds forbidding to many people who have never discovered the fun and excitement of it. There are men and women who have lived in London or Paris or in the desert and have climbed the highest mountain peaks, and they have written books to share their experiences with stay-at-homes like me. . . . Their books can tell me all about the place I have chosen—how it looks or how it looked in some former time, its history, its weather, its very smell and feel. The can show me the people who have lived there. . . . Sooner or later I come to feel that I know this faraway place and that I can move about in it as confidently as in my own kitchen. My imaginary people are at home there. And I myself have had the experience of stepping into another time and place. All this is research, and it is never dull. In fact, writing historical fiction is rather like living a double life.

"So you can understand why I must disagree with another saying. Writing, they say, is a lonely profession. I have never found it to be so. To be sure, I have sat for many long hours in a quiet room staring at a typewriter. . . . But it was not lonely. The room was filled with people, young and old, happy and sad, gentle and angry, all clamoring to be heard, all with something urgent to say. Sometimes I could hear their voices clearly and could only listen to the stories they had to tell. At other times the voices were dim and far away, a hint, perhaps, that I should visit the library again. Often, when the voices were interrupted, when the telephone or the doorbell rang or some household task demanded attention, it was with reluctance that I left these imaginary people who had become, as the days went by, almost as real as my own family. Often, they refused to be left behind; they followed me about, still talking, no matter what else I might be doing.

"No, writing is not lonely. It is a profession crowded with life and sound and color. I feel privileged to have had a share in it."

WRITINGS

NOVELS FOR YOUNG ADULTS

Calico Captive, 1957
The Witch of Blackbird Pond, 1958
The Bronze Bow, 1961
The Sign of the Beaver, 1983

NOVEL FOR ADULTS

The Prospering, 1967

NONFICTION

Child Life in New England, 1790-1840, 1961
Life in Colonial America, 1963

HONORS AND AWARDS

Notable Children's Books (American Library Association): 1957, for *Calico Captive*; 1958, for *The Witch of Blackbird Pond*; 1961, for *The Bronze Bow*; 1983, for *The Sign of the Beaver*

Newbery Medal (American Library Association): 1959, for *The Witch of Blackbird Pond*; 1962, for *The Bronze Bow*

Society of Colonial Wars Award: 1959, for *The Witch of Blackbird Pond*

International Board on Books for Young People Honor List: 1960, for *The Witch of Blackbird Pond*; 1964, for *The Bronze Bow*

Best Books of the Year (*School Library Journal*): 1093, for *The Sign of the Beaver*

Best Young Adult Books (American Library Association): 1983, for *The Sign of the Beaver*

Child Study Association Award (Bank Street College of Education): 1983, for *The Sign of the Beaver*

Children's Reviewers' Choice (*Booklist*): 1983, for *The Sign of the Beaver*

Outstanding Books of the Year (*New York Times*): 1983, for *The Sign of the Beaver*

Teachers' Choice (National Council of Teachers of English): 1983, for *The Sign of the Beaver*

Christopher Award: 1984, for *The Sign of the Beaver*

Scott O'Dell Award for Historical Fiction: 1984, for *The Sign of the Beaver*
Laura Ingalls Wilder Award: 1989, for her "distinguished, enduring contribution to children's literature"

FURTHER READING

BOOKS

Apseloff, Marilyn Fain. *Elizabeth George Speare,* 1991
Fuller, Muriel, editor. *More Junior Authors,* 1963
Gallo, Donald R., editor. *Speaking for Ourselves, Too: More Autobiographical Sketches by Notable Authors of Books for Young Adults,* 1993
Kingman, Lee, editor. *Newbery and Caldecott Medal Books: 1956-1965,* 1965
Hopkins, Lee Bennett. *More Books by More People: Interviews with 65 Authors of Books for Children,* 1974
Something about the Author, Vol. 62
Twentieth-Century Children's Writers, 1989
Who's Who in America, 1995

PERIODICALS

Current Biography 1959
Horn Book, Aug. 1959, p.265; Aug. 1962, p.336; July/Aug. 1989, pp.460 and 465
Library Journal, Apr. 15, 1959, p.1291; Mar. 15, 1962, p.1254

VIDEO

"A Visit with Elizabeth George Speare," Houghton Mifflin Author and Artist Series

Dr. Benjamin Spock   1903-
American Pediatrician, Psychologist, Writer,
Educator, and Political Activist
Author of *Baby and Child Care*

BIRTH

Benjamin McLane Spock was born May 2, 1903, in New Haven,
Connecticut. He was the oldest of the six children of Benjamin
Ives Spock, a successful corporate lawyer for the New Haven
Railroad, and Mildred Louise Stoughton Spock, a homemaker.
His brothers and sisters, from oldest to youngest, were Marjorie,
Betty, Anne, Bob, and Sally. The Spock family was relatively
wealthy, and young Ben grew up in a comfortable house in a
nice neighborhood.

YOUTH

Spock remembers his childhood as "plain, repressed, and strict." His mother was moralistic and domineering, and she set rigid rules that her children were expected to obey without question. For example, they were given specific amounts of certain foods to eat at mealtimes, and they were not allowed to snack. After dinner, they had to stay indoors until bedtime, while all the other neighborhood children went outside to play. However, Mildred Spock also had a tremendous love for babies that she passed on to her oldest son. "She was a dedicated mother, but an unnecessarily severe one," Spock says. "I'm sure that both of those factors came into play when I got interested in the psychological side of pediatrics." Spock admired his father, although there always seemed to be a great distance between them. His father usually worked long hours and never hugged or kissed the children. Nevertheless, Spock claims that "he was the one who inspired by example and built in me the obligation to be fair and reasonable, to be dependable, to be self-controlled ... and to be dignified."

Spock attended many different schools in his youth and experienced some unusual learning environments. Since his mother believed that fresh air was good for children, he went to an outdoor school for several years. Classes were held on an open platform in the teacher's backyard, regardless of the weather. Later he went to a private boys' school, Hamden Hall Country Day School in Connecticut, where he first began to enjoy playing sports. Hamden Hall only taught students through the tenth grade, however, so Spock completed his last two years of high school at the exclusive college prep school Phillips Academy in Andover, Massachusetts, which his mother felt would be more "wholesome" than the public high school. Throughout his private schooling, Spock had to write home every other day. Once, when he admitted in a letter that he had met a young woman who found him attractive, his mother decided that he had lost his ideals and that he should live at home during his first year of college. The strictness of his upbringing took a toll on Spock. "I was scared of both my parents, of all my teachers, of tough boys—and I was the kind that bullies quickly detected and picked on—and of barking dogs," he recalls. "I heard the expression 'mother's boy' and felt that it summed up my predicament and my personality."

EDUCATION

Since Spock grew up in New Haven and his father had graduated from Yale, he always knew that was where he would go to college. He wanted to make his mark on the university and become a true "Yale man" while he was there. During his first year of college, Spock lived at home and joined the track team as a high jumper. He was only a mediocre high jumper and did not find the event very exciting, but it was easy for him because he was 6'4" tall. One day, while he was working out in the gym, he ran into the captain of the Yale varsity crew team. Rowing was a sport of great prestige and tradition at Ivy League schools during those days, so Spock was awestruck by the encounter. "He looked me up and down—he was a very imposing and slightly arrogant person—and asked what sport did I go out for," Spock remembers. "I said high jumping, in my bashful way. And he said, 'Why don't you go out for a man's sport?' Well, instead of being insulted, I was very flattered that he thought I had the makings of an oarsman, so I rushed right over to the crew office and signed up. It happened that a new coach came in the next year with a new stroke, and those of us with less experience actually had an advantage. I was able to leapfrog over more experienced men."

Spock worked hard as an oarsman and steadily gained self-confidence in his remaining three years of college. Early morning practices and training table meals also gave him a good excuse to live on campus, so his social life improved as well. During his junior year, Spock advanced to become a member of the Yale varsity crew team. They defeated other American teams in the Olympic trials and were sent to Paris to represent the United States in the 1924 Olympic Games. The trip to France aboard a ship was Spock's first real experience of the world beyond New Haven, and he describes it as "a succession of delights." The team had to follow a strict training diet on board and go to bed early, but they still were treated like celebrities and got to dance with wealthy young women. When the team went on to win the Olympic Gold Medal in crew, Spock returned home knowing that he had made his mark as a Yale man, and that no one could call him a mother's boy anymore. He earned his bachelor's degree from Yale in 1925 and went on to study at the Yale Medical School.

CHOOSING A CAREER

Most of the time while he was growing up, Spock wanted to become an architect. But he also loved babies—just like his mother—and he enjoyed taking care of his younger brothers and sisters. He finally decided to become a doctor after he spent a summer during college as a counselor at a camp for crippled children. "I watched the orthopedic surgeon working with the children who had polio," Spock explains. "I realized how much he was helping them and I decided that I wanted to be a doctor."

Spock studied medicine at Yale for two years, but he did not enjoy his studies. He spent an entire year dissecting a cadaver, and much of his other work consisted of memorization. In addition, Spock says, "New Haven seemed dull, conventional, too full of my family's friends. Most of my college friends were now in New York." He decided to transfer to Columbia University, where he earned his M.D. in 1929. Living in New

York City exposed Spock to people and viewpoints that were very different from those of his family back in New Haven. He completed an internship in general medicine at Presbyterian Hospital in New York City in 1931, then served as a resident in pediatrics at the New York Nursery and Child's Hospital the following year. This hospital, which was located in a poor section of the city, allowed Spock to see firsthand some of the difficult problems faced by parents and children. Talking with patients there made him realize that he wanted to learn more about the psychology of raising children. In order to do this, Spock spent a year as a resident in psychiatry at New York Hospital, as well as many evenings training at the New York Psychoanalytic Institute. He thus became one of the only people in the country at that time to have trained both as a pediatrician and as a psychologist.

CAREER HIGHLIGHTS

Spock opened his own practice in New York City and began treating children in 1933. Unfortunately, this was during the depths of the Great Depression, when economic hardship meant that "people stopped having babies," according to Spock. When he did see patients, their families usually were not able to pay for his services. In fact, it took Spock three years before he earned enough money to pay the monthly rent on his small office. Later, however, Spock became a very popular doctor for children. He was very kind and sensitive with his young patients, and he spent a lot of time answering their parents' questions. Spock viewed his practice as an opportunity to learn about the interactions between parents and children. Spock was also one of the first pediatricians to try to make visits to the doctor less frightening for kids. For example, he stocked his waiting room with toys and built a little stairway and trapdoor for kids to climb through to get on the examining table.

In 1939 a publishing company contacted Spock about writing a book to help answer parents' questions about raising children. Even though he had only been in practice for a few years, the publisher sought him out because of his unique background in pediatrics and psychology. However, Spock felt that he was not ready to give advice at this time and turned the publisher down. In 1944 Spock interrupted his practice to join the U.S. Navy during World War II. During his two years in the navy, he served as a psychiatrist in New York and California. In his spare time, he began thinking more seriously about writing a book. By the time he was discharged from the navy as a lieutenant commander in 1947, he had already completed what would become one of the best-selling books of all time.

BABY AND CHILD CARE

In 1944, five years after he had declined his first offer from a publisher, Spock felt that he had finally learned enough by listening to parents and treating children to write a book. He wanted it to read easily, as if he were talking to a parent in his office, so he dictated most of the book aloud to his wife, Jane. This approach made Spock's book, *Baby and Child Care* (1946), very different from most of the guides for new parents that were available at that time. "Most doctors can't help using a condescending tone and can end up putting the fear of God into inexperienced parents by implying there might be fatal results if they are careless," Spock explains. "By contrast, my book assumes parents are sensible people."

At that time, most baby-care books recommended a very stern and rigid approach toward children. For example, parents were told to feed their babies on a strict schedule, every four hours, and to make sure they ate every bite. They were also warned not to hug or kiss their children too much, because excess affection might make them spoiled. "I wanted to be supportive of parents rather than to scold them," Spock notes. "Instead of just telling a parent what to do, I usually tried to explain what children are like at different stages of development, what their drives are, so that the parent would know what to expect and could act on his knowledge. The book set out very deliberately to counteract some of the rigidities of pediatric tradition." Spock's new outlook on parenting was clear from the book's now-famous opening words: "Trust yourself—you know more than you think you do."

Immediately after it was published, *Baby and Child Care* earned praise for answering parents' common questions in a reassuring way. Even though the publisher did very little advertising, word-of-mouth led to the sale of 750,000 copies in the first year. Spock initially attributed the book's success to good timing, since in 1946 "couples reunited after the war were eager to start families, and the baby boom was underway." It soon became clear that the book would be a phenomenal success, however, as it went on to sell an average of one million copies per year. By 1969 it had become the best-selling book ever by an American author, and by 1992 it had sold over 40

Benjamin Spock, M.D., and Michael B. Rothenberg, M.D.

Dr. Spock's
Baby and Child Care
6th Edition
Fully Revised and Updated for the 1990s

million copies in 39 languages—making it the second-best selling book of all time, after only the Bible. In order to keep up on current issues, Spock has updated his book every ten years or so since its first publication. The latest edition, which appeared in 1992 under the title *Dr. Spock's Baby and Child Care,* was co-authored by Dr. Michael B. Rothenberg, a Seattle pediatrician and Spock's former student. It includes new sections on such contemporary concerns as the father's role in pregnancy and delivery, the benefits of cloth vs. disposable diapers, the problems faced by working mothers, the best way to warn children about AIDS, and methods of coping with homosexual teenagers.

Following the success of his book, Spock found that he had many new demands on his time. He closed his practice in 1947 to concentrate on writing, teaching, and research. He moved to Minnesota that year, where he worked as a pediatrician and psychologist at the Mayo Clinic and the Rochester Child Health Project. He also taught classes at the University of Minnesota. In 1951 he moved to Pennsylvania, where he taught child development at the University of Pittsburgh, and in 1955 he moved again to Cleveland, where he taught at Western Reserve University. Also during these busy years, Spock wrote a monthly advice column for mothers that appeared first in *Ladies Home Journal* and then in *Redbook.* In 1967 Spock retired from teaching to pursue what had become, by then, a pressing interest for him: political activism.

BECOMING A PROMINENT POLITICAL ACTIVIST

Throughout the early part of his life, Spock did not pay much attention to politics. He originally held conservative views, like his parents and most others in New Haven, but his views gradually changed as he moved away from home and came into contact with many different people. He became a Democrat in the 1930s because he supported President Franklin D. Roosevelt's New Deal programs, which were intended to put Americans to work and help the country recover from the Great Depression. From that point on, Spock's views remained fairly liberal, but still he did not become involved directly with politics.

This situation changed during the 1960s. Spock endorsed John F. Kennedy for president because he liked Kennedy's proposal for a Medicare program that would provide health care coverage for the poor. Shortly after he won the election, however, Kennedy announced that he would renew American testing of nuclear weapons in order to keep up with the Soviet Union. Spock strongly opposed nuclear testing, both because he felt the nuclear fallout was harmful and because he felt weapons testing increased the likelihood of a nuclear war. "It seemed clear that the buildup would continue until there was a nuclear war or a nuclear accident," Spock says. "I realized that if we didn't have a test ban treaty, more and more children, not only in America but around the world, would die of cancer and leukemia or be born with mental and physical defects from fallout radiation. So I saw that it was a pediatric issue."

Spock soon joined the National Committee for a Sane Nuclear Policy (SANE), and he acted as the organization's co-chairman from 1963 to 1967. Members of SANE demonstrated against nuclear weapons and nuclear power plants around the country, trying to raise public awareness of their dangers. For his part, Spock appeared in a full-page advertisement in the *New York Times* under the headline "Dr. Spock Is Worried." Along with a picture of Spock holding a child on his lap, the advertisement contained information about how nuclear fallout led to unsafe levels of radiation in American milk supplies, which increased the number of babies born with birth defects. The ad also explained how the threat of a nuclear war made children fearful and nervous and harmed their development. Spock found that fans of his book had a hard time accepting him as a political activist. "Some people still imply that I somehow turned my back on pediatrics by becoming a political activist," he admits. "But pediatrics is not just vaccines and wonder drugs, or trying to help parents deal with thumb-sucking. It also has to do with public health in the broadest sense, and with working to prevent wars so that young people are not sacrificed by the millions."

In accordance with this philosophy, Spock became an active participant in the anti-war movement in 1965, when President Lyndon Johnson went back on his promise to work for peace and instead escalated the conflict in Vietnam. Spock says he felt "betrayed and outraged" by Johnson's actions, and he wrote numerous letters to the president but saw no results. Finally, Spock joined other protesters on the streets in demonstrations against the war. "What is the use of physicians like myself trying to help parents to bring up children healthy and happy, to have them killed in such numbers for a cause that is ignoble?" Spock asks. "We must stand up in opposition to the government's illegal, immoral, and brutal war."

At first, given his strict, conservative upbringing, Spock found protesting very embarrassing, "like one of those bad dreams where suddenly you are downtown without any clothes on," as he recalls. In fact, he did look out of place at the front of scruffy groups of marchers in his trademark blue pin-striped suit and tie. Gradually, however, as his belief in the cause grew, Spock became more militant. He was arrested for the first time in 1967, during a protest in Manhattan, and he went on to be arrested more than a dozen times during protests against nuclear weapons, the Vietnam War, and the plight of the homeless. In 1968, Spock was put on trial in Boston, along with several other prominent men, for conspiring to convince others to resist the military draft. The trial came about because Spock had signed a document known as the "Call to Resist Illegitimate

Authority." It argued that the war in Vietnam was illegal because it had not been officially declared by Congress, and it encouraged young men to refuse to participate in the war if they were drafted. The government was embarrassed by the number of young men who resisted the draft, so they pressed charges against the most prominent people who had signed the document. Spock was found guilty and sentenced to two years in jail and a $5,000 fine, but his conviction was overturned on appeal in 1969 before he had to serve his sentence.

By the 1970s, Spock had become "a hero to the young and the radical," according to one observer. He even ran for president in 1972 as the candidate of a small political group known as the People's Party. Spock's platform advocated withdrawing American troops abroad, providing free medical care for all Americans, eliminating tax loopholes for the rich, legalizing marijuana, and ensuring equal rights for women and homosexuals. Spock agreed to run mainly to draw attention to the party's goals, so he was only placed on the ballot in ten states. He received about 80,000 votes.

As he became more prominent politically, Spock made some enemies among conservative leaders, who blamed him for "the youth revolt of the sixties, which they felt was the result of the permissive attitude in child rearing that Spock encouraged," according to one writer. The Reverend Norman Vincent Peale, for example, charged that Spock's book had led to "the most undisciplined age in history." Spock refutes this charge, claiming that it comes from a misunderstanding of his work. "A lot of Americans still think that my advice is to let children do anything, that it's all right to let them act uncooperative or impolite, that I smile benignly on that," Spock says. "Right from the start, the book said give your children firm, clear leadership, ask them for politeness and cooperation. Respect your children, but ask them for respect also. There was nothing in it about giving children anything they want."

DR. SPOCK'S LEGACY

Summing up Spock's accomplishments as a pediatrician, writer, and activist, one observer called him "a national treasure" and "arguably the most influential American alive today." Spock had a profound and lasting effect on American children, who were raised very differently than their parents thanks to his best-selling book. And that same generation is raising their own children on his advice. He also led the way for Americans from all walks of life to become politically active and try to make the country a better place to raise children. Spock enjoyed working with young people during protests against the Vietnam War. When the war ended, however, he was disappointed to find that very few maintained their idealism and continued working for change. "I had the idea that young people had got hold of some fundamental truths—such as the hollowness of materialistic society. They used to say things like why do we have to get into this dog-eat-dog competitiveness in America? Why don't we work cooperatively? Why do we have to strive so hard to get money and goods? Why don't we see how simply we can live?" Spock recalls. "I thought these were wonderful ideals, and that the young, having discovered them, would go on with them, and that they would be passed down to succeeding generations. But it certainly was not! Within a couple of years of the withdrawal of American troops from Vietnam, I happened to be talking to students at Yale, and I asked them what they were thinking about. They said grades. It was rather chilling and shocking to me that it could happen so fast."

In fact, the tendency for students to worry about grades bothers Spock a great deal. "The purpose of education should not be to produce conformists in an unjust society, but to produce skeptics and protestors," he said at a graduation ceremony. "I'd love to tell you not to worry about grades in college, to forget the whole thing. But life isn't like that, so you will have to spend part of your time getting good grades. But try to spend most of your time looking for truth—not taking someone else's word for it, but by searching, in the library and in your life." He recommends that young people return to the basic values of kindness, loyalty, and service to the community. "We live in a sick society," he continued. "Ask yourself, how can I serve this country and this world, which has such serious problems?"

Spock remains a prominent social activist in his 90s. In 1994, he published *A Better World for Our Children: Rebuilding American Family Values*, which outlines his thoughts on the various problems he sees in American society. "I'm really concerned about such things as increasing violence, the fact that a lot of kids go to high school with either knives or guns. I'm concerned that there are millions of American children who are getting their ideals about life from television," Spock says. He also expresses concern about the high divorce rate, the lack of adequate day care facilities, and the number of homeless families in America. "If we allow the strains of our society to worsen, then living here will be ever more painful. But if we realize that in our democracy we *can* control our society, by guiding our children and using our political power, we can turn all these disheartening trends around," Spock notes. "I think it is literally true that man can't live by bread alone. You have to believe in something."

MARRIAGE AND FAMILY

Spock married Jane Davenport Cheney, whom he met during his Yale days, on June 25, 1927. The couple had two children: Michael, who became a museum director; and John, who became an architect. Even though both his children are well-adjusted and successful, Spock regrets that he moved his family so often and did not spend more time with them. "One of my great regrets is that I didn't fully enjoy my sons," he admits. "One thing that makes me sad is that men haven't learned more about balancing careers and families. It's horrible that they think it's all right to be working all evening instead of being at home with their families." Spock and his first wife were divorced in 1976.

On October 6, 1976, he married Mary Morgan, an "ardent feminist" 41 years younger than himself. Mary Morgan had a daughter from a previous marriage, Ginger, who was 11 when her mother married Spock. Spock found it very difficult to be a stepfather, calling it "the most difficult relationship of my life." Their first years together were very stormy and troubled, but they did become close many years later. When Ginger was married, she asked Spock to walk her down the aisle.

HOBBIES AND OTHER INTERESTS

Spock loves sailing, and for many years he spent his summers on a sailboat in Maine and his winters on a sailboat in the Caribbean. After he had a pacemaker installed in 1987 and suffered a mild stroke in 1989, however, his doctors recommended that he stick to dry land. "My Boston doctors were appalled at the idea of a man my age being at sea with only a wife half his size to help him," Spock recalls. Now he and his wife take long motor home trips instead, including one all the way down the Pacific Coast in 1994. Spock also follows a strict daily routine in order to maintain his health. For example, he and his wife meditate every morning and participate in a psychoanalysis session every afternoon. They eat only macrobiotic meals, consisting of vegetables and grains, and they follow an exercise program consisting of swimming, walking, and massage. This healthy lifestyle has helped Spock to remain active and to look at least 20 years younger than his actual age of 92.

HONORS AND AWARDS

Olympic Rowing: Gold Medal, 1924
E. Mead Johnson Award for Research in Pediatrics (The American Academy of Pediatrics): 1948
SANE Education Fund/Consider the Alternative Peace Award: 1963, 1988

WRITINGS

Baby and Child Care, 1946 (sixth revised edition, with Dr. Michael B. Rothenberg, published as *Dr. Spock's Baby and Child Care,* 1992)
A Baby's First Year (with J. Reinhart and W. Miller), 1954
Feeding Your Baby and Child (with M. Lowenberg), 1955

Dr. Spock Talks with Mothers, 1961
Problems of Parents, 1962
Caring for Your Disabled Child (with M. Lerrigo), 1965
Dr. Spock on Vietnam (with Mitchell Zimmerman), 1968
Decent and Indecent: Our Personal and Political Behavior, 1970
A Teenager's Guide to Life and Love, 1970
Raising Children in a Difficult Time, 1974
Spock on Parenting, 1988
Spock on Spock: A Memoir of Growing Up with the Century (with Mary Morgan), 1989
A Better World for Our Children: Rebuilding American Family Values, 1994

FURTHER READING

BOOKS

Bloom, Lynn Z. *Dr. Spock: Biography of a Conservative Radical,* 1972
DeLeon, David. *Leaders from the 1960s: A Biographical Sourcebook of American Activism,* 1994
Dubois, Diana. *My Harvard, My Yale,* 1982
Kaye, Judith. *The Life of Benjamin Spock,* 1993 (juvenile)
McGuire, William, and Leslie Wheeler. *American Social Leaders,* 1993
Michalek, Irene. *When Mercy Seasons Justice: The Spock Trial,* 1972
Milford, Jessica. *The Trial of Dr. Spock,* 1969
Spock, Benjamin. *Spock on Spock: A Memoir of Growing Up with the Century,* 1989
Zuckerman, Michael. *Almost Chosen People: Oblique Biographies in the American Grain,* 1993

PERIODICALS

American Health, June 1992, p.38
Boston Globe, Oct. 4, 1994, p.59
Current Biography 1969
Los Angeles Times, Aug. 31, 1994, p.E1
Nation, Feb. 5, 1990, p.152
New Orleans Times Picayune, Nov. 7, 1984, p.C3
New York Times, Mar. 5, 1992, p.C1
Newsweek, Mar. 4, 1985, p.10; Winter/Spring 1990, p.106; Oct. 27, 1994, p.84
Parenting, May 1993, p.80
People, Jan. 18, 1982, p.42; May 13, 1985, p.139
Redbook, Apr. 1981, p.40; May 1987, p.19
Yankee, Dec. 1984, p.74

ADDRESS

P.O. Box 1268
Camden, ME 04843-1268

Jonathan Taylor Thomas   1982-
American Actor
Plays Randy on "Home Improvement"

BIRTH

Jonathan Taylor Thomas was born Jonathan Weiss on September 8, 1982, in Bethlehem, Pennsylvania, to Stephen and Claudine Weiss. He has a 17-year-old brother, Joel. When he was five, Jonathan's family moved to Sacramento, California, where his father worked as an industrial sales manager.

YOUTH

Even at 18 months Jonathan "seemed older than his age, and really outgoing," said his mother, Claudine. "Everyone kept saying,

'Wow! Why don't you get him on television?'" Soon, they did. At seven, Jonathan began working as a fashion model and appearing in industrial films. Then he moved on to the Chatauqua Theater in Sacramento, in a double role as Tiny Tim and young Scrooge in *Scrooge*. He soon landed a commercial for Burger King and a part in a television series as Kevin on "The Bradys." "It didn't last very long," he said of the CBS take-off on the popular early-1970s TV show, "The Brady Bunch." "It bombed." Then he auditioned for "Home Improvement." He didn't know, at first, that the show was going to be an instant hit, but he thought the script was funny.

EDUCATION

Thomas is a seventh grader in an advanced program for gifted students in the Los Angeles Public Schools. During shooting, he works three weeks and then gets one week off. His school sends the work to the set, and a tutor helps him fulfill the three hours per day study time required by law. "We have posters, just like regular school," he says, "but (classes are) in a trailer, and we have cubicles. At lunch time we have to hurry and eat because we have a PE coach that comes to do gym." When on "hiatus," breaks during the year when shooting does not take place, Jonathan attends public school. His favorite subjects are history, geography, and science, and he is a straight "A" student.

"I keep my grades up because you never know how your acting is going to go," he recently told a *Los Angeles Times* interviewer. Keen on building a solid future, he explained the pitfalls of what he terms "The Child Actor Syndrome": "you have these kid actors who grew up and a bunch of years later they're on [TV talk shows] crying that they never had any time, that they were totally corrupted by show business. Probably most of them didn't have much to fall back on. It's easy to get twisted around in this crazy business." Thomas, an avid reader and well-informed on topics ranging from the importance of soccer in Brazilian culture to the beauty of the Seychelles Islands, plans to finish school and go to college. He believes that getting a good education is important.

CAREER HIGHLIGHTS

"HOME IMPROVEMENT"

The top-rated comedy series "Home Improvement," which debuted on September 7, 1991, features the Taylor family, three boys and their parents. Randy (Thomas) and his older brother, Brad (Zachery Ty Bryan), are in junior high school. Good buds, they ride the school bus together, like the same kind of music, and are beginning to notice girls. But they still get into plenty of trouble. Brad and Randy, whom Thomas calls "a huge con artist," love to pick on their younger brother, Mark (Taran Noah Smith), who is always struggling to fit in. Their father, Tim Taylor (played by comedian and star of the show Tim Allen), hosts a local do-it-yourself cable show, "Tool Time." Because his on-air projects often go awry, the kids scatter whenever Tim whips out any tools at home, keeping the family in a constant uproar. Tim is often at odds with Randy's mother, Jill (Patricia Richardson), while she struggles to maintain a household with four rambunctious males and study for a doctorate in psychology and family counseling.

Praised for his maturity, manners, and professionalism, Thomas is very different from his character Randy, who can be scheming nasty, and rude. Yet Randy is also, in Thomas's words, "intelligent, bright, clever, [and] articulate." He does acknowledge some similarities between them. "[We're] both mischievous and we like to have a good time, but I don't go to the extent that he would." In one episode, he related his own feelings about height when Randy was worried about being too short, but said, "I'm four-foot-eight. I won't be short and stumpy forever, though, because my dad's six feet tall and my brother is five-eleven."

The blue-eyed, blond-haired actor says he does not have any trouble memorizing his lines in the five days preparation time before each show. The script arrives on Mondays and the show is taped on Fridays. "You

get into the rhythm of reading the script and you can interpret it very easily," he says. On Mondays the actors, writers, and producers sit around a table, read the script, and "punch up" the jokes if they are not funny enough. The middle of the week is spent rehearsing in front of a small audience. By Friday each scene is rehearsed about three times before the show is performed in front of an audience of 200 to 300 people. Now in its fourth season, the series, which tops the charts as America's favorite television show, is taped at the Walt Disney Studios in Burbank, California. Thomas gets nervous before each taping, pointing out, "You can do this a million times and you are still going to be nervous, because you can't beat stage fright." Even Tim Allen still gets nervous, "and he's been doing stand-up comedy for 13 years."

When asked how he feels about being on a hit television series with millions of viewers, Thomas simply says that he wants to be considered "just a normal kid." He doesn't think of himself as different or special. Apparently, though, his fans do: the young actor receives about 200 fan letters each week, filling up five big boxes. The experience of being on a television show has broadened his horizons and opened him up to different things. He says it is a lot of fun, but a lot of work, too, sometimes taking in as many as 9 ½ hours a day, including a full day's schoolwork. On a particularly long day he might say, "I wish I were with my friends at a movie."

THE LION KING

Thomas didn't expect, "ever in a million years, to be doing television *and* movies." But experience from "The Bradys" and "Home Improvement" helped him win the role as the voice of young Simba in the Disney animated film *The Lion King*, which premiered June 24, 1994. Set in Africa, this film is Disney's 32nd full-length animated feature and its most successful animated film to date. Thomas shared his part with three other actors: Matthew Broderick took over when Simba reached adulthood, and the singing was provided by Jason Weaver (as a cub) and ex-Toto member Joseph Williams (as an adult).

Like Randy on "Home Improvement," Thomas recognizes similarities that he shares with the character. Thomas describes Simba as "real curious fun-loving, always getting into mischief." Those traits, coupled with the "miraculous timing" that Patricia Richardson of "Home Improvement" says he is blessed with, were exactly what *Lion King* producer Don Hahn had in mind. "We had this role for a scrappy young kid to play Simba, and we looked at dozens and dozens of actors before choosing Jonathan," Hahn said. "But we saw him on "Home Improvement" and just thought his voice was right. It gives him a very distinctive character." Thomas stole the show, according to *Superstars Datebook*, but his voice took a beating. "We had to make it sound like he was being flung down chutes in the elephant graveyard and being chased by wildebeests. We would rough him up at the microphone and try to make him out of breath." Thomas relied on hot tea with lemon and honey to soothe his throat.

Thomas filmed the hour-long takes for *The Lion King* alone in a soundstage on the same lot as "Home Improvement." The experience was vastly different from the rowdy clowning around Thomas enjoys on the set of "Home Improvement," and he admits the transition was difficult. He was so isolated, in fact, that he never met co-stars James Earl Jones

(Mufasa) or Jeremy Irons (Scar). And it wasn't until Thomas saw the movie that he realized how closely Disney animators had patterned young Simba's physical characteristics after his own. "I noticed a lot of my expressions in Simba," noted Thomas. "When I saw the movie with my mom, she said, 'That's what you do when you get sad. That's what you do when you're happy.' It's pretty cool to be immortalized in a Disney classic."

MAN OF THE HOUSE

Thomas recently co-starred in his first live-action movie, *Man of the House*, another Disney film, which premiered in February 1995. He played Ben Archer, a mischievous 11-year-old determined to get rid of a would-be future stepfather, played by Chevy Chase. Ben's mother, Sandra Archer, is played by Farrah Fawcett. "Ben's a nice guy who's a little rough around the edges," Thomas commented during filming, "he's had a tough life. His father left when he was six and it was really hard on him and his mother. He's always been able to get rid of the guys his mom dated, but this guy (Chevy Chase) poses a challenge." To discourage Jack, Ben pressures him to join the YMCA's Indian Guides program and learn outdoor games. While Jack is initially cool to the idea, their experiences together help to create a genuine friendship.

During one unusual scene, Thomas had to carry a tree branch holding a beehive with 100,000 bees in it. The bees were ordinary honey bees provided by a professional beekeeper. Rendered harmless by powerful chemicals, the bees did not sting Thomas, but he said, "I did get a bee in my ear."

The movie was made in Vancouver during his 1994 summer vacation, but Thomas still found time to have fun, enjoying lessons in throwing a tomahawk, canoeing, archery, and rain dancing for the movie. He even got to go fishing, his favorite activity. "When I got into this business, my mom was worried that I wouldn't have enough free time to be a kid, so there's always that balance of work and play." The day after Thomas returned home, he resumed work on "Home Improvement."

TOM SAWYER

Thomas's next movie role is as Tom Sawyer, in a film based on the classic novel by Mark Twain. The movie is scheduled to begin filming in mid-June 1995 and to be released in fall 1995. Thomas is looking forward to filming close to home in Los Angeles and in a part of the country he has yet to explore, Huntsville, Alabama. Brad Renfro has been cast as Huck Finn, but the part of Becky has not yet been filled. Thomas says he loves the idea of appearing in an historical film. "I love great books, I love history, and the idea of dressing up in costumes from the 1800s."

HOME AND FAMILY

Thomas lives outside of Los Angeles with his mother, brother Joel, his Lhasa Apso dog Mac, "a short, pudgy guy," and two cats, Samantha and Simba. His parents divorced in 1991, and his father now lives in northern California. When Thomas can take a break from his acting schedule, he likes to visit his father, go see his grandmother back in Pennsylvania, or just "hang out with his family" at home. He credits his mother with keeping him on track, and she praises his intelligence and ability to keep everything in balance. Nowadays, he chooses his friends carefully because "you have to make sure they're not just friends with you because of who you are."

HOBBIES AND OTHER INTERESTS

Thomas loved traveling to Canada to make *Man of the House* and enjoys promotional trips for "Home Improvement," but the real reason he likes to travel is to go fishing. It is his favorite pastime, and he has fished off the coast of Mexico (once snagging a huge three-foot yellowtail), caught salmon and halibut in Alaska, and coaxed marlin and kingfish out of the waters of Hawaii and the Caribbean. When he heard that "Home Improvement" was airing in Australia, he wanted to go there, too, so that he could fish in New Zealand, where he read the fishing is great.

His favorite sports are basketball, tennis, snow skiing, and soccer, which he has played since the age of four. Some quiet pastimes include collecting sports cards and postage stamps and reading books by Gary Paulsen and Art Spiegelman. A vegetarian, Jonathan's favorite food is pasta and his favorite meal is ravioli with salad and garlic bread. His brother still eats meat, though, and whenever Jonathan catches Joel eating a hamburger, he sneaks up behind him and yells, "Mooooo!"

SELECTED CREDITS

ON STAGE

Scrooge, 1989

ON TELEVISION

"The Bradys," 1990
"Home Improvement," 1991 to present
"What If I Were Home Alone," 1994
"A Sea World Summer Safari," 1994

ON FILM

The Lion King, 1994 (voice of Simba)
Man of the House, 1995

VOICE RECORDINGS

"Spot the Dog" video cartoon, 1994 (voice of Spot)
"Scooter's Magic Castle" CD-ROM, 1994 (voice of Scooter)

FURTHER READING

BOOKS

The Superstars Datebook, 1995

PERIODICALS

Chicago Tribune, June 12, 1994, p.30
Houston Post, July 4, 1994, p.B2
Los Angeles Times, Aug. 23, 1994, p.C1
Newsday, Feb. 13, 1994, Section 2, p.1
People, Jan. 24, 1994, p.15; Aug. 1, 1994, p.49
Teen Beat All Stars, June 1995, p.12
Tiger Beat, June 1995, p.13

ADDRESS

"Home Improvement"
2040 Avenue of the Stars
Los Angeles, CA 90067

BRIEF ENTRY

Vicki Van Meter 1982-
American Teenage Pilot

EARLY LIFE

Victoria Van Meter, known as Vicki, was born on March 13, 1982, in Meadville, Pennsylvania, a small town in the western part of the state, about 100 miles north of Pittsburgh. Vicki is the youngest of three children of Jim Van Meter, a stockbroker, and Corinne Van Meter, a homemaker. She has a sister, Elizabeth, and a brother, Daniel.

Vicki had a happy, unremarkable early childhood, attending the local public school, East End Elementary. A straight-A student, Vicki has always been adventurous and determined, according to her parents. She decided early on that she wanted to be an astronaut, and has clung to that decision ever since.

Vicki started flying quite by accident. In the fall of 1992, when Vicki was ten, she and her father were driving by the local airport and just happened to notice an advertisement for a new flight school. Jim Van Meter suggested to Vicki that since she wanted to be an astronaut, she might want to take a flying lesson, just to see if she liked it. Although Vicki was excited, her mother was scared. But as Corinne Van Meter later explained, "I didn't tell Vicki how scared I was. I thought that one lesson would be the end of it. But Vicki came out of the plane with a look of *power* on her face." Vicki was hooked.

Vicki continued with her flying lessons. She was so dedicated and determined in her approach that she impressed her teacher and soon passed ground school with straight-A's. She would have passed her pilot's exam, too, if she had been old enough. Instead, she'll have to wait until she is 16 to get her pilot's license.

MAJOR ACCOMPLISHMENTS

FLYING ACROSS THE UNITED STATES

Vicki made her first record-breaking flight in September 1993, at the age of 11—less than one year after she had started flying. She flew a small plane, a single-engine Cessna 172, across the United States, from Augusta, Maine, to San Diego, California. Although by law she had to have a licensed pilot at her side, he never touched the controls or helped her in any way. She was the youngest female pilot to fly across the U.S., and the youngest pilot ever to fly across the U.S. from East to West. That direction is considered the more difficult flight because it means flying against the wind. And in fact on part of the flight she had to fight her way through strong headwinds, turbulence, and airsickness. Because she was flying a small plane and because Federal Aviation Administration (FAA) regulations limited her to flying no more than eight hours each day, the trip took several days, with stops in Columbus, Ohio; St. Louis, Missouri; Oklahoma City, Oklahoma; Albuquerque, New Mexico; and Phoenix, Arizona. Her parents followed along on commercial flights, meeting her at each stop.

After that trip, Vicki decided that her next big flight would be across the Atlantic Ocean to Glasgow, Scotland. She trained hard all spring, driving with her dad each Friday to Columbus, Ohio. She would spend the weekend practicing in a single-engine Cessna 210, used for trans-Atlantic flights. The Cessna 210 is a heavier plane than the one Vicki had flown previously, and it's considered more difficult to handle. She practiced emergency procedures, including getting accustomed to the heavy survival suit she would have to wear while flying. If she had to make an emergency water landing, that suit would keep her warm and afloat for up to 24 hours in freezing cold water.

FLYING ACROSS THE ATLANTIC OCEAN

On June 4, 1994, the day after her graduation from sixth grade, Vicki started her flight across the Atlantic Ocean, with her parents again following along on commercial flights. Starting again in Augusta, Maine, Vicki made stops in Newfoundland, Canada, Greenland, and Iceland before arriving in Glasgow, Scotland. She handled all parts of the flight herself—navigation, fuel calculations, communications, takeoffs, landings, and the long, tedious hours flying over the ocean. The last leg of the trip, from Iceland to Scotland, proved to be a real challenge for the young pilot. Ice formed on the wings of the plane at her normal cruising altitude, between 3,000 and 7,000 feet. To get rid of the ice, she was forced to take the plane up above the clouds to about 13,500 feet. The lack of oxygen made her tired and dizzy, but she was able to finish the trip to Scotland without help from her co-pilot. In the process, she became the youngest female pilot to cross the Atlantic Ocean. Before returning home to Meadville she flew throughout Europe, making stops in England, France, Belgium, and Germany.

Many people encouraged and supported Vicki to help her reach her goals. Her school allowed her to take time off; her teachers worked with her after school to help her keep up with her work; and her parents gave their time and money to help. To date, the cost of Vicki's flying lessons, plus the expenses related to her two long flights, total $40,000. Her parents paid those expenses from money they had saved for her to attend college.

FUTURE PLANS

Vicki still hopes to be an astronaut. She would like to attend the United States Naval Academy, which many of the NASA astronauts attended. She recently had her first experience in a glider, and she's thinking about taking that up as well. But for now, as she explained shortly after completing her trans-Atlantic flight, Vicki's plans revolve around home, family, friends, and school: "I like to set goals and then work to accomplish them. So, I've accomplished my latest goal and people want to know what I'll do next.

"Well, I'd like to continue flying. . . but for now I'll take a break and maybe fly once a month to keep up my skills. But for now, I'd like to relax at home, enjoy the summer with my friends, play basketball with my brother in my backyard, and when school starts in the fall, I will concentrate on my studies because education is important to me.

"And I'll think about my next goal. I'm not sure right now what it might be, but anything is possible."

FURTHER READING

New Orleans Times Picayune, Sep. 21, 1993, p.A2
New York Times, Apr. 28, 1994, p.B1
Sports Illustrated, June 6, 1994, p.56

ADDRESS

Vicki Van Meter
Meadville, PA 16335

Heather Whitestone   1973-
Miss America
First Deaf Miss America
First Winner with a Disability in the
Pageant's History

BIRTH

Heather Whitestone was born on February 24, 1973, in Dothan, Alabama. Her father, Bill Whitestone, owns a furniture store. Her mother, Daphne Gray, was a homemaker when Heather was young. She is now a seventh-grade math teacher in Hoover, a suburb of Birmingham, Alabama. Daphne Gray has used her maiden name since she and Bill divorced when Heather was about 13. When interviewers ask her questions about her childhood, Heather never refers to her father; she speaks only of her mother.

Heather has two older sisters: Stacey, 25, a full-time mom, and Melissa, 24, a second lieutenant in the U.S. Air Force.

LOSING HER HEARING

Heather was born with perfectly normal hearing. In fact, she could hear just fine as an infant. She lost her hearing when she was about 18 months old. She received a vaccination for DPT (diphtheria, pertussis, and tetanus), a routine vaccination given to children. But Heather developed a high fever afterward. She was given medication to fight the fever, which her family long believed caused the nerve damage in her ears that resulted in hearing loss. But recently, doctors have determined that the nerve damage was caused, instead, by an infection of Hemophilus influenzae, a serious bacterial flu infection.

For Heather, the effects of the flu were profound. The 18-month-old toddler, who had been walking and talking, reverted to acting like an infant. She had to go through physical therapy to learn to move again. By the time she turned two, she seemed to be back to her old self. But the family learned otherwise at a Christmas gathering that year. As her mother tells it, "Heather was in the living room playing with some of her Christmas presents, and I was preparing brunch. I dropped some pans on the floor, and it made such a racket that everybody was startled—except Heather. She didn't flinch."

Tests showed that Heather was deaf. She had no hearing at all in one ear, and a very slight amount in the other—just five percent of normal hearing. Doctors were not optimistic for her future. They told her parents to teach Heather sign language and not to expect much from her. They didn't think she would get past third grade. But that was an attitude that her mother simply would not accept. Determined to find the best available options for her daughter, she set out to understand the communications issues facing the deaf.

COMMUNICATION AND EDUCATION FOR THE DEAF

For the deaf, choosing a means of communication is a crucial decision. The way in which deaf children are taught to communicate has a tremendous impact on their future, on what they will understand and on how they will be able to communicate throughout their lives. There are different viewpoints on the best way to educate deaf children. Debate on these educational viewpoints has extended back for over a century, and controversy continues to this day on the merits and pitfalls of the different approaches. Ultimately, each side argues that their approach increases communication abilities for the deaf and that the other approach limits them.

One view stresses the oral/aural approach. This view, which Heather ultimately adopted, emphasizes the spoken word. In this approach, the deaf learn to read lips (speech reading), they use hearing aids to amplify any residual hearing, and many also learn to speak. Learning to speak is much easier for those (like Heather) who were at one time able to hear and who learned the sounds of spoken English. Followers of this approach are less isolated from hearing society and more comfortable participating in mainstream culture, which, some believe, provides the deaf with greater opportunities.

The other view stresses the importance of sign language to deaf communication. This group, which embraces the deaf culture movement, rejects the notion that deafness is a disability. Instead, they view it as simply requiring a different means of communicating. And they contend that the best means, for deaf people, is American Sign Language, or ASL. Whereas Signed Exact English, or SEE, translates spoken English into hand gestures word-for-word, ASL, which also uses hand gestures, is based on concepts rather than individual words, and a single gesture can express a complex idea. ASL has such a different structure than spoken English, in fact, that it is considered a foreign language in some states. Many educators used to disparage ASL as vague, and deaf children were discouraged from learning it. Today, many linguists consider it a complex and subtle language with a sophisticated and nuanced grammatical structure. Within the deaf community, some oppose the use of lip reading as too limiting—there are some sounds and words that are impossible to distinguish through lip reading only. This group advocates the exclusive use of ASL, with translators, as necessary.

There are extremists on both sides of the debate, but many deaf people fall somewhere in the middle. According to David Stewart, director of the deaf education program at Michigan State University, "To say that signing or speaking, that one is better than the other, is simply taking an extremist position. It's great for stirring up sentiment and awareness, but it does little justice at portraying the realities of the world." And the reality is that the most important thing is effective communication, using whatever means in whatever combinations will best suit the individual.

MAKING CHOICES—HEATHER'S EDUCATION

These were the issues that Daphne Gray set out to understand as she researched educational options for Heather. She visited the Doreen Pollack Acoupedics Center at the Porter Memorial Hospital in Denver, Colorado. There, they emphasized lip reading and speaking, but not sign language. "I was so impressed with the children in the program," Daphne has said. "They were communicating with their voices and their lives seemed so full and rich." Ultimately, that was the approach that her mother chose for Heather. Daphne, along with a speech therapist, attended the program in Denver and then returned to Alabama to work with Heather.

It was hard, painstaking work. Heather had to practice with her mother for hours and hours to lip read and to speak. To learn a new word, she would practice saying it over and over, sometimes thousands of times. It took her six years to learn to correctly pronounce her own name. "After the doctor told her I would not go past the third grade, my mother made the decision for me to speak, and she spent hours working with me on my speech and my schoolwork," Heather recalls. "She never let me use my deafness as an excuse. We had a positive environment, where if you fail, just try again."

Heather enrolled in the local public school in Dothan. She also took ballet lessons, learning to count the beats to provide the rhythm for the dance. The discipline of learning to dance to a rhythm also helped her learn to speak according to a rhythm.

Despite her hard work, she was doing poorly in school. So when Heather was 11, her parents made the painful decision that she should leave home to attend the Central Institute for the Deaf (CID) in St. Louis. At CID, they focus on lip reading, speaking, and preparing children for life in mainstream society. Heather spent three years there. "It was wonderful," she says. "I was thrilled to be with girls my age." There were disadvantages, though—lots of homework and lots of rules, even more than at home. Heather's grades and her reading skills improved tremendously, though, and she returned to Alabama.

At about the same time, her parents' marriage was disintegrating. Heather, her mother, and her two sisters moved to Birmingham, Alabama. Heather started out attending the Alabama School of Fine Arts, where she continued studying ballet. She soon decided she wanted a more typical high school life, and she transferred to Hoover High School. It wasn't easy there. She was teased sometimes, and she had to work really hard on her school work, with her mother's help each night. But all that hard work paid off when she graduated with a 3.6 grade point average in 1991. She went on to the University of Montevallo in Montevallo, Alabama, for one year, and then transferred to Jacksonville State University in Jacksonville, Alabama, studying accounting.

FIRST PAGEANTS

To help pay the cost of college tuition, Whitestone began entering beauty pageants. In 1991, she entered a Junior Miss competition. She didn't win, but she earned enough scholarship money to pay the cost of tuition for her first year of college. Inspired by that success, she entered the Miss Alabama pageant, where she was named first runner-up in both 1992 and

1993. On June 18, 1994, she was crowned Miss Alabama, winning $4,800 in scholarship money and the chance to compete in the Miss America pageant.

THE MISS AMERICA PAGEANT

In September 1994, Whitestone traveled to Atlantic City, New Jersey, to take part in the Miss America Pageant. In the days leading up to the event, she won two of the preliminary competitions: swimsuit and talent. She was the 28th woman in the pageant's history to win those two events. Of those 28, 13 had gone on to win the crown.

On September 17, the night of the pageant, it was clear that she was the audience favorite. When she danced her talent number, a classical ballet choreographed to Sandy Patti's "Via Dolorosa," the audience gave her a standing ovation. All that was left was the live interview, the hardest part for Whitestone. At some pageants in the past, she had had trouble understanding the interviewer and had flubbed her answers. But not that night. When host Regis Philbin asked how she would motivate youth, she responded, "My good attitude helped me get through hard times and believe in myself." The audience went wild. Moments later, Whitestone was pronounced Miss America. At first, she didn't realize she'd won. But

as one of the other contestants signaled to her, she ducked her head to receive the crown and started to cry. As she took her ceremonial walk down the runway, she signed "I love you" to the audience.

Whitestone's pageant winnings are considerable: a new red Chevrolet Camaro convertible, a $35,000 scholarship, and the chance to earn at least $200,000 during her one-year reign as Miss America. It is a job that entails a great deal of traveling and public speaking. At first, some wondered if it wouldn't be a strain for a deaf person to hold this job. But on the day after the pageant, she showed her ability to master her new responsibilities. At a press conference, she deftly read lips and answered reporters' questions. When photographers' flash bulbs interfered with her ability to read lips, she gently asked them to stop taking pictures—and put to rest any doubts people might have about her ability to communicate. "I really believe the most handicapped [person] in the whole world is a negative thinker," she said. "I want to send a message: I believe that positive thinking is the solution."

Her approach has sparked controversy in the deaf community. While some rejoiced in her win, others argued that her use of speech and lip-reading rather than sign language set her apart, and that she should not represent deaf people. One explanation for the debate is offered by Sherry Duhon of Gallaudet University, the only liberal-arts college for the deaf in the world and a national center for deaf culture. "I'm sure Heather didn't expect to get involved in a political tussle," Duhon said. "I'm sure she's tried to satisfy both sides. . . . [But Heather] doesn't belong to either the hearing or the deaf community. We met, and I learned about her as a person. She's a sweet human being. And yes, she signed. But her signing skills show she was brought up in a hearing environment. She's not fluent, in other words." And that's important, Duhon explains, because "Among the deaf, status comes from using ASL, attending [deaf] schools, and coming from a deaf family. That's our culture. . . . That's why there's this disappointment in Heather."

The controversy put Heather on an emotional roller coaster ride. "I never imagined becoming Miss America would throw me into a communications war," Heather once said. "I feel caught between the hearing and deaf worlds. It's been very frightening." With time, though, she has been able to distance herself emotionally from her critics and return to her own hard-won sense of self. "I'm learning I have something to offer. And I'm learning there will be people who disapprove. That's all right. I've decided to be true to myself. I want to feel comfortable with myself. I am comfortable speaking. I am comfortable in my own voice."

HER PLATFORM

During her tenure as Miss America, Whitestone wants to convey her message to young people that anything is possible, and she holds herself up as both proof of that message and as inspiration for those with disabilities themselves. As Heather says, her mother always told her that the last four letters of American spell "I can." She plans to discuss her STARS program, for Success Through Action and Realization of Your Dreams. Like a star, her program has five points, as she explains here: "to have a positive attitude; to believe in your dreams, especially education; to face your obstacles, no matter how great; to work hard; [and] to build a support team" of parents, teachers, and friends. The goal of the program is to promote positive self-esteem, especially in young people. Motivating and encouraging people, both children and adults, is the focus of her reign as Miss America.

FUTURE PLANS

For the future, Whitestone has said that she plans to finish college and then become an accountant. She has also expressed a desire to work with children and has suggested that she may change her plans and become a math teacher. But no matter what career she follows, she says she wants a condo on the beach!

HOBBIES AND OTHER INTERESTS

In addition to dance, Heather enjoys sewing, bowling, hiking, and walking on the beach. But with the rigorous travel schedule that she'll follow as Miss America, she probably won't have much time for hobbies during her year-long reign.

MAJOR INFLUENCES

There are two people whom Whitestone looks to for inspiration. The first is her mother. As she says, "My mom is my inspiration. She worked with me every day. She never let me use my deafness as an excuse." The second person is Marva Collins, a well-known school teacher from inner-city Chicago. "She had the desire to help younger people with no hopes and no dreams, to make them feel unique. I want to do what she did. To look at abilities first, disabilities second."

HONORS AND AWARDS

Miss Alabama: 1994
Miss America: 1994

FURTHER READING

PERIODICALS

Birmingham Post-Herald, Sep. 26, 1994, p.B1
Chicago Tribune, Jan. 13, 1995, Chicagoland section, p.6
Detroit Free Press, Sep. 17, 1994, p.A1; Sep. 21, 1994, p.C1
New York Times, Sep. 19, 1994, p.A12; Sep. 26, 1994, p.B9; Oct. 27, 1994, p.C1
People, Oct. 3, 1994, p.48
Philadelphia Inquirer, Sep. 24, 1994, p.B1
Pittsburgh Post-Gazette, Oct. 2, 1994, p.M1
Time, Oct. 3, 1994, p.66

USA Weekend, Mar. 3-5, 1995, p.4
Washington Post, Sep. 19, 1994, p.D1

ADDRESS

The Miss America Organization
P.O. Box 119
Atlantic City, NJ 08404

OBITUARY

Pedro Zamora 1972-1994
Cuban-Born American AIDS Activist
Featured on MTV's "The Real World"

BIRTH

Pedro Zamora was born in a small town near Havana, Cuba, on March 1, 1972. His father, Hector, was a food-warehouse worker, while his mother, Zoraida, was a homemaker. Pedro, the youngest child, had two sisters and five brothers, Milagros, Maria Elena, Lazaro, Eduardo, Francisco, Jesus, and Hector Jr. Their family was quite poor.

Pedro rarely talked about his early life in Cuba. Accounts of his youth usually begin with his family's departure from Cuba for the United States.

CUBAN HISTORY

Cuba, like other islands in the Caribbean, was inhabited by native American Indian tribes when it was discovered by Christopher Columbus in 1492. Spanish settlers began colonizing the island in 1511. Over time, they developed an economy that relied on huge sugar plantations run on slave labor. That labor was provided first by the native Indians and later, beginning in 1517, by hundreds of thousands of African slaves. Cuba was a colony of Spain for about 400 years, until it won its independence in 1898. A series of authoritarian governments followed during the first half of this century, with occasional periods of democratic rule. There was ongoing political upheaval throughout this time. The United States repeatedly intervened in Cuban affairs, both to provide stability and to protect U.S. business interests there. Throughout all the changes in government, most Cubans lived in intense poverty.

THE CUBAN REVOLUTION

In 1959, Fidel Castro won a guerilla war against the regime of Fulgencio Batista. The Cuban Revolution reorganized the Cuban government and instituted a series of reforms patterned after those in the Soviet-bloc countries, creating the only Communist regime in the American hemisphere.

Under President Castro, Cuba has been isolated from many of its neighbors. His government restricted American economic and political influence on Cuban society. The United States and Cuba broke off diplomatic relations in 1961, after Castro took over American-owned businesses and banks. The U.S. retaliated with an economic embargo that eliminated trade between the two countries. It banned the export of American goods to Cuba and, more importantly, outlawed the importation of Cuban goods, notably sugar. The loss of its largest market for sugar, Cuba's largest export, seriously hurt the nation's economy.

Throughout the Cold War, Cuba was politically and economically aligned with the Communist countries of the Eastern bloc, the U.S.S.R. and its satellites in Eastern Europe; in fact, it depended heavily on Soviet military and financial aid, receiving billions of dollars in loans or gifts. With the fall of Communism and the dissolution of the U.S.S.R., Cuba has endured political isolation and economic difficulties.

THE MARIEL BOATLIFT

For the most part, Cuba has been a closed society, with very little emigration. Since the Revolution, Cubans have rarely been allowed to leave Cuba to move to other countries. There have been a few exceptions, though. One exception was the Mariel boatlift.

In 1980, the Cuban government allowed a group of people to leave Mariel, a northern seaport, for the United States. About 125,000 people eventually participated, sailing in boats large and small for southern Florida. The Zamora family—at least part of it—left Cuba in that boatlift.

At the time, the entire family expected to go, except for Pedro's oldest sister, who was married and planned to stay in Cuba. At the last minute, though, on the day the boat was loaded, four of his older brothers were forbidden to leave—a government official decided that they were too close to draft age. At first, Pedro's parents refused to go either, saying that they wouldn't leave their sons behind. But the boys insisted, saying that they wanted the younger children to have a chance for a better life in America. Like many Cubans, they all expected Castro to fall from power soon, and the family would be reunited then. The division of the family proved to be an ongoing heartbreak for all.

The Zamora family—Hector, Zoraida, eight-year-old Pedro, his 15-year-old sister Milagros, his 12-year-old brother Jesus, and his grandmother—made the 90-mile crossing on May 30, 1980. It was a miserable, stormy trip. Pedro was one of the lucky ones—he and his grandmother sat inside the tiny cabin. As he later described it, "It was really *the* worst day of my entire life. It was 25 hours of constant sickness." The rest of the family had it even worse. They sat outside on benches in the rain throughout the trip. They were jammed in so tightly that they couldn't move—even those who got seasick. Just across the deck, separated only by a rope, was a group of violent criminals, insane people, and the desperately ill. Castro was sending Cuba's outcasts to the U.S. to empty out its prisons, hospitals, and mental institutions.

YOUTH

The family settled in Hialeah, Florida, just west of Miami. They found a two-bedroom apartment, with the parents in one bedroom, Milagros and their grandmother in the second bedroom, and Pedro and Jesus on the fold-out couch in the living room. For Pedro, the biggest thrill was discovering the apartment complex's swimming pool—he had never seen a pool before. Pedro's father, Hector, soon found work mowing lawns, and later got a job in construction; his mother, Zoraida, went to work in a T-shirt factory. They were settled in, but they desperately missed the rest of their family.

Pedro soon started school—in English, of course, although he arrived speaking only Spanish. The Mariel refugees had been spread around the classrooms, to force the children to adapt, and there was only one other

Spanish-speaking child in his class. With the help of his supportive teachers and classmates, he soon started picking up English.

As the baby of the family, Pedro was especially close to his mother. They spent a lot of time together, playing card games and Chinese checkers, watching movies, and listening to Cuban music.

When Pedro was eleven, his mother noticed that a mole on her face was changing shape. It was cancer, and it soon spread. She died about two years later, when he was only thirteen. For Pedro, and the rest of the family, her loss was devastating. "Her death affected everything," his sister Milagros later said. "She was the one who kept things together. She was the leader of the family. When she died, it was very hard. We separated, even though we were together, and we each worked out our problems our own way."

THE AIDS DIAGNOSIS

Zamora first learned of his illness after he donated blood to the Red Cross. Soon afterward, on November 9, 1989, he received a letter from the Red Cross saying that there was a problem with the blood and requesting that he come in for testing. He was only 17.

At first he tried to deny it. He procrastinated for two months, ignoring the letters and delaying going in. Finally, he went in for the blood test. The results were positive: he had HIV (Human Immunodeficiency Virus), the virus responsible for AIDS (Acquired Immune Deficiency Syndrome). HIV weakens the immune system and leaves it vulnerable to infection. HIV can remain dormant for years: a person who is infected may not know it for years, until they start to develop symptoms, and may infect many other people in the process. AIDS, caused by HIV, is associated with a wide range of symptoms: first, fever, weight loss, diarrhea, and fatigue; later, a whole host of infections, neurological illnesses, and cancers. AIDS is fatal.

When Zamora heard the results, he was devastated. But it was his sister's birthday, and he didn't want to ruin it for her. He went to the family party and didn't tell anyone, never let them guess that anything was wrong. Several weeks later, he shared the news with his family: that he was gay, and that he had HIV. His family was stunned by the news, and devastated by his illness.

In April 1990, shortly before he was to graduate from high school, he developed shingles, an acutely painful viral infection that causes blisters on the skin. He missed two months of school, which he had to make up in summer school. He received his diploma in the fall of 1990 from Hialeah High School.

BECOMING AN ACTIVIST

At about the same time, Zamora was becoming an activist. Through several local AIDS prevention groups, he began doing public information lectures for schools and for civic, religious, and corporate groups. But by far, it was in schools that he initially had his greatest impact. A teenager himself, young, good-looking, and apparently healthy, Zamora was able to reach his teenage audience, to make them realize that it really could happen to them. "Teenagers think they're immortal, that they can never get AIDS, that they can never get cancer, that they'll live forever," he explains. "I know. I was one of those teenagers. I was wrong." His lectures were blunt about sex, but he also personalized the illness for his listeners, talking about himself and his feelings about being sick. Through these talks, he helped to ease the social stigma of having AIDS. For many, Zamora gave AIDS a human face. He was a gifted speaker, honest and genuine and moving. He often left his audience in tears. He made it easy to talk about AIDS.

His reputation as a speaker continued to grow. Zamora soon moved on to the national level as well, aided in part by a sympathetic 1991 profile in the *Wall Street Journal*. He was quickly becoming one of the country's leading educators on AIDS. He served on eight AIDS awareness committees on the local, state, and national level; spoke before a committee of the U.S. Congress; attended an international AIDS conference; testified before the Presidential Commission on AIDS; told his story on the NBC "Today" show; sat on several boards of national organizations; and was featured in a 1992 public service campaign on AIDS prevention by the Centers for Disease Control. As Donna Shalala, the secretary of Health and Human Services, described him, "He is more than an AIDS educator. He has an ability to personalize this brutal illness. And he has reached everybody, across generations."

"THE REAL WORLD"

His outreach continued when he appeared on the MTV television show "The Real World." For this documentary series, MTV producers interviewed a host of young hopefuls, selected seven, set up this group of total strangers as roommates in an apartment, videotaped hundreds of hours of their activities and conversations, and then edited those videotapes down to a series of 30-minute shows. "A weekly real-life soap opera," according to the *Wall Street Journal*, with every argument and dramatic confrontation skillfully edited into each prime-time segment.

Zamora and six others were chosen from among 25,000 hopefuls to appear on the show's third season, broadcast in 1994. Most of those who auditioned for "The Real World" hoped to become actors or at least to become famous. According to one of the show's creators, "Pedro just wanted to spread his story."

In San Francisco with the others, much of his life became fodder for the TV-viewing audience: his health, the response of his roommates to learning that he had AIDS, his continuing work as an AIDS educator, and his new relationship with a local AIDS activist, Sean Sasser. The easy charm and approachability that had so captivated audiences for his speeches soon touched the nation as well.

For Zamora, "The Real World" proved to be an excellent opportunity to continue his AIDS education work in the most personally revealing way. As he once explained, "It's a great way to educate people [about AIDS], because when I go into a presentation, I'm only there for an hour. I talk about the times that I'm happy and have a lot of energy, or I can talk about the times that I'm sick and that I'm scared, but they can't see it. They're just seeing me speak about it. This was the perfect way to have people see it all. I had cameras following me when I was at the park playing soccer with Judd [one of his roommates], and I had cameras with me when I was talking to the doctor and not feeling well. It's important, especially for young people, to see me living with six other people and to see that we could get along. Yes, some issues came up about HIV and AIDS, but it wasn't a big deal. We discussed them, we talked about them, and we moved on."

On August 17, 1994, shortly before a planned appearance on "CBS This Morning," Zamora became ill with a serious neurological disorder. Many people reacted with concern to the news of his illness. School children in Miami held bake sales to help pay for his medical care— Pedro had no health insurance. MTV contributed heavily to his medical expenses and set up a trust fund for his health care, and millions of fans responded. President Bill Clinton called to wish him well. And officials of the U.S. government worked to obtain visas to allow the members of his family still in Cuba to travel to the U.S. to see him. Zamora was reunited with his family just weeks before his death in Miami, Florida, on November 11, 1994.

HIS LEGACY

Zamora had a powerful impact on so many people. For some, the impact was very personal. "Please know this," one young gay man wrote from North Carolina, "If you never helped one other person, if you never made a difference in anyone's life, you made all the difference in mine." For others, it was his emphasis on tolerance, compassion, and humanity. As one woman wrote from South Carolina, "I never thought *anyone* could change my opinion on homosexuals and AIDS. Because of you, I've seen the human side of something that once seemed so unreal to me." For still others, as for this man from Puerto Rico, it was the inspiration that he offered to others: "I think you made me realize something very important in life. That we as individuals have the power to inspire, educate, influence, and move people to act or think in a positive way, and it can all be done with love. At least that's what I learned from you."

FURTHER READING

PERIODICALS

Detroit Free Press, Nov. 12, 1994, p.A16
Miami Herald, Mar. 4, 1993, p.F1; Nov. 12, 1994, p.A1
New York Times, Nov. 12, 1994, p.A8
People, Nov. 28, 1994, p.185
Wall Street Journal, Sep. 4, 1991, p.A1; Oct. 21, 1994, p.A1; Nov. 14, 1994, p.A3

Photo and Illustration Credits

Oksana Baiul/Photos: AP/Wide World Photos.

Jean-Bertrand Aristide/Photos: AP/Wide World Photos.

Benazir Bhutto/Photo: AP/Wide World Photos.

Jonathan Brandis/Photos: NBC Photo by Chris Haston; NBC Photo by Richard Foreman.

Warren Burger/Photos: Photo by Robert S. Oakes, National Geographic Society, Collection of the Supreme Court of the United States.

Ken Burns/Photo: General Motors/Al Levine

Candice Cameron/Photo: Schultz Bros. Photography.

Jimmy Carter/Photos: Charles Plant; Julie Lopez/Habitat for Humanity International.

Agnes de Mille/Photos: © Joseph Marzullo/Retna Ltd.; Photo by Maurice Seymour, © Ronald Seymour, Inc.

Placido Domingo/Photo: Peter Weissbech.

Patrick Ewing/Photo: George Kalinsky.

John Goodman/Photo: Edie Baskin/ABC.

Amy Grant/Photo: Albert Sanchez.

Jesse Jackson/Photo: AP/Wide World Photos.

James Earl Jones/Photo: Michael Jacobs.

Julie Krone/Photo: Michael J. Marten.

David Letterman/Photo: Christopher Little/CBS.

Heather Locklear/Photo: Dana Fineman.

Reba McEntire/Photos: Peter Nash; AP/Wide World Photos.

Cosmas Ndeti/Photos: AP/Wide World Photos.

Hakeem Olajuwon/Photos: Layne Murdoch/NBA Photos; Nathaniel S. Butler/NBA Photos.

Ashley and Mary-Kate Olsen/Photos: Craig Sjodin.

Appendix

This Appendix contains updates for individuals profiled in Volumes 1, 2, 3, and 4 of *Biography Today*.

* YASIR ARAFAT *

In September 1995, Arafat and Israeli Prime Minister Yitzhak Rabin signed an agreement that transfers control of most of the territory known as the West Bank from Israeli to Palestinian control. The accord calls for the withdrawal of Israeli troops from most of the West Bank by March 30, 1996. They will be replaced by an elected Palestinian council. Arafat signed the agreement in a White House ceremony attended by heads of state from all over the world. He said that the accord "demonstrates the irreversibility of the peace process," and he called it "the peace of the brave." There is still concern over terrorist activity by both Israelis and Palestinians opposed to the accord, who continue acts of violence against one another. Arafat and Rabin both pledged to try to control the violence and prevent further bloodshed.

* BONNIE BLAIR *

Bonnie Blair, winner of more Olympic gold medals than any other American woman, retired from the sport of speed skating in March 1995. In her last season on the speed skating circuit, Blair won the overall World Cup title in her signature races, the 500 meters and 1,000 meters, and also placed first in both events in the World Sprint championships. Blair skated her final races in Calgary, Alberta. She was in true championship form, as she placed first in both the 500- and 1,000-meter races, including a personal best in the 1,000. She thanked the crowd for a "lifetime of memories." Blair said she was retiring "because something inside of me says it's time. Now I can walk away and know I'm going to be happy because I've accomplished everything I dreamed of in the sport." She plans to do motivational speaking, coaching, and she may go back to college.

* CONNIE CHUNG *

Chung was dismissed from her co-anchor position on the CBS Evening News in May 1995. She was also dropped as the host of "Eye to Eye with Connie Chung." According to most reports, the network had hired Chung to help boost the ratings of the Evening News, and when she failed to do so after a year and a half as co-anchor, she was dropped. Chung claimed her firing was sexist, a charge the network denied. Her former co-anchor, Dan Rather, wished Chung well on the air, but off camera made comments to reporters in which he questioned her abilities. The relationship between the former colleagues soured, becoming, in the words of one journalist, "one of the more extraordinary displays of public venom ever seen among high-profile TV journalists." Four days after her dismissal, Chung learned that she and her husband, TV talk show host Maury Povich, had finally been successful in their plans to adopt a baby. They are now the parents of a son, Matthew Jay Povich. According to a former CBS colleague, Chung will probably "go underground for a while and just enjoy motherhood."

* BILL CLINTON *

During the past year, Clinton has announced that he will run for reelection. As he tours the country making speeches and raising money, Clinton is hoping to confront what he perceives as the confusion and uncertainty many Americans are feeling. In particular, he cited their anger over governmental policies, job uncertainty, and unease with the pace of technological change in modern society. Over the past year he has had to contend with a more conservative Republican congress that has begun to dismantle many democratic-sponsored programs, including welfare, and reforms to other government programs, such as Medicare. In 1995 Clinton was also involved with trying to broker a peace in the continuing war in Bosnia and once again hosted the signing of a peace agreement between the PLO and Israel. He considers the U.S. efforts in Bosnia and the Middle East "examples of the imperative for United States leadership."

* HILLARY CLINTON *

Hillary Clinton attended the U.N. World Conference on Women in September 1995 in Beijing, China. Although her visit was virtually ignored by Chinese officials, Mrs. Clinton took the opportunity during her speech before the U.N. group to indirectly condemn China's policies toward women. "If there is one message that echoes forth from this conference, let it be that human rights are women's rights," she said. On China's reproductive policies, she said this: "It is a violation of human rights when women are denied the right to plan their own families, and that includes being forced to have abortions or being sterilized against their will." She also condemned China's treatment of some 23,000 women delegates representing non-governmental organizations, who had been harassed and intimidated by Chinese officials throughout their stay in China.

* POPE JOHN PAUL II *

The Pope has continued to travel the world and plans to visit the U.S. in October, 1995. His five-day trip to the U.S. includes stops in the cities of New York, Newark, and Baltimore. In addition to holding religious services at Giants Stadium and Central Park in New York and Camden Yards in Baltimore, the Pope also plans to visit a small soup kitchen in Baltimore, hoping to draw Americans' attention to the plight of the poor and homeless in the U.S.

* MICHAEL JORDAN *

In a career that continues to hold surprising changes and reversals, Michael Jordan left professional baseball in early 1995. After reporting to spring training for the Chicago White Sox, Jordan said he was retiring from the sport of baseball because the baseball strike hampered his development as a player. A week after that announcement, Jordan returned to professional basketball—in the middle of the 1994-95 season—and rejoined his old team, the Chicago Bulls. His first outing with the Bulls was against the Indiana Pacers. Millions of fans watched on television as one of the most popular sports figures of all time returned to the sport he had dominated for years. Jordan's play in 1995 was not enough to bring the Bull's back to championship caliber, however. They lost in the playoffs to the Orlando Magic.

* JOE MONTANA *

After 16 seasons of professional football, Joe Montana announced his retirement from the game in April 1995. Montana held a press conference in San Francisco, where he had led the 49ers to four Super Bowls. He chose that site rather than Kansas City, where he played for the Chiefs for his last two seasons, because San Francisco is where he plans to live after retirement. His future plans include devoting more time to his family as well as to hobbies like flying, golf, archery, and wine making. He is also talking to several networks about broadcasting possibilities and he continues to appear in ads for numerous products. After a career that included 40,551 passing yards, 273 touchdown passes, and three MVP awards for Super Bowl play, Montana said he'd lost the desire to keep playing. "It felt like a job, and that's when I told myself it was time," he said. "I've got a lot of new things happening in my life I'm excited about. One thing, and it sounds simple, is just not being on a schedule. To just relax—that's something I've never been able to do."

* ROSS PEROT *

On September 25, 1995, Perot announced that he was forming a new political party, the Independence Party. Making his announcement on the Larry King Show, Perot stated he was disgusted with both major political parties and said his party would run a candidate for president and try to influence congressional races as well. Perot claimed he had no particular candidate in mind, and would not rule out running himself. When asked about the possibility of choosing former General Colin Powell for the position on his new party's ticket, Perot said "certainly we want people of that stature and quality." The party must now become certified in all the states in order to appear on the ballot for 1996. When the party is certified, it would field candidates through a national convention,

357

according to Perot. He said the party platform would be similar to that of his political organization, United We Stand, which is focused on reforms in campaign financing and lobbying, as well as balancing the federal budget.

* COLIN POWELL *

On November 8, 1995, Colin Powell held a press conference to announce that he would not be a candidate for president in 1996. His decision ended nearly two years of speculation that he might seek the highest political office in the U.S. Even though he had never announced his candidacy, grass roots organizations had sprung up across the country to organize voters on his behalf, and public opinion polls showed him running ahead of declared Republican candidates Bob Dole and Phil Gramm.

Despite the strength of public support, Powell said that he did not have the "passion and commitment" necessary to run for office. He also cited the welfare of his family, and the "sacrifices and changes" that would have occurred in their lives if he had run.

Powell did not rule out the possibility of running in the next election, saying "the future is the future." Although he had never declared a party affiliation before, he stated that he would now join the Republican Party and work to "broaden its appeal," particularly to African Americans.

In thanking Americans for their support and encouragement, Powell said: "In one generation we have moved from denying a black man service at a lunch counter to elevating one to the highest military office in the nation and to being a serious contender for the Presidency. This is a magnificent country and I am proud to be one of its sons."

* YITZHAK RABIN *

As co-architect of the Israeli-PLO agreement that gives back most of the West Bank to Palestinian control, Rabin once again appeared in a White House signing in September 1995. The agreement calls for the withdrawal of Israeli troops from most of the towns and villages of the West Bank by March 30, 1996. Israeli control will be replaced by an elected Palestinian council. The signing was attended by heads of state from around the world, including Egyptian president Hosni Mubarak and Jordan's King Hussein, once bitter enemies of Israel. "Please take a good hard look," said Rabin. "The sight you see before you at this moment was impossible, was unthinkable just two years ago. Only poets dreamed of it, and to our great pain, soldiers and civilians went to their death to make this moment possible." Rabin also spoke of the continuing threat of terrorism to Israelis and Palestinians. "If all the partners to the peace making do not unite against the evil angels of death by terrorism, all that will remain of this ceremony are color snapshots, empty moments."

Rabin's words proved to be tragically prophetic: on November 4, 1995, he was assassinated in Jerusalem by a right-wing extremist, Yigal Amir. The assassin, a 25-year-old Israeli student, admitted the killing and said he had done it to stop the peace process that allowed the return of the occupied territories to the Palestinians.

Rabin was mourned around the world. His funeral in Jerusalem was attended by President Clinton and delegates from 80 countries, including President Mubarak, who made his first trip to Israel to attend the ceremonies. Rabin was eulogized by Clinton as a "martyr for peace" and by his one-time enemy King Hussein as "a brother, a colleague, and a friend."

* JONAS SALK *

Jonas Salk died June 23, 1995, of heart failure in La Jolla, California. He was 80 years old. His historic achievement in medicine was the development of the first vaccine against polio, which, along with the vaccine developed by Albert Sabin, virtually eradicated the disease in most parts of the world. Salk is also remembered as a tireless researcher into such diseases as cancer and AIDS. At the time of his death, he was working on a vaccine to combat the AIDS virus. "He was truly one of the great figures in American medicine in the area of vaccinology," said Dr. Anthony Fauci, one of the top AIDS experts in the U.S. "His contributions have been substantial and it is extraordinary that he continued to make substantial contributions literally until the day of his death, which is the way I think he would have wanted it."

* STEVEN SPIELBERG *

In late 1994, Spielberg announced that he was forming a new company, Dreamworks SKG, with David Geffen and Jeff Katzenberg. The three men are among the most powerful and wealthy in the entertainment industry. Geffen is a billionaire from the recording industry, and Katzenberg recently resigned from his position as head of the animated film division of Disney studios. The group plans to make records, TV shows, and movies. In a deal announced in March 1995, the three men announced that Dreamworks would take part in a joint venture with Microsoft to develop educational computer games and other interactive products.

Also in 1995, Spielberg received the Life Achievement Award from the American Film Institute, becoming the youngest director to receive the honor.

* BORIS YELTSIN *

Boris Yeltsin suffered a heart attack in July 1995. He returned to work a month later, as questions about his health, his handling of the continuing crisis in Chechnya, the Russian support of the Serbs in the war in Bosnia, as well as his ability to lead his own nation were voiced within Russia and around the world. Yeltsin plans to speak to the U.N. General Assembly in October 1995.

Name Index

Listed below are the names of all individuals profiled in *Biography Today*, followed by the date of the issue in which they appear.

General Index

This index includes subjects, occupations, organizations, and ethnic and minority origins that pertain to individuals profiled in *Biography Today*.

Gilbert, Sara, 93/Apr
Goodman, John, 95/Sep
royalty
Diana, Princess of Wales, 92/Jul
runner
Ndeti, Cosmas, 95/Sep
"Rush Limbaugh: The Television Show"
Limbaugh, Rush, 95/Sep
Russian
Fedorov, Sergei, 94/Apr;
94/Update
Gorbachev, Mikhail, 92/Jan;
94/Update
Yeltsin, Boris, 92/Apr;
93/Update
Russian Federation, president of
Yeltsin, Boris, 92/Apr;
93/Update
San Francisco 49ers
Rice, Jerry, 93/Apr
Young, Steve, 94/Jan
"Saturday Night Live"
Carvey, Dana, 93/Jan
science fiction literature
Asimov, Isaac, 92/Jul
Science Talent Search, Westinghouse
Pine, Elizabeth Michele,
94/Jan
scientists
Asimov, Isaac, 92/Jul
Hawking, Stephen, 92/Apr
Jemison, Mae, 92/Oct
McClintock, Barbara, 92/Oct
Ochoa, Severo, 94/Jan
Pauling, Linus, 95/Jan
Ride, Sally, 92/Jan
Salk, Jonas, 94/Jan
Thomas, Lewis, 94/Apr
scientology
Alley, Kirstie, 92/Jul
Seinfeld, Jerry, 92/Oct
"SCTV"
Candy, John, 94/Sep

"seaQuest DSV"
Brandis, Jonathan, 95/Sep
Secretary General of the United Nations
Boutros-Ghali, Boutros, 93/Apr
Secretary of Housing and Urban Development, U.S.
Cisneros, Henry, 93/Sep
Secretary of Interior, U.S.
Babbitt, Bruce, 94/Jan
Secretary of Labor, U.S.
Dole, Elizabeth Hanford, 92/Jul
Secretary of State, U.S.
Baker, James, 92/Oct
Secretary of Transportation, U.S.
Dole, Elizabeth Hanford, 92/Jul
Secretary of Treasury, U.S.
Baker, James, 92/Oct
"Seinfeld"
Seinfeld, Jerry, 92/Oct
sexual harassment
Hill, Anita, 93/Jan
"Simpsons, The"
Groening, Matt, 92/Jan
singers
Abdul, Paula, 92/Jan
Anderson, Marian, 94/Jan
Battle, Kathleen, 93/Jan
Brooks, Garth, 92/Oct
Carpenter, Mary Chapin, 94/Sep
Cobain, Kurt, 94/Sep
Domingo, Placido, 95/Sep
Estefan, Gloria, 92/Jul
Grant, Amy, 95/Jan
Guy, Jasmine, 93/Sep
Hammer, 92/Jan
Houston, Whitney, 94/Sep
Ice-T, 93/Apr
lang, k.d., 93/Sep
McEntire, Reba, 95/Sep
Queen Latifah, 92/Apr
Salt 'N' Pepa, 95/Apr
Smith, Will, 94/Sep
"60 Minutes"
Bradley, Ed, 94/Apr

Places of Birth Index

The following index lists the places of birth for the individuals profiled in *Biography Today*. Places of birth are entered under state, province, and/or country.

Birthday Index

January

2 Asimov, Isaac (1920)
4 Naylor, Phyllis Reynolds (1933)
8 Hawking, Stephen W. (1942)
9 Menchu, Rigoberta (1959)
  Nixon, Richard (1913)
12 Limbaugh, Rush (1951)
17 Cormier, Robert (1925)
  Jones, James Earl (1931)
21 Domingo, Placido (1941)
  Olajuwon, Hakeem (1963)
22 Chavis, Benjamin (1948)
25 Alley, Kirstie (1955)
28 Gretzky, Wayne (1961)
29 Gilbert, Sara (1975)
  Winfrey, Oprah (1954)
31 Ryan, Nolan (1947)

February

1 Spinelli, Jerry (1941)
  Yeltsin, Boris (1931)
3 Nixon, Joan Lowery (1927)
4 Parks, Rosa (1913)
6 Zmeskal, Kim (1976)
7 Brooks, Garth (1962)
8 Grisham, John (1955)
10 Norman, Greg (1955)
12 Blume, Judy (1938)
15 Groening, Matt (1954)
17 Anderson, Marian (1897)
  Jordan, Michael (1963)
18 Morrison, Toni (1931)
20 Barkley, Charles (1963)
  Cobain, Kurt (1967)
  Crawford, Cindy (1966)
21 Carpenter, Mary Chapin (1958)
24 Jobs, Steven (1955)
  Whitestone, Heather (1973)
25 Voigt, Cynthia (1942)
28 Andretti, Mario (1940)
  Pauling, Linus (1901)

March

1 Rabin, Yitzhak (1922)
  Zamora, Pedro (1972)
2 Gorbachev, Mikhail (1931)
  Seuss, Dr. (1904)
3 Hooper, Geoff (1979)
  Joyner-Kersee, Jackie (1962)
10 Guy, Jasmine (1964)
  Miller, Shannon (1977)
12 Hamilton, Virginia (1936)
13 Van Meter, Vicki (1982)
15 Ginsburg, Ruth Bader (1933)
16 O'Neal, Shaquille (1972)
17 Nureyev, Rudolf (1938)
18 Blair, Bonnie (1964)
  de Klerk, F. W. (1936)
  Queen Latifah (1970)
20 Lee, Spike (1957)
22 Shatner, William (1931)
25 Steinem, Gloria (1934)
26 O'Connor, Sandra Day (1930)
28 James, Cheryl
  McEntire, Reba (1955)
30 Hammer (1933)
31 Chavez, Cesar (1927)
  Gore, Al (1948)

April

2 Carvey, Dana (1955)
4 Angelou, Maya (1928)
5 Powell, Colin (1937)
12 Cleary, Beverly (1916)
  Doherty, Shannen (1971)
  Letterman, David (1947)
13 Brandis, Jonathan (1976)
14 Rose, Pete (1941)
19 Hart, Melissa Joan (1976)
28 Baker, James (1930)
  Duncan, Lois (1934)
  Hussein, Saddam (1937)
  Leno, Jay (1950)

389

April, continued

29 Agassi, Andre (1970)
Seinfeld, Jerry (1954)

May

2 Spock, Benjamin (1903)
9 Bergen, Candice (1946)
14 Smith, Emmitt (1969)
15 Zindel, Paul (1936)
17 Paulsen, Gary (1939)
18 John Paul II (1920)
21 Robinson, Mary (1944)
26 Ride, Sally (1951)
27 Kerr, M.E. (1927)

June

1 Lalas, Alexi (1970)
4 Kistler, Darci (1964)
5 Scarry, Richard (1919)
6 Rylant, Cynthia (1954)
8 Bush, Barbara (1925)
Edelman, Marian Wright (1939)
Wayans, Keenen Ivory (1958)
10 Goodman, John (1952)
11 Cousteau, Jacques (1910)
Montana, Joe (1956)
12 Bush, George (1924)
13 Allen, Tim (1953)
14 Graf, Steffi (1969)
16 McClintock, Barbara (1902)
17 Gingrich, Newt (1943)
Jansen, Dan (1965)
18 Van Allsburg, Chris (1949)
19 Abdul, Paula (1962)
21 Bhutto, Benazir (1953)
Breathed, Berke (1957)
22 Bradley, Ed (1941)
23 Rudolph, Wilma (1940)
Thomas, Clarence (1948)
25 Carle, Eric (1929)
27 Babbitt, Bruce (1938)
Perot, H. Ross (1930)

July

1 Diana, Princess of Wales (1961)
Duke, David (1950)
McCully, Emily Arnold (1939)
2 Marshall, Thurgood (1908)
5 Watterson, Bill (1958)
10 Ashe, Arthur (1943)
11 Cisneros, Henry (1947)
White, E.B. (1899)
12 Cosby, Bill (1937)
Yamaguchi, Kristi (1972)
13 Stewart, Patrick (1940)
15 Aristide, Jean-Bertrand (1953)
16 Sanders, Barry (1968)
18 Mandela, Nelson (1918)
21 Reno, Janet (1938)
Williams, Robin (1952)
22 Hinton, S.E. (1948)
24 Krone, Julie (1963)
28 Davis, Jim (1945)
29 Burns, Ken (1953)
Dole, Elizabeth Hanford (1936)
Jennings, Peter (1938)
30 Hill, Anita (1956)

August

3 Roper, Dee Dee
5 Ewing, Patrick (1962)
9 Houston, Whitney (1963)
11 Haley, Alex (1921)
Hogan, Hulk (1953)
12 Martin, Ann M. (1955)
Myers, Walter Dean (1937)
13 Battle, Kathleen (1948)
Castro, Fidel (1927)
14 Berry, Halle (1967?)
Johnson, Magic (1959)
Larson, Gary (1950)
15 Ellerbee, Linda (1944)
19 Clinton, Bill (1946)
20 Chung, Connie (1946)
22 Schwarzkopf, H. Norman (1934)

People to Appear in Future Issues

Actors
Trini Alvarado
Richard Dean
  Anderson
Dan Aykroyd
Tyra Banks
Drew Barrymore
Levar Burton
Cher
Kevin Costner
Tom Cruise
Jamie Lee Curtis
Geena Davis
Matt Dillon
Michael Douglas
Larry Fishburne
Harrison Ford
Jody Foster
Richard Gere
Tracey Gold
Graham Greene
Tom Hanks
Mark Harmon
Michael Keaton
Val Kilmer
Angela Lansbury
Joey Lawrence
Martin Lawrence
Leon
Christopher Lloyd
Kellie Martin
Marlee Matlin
Bette Midler
Alyssa Milano
Demi Moore
Rick Moranis
Eddie Murphy
Bill Murray
Liam Neeson
Leonard Nimoy
Sean Penn
Phylicia Rashad
Keanu Reeves
Julia Roberts
Bob Saget
Arnold
  Schwarzenegger
Christian Slater
Jimmy Smits
Wesley Snipes
Sylvester Stallone
Mario Van Peebles
Damon Wayans
Bruce Willis
B.D. Wong

Artists
Mitsumasa Anno
Graeme Base
Maya Ying Lin
Yoko Ono

Astronauts
Neil Armstrong
James Lovell, Jr.

Authors
Jean M. Auel
Lynn Banks
Gwendolyn Brooks
John Christopher
Arthur C. Clarke
John Colville
Paula Danziger
Paula Fox
Patricia Reilly
  Gibb
Jamie Gilson
Rosa Guy
Nat Hentoff
Norma Klein
E.L. Konigsburg
Lois Lowry
David Macaulay
Stephen Manes
Norma Fox Mazer
Anne McCaffrey
Gloria D. Miklowitz
Marsha Norman
Robert O'Brien
Francine Pascal
Christopher Pike
Daniel Pinkwater
Ann Rice
Louis Sachar
Carl Sagan
J.D. Salinger
John Saul
Maurice Sendak
Shel Silverstein
Amy Tan
Alice Walker
Jane Yolen
Roger Zelazny

Business
Minoru Arakawa
Michael Eisner
Wayne Huizenga
Donna Karan
Phil Knight

Estee Lauder
Anita Roddick
Donald Trump
Ted Turner
Lillian Vernon

Cartoonists
Lynda Barry
Roz Chast
Greg Evans
Nicole Hollander
Charles Schulz
Art Spiegelman
Garry Trudeau

Comedians
Billy Crystal
Steve Martin
Eddie Murphy
Bill Murray

Dancers
Debbie Allen
Mikhail
  Baryshnikov
Gregory Hines
Twyla Tharp
Tommy Tune

**Directors/
  Producers**
Woody Allen
Steven Bocho
Ken Burns
Tim Burton
Francis Ford
  Coppola
Ron Howard
John Hughes
George Lucas
Penny Marshall
Leonard Nimoy
Rob Reiner
John Singleton

**Environmentalists/
  Animal Rights**
Marjory Stoneman
  Douglas
Kathryn Fuller
Lois Gibbs
Wangari Maathai
Linda Maraniss
Ingrid Newkirk
Pat Potter

Journalists
John Hakenberry
Dan Rather
Nina Totenberg
Mike Wallace
Bob Woodward

Musicians
Basia
George Benson
Ruben Blades
Clint Black
Boyz II Men
Bono
Edie Brickell
James Brown
C & C Music Factory
Mariah Carey
Ray Charles
Chayanne
Natalie Cole
Cowboy Junkies
Billy Ray Cyrus
Def Leppard
Gerardo
Guns N' Roses
Ice Cube
India
Janet Jackson
Jermaine Jackson
Winona Judd
Anthony Kiedis
Kitaro
Kris Kross
KRS-One
James Levine
LL Cool J
Andrew Lloyd Webber
Courtney Love
Lyle Lovett
MC Lyte
Madonna
Barbara Mandrell
Branford Marsalis
Paul McCartney
Riba McEntire
Midori
Morrissey
N.W.A.
Jessey Norman
Sinead O'Connor
Teddy Pendergrass
Itzhak Perlman
David Pirner
Prince

Public Enemy
Raffi
Bonnie Raitt
Red Hot Chili Peppers
Lou Reed
R.E.M.
Trnt Reznor
Kenny Rogers
Axl Rose
Run-D.M.C.
Paul Simon
Sting
Pam Tillis
Randy Travis
Terence Trent d'Arby
Travis Tritt
U2
Vanilla Ice
Stevie Wonder
Trisha Yearwood
Dwight Yoakum

Politics/
  World Leaders
Madeleine Albright
Jean-Bertrand Aristide
Harry A. Blackmun
Jesse Brown
Ronald Brown
Pat Buchanan
Mangosuthu Buthelezi
Violeta Barrios
  de Chamorro
Shirley Chisolm
Jean Chretien
Warren Christopher
Edith Cresson
Mario Cuomo
Robert Dole
Dalai Lama
Mike Espy
Louis Farrakhan
Alan Greenspan
Vaclav Havel
Jack Kemp
Bob Kerrey
Kim Il-Sung
Coretta Scott King
John Major
Imelda Marcos
Slobodan Milosevic
Mother Theresa
Manuel Noriega
Hazel O'Leary

Leon Panetta
Federico Pena
Robert Reich
Ann Richards
Richard Riley
Phyllis Schlafly
Pat Schroeder
Aung San Suu Kyi
Donna Shalala
Desmond Tutu
Lech Walesa
Eli Weisel
Vladimir Zhirinovsky

Royalty
Charles, Prince of
  Wales
Duchess of York
  (Sarah Ferguson)
Queen Noor

Scientists
Sallie Baliunas
Avis Cohen
Donna Cox
Jane Goodall
Stephen Jay Gould
Mimi Koehl
Deborah Letourneau
Philippa Marrack
Helen Quinn
Carl Sagan
Barbara Smuts
Flossie Wong-Staal
Aslihan Yener
Adrienne Zihlman

Sports
Jim Abbott
Muhammad Ali
Michael Andretti
Boris Becker
Barry Bonds
Bobby Bonilla
Jose Canseco
Jennifer Capriati
Michael Chang
Roger Clemens
Randall Cunningham
Eric Davis
Clyde Drexler
John Elway
Chris Evert
George Foreman

Zina Garrison
Florence Griffith-
  Joyner
Anfernee Hardaway
Rickey Henderson
Evander Holyfield
Brett Hull
Raghib Ismail
Jim Kelly
Petr Klima
Carl Lewis
Mickey Mantle
Willy Mays
Paul Molitor
Joe Montana
Jack Nicklaus
Joe Paterno
Kirby Puckett
Mark Rippien
David Robinson
Deion Sanders
Monica Seles
Daryl Strawberry
Danny Sullivan
Vinnie Testaverde
Isiah Thomas
Mike Tyson
Steve Yzerman

Television
  Personalities
Andre Brown
  (Dr. Dre)
Katie Couric
Phil Donahue
Ed Gordon
Arsenio Hall
Joan Lunden
Dennis Miller
Diane Sawyer
Jon Stewart
Paul Zaloom

Other
James Brady
Johnnetta Cole
David Copperfield
Jaimie Escalante
Jack Kevorkian
Wendy Kopp
Sister Irene Kraus
Jeanne White

BUSINESS REPLY MAIL

First Class Mail   Permit No. 174   Detroit, MI

Postage will be paid by addressee

Omnigraphics, Inc.

Attn: Order Dept.
Penobscot Building
Detroit, MI 48226

BUSINESS REPLY MAIL

First Class Mail   Permit No. 174   Detroit, MI

Postage will be paid by addressee

Omnigraphics, Inc.

Attn: *Biography Today,* Editor
Penobscot Building
Detroit, MI 48226

ON-APPROVAL ORDER FORM

Please send the following on 60-day approval:

Copies

BIOGRAPHY TODAY
_____ ISSN 1058-2347 . . . . $46.00/year (3 issues)

_____ _Standing Order_

_____ 1992 Hardbound Annual 48.00
_____ 1993 Hardbound Annual 48.00
_____ 1994 Hardbound Annual 48.00

_____ _Standing Order_

_____ Annual Subscription
(3 issues and hardbound annual) 92.00

_____ _Standing Order_

_____ Individual Issues 16.00

_____ **BIOGRAPHY TODAY AUTHOR SERIES** 30.00

☐ Payment enclosed, ship postpaid   ☐ Bill us, plus shipping

Institution _____

Attention _____

Address _____

City _____

State, Zip _____

Phone (_____) _____

We want to cover the people _you_ want to know about in _Biography Today._ Take a look at the list of people we plan to include in upcoming issues. Then use this card to list other people you want to see in _Biography Today._ If we include someone you suggest, your library wins a free issue, and you get one to keep, with our thanks.

People I'd like to see in BIOGRAPHY TODAY:

_____

_____

_____

_____

Name _____

Institution _____

Address _____

City _____

State, Zip _____

For Reference

Not to be taken from this room